Globalization and Gov

MW00976846

"This volume edited by Prakash and Hart is a first-rate piece of work, a highly valuable contribution to the IPE and globalization literature. It is an excellent collection of conceptually elegant and empirically rich essays, and is one of the very few books systematically to examine the impact of globalization on multiple facets of governance."

Sylvia Ostry, *University of Toronto*

Globalization and Governance is a completely up-to-date, impartial survey of a variety of perspectives on what constitutes governance, how globalization might impact on governance, and the state. Eleven essays and a thorough introduction provide a theoretical framework and a literature overview. Unlike most books on the subject, this does not espouse any ideological agenda and examines the topical subject of globalization in a conceptually rigorous way.

This refreshingly impartial collection is written for researchers and post-graduate students of political science and international relations, international political economy, or world politics.

Aseem Prakash is Assistant Professor, Department of Strategic Management and Public Policy at the School of Business and Public Management; Department of Political Science; and the Elliott School of International Affairs, The George Washington University. **Jeffrey A. Hart** is Professor of Political Science at Indiana University, Bloomington.

Routledge/RIPE Studies in Global Political Economy

Series editors: Otto Holman, Marianne Marchand (*Research Centre for International Political Economy, University of Amsterdam*) and Henk Overbeek (*Free University, Amsterdam*)

This series, published in association with the *Review of International Political Economy*, provides a forum for current debates in international political economy. The series aims to cover all the central topics in IPE and to present innovative analyses of emerging topics. The titles in the series seek to transcend a state-centred discourse and focus on three broad themes:

- the nature of the forces driving globalization forward
- resistance to globalization
- the transformation of the world order.

The series comprises two strands:

The *RIPE Studies in Global Political Economy* aims to address the needs of students and teachers, and the titles will be published in hardback and paperback. Titles include:

Transnational Classes and International Relations
Kees van der Pijl

Gender and Global Restructuring:
Sightings, Sites and Resistance
Edited by Marianne H Marchand and Anne Sisson Runyan

Global Political Economy
Contemporary Theories
Edited by Ronen Palan

Ideologies of Globalization
Contending Visions of a New World Order
Mark Rupert

Routledge/RIPE Studies in Global Political Economy is a forum for innovative new research intended for a high-level specialist readership, and the titles will be available in hardback only. Titles include:

1. Globalization and Governance*
Edited by Aseem Prakash and Jeffrey A. Hart

2. Nation-States and Money
The Past, Present and Future of National Currencies
Edited by Emily Gilbert and Eric Helleiner

3. The Global Political Economy of Intellectual Property Rights
The New Enclosures?
Christopher May

* Also available in paperback

Globalization and Governance

Edited by
Aseem Prakash and Jeffrey A. Hart

London and New York

First published 1999
by Routledge
11 New Fetter Lane, London EC4P 4EE

Simultaneously published in the USA and Canada
by Routledge
29 West 35th Street, New York, NY 10001

Reprinted 2000

First published in paperback 2000

Routledge is an imprint of the Taylor & Francis Group

Typeset in Baskerville by
BC Typesetting, Bristol
Printed and bound in Great Britain by
Biddles Ltd, Guildford and King's Lynn

British Library Cataloguing in Publication Data
A catalogue record for this book is available from the British Library

Library of Congress Cataloging in Publication Data
A catalog record for this book has been requested

ISBN 0–415–24249–5 (Pbk)
     0–415–21604–4 (Hbk)

To our colleagues at Indiana University, Bloomington

Contents

Series editors' preface

This second volume in the *RIPE Series in Global Political Economy* illustrates the ongoing lively debates in the field of International Political Economy (IPE) about the nature and implications of globalization. Interestingly enough, in recent years the debates about globalization have started to show an intercontinental bifurcation between North American (primarily US) and European (including British) debates. One of the reasons for this bifurcation is a drifting apart of scholars on both sides of the Atlantic in terms of their theoretical, epistemological, and ontological concerns.

In this volume, editors Aseem Prakash and Jeffrey Hart try to partially bridge this gap between different research traditions by organizing the collection's theme of globalization and governance around the debate between neo-institutionalists and constructivists. Whereas representatives of the rational actor-informed neo-institutionalist approach are mostly US-based scholars, the constructivist approach (or rather approaches) seems to provide some common ground for scholars from both continents to meet. As such the collection not only brings together a group of very prominent IPE scholars, but it also makes an important contribution to rekindling debates and exchanges between different research traditions. In so doing the editors are addressing two major concerns of heterodox (or new) political economy as it was originally formulated in the first issue of the *Review of International Political Economy*: first, to develop explanations which address both structure and agency; second, to rethink the foundations of IPE against the backdrop of globalization. The volume's theme of globalization and governance provides the focal point for addressing these concerns.

Processes of globalization have called into question the efficacy and relevance of existing governance structures. The search for new structures is one of the guiding themes of this collection, whereby contributing authors attach varying importance to actors or structures. The collection illustrates how globalization forces IPE scholars from distinct research traditions to reformulate and re-articulate their theoretical views. Even an actor-oriented neo-institutionalist approach now has to take structural factors into consideration.

Furthermore, the state as a basic unit of analysis has lost much of its primacy in understanding and explaining new global governance structures.

Also, the implicit territorial foundation of state sovereignty is increasingly challenged. The authors in this volume all discuss similar questions, even though their individual theoretical positions make them come up with very different answers. They all show, however, that processes of globalization fundamentally transform the ways in which law, politics, economics, and social relations are structured and governed, and reshape the boundaries between public and private regulation and between domestic and international governance.

We are confident that *Globalization and Governance* will prove to be an indispensable book for any serious student of these questions.

Otto Holman
Marianne Marchand
Henk Overbeek
Amsterdam, April 1999

Contributors

Alfred C. Aman, Jr. Professor and Dean, School of Law, Indiana University, Bloomington.

Philip G. Cerny. Professor of International Political Economy, University of Leeds, United Kingdom.

Ian R. Douglas. Fulbright Fellow, Watson Institute for International Studies, Brown University, Providence.

Michele Fratianni. W. George Pinnell Professor of Business Economics and Public Policy, Kelley School of Business, Indiana University, Bloomington.

Peter M. Haas. Professor, Department of Political Science, University of Massachusetts, Amherst.

Jeffrey A. Hart. Professor, Department of Political Science, Indiana University, Bloomington.

Stephen J. Kobrin. William H. Wurster Professor of Multinational Management, Director, The Joseph H. Lauder Institute of Management and International Studies, The Wharton School, University of Pennsylvania, Philadelphia.

Robert T. Kudrle. Professor, Hubert Humphrey Institute of Public Affairs and School of Law, University of Minnesota, Minneapolis.

David A. Lake. Professor, Department of Political Science, University of California, San Diego.

Michael D. McGinnis. Associate Professor, Department of Political Science, Indiana University, Bloomington.

Aseem Prakash. Assistant Professor of Strategic Management and Public Policy at the School of Business and Public Management; Department of Political Science; and the Elliott School of International Affairs, The George Washington University, Washington, DC.

Wayne Sandholtz. Professor, Department of Politics and Society, University of California, Irvine.

Preface

This volume is part of a series of books that examine the impact of economic globalization on governance. We have been interested in the various aspects of international political economy and one of the issues that fascinated us was how economic globalization impacts the extant governance institutions at multiple levels of aggregation and across policy arenas. We began preliminary discussions on this subject during Spring 1995 focusing on four key questions: is economic globalization a fad, how best to conceptualize it, how did it originate, and what may be its implications? We were initially frustrated because, although economic globalization prominently features in both the academic and the popular discourses, the term was being used loosely and therefore its implications were not well understood.

However, this was also an opportunity to learn and reflect more on this subject. To rigorously examine the meaning and governance implications of globalization, we organized two joint panels on "Governance Structures for the Twenty-First Century," at the 1996 annual meeting of the International Studies Association in San Diego, April 16–20. The following presented papers at these panels: Philip Cerny, Ian Douglas, Lorraine Eden, Joseph Grieco (in absentia), Peter Haas, Stephen Kobrin, Robert Kudrle, and Wayne Sandholtz. We were fortunate to have excellent discussants in Susan Strange and David Lake. The quality of the papers was outstanding and we decided to organize another meeting to further discuss their revised versions and to examine the possibility of turning them into an edited volume.

With the financial support from Indiana University, Bloomington and Purdue University we convened a workshop in Indianapolis on October 12– 13, 1996. We are grateful to the following for financial support: African Studies Program, Center for International Business Education and Research, Department of Political Science, East Asian Studies, Institute for Developmental Strategies, Office of the Dean of International Programs, Research and University Graduate School, School of Law, West European Studies, Workshop in Political Theory and Policy Analysis (all Indiana University) and Center for International Business Education and Research (Purdue University). The following presented papers at this workshop: Alfred Aman, Philip Cerny, Ian Douglas, Michele Fratianni, Peter Haas, Jeffrey Hart,

Stephen Kobrin, Robert Kudrle, David Lake, Aseem Prakash, and Wayne Sandholtz. The workshop participants received valuable comments from the following discussants/session chairs: Roberta Astroff, York Bradshaw, John Daniels, Lawrence Davidson, James Dworkin, Charles Lipson, Michael McGinnis, Philip Morgan, Elinor Ostrom, Brian Pollins, Larry Schroeder, and Keith Shimko. Loretta Heyen provided able administrative support in organizing this workshop.

Based on the input at the Indianapolis meeting, these papers were revised in 1997. Marilyn Grobschmidt provided valuable editorial support for turning them into a typescript ready for submission to a publisher. By Fall 1997, one of us (Aseem) had moved to Washington, DC. However, the technological wonders of the information society, especially e-mail, enabled us to carry on the conversation among ourselves, with the contributors to this volume, and with Routledge's editors. Based on the feedback from three anonymous reviewers, and the editors of Routledge's *RIPE Series in Global Political Economy*, Marianne Marchand and Henk Overbeek in particular, these papers were subjected to a second round of revisions in Summer 1998 and accepted for publication in October 1998. David Herman and Sue Seeley provided valuable editorial and technical support in this round of revision.

We are grateful for the permission to reprint the revised versions of the following previously published materials:

1   Stephen J. Kobrin (1998) "Back to the Future: Neomedievalism and the Postmodern Digital World Economy," *Journal of International Affairs*, 51(2): 361–86. Reproduced by permission of the *Journal of International Affairs*.
2   Jeffrey A. Hart and Aseem Prakash (1997) "Strategic Trade and Investment Policies, Implications for the Study of International Political Economy," *World Economy*, 20(4): 457–76. Copyright © Blackwell Publishers Ltd. Reproduced by permission of the publishers.
3   Alfred C. Aman (1997) "Administrative Law for a New Century," in Michael Taggart, editor, *The Providence of Administrative Law*, pp.118–34, Oxford: Hart Publishing. Reproduced by permission of Hart Publishing Ltd.

As we look back, editing this volume has been a very enriching and intellectually stimulating experience. It helped us to better understand the key theoretical issues involved in the study of economic globalization. Importantly, it brought us into close contact with leading scholars in the field of international political economy, a privilege that very few people have.

This volume is dedicated to our colleagues at Indiana University, Bloomington who, in various capacities, supported us and made this project possible.

Aseem Prakash and Jeffrey A. Hart
October 1998

Globalization and governance: an introduction

Aseem Prakash and Jeffrey A. Hart[1]

This volume contributes to an understanding of the implications of globalization by examining three sets of issues. First, what is meant by governance in the study of international relations and international political economy? Two competing perspectives – the new institutionalist and the constructivist – are presented. Second, how will the processes of globalization impact on governance? Are territorial-based systems of governance obsolete or increasingly incapable of efficiently and equitably performing the functions expected of them by actors (whether citizens or firms) living in their jurisdictions? What kinds of changes can we expect? What are the politics of such changes? Third, what kinds of policy innovations at the country-level may be required and are politically feasible in the domains of administrative law, tax policy, monetary policy, and trade and industrial policies to deal with the challenges of globalization?

Both globalization and governance are contested terms with respect to their meanings, etiologies, and implications. Some even dismiss globalization as a fad (Chase-Dunn, 1994). Unlike other works on these questions, this volume does not advocate any particular perspective on globalization, governance, or the linkage between them. We endeavor here only to identify the areas of agreement and disagreement among the scholars contributing to this volume and to learn from their debates.[2] To structure these debates, we provide our own definitions of both globalization and governance below.

First, what is governance and what are the key units of governance in the study of international political economy? It is almost a cliche to point out that international relations scholars (and to a certain extent domestic politics scholars as well) tend to focus on the state as the pre-eminent unit of governance – the primacy of "methodological nationalism"(Cerny, 1997) in the study of politics. This focus was perhaps appropriate in the examination of issues of national security, given that the state did not have many credible economic or political rivals in that arena. Consequently, scholars tended to treat governance as synonymous with government. The pendulum, however, seems to have swung to the other end; some scholars believe that governments are now marginal players (or will soon become marginal) in the international political economy (Strange, 1996; Ohmae, 1991). We return to this debate later. For now, we define governance simply as organizing collective action. In the instrumental sense, governance entails the establishing of institutions; institutions being the rules of the game that permit, prescribe, or prohibit certain actions (Ostrom, 1986; North, 1990).[3] Formal organizations are often required to establish, monitor, and enforce rules, as well as to resolve disputes.[4] Nevertheless, institutions may operate successfully without organizations and one should not assume a one-to-one correspondence between them. It is also important to note that the traditional notions of the state do not explicitly distinguish between its organizational and institutional dimensions. This volume focuses primarily on the institutional dimensions – the rules and policies and how they are affected by the processes of globalization.

By altering incentives, governance institutions encourage actors to adopt strategies that overcome collective action dilemmas. Successful collective action enables actors to cooperate in pursuing their individual and communal goals. The eventual outcome could be Hicks-Kaldor superior (generating net benefits at the aggregate level) if not pareto-superior (at least one participant is better off and no one is worse off than the *status quo*). However, if the benefits and the costs are asymmetrical across actors, institutional evolution and change could be conflictual. Institutions are therefore political artifacts. Also, once established, institutions may take on a life of their own and become political actors in their own right (Keohane, 1984). In some instances, institutions may be established even though they are Hicks-Kaldor inferior: the losses of the "losers" outweigh the benefits of the "winners," but the latter can impose their preferences. Since institutions consequent to such collective action may not be efficiency-enhancing (Libecap, 1989; North, 1990; Knight, 1992), it is important to examine how governance institutions evolve, whose preferences they reflect, and how they influence human behavior.[5]

This conceptualization of governance is not limited to governments since other social institutions may provide governance services as well. As societies become more complex with modernization and industrialization, the opportunities for both governmental and non-governmental governance increase. Thus, one can witness governance within private organizations, such as business enterprises, as well as within less formally organized communities.[6] Some of the key issues in the study of governance are: what is the most efficient and equitable way to provide governance services, through what institutional means, and for which aggregations of individuals?

This volume examines the impact of economic globalization on governance. Globalization or transnational integration, whether conceptualized at the level of the world system, a country, a sector/industry, or a firm, needs to be differentiated from internationalization. With a firm as his unit of analysis, Kobrin (1991) points out that international firms produce in a single country and ship their products worldwide to independent distributors or source raw materials and intermediate products from independent suppliers abroad. On the other hand, transnationally integrated firms exploit assets through internalization within the firm. They rely less on independent distributors or suppliers.[7] A similar distinction may be made at the country-level between an international and a global economy (Metaph and Michalet, 1978, cited by Mittleman, 1996). In an international economy, cross-national trade and investment flows are regulated by the state, or supra-national institutions established by states. In contrast, production in a global economy is organized in cross-border networks or value-chains largely out of the control of states. Since a significant proportion of cross-border trade takes place within firms, cross-border networks supersede resource allocation by markets as well.

Though globalization has many dimensions, economic and non-economic, this volume focuses primarily on economic globalization and how it affects governance at the country-level.[8] This is because currently there is better evidence for economic globalization than other forms of non-economic globalization.[9] The contributors to this volume have agreed to employ the term globalization to refer to a set of processes leading to the integration of economic activity in factor, intermediate, and final goods and services markets across geographical boundaries, and the increased salience of cross-border value chains in international economic flows.[10] This of course leads to the question: how do we measure globalization, and at what stage of integration can we claim that a country is indeed globalized?

Ipso facto globalization refers to processes that potentially encompass the whole globe. The process does not have to have actually encompassed the whole globe to be associated with the phenomenon of globalization but there has to be at least a potential for its omnipresence. Thus, one should be able to identify the degree to which a particular globalization process has actually attained globality. This again calls for efforts to measure or assess the extent of globalization, and on this count, justifies our focus on economic globalization.

There are three approaches to assess levels of economic integration of a country. First, by examining the extent of institutional convergence or harmonization across countries (Berger and Dore, 1996); second, by focusing on the salience of the international flows compared with the domestic ones (Wade, 1996); and third, by evaluating the outcomes of integration in terms of converging prices of goods, services, and factors (Keohane and Milner, 1996).

Convergence or harmonization of domestic economic institutions reduces obstacles (or transaction costs) to cross-border economic flows. The recent trends in regional and global trade, monetary, and investment agreements signify efforts to reduce transaction costs of cross-border flows. Harmonization or convergence therefore constitutes a necessary condition for globalization. Of course, even if economic and political institutions are harmonized, there is no guarantee that economic actors will indeed undertake cross-border flows. It is therefore important to examine to what extent economic actors have taken advantage of such opportunities. This can be assessed by examining ratios such as foreign trade to GDP (gross domestic product), foreign direct investment(FDI) to GDP, net foreign investment to domestic assets, and FDI to gross domestic investment. In addition, we also suggest measuring cross-border flows of factors of production (land, labor, capital, entrepreneurship, and technology). Once these multiple indicators have been developed, the salience of cross-border flows relative to domestic ones can be better assessed.[11] This is not to say that all flows have similar impacts on domestic politics in a given country or across countries. Countries differ in endowments to negotiate with demands placed by different flows: as the recent economic turmoil in East Asia suggests, countries with substantial foreign exchange reserves (such as China and Taiwan) have greater leeway in influencing their exchange rates and therefore domestic interest rates, than countries with meager reserves (Indonesia and Malaysia). Further, the domestic impact also differs across flows: rising capital flows have a greater constraining influence on fiscal and monetary policy than trade flows (Frieden and Rogowski, 1996).

Third, we need to examine if increased cross-border flows translate into similar levels of prices across jurisdictions. For example, have the rising levels of cross-border capital flows resulted in equalization of real (covered) interest rates? Or, given that labor is theoretically mobile, say within the European Union, has the price of labor converged in member countries? Thus, based on the three categories of indicators, we can assess the levels of globalization at the country level.

Globalization as an independent and a dependent variable

We hypothesize that globalization processes (as dependent variables) were initiated and encouraged by four categories of factors: technological change, spread of market-based systems, domestic politics, and inter-state rivalries.[12] Globalization processes could lead to new or modified governance institutions as they move more toward genuine globality. This is because to capitalize on the opportunities created or to reduce the costs imposed by globalization processes, actors may have the incentives and the resources to modify extant governance institutions or create new ones. Thus, in time, globalization processes will become the independent variables and the new or modified institutions of governance will become the dependent variable. Of course, over time, changes in governance will unleash new forces that may, in turn, impact on the pace and extent of globalization processes. This is summarized in Figure 1.

Globalization as a dependent variable

In this section we briefly review the literature on globalization as a dependent variable and in the next section as an independent variable. If globalization is a consequence, who or what initiated it and for what reasons? We have

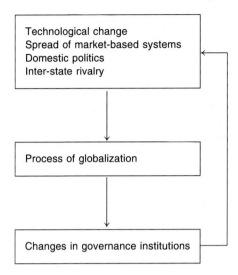

Figure 1 Globalization as independent and dependent variable

already identified four possible culprits: technological change, the spread of market-based systems, domestic politics, and inter-state rivalries. For example, some authors argue that globalization is primarily an outcome of technological change; the latter being necessary and sufficient for explaining the acceleration of such processes. As a corollary, globalization processes driven by technological change are unstoppable unless some new techno-logical breakthroughs reverse the existing trajectories. Structural and domestic politics-based explanations emphasize the role of conscious human agency in encouraging such processes. The latter do not ignore the contri-butions of technological change; rather, they treat it as only a facilitating condition, or at most, a necessary condition. We briefly discuss these explanations below.

Technological change

Some view globalization processes as outcomes of technological advances, especially in telecommunications, information, and transportation tech-nologies. The level of investment in information technology has reached gigantic proportions: in the United States, information technology accounts for 45 per cent of all business equipment investment (Barshefsky, 1998). Technological advances have enabled firms to delocalize and fragment value-addition processes, thereby locating the various stages across territorial jurisdictions (Sjolander, 1996). The digitization of information flows com-bined with the spread of fast packet switching for data and voice communica-tions has led to a contraction of space and time (Mittleman, 1996) enabling economic actors to communicate across great distances in real time. The rapid advances in ground, sea, and air transportation have facilitated inter-national trade by making movements of goods and services cheaper and faster. A good example would be the invention of the wide-bodied jet aircraft, the jumbo jet, which makes the shipping of small and light objects (including people) by air considerably cheaper than shipping those same objects by sea (previously the cheapest alternative). Therefore, in this view, accelerating globalization processes are not conscious policy artifacts; they are *faits accompli* of a technology-driven economy.

Another argument associating globalization with technological change starts with the observation that intra-industry consolidations often have effects that cross national boundaries. Thus, when Chrysler had to downsize its operations in the late 1970s, employees in France and Britain had to bear some of the costs. Similarly, its merger with Daimler-Benz will significantly impact on its US operations. More recently, American employees of the troubled French defense and electronics company, Thomson CSF, faced job cuts when the French government decided to privatize the firm in 1996. Similarly, the Boeing Corporation worked collaboratively with contracting firms in Europe and Asia to build its latest wide-body jet aircraft, the 777, effectively making it a multinational enterprise. The need for such firms to operate in more than one industrialized region is increasingly viewed as an outcome of skyrocketing research and development (R&D) costs: the mini-mum efficient scale to amortize such large R&D investments is greater than any single national or regional market can offer (Kobrin, 1995). Ohmae also notes that:

> As automation has driven the variable cost of labor out of production, manufacturing has increasingly become a fixed-cost activity. . . . In a fixed-cost environment, the focus switches to maximizing marginal con-tributions to fixed costs – that is, boosting sales. This new logic forces managers to amortize their fixed costs over a much larger market base and this drives them towards globalization.
>
> (1991: 6–7)

Spread of market-based systems

Technological change, however, is only part of the story. Since markets and market-supporting governance are important in fostering and disseminating technological innovations, the spread of market-based systems and explicit governmental policies for promoting technological innovation have acceler-ated globalization processes. Drawing upon Polanyi's (1957) contention that economic relations, especially the notion of free markets, are rooted in specific political philosophy, Scott argues:

> [I]t remains insufficient to analyze globalization exclusively as though it were the outcome of social and economic processes, however complex.

> Globalization must be seen in part at least as the outcome of an idea, and specifically the idea of a free market; "free" in the sense of freed from political, social, or "*gemeinschaftlich*" constraints.
>
> (1997: 9; italics in original)

Therefore, an important cause for the pace and extent of globalization processes is the increasing legitimacy and spread of market-based systems for allocation and exchange both within and between countries. With the expertise and legitimacy of the state to intervene in the domestic economy increasingly under attack, there are calls for deregulation and privatization. As Evans (1997) points out, state bureaucracies are now blanket labeled as either corrupt or vulnerable to "capture" by vested interests.

The same logic is applied to assessing state intervention in international economic activity, adding to the demands for reducing state-created institutional obstacles to flows of goods, services, and investments.[13] This of course has often led to establishing regional and global institutions. Paradoxically, supra-national bureaucracies are not viewed as having the same problems as national bureaucracies. One expects that due to greater physical and cultural distance between transnational bureaucrats and the governed, and the lack of democratic accountability (or even accountability to the market), they will suffer from even greater principal-agent conflicts (Berle and Means, 1932). Until recently, the ability of states in the developing countries to manage their economies was criticized widely in the United States but not the ability of the World Bank's or the International Monetary Fund's (IMF's) bureaucracies. The recent East Asia crisis, however, has changed this. There are now calls for greater accountability and transparency of the decision-making processes of the World Bank and the IMF.[14]

The deregulatory agenda has resonated well with the ideological thrust of the neo-liberal political forces that rose to power in the United States and the United Kingdom in the 1980s. This alliance received further ideological and policy legitimacy with the end of the Cold War, interpreted by them as the triumph of market-based systems over centrally planned systems. The defeat of the Republicans in 1992 and 1996 by the "New Democrats," led by William Jefferson Clinton, and the defeat of the Tories in 1997 by Tony Blair's "New Labour," has not altered this situation significantly. Recent developments also suggest that the victory of the Socialists in France, not withstanding their pledge to prioritize jobs over deficit reduction, will not alter the neo-liberal thrust of the French economy. In the 1997 European Union (EU) summit in Amsterdam, the French proposal for a launching public works programs to create jobs did not find support and the "stability pact" that stipulates deficit reduction as the top EU priority could not be dethroned. Not surprisingly, Tony Blair and Helmut Kohl spoke out against the French proposal. Mr Blair noted that "the European Union's role in employment is to encourage the exchange of ideas and best practice, and not to launch major new spending programs" (*New York Times*, 1997b).

A widespread adoption of market-oriented policies across countries suggests globalization of the model of a liberal economy. However, the adoption of a specific economic model *per se* does not suggest globalization. For example, the universal adoption of a state interventionist model will not facilitate globalization (Berger, 1996). As Hart and Prakash argue in this volume, states may now have greater incentives to intervene in technologically intensive industries in a globalizing world economy in order to create domestic "architectures of supply."

Domestic political economy

Another category of explanations focuses on the role of conscious policy interventions in initiating globalization processes; domestic political and economic actors are viewed as the key driving forces behind such policy changes. The main actors in such "second-image" explanations are domestic firms with substantial export interests, multinational enterprises (MNEs), and financial traders. The policy changes advocated by these actors are of three kinds: encouraging internationalization of the domestic economy through the liberalization of trade and investment regimes, deregulation of domestic regulated markets, and liberalization of domestic financial markets.

As discussed previously, deregulation and privatization, especially of government-controlled utilities and state enterprises, has become a major factor in accelerating transnational capital flows in recent years, often through mergers and acquisitions (Julius, 1990; UNCTAD, 1995). For example, in the first six months of 1998 only, the value of mergers and acquisitions in the United States is projected to reach $910 billion ($1.3 trillion worldwide), equal to 1997 (full year level) and about ten times the 1988 (full year) level (*New York Times*, 1998). Previously, such consolidations were discouraged by anti-trust laws or competition policy, governmental ownership of utilities and state enterprises, and active opposition to foreign ownership. Once such restrictions were lifted, there was an upsurge in cross-national mergers, acquisitions, and alliances. Of course, the success of domestic forces in pushing through deregulation shows considerable variation across countries and issue areas. In the case of financial deregulation, the degree of central bank independence was often the crucial factor in determining the extent and character of financial liberalization (Goodman, 1992). In the case of telecommunications services in western Europe, the power of telecommunications workers' unions is often cited as a factor inhibiting deregulation.

Inter-state rivalry

Cerny (1997: 251) declares that "the transformation of the nation-state into a 'competition state' lies at the heart of political globalization," thereby implying that globalization processes may have been encouraged by inter-state rivalries.[15] Such "third-image" explanations treat technology-based and domestic political economy-based explanations as being under-specified since they cannot explain the timing and character of state policies that led to deregulation and financial liberalization. To have fully specified explanations, these theories suggest a focus on state preferences and strategies. For example, policy harmonization across countries, forced or voluntary, exemplifies the critical role of inter-state rivalry in facilitating globalization processes. In the Structural Impediments Initiative talks between Japan and the United States (1989–1990), the US negotiators demanded changes in Japanese domestic economic policies which were perceived to rig the market against foreign economic actors (Kahler, 1996; Kosai, 1996). Such forced policy harmonization sought to integrate some of the protected sectors of the Japanese economy with the world economy.

Consider the role of conscious state policies in fostering the processes of financial globalization.[16] The Interest Equalization Tax of 1963 was the first milestone in this direction. This tax was imposed by the US government to discourage the sale of foreign bonds on the New York Stock Exchange. However, it led to the unanticipated creation of the Eurocurrency markets. The second milestone was the jettisoning of the fixed interest rate mechanism by the Federal Reserve of the United States in the early 1970s. The third was the surge in private foreign lending, again with the blessing of the US government, to recycle petro-dollars. The subsequent debt crisis of the 1980s almost led to a global banking crisis. The IMF–World Bank Structural Adjustment Programs, again inspired by the US desire to protect its domestic international banking industry, forced many developing countries to adopt policies to deregulate and privatize government utilities, to attract foreign direct investment (FDI), and to open up their domestic markets for imports. The fourth milestone was the "big bang" of London in 1987 that led to competitive deregulation of the financial markets, with each country attempting to attract mobile capital (Helleiner, 1994).

The General Agreement on Tariffs and Trade (GATT) is another example of state interests guiding the pace and direction of the processes of globalization. Until the Tokyo Round of the GATT, the United States pushed primarily for tariff reductions. This served the interests of US-based firms since they had competitive advantages in manufacturing. Once non-tariff barriers became important impediments to trade in services, and violations of intellectual property rights became a key concern for US exporters, the United States urged agreements on these issues as well. This began in the Tokyo Round and culminated in the Uruguay Round. In February 1997, the US succeeded in pushing through a global agreement for a complete phase-out of tariffs on information products (*New York Times*, 1997a).

In part, the North American Free Trade Agreement (NAFTA) and the renewed urgency in Europe towards integration can also be viewed as state responses to economic globalization. With the Maastricht treaty, Europe sought to regain its competitive edge against the US as well as Japan/East Asian firms. NAFTA, in turn, can be interpreted as an American response to

European integration. Further, moves to expand NAFTA to South America and the possibility of turning the Asia Pacific Economic Cooperation into a free trade area also suggest that inter-state rivalry is important in encouraging integration. A related issue that emerges is whether the current trends point toward regionalization rather than globalization of the world economy. Further, whether regionalization is a "building bloc" or a "stumbling bloc" (Lawrence, 1995) towards globalization. Since regionalization may also represent a decline of multilateralism (Gilpin, 1987), another key issue is whether multilateralism is necessary for globalization. If so, will the processes of globalization be impeded by the trend towards minilateralism, bilateralism, and unilateralism?

A key agent of globalization is the "stateless" MNE. However, MNEs are really not stateless: they continue to retain their national character and there is little convergence in the fundamental strategies on locating the core research and development (R&D) facilities, internal governance, and long-term financial structures (Pauly and Reich, 1997).[17] States, therefore, continue to have strong incentives to promote firms that are closely identified with their territorial jurisdictions. They are now actively engaging in commercial diplomacy, and ensuring a fair deal for their firms has become a key item on international agendas. It is fairly common for large business delegations to accompany dignitaries in their international junkets. The commercial outcomes are often advertised as important achievements of such trips.

Both internal and external deregulation, important pillars of globalization processes, have been actively encouraged by international organizations such as the World Bank, the International Monetary Fund, and the World Trade Organization. Many view such organizations as serving the interests of particular countries, promoting so-called Anglo-Saxon capitalism, thereby becoming tools in inter-state rivalry. In this context, it is important to note that, while many countries believe that globalization serves US interests, many Americans believe that the US is a prisoner of the globalization processes. Milner notes:

> But some claim that globalization is not only a creation of the United States but also a creature controlled by it. Countries such as France and Malaysia have vehemently expressed the view that globalization is basically the extension of American economic practices and ideals to the world, and a tool for the exercise of American power. . . . Ironically, many Americans see globalization as beyond their country's control. Indeed, in their eyes, the United States is ever more constrained by global forces, just like everyone else.
>
> (1998: 121)

To summarize, it appears that globalization processes have been encouraged by all four factors even though there is still much debate over their relative importance. For example, Beinart (1997) sees global integration since World War II as stemming more from politics than from technology. According to Beinart, there have been two important institutional shifts attributable to politics: establishment of liberal trading and monetary regimes in the late 1940s and the abolition of controls over the movement of foreign capital in the 1970s. Mittleman (1996), in contrast, views globalization processes as primarily market induced and not policy led.

We view technological progress as a necessary condition without which policy interventions would be less successful in fostering globalization processes. However, the political support of domestic constituencies, the response of governments to inter-state rivalries, and the spread of market-based systems have also been critical. An interesting future research agenda then would be to identify economic sectors with varying strengths of globalization processes and to test hypotheses for teasing out the relative contribution of the four independent variables. This would enable us to identify conditions under which different independent variables had the greatest impact on globalization processes. Having discussed globalization processes as dependent variables, we now treat them as independent variables and examine their impact on the institutions of country-level governance.

Globalization as an independent variable

How will globalization impact governance at the country-level? Will the Westphalian system and the Keynesian welfare state survive its onslaught?[18] Do we expect changes in domestic institutions to vary across policy areas and across states? How will the power of domestic actors impact on these changes? What may be the impact of extant institutions, especially the political institutions, that privilege certain actors over others? Will "strong" states be more successful in adapting domestic institutions to the demands of footloose capital? Will the corporatist structures that were designed to produce policy consensus in the wake of rapid economic change survive the test of globalization(Katzenstein, 1985)? Clearly, there are no simple answers to the above questions and assessing the impact of globalization at the country-level is a complex task.

In the Westphalian system, the state is the major agency to supply collective goods and state-centric security considerations play a dominant role in international relations. The notion of a welfare state is predicated on the "embedded-liberalism" social compact (Ruggie, 1982) and the Keynesian philosophy that markets are not self-regulatory. The former suggests that costs imposed by liberalized trade on labor and other domestic actors are to be offset by side-payments in the form of social safety nets such as unemployment insurance, old-age insurance, welfare payments, and other redistributive social policies.

There are three broad categories of views on how globalization may impact on the Westphalian system and the welfare state. First, it is suggested that the nation-state will wither away; perhaps, not physically but in terms of policy options it can effectively exercise in the economic realm. Further, in the emerging "new world order," economics will increasingly dominate security considerations. Thus, globalization heralds the demise of both the Westphalian system and the welfare state. The second perspective, in contrast, views business-as-usual for the state. It is suggested that the existing instruments of economic policy, perhaps with some modifications, are sufficient to handle the challenges posed by globalization. Further, the security imperatives of international relations will remain important. The third perspective is that the state will neither wither away nor remain unchanged. Rather, states will rearticulate themselves by shedding some political and economic functions and adopting new ones. Also, though national security considerations will remain important, a new perspective on security will evolve.

Since the pace and extent of changes in governance institutions will vary across states and sectors, an important research area is the development and testing of hypotheses to explain such sectoral as well as country-level variations. The reader will note that we had raised a similar issue previously in the discussion on globalization as a dependent variable. We believe that for the discourse on globalization to evolve into a coherent research program, it is important that scholars study the impact of globalization on institutions of governance representing multiple levels, particularly, the country and the sectoral levels. We now elaborate on the three categories of response to the processes of globalization.

The end of the Westphalian and the welfare state

Some suggest that the Westphalian system is on its last leg, and the world is heading towards some sort of a new political order that resembles the (non-state-centered) medieval period. For these scholars, the arrival of a "borderless world" (Ohmae, 1991) is imminent. This global village will be governed by supra-national institutions and the European Union is often identified as a plausible model. Others suggest that the new governance institutions will resemble an order with governance at both the subnational and the supra-national levels and citizens having loyalties to multiple jurisdictions (Kobrin, this volume).

Since the ability of the state to influence economic processes is predicted to greatly diminish, what policies should be adopted to enhance the economic welfare of citizens, particularly the ones that no longer have a "voice," cannot "exit," and have little hope of successfully employing "loyalty" to change the system from within (Hirschman, 1970)? It is recommended that governments should focus on retaining and attracting investments from MNEs. A key strategy is to upgrade the country's human capital – the assumption being that MNEs tend to invest in countries with a skilled workforce (Reich, 1992). For such scholars, globalization has either arrived or its arrival is imminent; it is an inexorable force, merciless to those who defy its logic (O'Brien, 1992).

It is also predicted that the Westphalian system of security-conscious states will give way to a new world order where economics will prevail over politics. Echoing the ideas popularized by Normal Angell ([1910] 1933) on the eve of World War I, they suggest that national security will not remain a critical factor in international relations. Ohmae notes that:

> Under cold war assumptions, government officials fall back on arguments that countries have to be prepared for emergencies – that is, war. Inefficient industries are subsidized in the name of national security. . . . Meanwhile, Singapore and Hong Kong don't worry about ifs. In theory Singapore can't exist because it has no insurance, either in the form of military or strategic (read protected) industries. Yet, it enjoys current prosperity. I believe that the Singaporean solution is the right one, because in the global economy, economic linkage increases security.
>
> (1991: 13–14)

Further, since globalization processes have led to the spread of democracy, and democracies almost never fight each other (Russett, 1993), national security will be relegated to economic issues. However, the recent enlargement of the North Atlantic Treaty Organization, the strife in the Balkans, the continuing stalemate in the Middle East, and more recently, the nuclear blasts in the Indian subcontinent suggest that security considerations remain important in international relations.[19] The recent controversies in the US involving the sale of dual-use technology to China remind us that many key policy makers actively resist the idea that commercial considerations should prevail over national security issues.

The resilient state

Others question the fuss over globalization, whether governments have actually become so powerless compared to the MNEs and financial markets, and whether the "stateless corporation" has indeed arrived. For them, the state-centered Westphalian model still holds, governments continue to remain powerful in the economic sphere, and the national origins of MNEs remain important for both business strategy and public policy (Tyson, 1991; Carnoy *et al.*, 1993; Pauly and Reich, 1997). Further, the novelty of the levels of economic integration is also questioned: based on trade and capital flows as proportions of the GDP, economies were perhaps more globalized on the eve of World War I (Krugman, 1989). Japan exported a greater proportion of its total production during the interwar period than it does currently (Rodrik, 1997). In spite of the rhetoric that market forces will coerce governments to shrink welfare payments, evidence does not suggest radical restructuring of the welfare state (see below). Thus, the proclamations of the imminent arrival of a globalized economy are viewed as ruses to undermine the power of labor and other supporters of an activist state. If there are discernible trends towards globalization and downsizing of the welfare state, they recommend politically resisting them from "above" (transnational alliances) and from "below" (local level opposition) (Boyer and Drache, 1996; Gills, forthcoming).

Kudrle, in his chapter for this volume, disputes that economic integration has narrowed the scope of effective policy instruments that states can employ to advance the welfare of their citizens. He debunks four common misperceptions: "reinventing government" can be attributed to globalization, devolution is a manifestation of globalization, after-tax income inequality in industrialized countries has increased due to foreign trade, and deregulation has been forced by globalization. He concludes that most of the challenges associated with globalization admit to effective responses at the national level. Also, those that cannot be handled at the national level can often be dealt with by cross-national policy harmonization.

Krugman (1994) also challenges the widespread belief that globalization is the cause of economic miseries in the industrialized world. He argues that increases in global trade are not the main culprit in the increasing inequalities or the shrinking size of middle income groups in industrialized countries – only 20 per cent reduction in the earnings of low-skilled American workers can be attributed to international trade. Rather, the causal variables are slow growth in domestic productivity, and increases in demand for skilled labor relative to that of unskilled labor. Thus, if globalization has not caused the alleged domestic problems, there is little reason for radically altering the extant systems of governance.

A critical interpretation of the continued importance of state is provided by Falk. He notes that:

> [T]he policy orientation of the state has been pulled away from its territorial constituencies and shifted outwards, with state action characteristically operating as an instrumental agent on behalf of non-territorial regional and global market forces. . . . This partial instrumentalization of the state was evident in the Gulf War, properly regarded as the first post-modern war, where the extraordinary mobilization of military capabilities was responsive to severe global market anxieties about the price of oil and the future control of Gulf oil reserves.
>
> (1997: 129)

The rearticulated state

The third set of scholars believe that given the pressures from the processes of globalization, states will not be able to do business-as-usual. They will not collapse either; rather, they will rearticulate themselves by modifying their institutions and policies. Further, though national security concerns will remain important in international relations, the notion of security itself will be reformulated and acquire new dimensions.

That new governance institutions will evolve does not necessarily imply that they will be superior or more efficient in some sense to the *status quo*. First, it is difficult to expect that "boundedly rational" (Simon, 1957) actors confronting a world of frenzied technological change (a corollary being that full and complete information is not possible due to both actor-level and structural reasons) can ever devise such institutions in a single iteration. Clearly, the rearticulation will have to be an incremental process. Second, for the rearticulation to be successful (rather than dysfunctional) in meeting the challenges of globalization, state bureaucracies must have the incentives and the abilities to regenerate themselves. They should also be able to overcome the opposition from social actors interested in preserving the *status quo*. Further, they may need to actively involve non-state actors (often with different preferences and endowments) in institutional design and implementation. The politics of rearticulation is complex, and is further complicated by the incomplete understanding of the nature and architecture of the desired institutions.

Nevertheless, two types of modifications are suggested. First, in view of the persistent budgetary deficits and the opposition to both inflation and higher taxation, states will eventually downsize some functions, primarily the social policies traditionally associated with the Keynesian welfare state. They will also adopt new ones, especially to safeguard the interests of their domestic firms in increasingly global markets. This is rooted in the belief that, in order to enhance the economic wellbeing of their citizens, states now increasingly compete for world market shares in key industries (Stopford and Strange, 1991; Strange, 1995). For example, industrialized countries will become aggressive in devising institutions or modifying the extant ones that will protect intellectual property rights, open foreign markets for trade in services, and minimize restrictions for FDI (Sell, forthcoming). Second, states will delegate some of their functions upwards to supra-national institutions as well as downwards to local governments. Thus, federalism and creating of supra-national institutions (regional and global) will go hand-in-hand.

Which functions states shed or adopt depends significantly on structural constraints (for example, commitments to international institutions such as the World Trade Organization), the economic costs of not doing so, and domestic politics. Processes of globalization create "winners" and "losers" in the domestic political economy. That foreign trade asymmetrically benefits factors of production (Rogowski, 1989; Midford, 1993), sectors or industries (Magee, 1980; Frieden, 1991), and firms (G. Helleiner, 1977; Milner, 1988) is well established: for example, factors employed intensively in import-competing industries lose, and factors employed intensively in exporting industries gain. In a pluralistic society, losers can be expected to oppose globalization processes, and winners to support them. Public policy is an outcome of such conflicting pulls and pressures filtered through multiple institutions.

As suggested above, welfare provision is expected to be eventually downsized. It is argued that financial markets punish states that are profligate and run chronic budgetary deficits. Further, there are signs of citizen dissatisfaction with high taxes as well. Footloose MNEs are also allegedly ready to locate to countries that offer low tax rates. On this count, the roll back of the welfare state should be imminent. However, data for the 1980s suggest that the welfare state has turned out to be quite resilient: the share of welfare payments as a proportion of GNP has not declined significantly (Pierson, 1996). One reason is that the growth of the welfare state since World War II has transformed the politics of social policy; with concentrated and tangible losses but diffused and uncertain benefits, welfare cutbacks are politically unrewarding. Data also suggests that countries with strong economies and/ or significant exposure to external trade have strong welfare states (Cameron, 1978; Rodrik, 1997). This is partly attributed to the increasing capacities of states to fund such redistributive policies as well as the need to placate the losers from free trade (Ruggie, 1982). Further, as suggested by McGinnis in this volume, for any governance system to survive in the long run, it must build legitimacy. This is often done by redistributing some of the gains of collective action from winners to losers. Globalization processes, with their emphasis on quick changes in production technologies and increased exposure to foreign trade, will create many losers. Consequently, institutionalized mechanisms for redistribution or side-payments are required. The existing governance institutions, particularly the state, may be better placed to provide such redistributive services than any new ones. Thus, even on efficiency consideration, the extant institutions of the state may turn out to be efficient providers of welfare services due to their lower start-up costs. This discussion again suggests that the politics of rearticulation is complex. This is not to say that globalization processes have little impact on economic policies due to domestic politics – welfare reforms remain on active agendas in most industrialized countries. Rather, it is important to appreciate that the impact of globalization on domestic governance is mediated through a variety of institutions and contested terrains.

The second modification is that by upwards and downwards delegation of some functions, states will become structurally and functionally differentiated. Thus, as Cerny argues in his chapter for this volume, a single level structural hegemony – statism, regionalism, or multilateralism – will not prevail. Rosenau (1997) also predicts "fragmegration" (the co-occurrence of fragmentation and agglomeration) of governance institutions. The logic is that the Westphalian state is no longer the most efficient unit of aggregation for supplying various collective goods. This resonates well with the Public Choice literature of the 1960s and 1970s that argued in favor of constitutional federalism. Their main contention was that federalism has an efficiency-based rationale since different collective goods are efficiently provided at different scales, the national scale being only one of them (Ostrom *et al.*, 1961).

For Evans (1997), the re-articulation of the state could take two paths. First, to survive, states become meaner and more repressive. Second, states could develop capacities to co-produce collective goods with their citizens. He points out that in the post World War II era, states took upon themselves more functions and responsibilities than they could handle. Thus, the attrition of the state is a corollary of the "capacity gap." He, however, notes that the capacity gap cannot be bridged by old strategies, particularly because of the hostile ideological climate; the return of the pendulum is therefore unlikely. His preferred strategy and outcome is:

> Engaging the energy and imagination of citizens and communities in the co-production of services is a way of enhancing the states' ability to deliver services without having to demand more scarce material resources from the society. . . . Since such a strategy simultaneously rewards the reinvigoration of civil society, thereby augmenting the reservoir of the potential participants in co-production, it is certainly subject to increasing returns.
>
> (1997: 86)

Reiterating the theme of re-articulation, Hart and Prakash, in chapter 9 of this volume, contend that states have incentives to reconfigure themselves. For them, the hallmark of globalization is the "technologization" of trade, that is, the increasing salience of high-technology products in global trade. This creates incentives for states to employ strategic trade and investment policies (STIPs) for developing domestic "architectures of supplies" (Borrus and Hart, 1994) in critical technologies. Imperfect markets create a potential for super-normal profits and such interventions may shift these profits from foreign to domestic firms. Since "architectures of supplies" may provide high-technology firms located in a country adequate and timely access to new technologies, they will become a major "pull-factor" attracting investment from both domestic and foreign MNEs (also see Porter, 1990; Ohmae, 1991).

Having discussed globalization as an independent variable and governance as a dependent variable, we now briefly describe the structure of this volume.

The structure of the volume

This volume is divided into three parts. Part I deals with the concepts and politics of governance in the context of globalization. Authors present two perspectives on governance: new institutionalist (David Lake and Michael McGinnis) and sociological (Wayne Sandholtz and Peter Haas). In addition, Ian Douglas examines the politics of the globalization and governance discourse.

Part II focuses on the impact of globalization processes on the Westphalian state. Three perspectives are presented. Stephen Kobrin argues that the Westphalian system will give way to a new political organization that, metaphorically speaking, resembles the medieval order. His contention is that since territorial sovereignty has not been privileged historically, looking back may help us to look forward. In contrast, Robert Kudrle argues that the policy instruments at the disposal of the states are sufficient to deal with the challenges posed by globalization. Philip Cerny provides a perspective on the re-articulation of the state. Cerny predicts that the state will become functionally and structurally differentiated.

In Part III, authors focus on policy response in the realms of trade and investment policies, administrative law and monetary policy. Hart and Prakash argue that globalization creates incentives for states to employ strategic trade and investment policies to promote high-technology industries. Alfred Aman provides a perspective on the impact of globalization on administrative law. Michele Fratianni examines the introduction of the Euro as a response to globalization processes.

In the concluding chapter, we first summarize the findings and the lessons learned from this volume. Then, we briefly discuss an agenda for future research to examine how various actors are coping with globalization and to draw lessons from the successful and unsuccessful coping strategies.[20]

Notes

1 We thank Yu-che Chen, Phil Cerny, Ray Eliason, Marilyn Grobschmidt, Bob Kudrle, David Lake, Marianne Marchand, Mike McGinnis, Henk Overbeek, and the three anonymous reviewers for their comments and Jennifer Baka for her research assistance.

2 This volume is the first study of a research program that examines the impact of globalization on governance. We are also working on two other edited volumes tentatively entitled "Coping with Globalization" and "Responding to Globalization". Scholars often assume that globalization is either essentially beneficial or disruptive. We view such perspectives as representing the polar ends of the "response to globalization" continuum and these volumes seek to examine other responses as well. They therefore focus on the "coping" strategies of governments and firms, evaluating the success of such strategies, and drawing lessons from them.

3 For a detailed analysis of the various notions of institutions, see Crawford and Ostrom (1995). In a new-institutionalist perspective, regimes and institutions are functional equivalents: they facilitate collective action by encouraging information flows, provide arenas for bargaining, and establish mechanisms for monitoring and enforcing contracts (Krasner, 1982; Keohane, 1984; Young, 1986). For a sociological perspective on institutions, see Scott (1987), March and Olsen (1989), DiMaggio and Powell (1991), Oliver (1991) as well as the papers by Sandholtz and Haas in this volume. For a comparison of the new-institutionalist and sociological perspectives, see Keohane (1988) and Ostrom (1991).

4 Even the virtual organizations that exist only in the cyberspace have budgets, personnel, etc.

5 Some scholars do not view firms as efficiency-enhancing institutions; rather, they view firms as instruments of capital to dominate labor (Marglin, 1974; Perrow, 1979; Edwards, 1979).

6 For example, firms are units of governance for organizing economic activity. As Coase (1937) pointed out, firms economize on transaction costs associated with the functioning of markets. Williamson (1985) also views firms as governance structures to economize costs associated with opportunism of labor given asset-specificity and bounded-rationality.

7 For a review of the literature on measuring globalization at the firm level, see Sullivan (1994). For a critique of Sullivan, see Ramaswamy *et al.* (1996). For a discussion on measuring globalization at the sector or industry level, see Makhija *et al.* (1997).

8 The literature on non-economic dimensions of globalization is rather vast. For example, key works on the subject of cultural globalization include Featherstone (1990), Robertson (1992), Abramson and Inglehart (1995), Appadurai (1996), and Lipid and Kratochwil (19997).

9 This of course raises important epistemological questions such as what constitutes evidence and how do we test hypotheses. Further, it is also argued that globalization as an ideology plays a critical role in sustaining globalization as a phenomenon (Robertson, 1992; also see Douglas' chapter in this volume).

10 Our definition is more spartan than Mittleman's (1996: 2). For him, globalization manifests as

> spatial reorganization of production, the interpenetration of industries across borders, the spread of financial markets, the diffusion of identical consumer goods to distant countries, massive transfer of populations within the South as well as from the South and the East to the West, . . . and an emerging world-wide preference for democracy.

Unlike our conception, Palan and Abbot view globalization "not as a quantitative change denoting the global integration of markets but as a qualitative change which implies an intensification and extension of capitalist relationships" (1994: 19). We, however, believe that "intensification" and "extension of capitalist relationships" emanate from integration of markets; the latter being a necessary (and perhaps sufficient as well) condition for the former.

11 For an elaboration of this argument, see Prakash and Hart (1998). Also see Wade (1996) on assessing the levels of globalization.

12 An important question then is: can these four factors also lead to reversal of globalization? For example, can new developments in the domestic sphere lead to conditions whereby countries start withdrawing from the global economy? This poses a broader question: is globalization reversible? If history is any guide, perhaps it is. Globalization measured in terms of trade and capital flows peaked on the eve of World War I and reached its lowest point in the 1940s (Milner, 1998). It again began an upward trajectory after World War II.

13 For a discussion on the important role of epistemic community of central bankers in ushering in financial deregulation, see E. Helleiner (1994).

14 The Republican criticism of the United Nations and its affiliated organizations such as UNICEF was of a different character. Specifically, many Republicans felt that the UN had been "captured" by anti-US groups, had lost its focus, and spawned a bloated bureaucracy.

15 For a discussion on the notion of a "competition state", see Palan and Abbot (1996), especially Chapters 1 and 2.

16 For an excellent review of literature on this subject, see Cohen (1996).

17 The relationship between MNEs, host and home governments is complex. The traditional model that suggests that home governments support their home-based MNEs and host governments view them as adversaries has been questioned. For a discussion on this subject, see Rugman and Verbeke (1998).

18 It is important to note that the Westphalian system is also under attack from a resurgence of civil society as well as the increasing emphasis on the "third sector" (Ostrom, 1990; Putnam, 1993). On the face of it, this should not impact on the globalization discourse. Further, many conservative critics of "big government" and proponents of "family values" and "communities" oppose globalization – Ross Perot and Patrick Buchanan being prominent examples. We contend, however, that these attacks have added to the undermining of the credibility of the Westphalian state and hence paved the way for privatization and deregulation. Thus, by choice or by accident, these movements have played into the hands of the supporters of globalization.

19 The clash of civilization thesis also suggests the continued importance of security issues. Huntington (1996), however, identifies the "civilization," and not the nation-state, as his unit of analysis.

20 This is also the thrust of the two other volumes we are co-editing as part of this research project.

References

Abramson, P.R. and R. Inglehart (1995) *Value Change in Global Perspective*, Ann Arbor, MI: University of Michigan Press.

Angell, Norman ([1910] 1933) *The Great Illusion*, New York: G.P. Putnam.

Appadurai, Arjun (1996) *Modernity at Large: Cultural Dimensions of Globalization*, Minneapolis, MN: University of Minnesota Press.

Barshefsky, Charlene (1998) "Internet Freedom," *The Washington Post*, A19, July 9.

Beinart, Peter (1997) "An Illusion of Our Time," *The New Republic*, October 20: 20–4.

Berger, Suzanne (1996) "Introduction," in Suzanne Berger and Ronald Dore, editors, *National Diversity and Global Capitalism*, pp.1–25, Ithaca, NY: Cornell University Press.

Berger, Suzanne and Ronald Dore, editors (1996) *National Diversity and Global Capitalism*, Ithaca, NY: Cornell University Press.

Berle, A. A. and G.C. Means (1932) *The Modern Corporations and Private Property*, New York: McMillan.

Borrus, Michael and Jeffrey A. Hart (1994) "Display's the Thing: The Real Stakes in Conflict Over High-Resolution Display," *Journal of Policy Analysis and Management* 13(1): 21–54.

Boyer, R. and D. Drache, editors (1996) *States Against Markets*, New York: Routledge.

Cameron, David (1978) "The Expansion of the Public Economy: A Comparative Analysis," *American Political Science Review* 72(4): 1243–61.

Carnoy, M., M. Castells, S. Cohen and F. Cardoso, editors (1993) *The New Global Economy in the Information Age*, University Park, PA: Pennsylvania State University Press.

Cerny, Philip G. (1997) "The Dynamics of Political Globalization," *Government and Opposition* 32(2): 251–74.

Chase-Dunn, Christopher (1994) "Technology and the Logic of World-Systems," in R. Palan and B.K. Gills, editors, *Transcending State-Global Divide: A Neostructuralist Agenda in International Relations*, Boulder, CO: Lynne Reinner.

Coase, R.H. (1937) "The Nature of the Firm," *Economica* IV: 386–405.

Cohen, Benjamin J. (1996) "Phoenix Risen: The Resurrection of Global Finance," *World Politics* 48 (January): 268–96.

Crawford, Sue E. and Elinor Ostrom (1995) "A Grammar of Institutions," *American Political Science Review* 89: 582–600.

DiMaggio, P.J. and W.W. Powell, editors (1991) *The New Institutionalism in Organizational Analysis*, Chicago, IL: The University of Chicago Press.

Edwards, Richards (1979) *Contested Terrains: The Transformation of the Workplace in the Twentieth Century*, New York: Basic Books.

Evans, Peter (1997) "The Eclipse of the State? Reflections on Stateness in an Era of Globalization," *World Politics* 50(1): 62–87.

Falk, Richard (1997) "State of Siege: Will Globalization Win Out?" *International Affairs* 73(1): 123–36.

Featherstone, M., editor (1990) *Global Culture*, Thousand Oaks, CA: Sage.

Frieden, Jeffrey A. (1991) "Invested Interests: The Politics of National Economic Policies in a World of Global Finance," *International Organization* 45: 425–51.

Frieden, Jeffrey A. and Ronald Rogowski (1996) "The Impact of the International Economy on National Polices: An Analytical Overview," in Robert O. Keohane and Helen V. Milner, editors, *Internationalization and Domestic Politics*, pp.25–47, Cambridge: Cambridge University Press.

Garrett, G. and Peter Lange (1991) "Political Response to Interdependence: What's Left for the Left," *International Organization* 45(4): 539–64.

Gills, Barry K., editor (forthcoming) *Globalization and the Politics of Resistance*, London: Macmillan.

Gilpin, Robert (1987) *Political Economy of International Relations*, Princeton, NJ: Princeton University Press.

Goodman, John B. (1992) *Monetary Sovereignty: The Politics of Central Banking in Western Europe*, Ithaca, NY: Cornell University Press.

Helleiner, Eric (1994) *States and the Reemergence of Global Finance*, Ithaca, NY: Cornell University Press.

Helleiner, Gerald K. (1977) "Transnational Enterprises and the New Political Economy of U.S. Trade Policy," *Oxford Economic Papers* 29: 102–16.

Hirschman, Albert O. (1970) *Exit Voice, and Loyalty*, Cambridge, MA: Harvard University Press.

Huntington, Samuel, P. (1996) *The Clash of Civilizations and The Remaking of World Order*, New York: Simon and Schuster.

Julius, DeAnne (1990) *Global Companies and Public Policy*, New York: Council on Foreign Relations Press.

Kahler, Miles (1996) "Trade and Domestic Differences," in Suzanne Berger and Ronald Dore, editors, *National Diversity and Global Capitalism*, pp.298–332, Ithaca, NY: Cornell University Press.

Katzenstein, Peter J. (1985) *Small States in the World Markets: Industrial Policy in Europe*, Ithaca, NY: Cornell University Press.

Keohane, Robert O. (1984) *After Hegemony*, Princeton, NJ: Princeton University Press.

Keohane, Robert O. (1988) "International Institutions, Two Approaches," *International Studies Quarterly* 32: 379–96.

Keohane, Robert O. and Helen V. Milner, editors (1996) *Internationalization and Domestic Politics*, Cambridge: Cambridge University Press.

Knight, Jack (1992) *Institutions and Social Conflict*, Cambridge: Cambridge University Press.

Kobrin, Stephen J. (1991) "An Empirical Analysis of the Determinants of Global Integration," *Strategic Management Journal* 12: 17–31.

Kobrin, Stephen J. (1995) "Regional Integration in a Globally Networked Economy," *Transnational Corporations* 4(2): 15–33.

Kosai, Yutaka (1996) "Competition and Competition Policy in Japan: Foreign Pressures and Domestic Institutions," in Suzanne Berger and Ronald Dore, editors, *National Diversity and Global Capitalism*, pp.197–215, Ithaca, NY: Cornell University Press.

Krasner, Stephen J., editor (1982) *International Regimes*, Cornell, NY: Cornell University Press.

Krugman, Paul R. (1989) *Exchange Rate Instability*, Cambridge, MA: MIT Press.

Krugman, Paul R. (1994) "Competitiveness: A Dangerous Obsession," *Foreign Affairs* March/April: 28–45.

Lawrence, Robert Z. (1995) "Emerging Regional Arrangements: Building Blocs or Stumbling Blocs?," in Jeffrey A. Frieden and David A. Lake, editors, *International Political Economy*, pp.407–15, New York: St. Martin's Press.

Libecap, Gary D. (1989) *Contracting for Property Rights*, Cambridge: Cambridge University Press.

Lipid, Y. and F. Kratochwil, editors (1997) *The Return of Culture and Identity in IR Theory*, Boulder, CO: Lynne Rienner.

Magee, Stephen (1980) "Three Simple Tests of the Stolper-Samuelson Theorem," in Peter Oppenheimer, editor, *Issues in International Economics*, pp.138–53, London: Oriel Press.

Makhija, Mona V., Kwangsoo Kim and Sandra D. Williamson (1997) "Measuring Globalization of Industries Using a National Industry Approach: Empirical Evidence Across Five Countries Over Time," *Journal of International Business Studies* 28(4): 679–710.

March, James G. and Johan P. Olsen (1989) *Rediscovering Institutions: The Organizational Basis of Politics*, New York: Free Press.

Marglin, Stephen (1974) "What Do Bosses Do? The Origin and Functions of Hierarchy in Capitalist Production," *The Review of Radical Political Economy* 6: 33–60.

Midford, Paul (1993) "International Trade and Domestic Politics: Improving Rogowski's Model of Political Alignments," *International Organization* 47: 535–64.

Milner, Helen V. (1988) *Resisting Protectionism: Global Industries and the Politics of International Trade*, Princeton, NJ: Princeton University Press.

Milner, Helen V. (1998) "International Political Economy: Beyond Hegemonic Stability," *Foreign Policy* Spring: 112–23.

Milner, Helen V. and Robert O. Keohane (1996) "Internationalization and Domestic Politics: An Introduction," in Robert O. Keohane and Helen V. Milner, editors, *Internationalization and Domestic Politics*, pp.3–24, Cambridge: Cambridge University Press.

Mittleman, James H. (1996) *Globalization: Critical Reflections*, Boulder, CO: Lynne Reimer.

New York Times (1997a) February 16: A1.

New York Times (1997b) June 17: A1.

New York Times (1998) June 26: B1.

North, Douglass C. (1990) *Institutions, Institutional Change, and Economic Performance*, New York: Cambridge University Press.

O'Brien, Richard (1992) *Global Financial Integration: The End of Geography*, New York: Council for Foreign Relations.

Ohmae, Keinchi (1991) *The Borderless World*, New York: Harper.

Oliver, Christine (1991) "Strategic Responses to Institutional Processes," *Academy of Management Review* 16(1): 145–79.

Ostrom, Elinor (1986) "An Agenda in the Study of Institutions," *Public Choice* 48: 3–25.

Ostrom, Elinor (1990) *Governing the Commons*, Cambridge: Cambridge University Press.

Ostrom, Elinor (1991) "Rational Choice Theory and Institutional Analysis: Towards Complementarity," *American Political Science Review* 85(1): 237–43.

Ostrom, Vincent, Charles M. Tiebout and Robert Warren (1961) "The Organization of Governments in Metropolitan Areas: A Theoretical Inquiry," *American Political Science Review* 55: 831–42.

Palan, Ronen and Jason Abbot with Phil Dean (1996) *State Strategies in the Global Political Economy*, London: Pinter.

Pauly, Louis W. and Simon Reich (1997) "National Structures and Multinational Corporate Behavior: Enduring Differences in the Age of Globalization," *International Organization* 51(1): 1–30.

Perrow, Charles (1979) *Complex Organization: A Critical Essay*, Glenview, IL: Scott Foresman, and Company.

Pierson, Paul (1996) "The New Politics of the Welfare State," *World Politics* 48 (January): 143–79.

Polanyi, Karl (1957) *The Great Transformation: The Political and Economic Origins of Our Time*, Boston, MA: Beacon Press.

Porter, Michael E. (1990) *Competitive Advantage of Nations*, New York: Free Press.

Prakash, Aseem and Jeffrey. A. Hart (1998) "Political Economy of Economic Integration," *Business and the Contemporary World* X: 611–32.

Putnam, Robert D. (1993) *Democracy at Work*, Princeton, NJ: Princeton University Press.

Ramaswamy, Kannan, K. Galen Kroeck and William Renforth (1996) "Measuring the Degree of Internationalization: A Comment," *Journal of International Business Studies* 27(1): 167–77.

Reich, Robert B. (1992) *The Works of Nation*, New York: Vintage Books.

Robertson, Roland (1992) *Globalization, Social Theory, and Global Culture*, Thousand Oaks, CA: Sage.

Rodrik, Dani (1997) *Has Globalization Gone Too Far?* Washington, DC: Institute for International Economics.

Rogowski, Ronald (1989) *Commerce and Coalitions: How Trade Affects Domestic Political Alignments*, Princeton, NJ: Princeton University Press.

Rosenau, James N. (1997) *Along the Domestic-Foreign Frontier: Exploring Governance in a Turbulent World*, Cambridge: Cambridge University Press.

Ruggie, John G. (1982) "International Regimes, Transactions and Change: Embedded Liberalism in the Postwar Economic Orders," *International Organization* 36 (Spring): 379–415.

Ruggie, John G. (1993) "Territoriality and Beyond: Problematizing Modernity in International Relations," *International Organization* 47 (Winter): 139–73.

Rugman, Alan M. and Alain Verbeke (1998) "Multinational Enterprise and Public Policy," *Journal of International Business Studies* 29(1): 115–36.

Russett, Bruce (1993) *Grasping the Democratic Peace: Principles for a Post-Cold War World*, with the collaboration of Antholis, William, Carol R. Ember, Melvin Ember, and Zeev Maoz, Princeton, NJ: Princeton University Press.

Scott, Alan, editor (1997) *The Limits of Globalization*, London and New York: Routledge.

Scott, W.R. (1987) "The Adolescence of Institutional Theory," *Administrative Science Quarterly* 32: 493–511.

Sell, Susan (forthcoming) "The Future of the WTO," in Richard Stubbs and Geoffrey Underhill, editors, *Political Economy and the Changing Global Order*, New York: St. Martin's Press.

Simon, Herbert A. (1957) *Administrative Behavior*, New York: Macmillan.

Sjolander, Claire T. (1996) "The Rhetoric of Globalization: What's in the Wor(l)d?" *International Journal* LI (Autumn): 603–16.

Stopford, John and Susan Strange (1991) *Rival States Rival Firms*, Cambridge: Cambridge University Press.

Strange, Susan (1995) "The Defective State," *Daedalus* 124(2): 55–74.

Strange, Susan (1996) *The Retreat of the State: The Diffusion of Power in the World Economy*, Cambridge: Cambridge University Press.

Sullivan, Daniel (1994) "Measuring the Degree of Internationalization of a Firm," *Journal of International Business Studies* 25(2): 325–42.

Tyson, Laura D'Andrea (1991) "They Are Not Us," *The American Prospect* 4, Winter.

United Nations Conference on Trade and Development/UNCTAD (1995) *World Investment Report*, Geneva: United Nations.

Wade, Robert (1996) "Globalization and its Limits: Reports of the Death of the National Economy are Greatly Exaggerated," in Suzanne Berger and Ronald Dore, editors, *National Diversity and Global Capitalism*, pp.60–88, Ithaca, NY: Cornell University Press.

Wall Street Journal (1997) January 3.

Williamson, Oliver E. (1985) *Economic Institutions of Capitalism*, New York: Free Press.

Young, Oran R. (1986) "International Regimes: Towards a New Theory of Institutions," *World Politics* 39: 104–22.

Part I

The concepts and politics of globalization and governance

This section carries on a dialogue between the advocates of two different perspectives on governance: the new-institutionalists (David Lake and Michael McGinnis) and the constructivists (Wayne Sandholtz and Peter Haas). The fifth paper by Ian Douglas critically evaluates the broader public debate on globalization and governance.

Scholars of international relations often argue that domestic governance is characterized by a hierarchy of institutions with the state at the top, while international politics is anarchic involving competition among juridically sovereign countries. Employing a new-institutionalist perspective, David Lake challenges this anarchy–hierarchy divide. He finds this notion to be overly restrictive since the anarchy–hierarchy continuum operates both at the international and the domestic levels. Consequently, a wide variety of governance structures are present at these levels.

In the introductory essay, we defined governance as the organization of collective action. Lake's notion of governance differs from ours in that he equates governance with contracting only. According to Lake, organizing collective action involves two analytically separate processes: bargaining and contracting. Bargaining divides the available costs and benefits between actors, while contracting enforces the bargains that have been reached. For him, the crux of governance lies in contracting. Further, since central to contracting is the right to residual control, hierarchies emerge whenever this residual control is lodged in only one party to a contract.

Lake then argues that the location of governance structures on the anarchical–hierarchical continuum is a function of three variables: scale economies, expected costs of opportunism, and governance or agency costs. Scale economies reflect gains from cooperation. However, any cooperative endeavor can be undermined by the fear of opportunistic behavior; that the other actor will manipulate the contract to its advantage. And the cost of opportunistic behavior varies with the relational-specificity of assets. Though hierarchies are expected to mitigate the costs of opportunism, they suffer from governance costs due to principal-agent conflicts (agency costs) as well as potential for exploitation by hierarchical superiors (managerial opportunism). Hence the location of any governance structure on the hierarchy–anarchy continuum reflects the efficient trade-off between govern-ance costs, on one hand, and the potential gains from cooperation and lower-ing costs of opportunism, on the other.

Finally, Lake suggests that globalization processes have been facilitated by specific kinds of domestic governance structures of early industrializers – particularly, Britain and the United States. These *laisser-faire* economies were characterized by large numbers of small private actors with non-specific assets and the liberal order vested substantial residual rights in them. By virtue of their hegemonic position in the international political economy, Britain and the United States could mold the anarchical system in the image of their domestic political economies. This left large unclaimed political spaces in the international arena, and globalization results because non-state economic actors such as the multinational corporations occupy these vacant spaces. Lake then comes up with a counterfactual conclusion that if, as a response to the processes of globalization, more hierarchical forms of supra-national governance structures were to emerge, such structures would under-mine anarchy, the main condition facilitating these processes.

Lake views transaction cost efficiencies as defining organizational types. Michael McGinnis argues otherwise. Although he also employs a new-institutionalist perspective, he reaches a different set of conclusions on the desired determinants of any organizational type. McGinnis' basic premise is that any conceptualization of governance needs to be broken down into its constituent service components. Corresponding to the three basic human needs of wealth, physical security, and emotional attachment, he identifies three realms of collective action: economic-productive, coercive-protective, and social-communal. The fourth realm – political-governance – provides services for coordinating the other three realms. His important insight is that no single realm can by itself solve its collective action dilemmas; it needs to draw upon resources from other realms. McGinnis notes that by definition, agents of an organization in one realm control resources relevant to the moti-vation defined as the most central to that realm. That is, agents of firms have direct access to economic resources but not to coercion, and police officers can dispense coercion much easier than bribes. Since extracting additional resources on the basis of any single motivation ultimately faces diminishing marginal returns, agents in one realm have incentives to access the resources under the control of agents in the other realms.

In the Hobbesian conception of a state all four realms are concentrated within a single organizational structure, the Leviathan. This is also a basic premise of the Westphalian system. By challenging this monopolization, globalization processes force changes in existing governance structures. What will the new structures look like and will they, *à la* Lake, minimize transaction costs as determined by scale economies, costs of opportunism, and governance costs?

McGinnis identifies two elements of the costs of maintaining a governance organization: start-up costs in establishing new organizations and the govern-ance costs to which Lake alludes in his chapter. According to McGinnis, for any governance system to survive in the long run, it must build legitimacy. This is often done by redistributing some of the gains of collective action from winners to losers. Globalization processes, with their emphasis on quick changes in production technologies and increased exposure to foreign trade, will create many losers in the domestic economy. As a result, institutionalized mechanisms for redistribution are required to maintain legitimacy. The exist-ing institutions of governance, particularly the state, may be better placed to provide such redistributive services than any new ones. He feels that even though such extant institutions may not minimize governance costs, they may be better placed for providing redistributive services due to their lower start-up costs. As a result, such institutions are well placed to survive the onslaught of the processes of globalization.

Both Lake and McGinnis employ a new-institutionalist perspective in that they view human behavior as being rational or consequence-driven. Rational behavior means that individuals assess the costs and benefits *prior* to action. The central assertion of new-institutionalism is that institutions affect behavior by altering the incentives facing actors. Importantly, institutions are viewed as human artifacts that can be established, strengthened, weakened, or abolished. In contrast to a consequence-based approach, Wayne Sandholtz presents a sociological rule-based perspective on govern-ance. Sandholtz criticizes the transactions cost approach, questioning its empirical validity. He claims that there is little reliable data on transaction costs, how institutions actually lower or raise them, or how actors change their behaviors in response to reductions or increases in transaction costs.

In contrast to the new-institutionalists who subscribe to a methodological individualism in which agents are ontologically superior to structures, Sandholtz advocates employing a constructivist perspective where individual and social structures have equal ontological status. One of the limitations of the rationalist approach is that it takes as given the social and institutional foundations of "interests" and "utility." Constructivists assert that actors have interests or goals only in the context of social relations that produce shared meanings and values. Thus, for Sandholtz, institutions are much more than bargaining forums where utility-maximizing states with autono-mous preferences construct arrangements for minimizing transaction costs.

A rule-based approach views individual behavior as being driven by heuris-tics and orientations. The dominant mode of decision making is by analogy and not by cost-benefit calculations. Decisions depend crucially on beliefs and values and the ways issues get framed. This is even more pronounced in organizations where individual behavior is guided by routines and standard operating procedures. Since international relations is conducted primarily among such organizations, a rule-based approach is more appropriate than a consequence-based approach for examining international issues like globalization. Sandholtz suggests three basic clusters of rules in the study of international relations: (1) state system rules that establish states as juridically sovereign; (2) liberal rules that define the authority between the state and the individual; and (3) technical rules that define how individuals and communities relate to the natural environment.

How may we apply a constructivist perspective to a particular issue area of international governance? In his chapter, Peter Haas examines the role of ideas in shaping the institutions of international environmental governance. Haas' chapter has a lot in common with those of the new-institutionalists in this volume in that he suggests a functionalist explanation of institutional emergence. On the other hand, along with Sandholtz, he emphasizes the importance of ideas in shaping these institutions. For him, ideas precede and justify practices; "epistemic communities" are the intervening variable between them. Epistemic communities are "networks of professionals who share common normative and causal beliefs, accept common truth-tests and are engaged in a common policy enterprise." According to Haas, explanations that focus only on technological changes for explaining observed changes in practices are under-specified. He identifies four elements necessary for any governance system: (1) a set of commitments specifying rights and responsibilities, rules and procedures for realizing these commitments; (2) a set of actors to participate in decision-making rules; (3) a set of formal institutions to coordinate activities; and (4) a procedure for adjudicating disagreements.

In the absence of epistemic communities, governance in international relations is primarily state-centered. However, in environmental governance there is a powerful global epistemic community that holds governments accountable to new standards of environmental behavior. Consequently, a stable set of expectations has been established that is becoming more comprehensive over time. The norms, rules and strategies for environmental governance are no longer widely contested.

Any discussion of global governance would be incomplete without a consideration of the politics at stake. That the notion that "global governance" carries positive value is worthy of further investigation. That it often runs hand-in-hand with discourses of democratization, empowerment and the fragmentation of state power, gives this notion an extra political edge. How did global governance become an object of knowledge, and to what problem does it provide a solution?

Clearly concerned by the popularization of the notion of "global governance," Ian Douglas interrogates its rhetoric, suggesting that behind its silent ascent lies a hidden history of political intervention. From the Foucauldian hypothesis that the development of political governance over the modern period has been characterized by the decentralization of power and the emergence of systems of self-constitution at the level of individuality (subjectification), as well as the channeling of energies into specific tasks validated by political reason (disciplines), Douglas argues that the very notion of a democratic global governance in which one is active and mobile (a globalized citizen), is a politicized one. He traces the ascent of this global rationality to the development of state power, employing Michel Foucault's critique of liberal philosophy, and Paul Virilio's analytics of "speed" to trace how globalism as a technical achievement (the contraction of the world's distance) is linked to the decentralization of political governance and the birth of industrial society.

What Douglas suggests is that "global governance" stands at the endpoint of the disappearance of state power. But unlike other authors (for example Kobrin and Cerny in this volume), he conceives of "disappearance" as an extension, rather than abrogation of modern practices of social power. The state, Douglas suggests, has emptied itself out; inscripting itself less in public spaces and more in the pace of public life. For him the contemporary commentators are not only making an observational mistake, but are making a fatal political one; one that merely prepares the ground upon which the universalization of political order will be staged. Douglas takes this universalization of political order (the endpoint of "global governance") to be the paralysis of humanity and the end of politics as well as history. In tracing the "genealogy of power" (governance) and the "genealogy of motion" (globalism), he aims to open a new space of reflection, and possible transformation, of the politics of globalization and governance.

1   Global governance

A relational contracting approach

*David A. Lake**

Governance and globalization have long been central concerns of international relations. Throughout the history of the discipline, scholars have
examined how states, groups, corporations, and other actors organize themselves politically within the international arena. This concern was most
recently manifested in the literature on international regimes (see Krasner
1983 and Keohane 1984). The end of the Cold War, the apparent growth of
supra-national institutions in Europe, and rising concerns with environmental degradation and other transborder externalities are now sparking a
broader inquiry into global governance. Likewise, for decades, scholars have
studied how economic flows, migration, and other interactions shape international politics, first in the work of Karl Deutsch and his collaborators (see
Deutsch, *et al.* 1957) and, later, in the literatures on transnational relations
and interdependence (see Keohane and Nye 1972 and 1977). The explosion
in the frequency, types, and magnitudes of transborder activities over the
last decade has stimulated new interest in globalization.

These two concerns are increasingly seen as linked. Globalization, it is commonly averred, is breeding new forms of governance, either in the guise of
impersonal markets (Strange 1996) or private, "sovereignty-free actors"
such as multinational corporations, transnational societies, and international
organizations (Rosenau 1990). While globalization is no longer expected to
render states obsolete (contrary to Kindleberger 1969 and Vernon 1971),
many analysts have nonetheless concluded that political authority within the
international system is becoming more diffuse. Susan Strange (1996, 84)
argues that "the reality of state authority is not the same as it once was."
Jessica T. Mathews (1997, 50) writes that:

> National governments . . . are sharing powers – including political, social,
> and security roles at the core of sovereignty – with businesses, with inter-
> national organizations, and with a multitude of citizens groups. . . . The
> steady concentration of power in the hands of states that began in 1648
> with the Peace of Westphalia is over, at least for a while.

Richard Rosecrance (1996) wryly observes that we now live in the age of the "virtual state."

Despite this long history and growing academic attention, the concept of governance and its relationship to globalization remain poorly understood. This paper offers a framework for thinking about issues of governance and globalization, and provides an interpretation of current and future trends in both domains. The analysis is intended to be suggestive rather than definitive, to place the study of governance and globalization on the right track rather than steer it into the final station. In this chapter, I develop three themes, taken up section-by-section below. All run contrary to the current conventional wisdom.

First, as a discipline, international relations typically employs an extremely attenuated definition of governance. Both yesterday and today, there is a wide variety of governance structures in international relations, including a fair number of hierarchies.

Second, current studies of global governance, embodied in the literature on international institutions, are plagued by selection bias. Once the full range of governance structures is properly conceptualized and a model developed, it becomes clear that we cannot generalize from international institutions to the larger question of global governance without taking this bias into account.

Third, globalization is the product of a particular form of governance rooted in the domestic political economies of the early industrializers. Based upon a "watchman" state, this domestic governance structure has been generalized to, and has created a large sphere of private activity within, the international arena. Together with the permissive conditions of a world system broken into separate, national "sovereignties" and technological change that reduces the costs of communication and transportation, this governance structure provides the foundation for globalization. In turn, there are immense sources of inertia in our present form of global governance. If some more hierarchic form of global governance were to emerge, it would encroach upon and possibly undermine the conditions necessary for globlization. By itself, globalization has little potential for transforming international relations.

What is global governance?

The term global governance lacks any accepted definition. As one analyst puts it:

> The word . . . presents dangers and opportunities to anyone who would reopen the question of global governance, though the term itself lacks in precision what it offers in its novelty. It is quite certain in most people' s minds that *governance is not government.* . . . But beyond that negative

stance, the concept of global governance needs to be clarified, amplified and, if thought desirable, made operational.

(emphasis in original; Desai 1995, 7)

The Commission on Global Governance (1995, 2) defines their subject as "the sum of the many ways individuals and institutions, public and private, manage their common affairs. It is a continuing process though which conflicting or diverse interests may be accommodated and co-operative action may be taken." Leon Gordenker and Thomas Weiss (1996, 17) define global governance as "efforts to bring more orderly and reliable responses to social and political issues that go beyond the capacities of states to address individually." Oran Young (1994, 15), in turn, defines governance as

> the establishment and operation of social institutions (in the sense of rules of the game that serve to define social practices, assign roles, and guide interactions among the occupants of these roles) capable of resolving conflicts, facilitating cooperation, or, more generally, alleviating collective-action problems in a world of interdependent actors.

James N. Rosenau (1992: 5) offers the most succinct and, in some ways, most insightful definition: "governance is order plus intentionality."

These definitions properly direct our attention to the interdependent nature of decision making and the attempt by actors to "manage" or produce more "orderly" responses to common problems. Nonetheless, they blur two analytically distinct political processes: bargaining, which divides the available costs and benefits between actors, and contracting, which enforces the bargains reached. It is the enforcement of bargains that we intuitively mean by the term governance.[1]

It is the design, construction, and maintenance of mechanisms to enforce agreed upon behaviors that lies at the heart of contracting, as a process, and governance, as both an analytic concept and the set of mechanisms actually employed. All contracts, or governance structures, include provisions for monitoring the behavior of others and safeguards for altering the incentives of others and, frequently, oneself (Williamson 1985). Governance structures may be formal, as found in written constitutions or ratified treaty documents, or informal, as in unwritten constitutions based on common law and precedent or some international regimes (Lipson 1991).

Bargaining and contracting are obviously related, with each dependent upon the other (see Fearon 1998). Some feasible bargains may lack any effective contract, and thus are impossible to reach in practice; knowing that the bargain cannot be enforced, actors will not agree to that division in the first place. The initial and on-going costs of the contract may also be greater than the joint gains, again rendering any bargain impractical. Different bargains, in turn, may require different sorts of contracts, and in a world of limited options the nature of the contract may follow simply from the bargain reached. Given the necessary relationship between bargaining and contracting, the two processes will often, in practice, unfold simultaneously. Moreover, since contracts will often determine which bargains are feasible, much of the negotiation or apparent "bargaining" between the actors may well be over alternative contracts, which then logically produce different substantive outcomes with different distributional consequences. Nonetheless, bargaining and contracting are analytically distinct processes. Contracting and governance are concerned not with the substance of agreements but with securing and enforcing those agreements.

Contracts specify, implicitly or explicitly, the rights of residual control retained by each party to the contract. This is a central feature of all governance structures, and it is the primary dimension of variation that I focus on in this chapter. In a world of bounded rationality or costly information, all contracts are necessarily incomplete (Williamson 1985). It is either impossible or too costly to specify actions required by the parties in all possible states of the world. Rights of residual control determine who decides what in these unspecified or unspecifiable futures (see Grossman and Hart 1986). It is important to emphasize that the term "right," as used here, does not necessarily imply a formal recognition by the parties to a contract of the authority to exercise control over the residual areas of decision; it can simply reflect an informal ability by one party to control the behavior of the other over some areas. Rights differ from mere influence, however, by constituting an enduring pattern of control within an on-going relationship.

Sovereign states, whatever agreements they may enter into, retain all residual rights of control; this is the "constitutional independence" that Alan James (1986) sees as the defining characteristic of sovereignty. Thus, states may agree to come to one another's aid in case of attack by a third state, but each is free to determine whether an attack has in fact occurred and how it will respond. Again, it is this vesting of residual rights in the contracting parties themselves that classifies states as independent or, in international relations terminology, sovereign. In an empire, on the other hand, all residual rights of control are vested in the imperial state. However extensive the autonomy granted to the colony, the imperial center retains the right to determine actions by the subordinate colony outside the designated areas. It is the lodging of residual rights of control in only one party to the contract that creates a hierarchy.

Rights of residual control also differ within states. Unlike in more centralized regimes, rights of residual control are divided across many actors in the United States, creating a decentralized or comparatively "flat" and "anarchic" political system. The tenth amendment to the constitution clearly specifies that all rights not otherwise specified "are reserved to the States, respectively, or to the people." Most state constitutions contain a similar provision. Thus, by design, residual rights of control are divided between "the people" and, in defined areas, the states or the federal government. These rights have also evolved over time, gradually shifting to the federal level. An important basis for this shift has been the vesting of the right to interpret the federal constitution in an entity of the federal government, namely the Supreme Court. Through the interpretations of the Court, the residual rights of the federal government have been progressively expanded and the rights of the states correspondingly shrunk.

Although the language of "contracting" is often understood to imply voluntary agreements between actors, governance and especially rights of residual control are highly political and intimately related to issues of power.[2] Power can be disaggregated into capabilities – the raw materials of power – and decision-making ability. Although international relationists, in general, tend to ignore the second attribute of power, both are necessary to its effective use. Capabilities matter only when the actor has the ability to decide to manipulate its resources to its advantage.

Residual rights of control, in turn, define the what the actor can and cannot decide, and thus are central to the structure of power and its use. For example, the trade dependence of an imperial state upon its colony gives the latter the capability to impose punishments or rewards upon the former, but the colony lacks the ability to decide to exercise that influence. Without an independent state to define autonomous goals and implement strategies, the colony lacks the ability to "decide." This formulation of power parallels definitions of structural or the second face of power (Lukes 1974). Politically weak and disenfranchised actors often have the capability to wield substantial influence, but in the absence of any political apparatus they lack the ability to choose to exercise their power; thus, their influence remains latent.

In addition, contracts are often founded on and maintained by coercion – further reflecting their basis in power.[3] Coercion can be understood as a substitute for the compromises that would be necessary in otherwise "voluntary" negotiations. In order to ensure that it cannot be exploited in the future by its partner, a state may insist upon detailed contractual provisions that ensure its ability to monitor and enforce an agreement. When faced with a coercive threat from its partner, however, that same state may capitulate and accept a much "weaker" contract – or even be forced into a relationship against its will. Even possible threats – the "shadow of force" – can alter the terms of a contract. As a result, contracts both aim to alter the incentives of the actors, and thus are an exercise of power, and reflect the power of the actors. In the presence of coercion, contracts need not be "fair," "equal" or pareto-improving. Indeed, although the subordinate party will seek to limit its exploitation as much as possible through the contract, the contract itself may be an instrument of its own subordination.

Implications

This conception of governance has at least three implications for our understanding of international relations. First, as frequently noted in the existing literature, governance is not equivalent to government or formal institutions. As Young correctly notes, there is nothing in the concept of governance "that presupposes the need to create material entities or organizations (that is, governments) to administer the rules of the game that arise to handle the function of governance" (1994, 15–16; see also Rosenau and Czempiel 1992). All contracts, whether formal or informal, constitute governance.

Second, governance is a variable. Anarchy, which vests residual rights in states, is but one form of international governance; hierarchy is a second form, and there are mixed types in-between (see Lake 1996 and 1999). Along this continuum, relationships vary in the rights of residual control retained by the actors. As relations move from anarchy to hierarchy, actors are ceding greater rights over more issue areas to their dominant partners. Even within states, moreover, variations in governance can occur, providing a useful basis for diachronic and synchronic comparisons. There is no reason, even within systemic theories of international relations, to treat anarchy as a constant and unchanging feature of the global environment. Nor does the distinction between hierarchy and anarchy cleanly distinguish domestic from international political systems (contrary to Waltz 1979; see Milner 1991). There are elements of anarchy in nearly all polities, just as there are elements of hierarchy in world politics. Both domestic and international political systems should be understood as varying along a continuum.

Empirically, and limiting ourselves to traditionally "international" interactions, there has been a wide variety of relations. Even in the security arena, where states might be expected to worry most about hierarchical ties, we observe historically a range of relationships, some of which – like spheres of influence – have long been part of international relation's lexicon but have not been integrated in our theoretical paradigms in any consistent way. Elsewhere, I have posed a continuum of security relationships, defined by decreasing rights of residual control possessed by the subordinate polity (Lake 1996 and 1999). This continuum ranges from anarchic *alliances* (each party remains fully sovereign), to *spheres of influence* (the subordinate member gives up the right to ally with states other than the dominant party), to *protectorates* (the subordinate member cedes rights over its foreign policy), to *informal empires* (a broad range of residual rights are transferred to the dominant state), to *empire* (nearly all rights of residual control are vested in the dominant state).

While examples of alliances and empires come readily to mind, the range of intermediate relationships is actually quite broad and almost obvious once depicted in these terms:

- under the aegis of the Monroe Doctrine, the United States has possessed a sphere of influence (at least) over all of Latin America from early in the nineteenth century;
- during the Persian Gulf War, the United States created a protectorate over Saudi Arabia and the other Gulf states; once American troops were deployed in the kingdom, the Saudis lost their ability to conduct an independent foreign policy toward Iraq;
- following World War II, the Soviet Union established an informal empire over the nominally sovereign but subordinate states of Eastern Europe; this informal empire collapsed only in 1989.

All of these examples are typically treated as anarchic relations, but simultaneously recognized as somewhat anomalous. The Warsaw Pact, for instance, was called an alliance by the member states and Western analysts, but the latter, at least, typically recognized that the label fitted poorly; the Soviet Union intervened deeply into the domestic political and economic affairs of the subordinate members. As these examples suggest, once we begin to look for variations in rights of residual control, we can readily see that, at least at the dyadic level, anarchy is not a constant. Instead, international politics can be more properly seen as a rich tapestry of relations of varying degrees of hierarchy.

Third, global governance is not limited to contracts between states. Two examples can help make this clear. Considerable attention has recently been devoted to the role of non-governmental organizations (NGOs) in monitoring international accords, particularly in the areas of the environment and human rights (for instance, Weiss and Gordenker 1996, Salamon 1994). Far from anomalous, using private groups to gather information and pull "fire alarms" (McCubbins and Schwartz 1984) is standard operating procedure for governments around the world – both in their domestic affairs and foreign relations. Rather than undertaking periodic monitoring themselves ("police patrols"), governments often empower groups and design political structures to induce groups with strong interests to perform this role. Affected economic groups, human rights organizations, and environmental activists (see Haas, this volume) all play important roles in monitoring national compliance with international commitments and, as such, are properly understood as part of the international contract regulating behavior in those areas.

Multinational firms have proliferated over the last fifty years through informal contracts with their home governments to secure their property rights abroad and often more formal contracts with host governments. Typically, agreements now cover a range of issues from ownership to export quotas and the training and promotion of local personnel. In the not too distant past, foreign direct investment often required hierarchical governance structures, especially in plantation agriculture and mineral extraction (Frieden 1994). With insecure property rights, large site-specific investments, but few firm specific assets, primary and raw material production was an easy target for nationalization. As a result, foreign investment required either direct or indirect rule by an investor country. Thus, foreign investment in extractive industries tended to occur within colonial or neo-colonial relationships, internalizing the investment in a formal or informal imperial relationship. As foreign investment in manufacturing increased over the early decades of the twentieth century, however, the need for political hierarchy diminished. Such investments were often not site-specific (the "footloose" multinational) but were highly firm-specific, resting on proprietary technology, firm reputation, or integration into a global production and marketing strategy. Since firm specific assets cannot be appropriated as easily by foreign governments, nationalization became far less effective and, therefore, less common. Multinational firms and governments, thus, could now contract independently over those aspects of the investment and production process that were more readily monitored and regulated by national authorities. Foreign direct investment ultimately became based on anarchic contracts between private firms and national governments (these agreements are possibly being codified into a multilateral agreement; see below).

Explaining global governance

Whenever actors cooperate, they must choose a relationship along the continuum of anarchy to hierarchy to govern their interactions. In this section, I briefly summarize a theory of relational contracting in international relations and discuss its implications for how we should study the effects of international institutions. Although I have developed the argument most fully for security relations (Lake 1996, 1997, 1999), I believe the theory is applicable also to cooperation in economic, environmental, and other affairs.

A theory of relational contracting

Theories of relational contracting, first developed in economics to explain the firm, are general theories of social relationships and, as such, can also be applied to politics (see Keohane 1984). As used here, the theory is informed by a central metaphor, namely, that the government is a firm producing goods and services in exchange for revenue. Whenever a government chooses to produce a good or service in association with another polity, it must choose a relationship to govern that cooperative enterprise. In this metaphor, an alliance is analogous to an arm's length contract between separate firms, while an empire is akin to integration within a single firm. The decision to cooperate and, if so, the choice between alternative governance structures, I argue, is a function of three main variables.[4]

Joint production economies determine the gains from cooperation, and thus form a crucial determinant of whether polities act unilaterally or pool their resources and efforts with others. Joint economies derive from technological scale economies, the division of labor, and positive externalities. They are always at least as great in cooperation as in unilateralism, but some technologies are utilized properly only in conjunction with others, the division of labor is possible only with partners, and actors can reduce redundant efforts only when positive externalities are "internalized" in some cooperative relationship. The greater the joint economies, the greater the resources saved by cooperation. Joint economies, in turn, are partly endogenous to the relationship; the less opportunistic their partners, the more deeply actors will invest in technologies, divisions of labor, and positive externalities that are contingent on the actions of those partners.

All actors are opportunistic, or self-seeking with guile (Williamson 1985). In any relationship, actors will seek to manipulate its terms to their advantage, abandoning, entrapping, or exploiting their partners whenever possible. The cost to an actor of opportunistic behavior by its partner is determined by the extent of its relationally specific assets (Klein *et al.* 1978). If it has incurred investments that are of value only in that relationship, such as dedicated plant and equipment for firms or overseas bases for states, opportunism will be very costly. The probability that a partner will act opportunistically, however, is a function of the governance structure or relationship the parties construct. Given some set of behaviors required by a contract, the ability to act opportunistically is determined by the rights of residual control. If the actor has no rights of residual control – no ability to decide anything outside the immediate terms of the contract – it cannot (or is significantly less able to) behave opportunistically; the decision whether to honor the contract and what to do when the contract does not specify action under some circumstance is entirely in the hands of the dominant partner. Thus, hierarchy reduces the probability that opportunism will occur. The *expected* costs of opportunism, holding joint production economies constant, decline as relations move from anarchy to hierarchy, creating an incentive for actors to create hierarchies when the potential costs or risks of opportunism are large.

Governance costs arise from the direct and indirect value actors place on the residual rights of control. In international relations, rights of residual control – embodied in the concepts of freedom, independence, and autonomy – are often valued on their own terms, as arguments in an actor's utility function. Residual rights of control may also be valued for their incentive effects. For a subordinate actor, any residual rights it cedes to a dominant actor will, presumably, be exercised to choose behaviors that it alone would not select. Any gains it receives from cooperation dependent upon the transfer of residual rights, therefore, will be less valuable to it, in the short run, and may lead to secondary distortions in its incentives in the long run. In order for the subordinate actor to cede rights to the dominant actor, it must either be compensated for the loss in autonomy and the distortions that are engendered by the dominant actor, or coerced, both of which, paradoxically, transfer the costs of hierarchy onto the dominant actor. The dominant actor, in turn, may also be required to bind itself not to act opportunistically toward the subordinate actor, reducing the value of the residual rights transferred to itself. In order to gain the compliance of the subordinate actor, the dominant actor may restrict its own powers or send some costly signal, imposing costs on itself in order to secure hierarchy over the other. Arising from both the need to compensate or coerce the subordinate actor and tie its own hands, the governance costs to the dominant actor escalate with hierarchy and deter actors from pursuing such governance structures.

As the expected costs of opportunism decline with hierarchy, while governance costs rise with hierarchy, there must exist some optimal relationship along the continuum defined above. The net gains from the optimal relationship are then assessed against the baseline gains from unilateralism. The greater the joint economies, the lower the expected costs of opportunism, and the lower the governance costs, the more likely actors will be to choose some form of cooperation. The lower (greater) the expected costs of opportunism or the greater (lower) the governance costs, the more likely actors will be to choose relatively anarchic (hierarchic) relations.

International institutions and governance

By focusing almost exclusively on anarchic international institutions, a specific form of governance, analysts have unwittingly created a significant selection bias in their studies of international relations. The theory just summarized implies clearly that conclusions based on extant international institutions cannot and should not be generalized to global governance (contrary to Murphy 1994, 1).[5]

Realists claim that international institutions are epiphenomenal (Krasner 1983; Strange 1983, and Mearsheimer 1994–95). Institutions do not prevent states from "defecting" and pursuing their self-interest whenever it serves their purpose. When institutions do appear to be effective, on the other hand, it is because the interests of states actually coincide. Likewise, neoliberal institutionalists have not been able to demonstrate conclusively that international regimes matter.[6] These conclusions are highly circumscribed.

As explained above, states enter into anarchic relationships only when the gains from cooperation are sufficiently large, the expected costs of opportunism by their partners are sufficiently low, and the costs of constructing more hierarchical structures are sufficiently high. In other words, we observe anarchic relations – e.g., international institutions – only when states reach the conclusion that an anarchic contract is the most cost-effective way to preserve the gains from cooperation against opportunism by their partners. When examining international institutions, then, we are selecting one of two sets of conditions.

In the first instance, the gains from cooperation are large and governance costs rise rapidly with hierarchy. Attracted by the gains from pooling resources and efforts with others, but repelled by the high costs of building and maintaining hierarchy, states choose anarchic relationships and accept high expected costs of opportunism by their partners. In this case, states anticipate that they will be exploited by their partners, but they also calculate that, on balance, the gains from cooperation are worth the risk. In this case, the institutions are not expected to be very constraining; that we observe lots of opportunistic behavior here is not surprising.

In the second instance, the gains from cooperation are low, but the expected costs of opportunism are even lower, perhaps because the interests of states are closely aligned, the realist case, or few specific assets are at risk. Under this circumstance, anarchy is sufficient because states believe it is unlikely that their partners will act opportunistically or, if they do, it will not be very costly. Thus, an anarchic form of cooperation is selected by states precisely because there is not much at risk. That the self-interests of states do not lead them to defect under this circumstance should not be surprising.

By examining the effects of extant international institutions on co-operation, then, we are selecting instances in which states are expected to defect, but the gains are nonetheless worth the risk, or the weak constraints of an anarchic governance structure are sufficient to safeguard the agreement. In both cases, we would draw the correct conclusion that institutions do not "matter," but it would be a mistake to conclude that governance, more generally, is unimportant. By examining international institutions, we do not observe cooperation that requires and occurs only within more hierarchic governance structures. Similarly, we do not observe cooperation that fails to occur because the gains are too small, the expected costs of opportunism are too large, or the governance costs of hierarchy rise too rapidly. Cooperation that occurs within extant international institutions is a product of the very features realists rely upon to demonstrate the epiphenomenal nature of institutions.

By similar logic, international institutions will have only a minimal effect on "transactions costs," an ambiguous label used in the literature to refer to both the expected costs of opportunism and governance costs. Wayne Sandholtz (this volume) and others criticize new-institutionalist accounts of international regimes because there is little direct evidence that transactions costs are reduced by such cooperative agreements. While transactions costs are notoriously difficult to measure, the selection bias introduced by studying only anarchic international institutions suggests a second and equally impor-tant problem. International institutions are likely to exist precisely in those areas where transactions costs are relatively modest, and thus hardest to observe. In the first instance noted above, the expected costs of opportunism may be large, but the governance costs in anarchy are comparatively low – each type of transactions costs offsets the other. In the second instance, both the expected costs of opportunism and governance costs in anarchy are negligible. Analysts look for the transactions costs-reducing effects of inter-national institutions exactly where they are hardest to find.

If we want to observe where global governance and relational contracting matters most, we need to expand our analytic horizons beyond existing international institutions to empires; multinational states, like the Soviet Union, that subsume numerous would-be polities; private actors, such as MNCs or NGOs; and other, more hierarchic entities. We also need to probe more effectively plausible counterfactuals: for instance, why are the United States and Canada two separate states or, for that matter, why is the United States not fifty independent countries? We have failed to look for such relationships and ask such questions only because of our collective fascination with and acceptance of anarchy as the organizing principle of international relations not only at the systemic level, where it of course still holds, but in the relations between states and other international actors. To see governance in action, we need a broader lens. The narrow one commonly used distorts our vision.

Governance and globalization

Globalization is one of the dominant trends of our time. Although, again, there is no consensus on what is meant by this term, it is usually associated with the following sorts of developments: the growth of political and economic interdependence at the world level; the erosion of space and local time as structures of economic life; and the homogenization of social life – especially at the elite level – through universal standards, products, and culture (see Mlinar 1992, 19–22; Boyarin 1994; Giddens 1990).

For many, globalization and global governance are intimately connected. As globalization occurs, states lose control over their destinies, problems become "bigger" than the capacities of individual governments, and states must delegate and possibly abdicate political authority to supranational entities with powers that more nearly coincide with the scope of the issues and actors to be managed. Thus, in this common view, globalization is a primary motor behind current trends toward expanded global governance (see Cerny 1995). In this section, I question this link between globalization and global governance and, in fact, reverse the causal arrow.

There are three necessary and, together, sufficient factors driving the process of globalization. First, as long recognized by world systems theorists, the rise of a global capitalist system was contingent upon the fragmentation of the international political system into competing states (Wallerstein 1979). The division of political authority into numerous units allowed private actors with non-site specific assets (i.e., internationally mobile assets) to "escape" national jurisdictions and play one state off against another, using the possibility of exit to negotiate for greater political freedom and larger rights of residual control (Bates and Lein 1985).

Second, until quite recently, most factors of production enjoyed only limited international mobility, restraining the process of globalization to small segments of the economy and society. Over the twentieth century, and over the last decade in particular, technological changes have reduced the costs of communication, transportation, and travel over distance, exposing much larger segments of the economy and society to deeper international interactions (see Kobrin, this volume; Mathews 1997).

Third, and perhaps most important for the purposes of this chapter, the domestic governance structures of the early industrializing states first created spheres of private activity and then helped generalize these spheres to the international arena. As I attempt to suggest in this final section, this particular form of domestic governance underlies globalization in a way that is seldom appreciated. These private actors are the prime movers behind globalization, integrating markets and societies, breaking the constraints of space and time, and erasing local variations. Multinational firms are exemplars, and under their actions globalization has reached farthest in the economic arena. Many NGOs, however, are also drivers of globalization; human rights organizations, for instance, propagate a universal standard of political and civil freedom that also reduces local variations in politics, societies, and cultures. To understand globalization, we must first understand how private actors established themselves within the domestic political economies of leading states.

I suggest below that there are, today, powerful vested interests who gain from this governance structure and, in turn, globalization. While globalization might appear to require new governance structures, there are important sources of inertia that thwart efforts to construct greater hierarchy at the global level. Somewhat paradoxically, were greater hierarchy to be achieved this would actually impede and possibly reverse the conditions for globalization.

The political origins of globalization

Private actors are central to the phenomenon of globalization. To probe the relationship between globalization and governance, therefore, it is appropriate to begin with an understanding of what we mean by "private." In terms commensurate with the conception of governance posed above, private actors can be defined by their possession of substantial rights of residual control. Just as we can distinguish between two separate firms and a single firm with two subsidiaries by who holds the rights of residual control, we can also distinguish between private and public actors by the vesting of these rights. While private actors may have many contractual obligations to the state, up to and including general loyalty, they nonetheless possess substantial residual rights. Public actors, on the other hand, lack such residual rights; they may have substantial authority delegated to them by the state, but residual rights are located in the state, not in the actors themselves. Between these two extremes, we can envision a continuum of quasi-public actors who have greater or lesser residual rights; "state-owned" firms, for instance, may have rights over pricing and production decisions, but not over wage, employment, or location determinations.

The predominance of private actors is, in part, a consequence of early industrialization in Britain and the United States and the generalization of this model of political organization to the international economy under their respective hegemonic reigns. As Alexander Gerschenkron (1962) first recognized, early industrialization required only a minimalist state. Recasting his argument in the terms of the theory above, early industrialization was led by small firms that generally lacked specific assets (see Kurth 1979; Landes 1998, 213–75). Without significant market power or strong incentives to exercise power, these early industrializing firms could not act opportunistically toward other social actors (such as labor) or the state itself. No strong political hierarchy was necessary to reduce the expected costs of opportunism or, to put it another way, increased hierarchy was more costly than the expected reduction in the costs of opportunism. Given the absence of large specific assets, anarchic state–society relations were sufficient. This resulted in a large private sphere that vested enormous residual rights in economic actors and produced the so-called liberal model.

As Gerschenkron also shows, late industrialization required larger scale economies within individual firms, which in turn produced significant firm specific assets and oligopolistic market structures. To achieve these greater scale economies required greater centralized direction of investment, thereby creating a role for the banks, in the case of Germany, and the state, in Russia and elsewhere. The presence of firm specific assets, however, also created a substantial risk of opportunism between firms and other social groups, especially labor, and firms and the state, all of whom could attempt to exploit each other. Thus, if late industrialization were to occur, the high expected costs of opportunism required a more hierarchical governance structure, a shift in the residual rights of control to the banks in Germany, who exercised control through firm debt, or to the state in others.[7] In the late industrializers, then, the private sphere was significantly smaller and economic actors retained substantially fewer rights of residual control. This model reached its extreme in the Soviet Union, as Gerschenkron also notes, where the state came to own all factors of production. In short, the firm specific assets characteristic of large-scale, late industrialization required more hierarchical governance structures within the domestic political economy.

Partly resting on the superior competitive abilities of their private firms, the hegemonies of the early industrializers helped to generalize their model of domestic governance to the international arena. Supporting their firms and, at least at the margin, helping to open foreign markets for their goods and investments, Britain and, later, the United States led the creation of "level playing fields" in which their producers could prosper (Gilpin 1977). In turn, the large private sphere of authority characteristic of their domestic governance structures was replicated at the international level, supporting and supported by a set of liberal rules governing exchange and factor movements (see Sandholtz, this volume).

Inertia

Governance structures within and between states endure because actors make ever greater relation-specific investments, and thus develop an interest in preserving the current structure (see Gourevitch 1999). As contracts, governance structures can and should be renegotiated as conditions evolve, depending on the rate of environmental change and the transactions costs of bargaining out a new set of rules and safeguards. Yet, we know that governance structures, particularly at the global level, are not continually renegotiated, even when conditions advance rapidly. The accumulation of relation-specific investments creates an important source of political inertia.[8]

Governance structures set the terms of political interaction between actors. They also produce sets of policies that may have differential rewards for investors. Anticipating the rules of the political game and the sets of policies they produce, actors make investments premised on their expectations of the future. If actors expect a large sphere of private activity, for instance, they will invest in assets which are most productive in that sphere. In making such investments, in turn, the actors acquire an interest in preserving the governance structure and the set of policies that follow from it. In other words, investors acquire specific assets – or "vested interests," in common parlance – based upon the current system and they will act politically to preserve that system. The *ex post* and *ex ante* political interests of investors differ and – although collective action problems also matter (see McGinnis, this volume) – it is this wedge that creates political inertia.

To help make this point clear, consider an example from American domestic politics. Following World War II, the United States government sought to encourage individual home ownership; accordingly, it offered a federal income tax deduction for interest paid on home mortgages, and millions of taxpayers took advantage of this incentive to purchase their own homes. Having made such a purchase, the incentives of these taxpaying voters changed: where prior to the policy they might have been agnostic if not hostile to tax incentives for home ownership, after their purchases they became vigorous advocates of continuing the deduction. Today, even the most strident advocates of tax reform usually recognize the political necessity of maintaining the home mortgage interest deduction.

At a more macro level, this same *ex ante* interest is reflected in the persistence of the early industrializing model in the United States, despite later challenges. Premised upon a large private sector that reflected the early American economy, the constitution left large residual rights of control to individuals and the states (see above). This large private sphere, in turn, was well suited for the requirements of early industrialization. Actors based their investments on the assumption of large residual rights of control, and subsequently acted to defend those rights when they later came under assault.

As scale economies increased with industrialization in the late nineteenth century, however, large firms and concentrations of economic power began to emerge. Although similar developments were occurring simultaneously in the late industrializers, either as cause or effect of greater state strength, in the United States the governance structure did not adapt. This was a particularly contentious period in American politics. Populists fought the trusts, especially the railroads, progressives attempted to mobilize the government to regulate business practices, and labor struggled to organize and bargain collectively (see Hofstadter 1955). Each group, in turn, won some successes: America's nearly unique anti-trust legislation was passed, some of the more egregious business practices of the era were mitigated, and the right to unionize was eventually recognized. However, the victories were limited. The watchman state was unable to obtain significantly greater control over the economy or adapt to the concentration of business. Big business used the existing rights of the already large private sphere to defend itself against greater public control, thereby retaining powers that in the late industrializers were being ceded to or exercised by the state. In addition, the opponents of business "pulled their punches." They wanted to preserve the large private sphere which was generally advantageous to them in other ways, so they limited their demands to those intended to counterbalance economic power but they never challenged the governance structure itself. Workers, for instance, demanded the right to organize and lobbied for new government regulations on business, but comparatively few became revolutionaries.[9] Thus, despite the changing nature of the economy, state and society remained autonomous and, at least compared to other countries going through similar economic transformations, relatively anarchic (Katzenstein 1978).

The same inertia that prevented the United States from developing greater "state capacity" is today preventing the realization of greater or more effective global governance. The private actors prospering in the interstices of political authority are not leading the charge for supra-national entities designed to regulate their behavior more effectively. They have grown out of and adapted to the current governance structure, and have little interest in seeing it overturned or even significantly modified. The already large private sphere, in turn, gives these international actors considerable leverage, which they can and will use to thwart efforts at fundamental reform.

Indeed, growing business and developed-country support for increased regulation of world markets can be understood not as a movement toward greater governance but as an attempt to expand further and solidify the large private sphere that already exists. This can be seen most clearly, perhaps, in the Multilateral Agreement on Investment (MAI), negotiated under the auspices of the Organization for Economic Co-operation and Development (OECD) and, at the time of writing, in diplomatic "limbo" due to stiff opposition from outside the business community.[10] The MAI is intended to be a comprehensive agreement covering all economic sectors and all forms of international investment. The MAI further seeks to ensure legal guarantees for investments against encroachments from all levels of government, including central, federal, state, provincial, and local authorities.

Much like the market-based legal systems of Britain and the United States, where laws are designed and intended to apply broadly to all members of particular classes, the MAI emphasizes the principles of non-discrimination and national treatment – that is, governments pledge to treat foreign investors and their investments no less favorably than they treat their own investors. In this way, the MAI seeks to level the playing field for domestic and foreign firms alike.[11]

At its core, the MAI seeks to prevent governments from exercising sovereign powers and intervening in markets for or against particular firms (or classes of firms). As the OECD itself recognizes, "as with all binding international agreements, this will moderate the exercise of national authority to a degree." At the same time, however, the MAI does not transfer powers to any authority higher than the state. Although the agreement is likely to contain a mechanism for dispute resolution that will follow judicial procedures, it is designed to adjudicate disagreements not to create new decision-making authorities. In short, the MAI constrains national governments and enlarges the private sphere within the international economy. It does not undermine the current system of international governance but actually serves to reinforce its anarchic structure.

What is true for the MAI holds equally for the new World Trade Organization and various regional trade agreements, such as the North American Free Trade Agreement. Governments are constrained from exercising sovereign powers but no higher authorities are created – in each case, further widening the private sphere within the international economy. Globalization and the regulation of international markets may constrain states and limit the policy instruments at their disposal, but the beneficiaries of this process are not clamoring for greater supranational authority and policy discretion. Quite the contrary.

The primary opponents of globalization, in turn, are those national actors who are disadvantaged by the new global trends. Even so, they too have vested interests in existing governance structures and are unlikely to support radical change. National governments have little incentive to give up their current rights of residual control to some new supranational authority; they may seek to seize or reclaim in the future rights now enjoyed by private actors, but they are unlikely to cede those rights to some other entity. National groups that are politically powerful enough to compel states to transfer residual rights to a supranational authority are likely to be the beneficiaries of existing national governance structures. Like the opponents of business in turn-of-the-century America, these powerful national actors have been privileged by the current governance structure and, though they may seek reform, they too will not seek revolution.

Ironically, those states most threatened politically by the large private sphere inherent in globalization – fundamentalist regimes, such as Iran, and their supporters – are the least likely supporters of more hierarchic global governance, at least until such structures can be made to mirror their own internal characteristics. Such states are, indeed, the potential revolutionaries who can gain only by seizing the levers of power and transforming governance structures. In this way, globalization exacerbates the "clash of civilizations," but not for the reasons usually given (Huntington 1993).

Finally, if supranational entities were to acquire some significant residual rights and a measure of hierarchical control, against expectations, this authority would likely impede further globalization. Globalization rests, at least in part, on the fragmentation of sovereignty. Consolidating political authority into new supranational structures would infringe upon the private sphere, restrict the residual rights of private as well as state actors, and thereby undermine the basis for globalization.

Globalization clearly does create transnational externalities of high political salience, including environmental degradation, worsening global distributions of income and wealth, ethnic conflicts and refugee problems that spread across national borders, and more (see McGinnis, this volume). It is the desire to cope more effectively with such problems that prompts demands for "greater" governance or more hierarchical structures. Developing an ability to cope more effectively with such problems, however, would give a new governance structure the simultaneous ability to control the actions of the private actors now prospering in the anarchic international system; mitigating environmental degradation, for instance, virtually requires such constraints. Were such restrictions to pass, however, investment in the activities that today underpin globalization would become less attractive compared to other alternatives. Far from being mutually reinforcing, globalization and global governance may well stand opposed to one another. We can expect the present structure of global governance to endure long into the future.

This is not to conclude, however, that our present governance structure is well suited for coping with the ever more complex world before us (see McGinnis, this volume). Along with globalization has come a variety of political, economic, and environmental externalities that increase the need for international cooperation (Cerny, this volume). Some form of supranational governance may well be necessary to deal with human migrations, economic crises, or environmental degradation. The vested interests of private actors and states, however, will prevent them from supporting new governance structures. In the future, states will find themselves both challenged to respond to common problems and constrained by the large private sphere deeply embedded into the current structure of global governance.

Contrasts, no conclusions

Relational contracting theories have been criticized for their functionalism (or their emphasis on "efficiency"), their inability to give precise operationalizations for key variables – such as transactions costs or information asymmetries (see Sandholtz, this volume), and their non-falsifiability. It is relatively easy – and many analysts have given in to the temptation – to concoct *post hoc* stories about why observed relationships and institutions are "efficient" for the parties involved. The real test of a theory of relational contracting comes from specifying concretely the range of institutional alternatives and the determinants of efficiency – around which there continues to be substantial debate and, thus, multiple theories united by a common approach. Such a test, however, does not require precise measures of transactions costs or information (contrary to Sandholtz, this volume). Rather, the relational contracting approach proceeds by identifying observable variables, such as specific assets, deducing behavioral consequences, and then testing these consequences against actual events. One need not observe gravity to verify its existence; it is known only by its effects. Likewise, social scientists do not need to observe the effects of each link in a causal chain. No theory can meet that standard, not even the constructivist approaches often favored by critics of rationalism, in general, and relational contracting, in particular.

In this chapter, I have emphasized problems of selection bias in the study of international institutions and, in turn, the need to consider alternative governance structures in any theory of governance. Only when the costs and benefits of alternative governance structures are understood can extant structures be explained. The analytic role of alternatives is, perhaps, one of the most important divisions between rationalist approaches to international politics, of which relational contracting theory is one variant, and constructivist approaches (see the chapters by Sandholtz and Haas, this volume). Rationalist theories are premised on the explicit contrasting of alternatives. While critics are correct that individuals and organizations may lack the cognitive capabilities assumed by some rationalists, the search for alternatives and the assessment of their relative costs and benefits constitutes the core of rationalist theories (Bueno de Mesquita 1996). When they arise, problems of selection bias, like that discussed above, are typically unintentional, caused more by the limitations of individual analysts who fail to consider the full range of possible outcomes than by the approach itself.

Problems of selection bias, however, are inherent in constructivism. This poses something of a paradox, of course, as constructivism arose partly in reaction to rationalism's privileging of existing institutions (e.g., anarchy, the state). Constructivists have been effective at problematizing extant institutions, but they have neither posed alternatives nor a theory of why only certain alternatives are chosen or constructed. They offer possibilities – arguing that different institutions might have been chosen – but not a theory of probabilities. This paradox, in turn, is rooted in the presumption found in most constructivist work that theory must incorporate and align itself with the self-understandings of the actors themselves. It is the practice of actors – and as Sandholtz (this volume) reminds us, the meaning attached by actors to practice – that guides their choices. In grounding theory in the self-understanding of actors, analysis itself becomes limited by that self-understanding. While the study of practice holds out the possibility that, for instance, states might have chosen to conduct themselves differently even under anarchy (Wendt 1992), the self-understanding of states cannot itself identify the range of possible alternatives to power politics – which by definition are not even envisioned by states. This suggests that constructivism, despite aspirations to the contrary, is fundamentally conservative in the classic sense of that term. Although they differ over the purpose of theory, rationalism and relational contracting theory – with their emphasis on alternatives taken and not taken – may have more in common with critical theories of international relations than commonly assumed.

Notes

* I gratefully acknowledge the comments of Steph Haggard, Jeff Hart, Steve Kobrin, Lin Ostrom, Bob Powell, Aseem Prakash, Arthur Stein, and Mike Tierney and the research assistance of Matthew Baum.

1 As the editors of this volume correctly note, my definition of governance is narrower than the organization of collective action, which includes both bargains about who bears what cost for the action and how to enforce the agreement. Nonetheless, their definition of governance as the "organizing [of] collective action" is quite close to my concept of contracting. Any institutionalized "rules of the game that permit, prescribe, or prohibit certain actions" have a formal or informal contract at their core (Prakash and Hart, Introduction, p. 2).

2 On "power" versus "efficiency" conceptions of contracting, with particular reference to hierarchy, see the exchange between Charles Perrow, Oliver Williamson and William Ouchi, and Alfred Chandler, reprinted in McCraw 1988, 432–64.

3 In his essay for this volume, Michael McGinnis implies that the continuum of anarchy to hierarchy developed here is defined by the level of coercion. Although hierarchy may often require some measure of coercion, anarchy, hierarchy, and the relationships in between are defined only by the rights of residual control retained by the parties to the contract.

4 McGinnis (this volume) adds the dimensions of consent and legitimacy to this analysis and, in turn, reaches different conclusions.

5 Downs *et al.* (1996) make a similar point about the depth of cooperation.

6 For a discussion of both problems of research design and successes to date, see Keohane and Martin 1995, 46–50.

7 There is a "chicken-and-egg" problem in Gerschenkron's analysis that is reproduced here: did late industrialization produce hierarchical political economies or did pre-existing hierarchies allow late industrialization to occur in some places but not others? While I lean toward the latter position, the answer to this puzzle does not affect the interpretation offered here.

8 On the problem of maladaption costs more generally, see North 1990. McGinnis, this volume, sees institutions as being very sticky and path dependent. Sandholtz, this volume, finds the source of inertia in rules which, in turn, shape other rules. Given that relationally specific assets, sticky institutions, and rules all point to the preservation of our current international governance structure, the existence of inertia itself cannot differentiate between these analytic alternatives.

9 This might be contrasted with Europe, where late industrialization and correspondingly greater concentrations of economic and political power created a deeper and more "revolutionary" struggle to control the state itself.

10 On the regulation of international business, see Graham 1996; and Rugman and Verbeke 1998. On the MAI, see the OECD's webpage at http://www.oecd.org/daf/cmis/mai/mainindex.htm.
11 Attempts to regulate markets even in an "even-handed" fashion will inevitably privilege some firms at the expense of others (see Stigler 1971; Peltzman 1976) That support for the MAI originates largely in the developed countries and in the largest international firms is not surprising, as these countries and enterprises will be the largest beneficiaries from "equal treatment."

References

Bates, Robert H. and Da-Hsiang Donald Lien (1985) "A Note on Taxation, Development, and Representative Government," *Politics and Society* 14: 53–70.

Boyarin, Jonathan (1994) *Remapping Memory: The Politics of TimeSpace*, Minneapolis, MN: University of Minnesota Press.

Bueno de Mesquita, Bruce (1996) "Counterfactuals and International Affairs: Some Insights from Game Theory," in *Counterfactual Thought Experiments in World Politics*, ed. by Philip E. Tetlock and Aaron Belkin. Princeton, NJ: Princeton University Press.

Cerny, Philip G. (1995) "Globalization and the Changing Logic of Collective Action," *International Organization* 49: 595–625.

Commission on Global Governance (1995) *Our Global Neighborhood*. New York: Oxford University Press.

Desai, Meghnad (1995) "Global Governance," in *Global Governance: Ethics and Economics of the World Order*, ed. by Meghnad Desai and Paul Redfern. New York: Pinter.

Deutsch, Karl W., *et al.* (1957) *Political Community and the North Atlantic Area: International Organization in the Light of Historical Experience*, Princeton, NJ: Princeton University Press.

Downs, George W., David M. Rocke and Peter N. Barsoom (1996) "Is the Good News About Compliance Good News About Cooperation?" *International Organization* 50: 379–406.

Fearon, James D. 1998. "Bargaining, Enforcement, and International Cooperation," *International Organization* 52: 269–305.

Frieden, Jeffry A. (1994) "International Investment and Colonial Control: A New Interpretation," *International Organization* 48: 559–93.

Gerschenkron, Alexander (1962) *Economic Backwardness in Historical Perspective: A Book of Essays*, Cambridge, MA: Harvard University Press.

Giddens, Anthony (1990) *The Consequences of Modernity*, Stanford, CA: Stanford University Press.

Gilpin, Robert (1977) "Economic Interdependence and National Security in Historical Perspective," in *Economic Issues and National Security*, ed. by Klaus Knorr and Frank N. Trager, Lawrence, KS: Regents Press of Kansas.

Gordenker, Leon and Thomas G. Weiss (1996) "Pluralizing Global Governance: Analytical Approaches and Dimensions," in *NGOs, the UN, and Global Governance*, ed. by Thomas G. Weiss and Leon Gordenker, Boulder, CO: Lynne Rienner.

Gourevitch, Peter (1999) "The Governance Problem in International Relations," in *Strategic Choice and International Relations*, ed. by David A. Lake and Robert Powell, Princeton, NJ: Princeton University Press.

Graham, Edward M. (1996) *Global Corporations and National Governments*, Washington, DC: Institute for International Economics.

Grossman, Sanford J. and Oliver D. Hart (1986) "The Costs and Benefits of Ownership: A Theory of Vertical and Lateral Integration," *Journal of Political Economy* 94: 691–719.

Hofstadter, Richard (1955) *The Age of Reform: From Bryan to F.D.R.*, New York: Vintage.

Huntington, Samuel (1993) "The Clash of Civilizations?" *Foreign Affairs* 72, 3: 22–49.

James, Alan (1986) *Sovereign Statehood: The Basis of International Society*, Boston, MA: Unwin and Hyman.

Katzenstein, Peter J., ed. (1978) *Between Power and Plenty: Foreign Economic Policies of Advanced Industrial States*, Madison, WI: University of Wisconsin Press.

Keohane, Robert O. (1984) *After Hegemony: Cooperation and Discord in the World Political Economy*, Princeton, NJ: Princeton University Press.

Keohane, Robert O., and Joseph S. Nye, eds. (1972) *Transnational Relations and World Politics*, Cambridge, MA: Harvard University Press.

Keohane, Robert O., and Joseph S. Nye (1977) *Power and Interdependence: World Politics in Transition*, Boston, MA: Little, Brown.

Keohane, Robert O. and Lisa L. Martin (1995) "The Promise of Institutionalist Theory," *International Security* 20, 1: 39–51.

Kindleberger, Charles. P. (1969) *American Business Abroad*, New Haven, CT: Yale University Press.

Klein, Benjamin, Robert G. Crawford and Armen A. Alchian (1978) "Vertical Integration, Appropriable Rents, and the Competitive Contracting Process," *Journal of Law and Economics* 21: 297–326.

Krasner, Stephen D., ed. (1983) *International Regimes*. Ithaca, NY: Cornell University Press.

Kurth, James (1979) "The Political Consequences of the Product Cycle: Industrial History and Political Outcomes," *International Organization* 33: 1–34.

Lake, David A. (1996) "Anarchy, Hierarchy, and the Variety of International Relations," *International Organization* 50: 1–33.

Lake, David A. (1997) "The Rise, Fall, and Future of the Russian Empire: A Theoretical Interpretation," in *The End of Empire? Comparative Perspectives on the Soviet Collapse*, ed. by Karen Dawisha and Bruce Parrott, New York: M.E. Sharpe.

Lake, David A. (1999) *Entangling Relations: American Foreign Policy in its Century*, Princeton, NJ: Princeton University Press.

Landes, David S. (1998) *The Wealth and Poverty of Nations: Why Some Are So Rich and Some So Poor,* New York: W.W. Norton.

Lipson, Charles (1991) "Why Are Some International Agreements Informal?" *International Organization* 45: 495–538.

Lukes, Steven (1974) *Power: A Radical Approach*, London: Macmillan.

Mathews, Jessica T. (1997) "Power Shift," *Foreign Affairs* 76, 1: 50–66.

McCraw, Thomas K., ed. (1988) *The Essential Alfred Chandler: Essays Toward a Historical Theory of Big Business*, Boston, MA: Harvard Business School Press.

McCubbins, Mathew, and Thomas Schwartz (1984) "Congressional Oversight Overlooked: Policy Patrols versus Fire Alarms," *American Journal of Political Science* 2: 165–79.

Mearsheimer, John (1994–95) "The False Promise of International Institutions," *International Security* 19, 3: 5–49.

Milner, Helen (1991) "The Assumption of Anarchy in International Relations Theory: A Critique," *Review of International Studies* 17: 67–85.

Mlinar, Zdravko (1992) "Individuation and Globalization: The Transformation of Territorial Social Organization," in *Globalization and Territorial Identities*, ed. by Mlinar, Brookfield: Avebury.

Murphy, Craig N. (1994) *International Organization and Industrial Change: Global Governance since 1850*, New York: Oxford University Press.

North, Douglass C. (1990) *Institutions, Institutional Change, and Economic Performance*, New York: Cambridge University Press.

Peltzman, S. (1976) "Towards a More General Theory of Regulation?" *Journal of Law and Economics* 19: 211–40.

Rosecrance, Richard (1996) "The Rise of the Virtual State," *Foreign Affairs* 75, 4: 45–61.

Rosenau, James N. (1990) *Turbulence in World Politics: A Theory of Change and Continuity*, Princeton, NJ: Princeton University Press.

Rosenau, James N. (1992) "Governance, Order, and Change in World Politics," in *Governance Without Government: Order and Change in World Politics*, ed. by Rosenau and Ernst-Otto Czempiel, New York: Cambridge University Press.

Rosenau, James N. and Ernst-Otto Czempiel, eds (1992) *Governance Without Government: Order and Change in World Politics*, New York: Cambridge University Press.

Rugman, Alan M. and Alain Verbeke (1998) "Multinational Enterprises and Public Policy," *Journal of International Business Studies* 29, 1: 115–36.

Salamon, Lester M. (1994) "The Rise of the Nonprofit Sector," *Foreign Affairs* 73, 4: 109–22.

Stigler, George J. (1971) "The Theory of Economic Regulation," *Bell Journal of Economics and Management Science* 2: 137–46.

Strange, Susan (1983) "Cave! hic dragones: A Critique of Regime Analysis," in *International Regimes*, ed. by Stephen D. Krasner, Ithaca, NY: Cornell University Press.

Strange, Susan (1996) *The Retreat of the State: The Diffusion of Power in the World Economy*, New York: Cambridge University Press.

Vernon, Raymond (1971) *Sovereignty at Bay: The Multinational Spread of U.S. Enterprises*, New York: Basic Books.

Wallerstein, Immanuel (1979) *The Capitalist World Economy*, Cambridge: Cambridge University Press.

Waltz, Kenneth N. (1979) *Theory of International Politics*, Reading, MA: Addison-Wesley.

Weiss, Thomas G. and Leon Gordenker (1996) *NGOs, the UN, and Global Governance*, Boulder, CO: Lynne Rienner.

Wendt, Alexander (1992) "Anarchy is What States Make of It: The Social Construction of Power Politics," *International Organization* 46: 391–425.

Williamson, Oliver (1985) *The Economic Institutions of Capitalism: Firms, Markets, Relational Contracting*, New York: Free Press.

Young, Oran R. (1994) *International Governance: Protecting the Environment in a Stateless Society*, Ithaca, NY: Cornell University Press.

2 Rent-seeking, redistribution, and reform in the governance of global markets

*Michael D. McGinnis**

Governance entails provision of a range of services to some group of individuals or organizations. International relations theorists typically presume that a particular form of organization (the sovereign state) provides all aspects of governance, writing and enforcing laws and regulations as well as producing public goods. Globalization is said to be changing all that, as rapid economic and technological changes make it easier for individuals and private organizations to reach across national borders to devise new ways of organizing their collective endeavors. Other contributors to this volume discuss many examples of transnational governance that occur outside the direct control of national political authorities. In this chapter I question whether all this really constitutes a fundamental change in the nature of global governance.

The central thesis of this chapter is that different governance services have routinely been provided by a wide range of formal organizations and informal arrangements at all levels of social aggregation. The accelerating effects of globalization force international relations theorists to take off their blinders, to look past the supposedly all-encompassing state to confront the full array of governance organizations that have been there all along. In this process more analysts may come to realize that the concept of governance needs to be broken down into its constituent service activities, each of which can be provided by individuals or organizations specializing in the production or provision of that particular service. But this recognition of the multiplicity of service providers pre-dates the onset of globalization by many years, particularly in the literature on polycentric systems of governance at the metropolitan level (Ostrom, *et al.*, 1961; see McGinnis, forthcoming).

From this perspective, globalization does not threaten to transform the very nature of governance at the global level, since a complex array of governance organizations have already co-existed for a very long time. Instead, globalization directs our attention to the changing patterns of interactions among different forms of collective action organizations that provide a variety of governance services to diverse groups.

This chapter focuses on the behavior of these organizations. Other contributors to this volume direct attention to global trends, but it is also important to consider how particular organizations might respond to those trends, and how these responses in turn contribute to the furtherance or reversal of these trends. Lake and Cerny address exactly these questions with respect to the state as a whole; my concern is with the component organizations that comprise "the state," and their many competitors.

Along with the rest of the contributors, I focus on governance as it relates to market exchange. Governance facilitates the operation of a wide variety of exchange and other forms of interactions among the "consumers" of these services. One particularly important effect of governance is to reduce the costs of transactions experienced by individuals or organizations seeking to realize the joint gains from a mutually beneficial exchange. In effect, then, governance is a collective good. As such, any effort to arrange for governance necessarily confronts dilemmas of collective action.

This chapter draws on two efforts to systematize the multi-disciplinary literature on collective action. Lichbach (1996) organizes the full range of "solutions" to collective action dilemmas under four paths to "social order": market, contract, hierarchy, and community. Elsewhere I posit four "realms" of collective action, classifying organizations according to whether their primary activities are economic-productive, coercive-protective, social-communal, or political-governance (McGinnis, 1996). In both frameworks, particular attention is given to the ways in which solutions in different categories or organizations in different realms act to reinforce each other. It is this interaction among multiple forms of collective action that lies at the heart of the method of analysis outlined in this chapter.

In the modern state, national political authorities have managed to combine a significant portion of activities from all four realms into a single arena of interaction. Politicians seeking elective office, and the bureaucrats they appoint, hold sway over a broad array of economic, social, political, and coercive issues. In each of these areas, however, other organizations cannot be overlooked.

The importance of economic corporations is self-evident, and recent trends in domestic and international affairs remind us all of the political importance of religious organizations. Even the coercive function of states has been challenged, albeit in a limited fashion, by the intervention of mercenary organizations in some African conflicts (Rubin, 1997). Intergovernmental organizations have come to play important roles, but it may be especially important to acknowledge the increased role of sub-national governments in competitive efforts to attract foreign investment. Yes, the state as such is increasingly under challenge, but those in positions of national political authority also have access to a wide array of resources. It is the state's location at the nexus of economic, social, coercive, and political realms of interaction that makes it seem so dominant, and so under siege.

Once one realizes that the state never achieved complete monopoly in any of these arenas of interaction, then its current difficulties in responding to the pressures of globalization can be understood in context. The co-existence of multiple service providers suggests that, in some circumstances, it may be useful to talk of a "market" in governance services. Globalization imparts important changes to the structure of governance markets, but these changes may fall well short of a fundamental transformation.

Pre-existing organizations are well placed to expand their range of services, so any one provider of governance services may come to provide a diverse array of governance services to overlapping or even distinct groups. Since the ways in which diverse services are combined in particular organizations directly affect that organization's performance, we can say that "institutions matter." Of particular importance is the combination of services typically provided by the modern welfare state.

As detailed elsewhere in this volume, market globalization is a general process by which exchanges across national boundaries become much more frequent in all kinds of markets (as well as other forms of social interaction). As a consequence, workers lose jobs, once-successful products lose market shares and fixed capital assets become obsolete. The scope of the problem market globalization sets for governance at the international level has been aptly summarized by the editors of this volume:

> If the world economy is becoming more "global," and the international political system remains, for the most part, rooted in a decentralised (or anarchic) system of governments of nation-states, then the mismatch between global markets and national governance is sure to create important problems of control and accountability for those governments and possibly unacceptable levels of uncertainty for globally operating actors, particularly the global business enterprises on whom our overall prosperity allegedly depends.
>
> (Hart and Prakash,1996: 207)

Elsewhere in this volume, Lake demonstrates that this mismatch between the scale of state-based governance and the actual scale of economic activity is the fundamental driving force behind the impetus for globalization itself. To some extent, this same "mismatch between global markets and national governance" was present at the very origins of the modern world economy (Wallerstein, 1974). Kobrin (this volume) examines the complex nature of governance in the medieval age, out of which the modern conceptualization of state-centered governance emerged. He envisions an impending transformation of the modern system back to a system resembling medieval Europe. Similar claims have been made before: two decades ago, even so prominent a realist as Bull (1977) warned of an impending "neo-medieval" world order. Deeper continuities also need to be acknowledged. Berman

(1983), for example, argues that a multiplicity of co-existing governance services (in his case alternative legal orders) is the defining characteristic of Western civilization, both medieval and modern.

The conceptualization of governance outlined in this chapter lies between the frameworks used by the authors of the immediately preceding and following chapters. Lake conceptualizes market governance in terms of transaction cost minimization, whereas Sandholtz locates rules at the heart of the process of governance. Lake posits a congruence between the characteristics of the uncertainty facing actors in a given sector of the world economy and the nature of governance related to that sector; Sandholtz sees a fundamental tension between the rule systems of liberalism, sovereignty, and technical rationality. To complement their macro-level perspectives, this chapter focuses on organizational response to changing macro-level conditions.

Sandholtz synthesizes important aspects of the rational choice and rule-directed approaches to the study of governance. Although he acknowledges that rules do not automatically determine behavior, he argues that by shaping common expectations rules effectively constrain individual and organizational behavior. He further argues that rules have a certain logic, and that tensions among the rules associated with liberalism, sovereignty, and technical rationality must be considered in any evaluation of the consequences of globalization.

In this chapter I argue that organizations have a certain logic, as well as a central purpose. Those organizations that step outside this range of expected behavior face increased costs of transactions, for they must find some way to assuage the concerns of their potential customers or supporters. They may also face competition from other organizations offering similar services that have core functions located in other sectors. In short, globalization induces dynamic patterns of contention among different forms of organizations.

The modern state is a multifaceted, multi-purpose organization that is potentially vulnerable to challenge from sectoral or other narrowly focused organizations. But national authorities have recourse to a uniquely complete complement of resources: economic, coercive, and social.

Consider the state's role in regulating business practices in a given sector of the economy. In many instances actors in that sector themselves can do a more effective job of developing and implementing a common set of standards. When state authorities interfere with these arrangements, they do so in the name of distributive justice. Elsewhere in this volume, Cerny argues that redistribution is no longer the exclusive purview of political authorities but is instead carried out in a broad array of organizational contexts. Still, as long as the symbolism of nationalism remains influential, national political authorities will retain a unique advantage in justifying extractions for redistributive purposes. The basic conclusion of this analysis is that those governance organizations or networks of related service providers that most effectively combine the provision of economic-productive, coercive-protective, and social-communal services are most likely to survive and prosper. In short, stable governance requires a capacity for redistribution and reform.

Approaches to the analysis of market governance

The term "market governance" is here used to include any activities that facilitate the making, implementation, and enforcement of economic exchanges. In the public policy literature government is conceptualized as a collective response to market failures. In a widely used textbook on public policy, Weimer and Vining (1989: 90) list four general categories of market failures: public goods, externalities, natural monopoly, and information asymmetry. The first three categories have long been recognized as a legitimate role for government, even among the most ardent opponents of excessive governmental intervention (Friedman, 1963). Since public goods, by their very nature, are unlikely to be provided by private action, governments must either directly produce or indirectly procure many public goods. Governments also deal with the conflicts of interests generated by externalities, in which some economic exchange has a negative impact on the welfare of parties not directly involved in that exchange. Governments also provide monitoring and regulation of natural monopoly, as well as establishment of artificial monopolies.

Weimer and Vining's inclusion of information asymmetry as a major category of market failure provides a theoretical foundation for governmental efforts to protect individuals from being exploited by those with better information about the quality of a product. Such asymmetries can make parties much less reluctant to engage in an exchange. By acting to offset these asymmetries, or to protect parties against the excessive opportunism of other parties, governments can facilitate economic exchange in markets characterized by information asymmetries.

Scholars of "new institutional economics" or "transaction costs economics" have explicated the basic problems of market governance. North (1981, 1990) emphasizes that a clear definition of property rights is essential before market processes can operate at anywhere near efficient levels. That it is also necessary to facilitate the implementation of economic exchanges of a long-term nature has been the focus of research on transaction costs pioneered by Williamson (1975, 1985, 1996). In contrast to mutual exchange on spot markets, actors considering entering into long-term contracts must be concerned about the potential costs of opportunism, that is, the danger that the other party may take advantage at some later date of the relationship then being contemplated. In the absence of some means of recourse should a contract be broken, many otherwise mutually beneficial exchanges would not be made.

In some circumstances it may be cost-effective to integrate different activities within a single hierarchical organization (a firm), but in many other cases some "hybrid" form of economic organization based on long-term contracts is more suitable. Williamson concludes that the most efficient form of economic organization is determined by the degree of asset specificity entailed in that exchange, the frequency and uncertainty of interactions between these parties, and the ease of measuring quality and monitoring performance.

If a governance structure can be established that reduces the likelihood or the expected costs of opportunism, then markets can operate more efficiently. For Williamson, governance is basically a form of contract that ensures that other contracts can be enforced. This chapter argues that governance is more complicated than that analogy suggests.

The international political economy consists of a series of (relatively) separable sectors. Lake (1996; this volume) argues that the nature of the governance structure in each sector is systematically related to the characteristics of that sector, in a manner to be detailed more fully below. Just as Waltz (1979) used the standard microeconomic understanding of firms and markets to justify his fundamental distinction between hierarchy and anarchy, Lake uses Williamson's general conceptualization of economic organization to argue that international relations theorists need to expand their understanding of the range of governance options beyond the standard dichotomy between hierarchical states and anarchical systems.

Lake draws attention to the efforts of privileged actors to retain their advantageous position. He points out that transaction cost structures are shaped by political struggles, in which the haves can exploit their advantages over the have-nots. In effect, Lake incorporates some consequences of political competition and coercion into Williamson's transaction costs framework.

In this chapter I emphasize another side of the political equation, namely, the efforts of groups injured by the operation of the existing system to work within that system to redress their grievances. My concern is with those groups whose grievances are considered legitimate by all actors operating within the extant governance structure. Any form of governance requires both coercion and consent, and responses to globalization will require the consensual participation of actors whose interests are materially hurt by that participation.

Bringing consent and legitimacy back into the picture helps fill in the intermediate steps in Lake's continuum between anarchy and hierarchy. At the anarchical side governance depends exclusively on the consent of the governed; as we move towards the hierarchical side coercion becomes more important, but consent is never entirely absent.

A complicating factor is the sense of community that participants feel towards each other. Groups that share common beliefs, expectations, values, and norms will find it easier to coordinate their actions, whatever the level of coercion available to their agents. Appeals to communal values can be particularly effective tools for the redress of grievances on the part of actors who are seen to have lost resources in an unfair or undeserved manner.

When combined with a capacity for coercion, redress of grievances can take the form of a redistribution of resources. In the longer run, reform of the overall governance regime can be driven by a combination of a shared sense of the morally unacceptable effects of existing institutional arrangements and the capacity to enforce changes in institutions and procedures.

The extent to which actors share common values or norms can be added as a second dimension orthogonal to the anarchical–hierarchical continuum. The latter is based primarily on the coercive capacities of agents of governance organizations, but community and coercive capacity are not entirely separable. Instead, they act in a complementary fashion to reinforce and extend the capacity for governance. To understand this interaction it is necessary to examine the forms of collective action involved in any form of governance.

International relations as collective action

Individuals (and organizations) pursue goals and the achievement of many of these goals requires the concerted action of a number of individuals (or organizations). As is well known, collective action is difficult. Many individuals prefer to enjoy the benefits of a collective good without contributing to its provision, if they can get away with it. Thus, for any group to act in unison, fundamental dilemmas of collective action must be overcome or addressed in some manner.

Establishment and maintenance of a formal organization requires attention to the costs of bargaining, monitoring the behavior of agents and members of that organization, and imposing sanctions for violations or shirking. (I use the term "organization" to denote a formal institutional structure that has been set up to realize the common interest of some group, while "institution" includes any formal or informal way in which individuals coordinate their activities.)

Collective action lies at the heart of all the organizations involved in international relations: national governments, multinational corporations or transnational enterprises, intergovernmental organizations (IGOs), nongovernmental organizations (NGOs), terrorist groups and even the military forces that so dominate realist accounts of international relations. None of these organizations is immune to the effects of ongoing dilemmas of collective action, and each has been shaped by different responses to these dilemmas.

The formation of organizations is only the first step, for the heart of international relations consists of interactions among organizations. Here the dilemmas of collective action recur in a slightly different guise, for agents seeking to collaborate for broader purposes also face incentives to let agents of other organizations (or the members of their own organization) bear the brunt of the costs of their collaboration.

Other scholars have investigated the relevance of collective action to international relations theory, but not in as sustained or systematic a manner as is attempted here. For example, analysts of international regimes have used concepts of collective action theory to analyze the ways in which national governments cooperate in trade, commerce, and technical areas (Keohane, 1984). The emerging importance of global environmental issues further highlights those dilemmas of collective action underlying the "tragedy of the commons" and other motivations for the management of common-pool resources (Ostrom, 1990). In this chapter I hope to contribute towards a more systematic application of collective action theory to international relations.

Lichbach (1996) classifies the many "solutions" to dilemmas of collective action offered by social scientists and philosophers into four categories: market, contract, community, and hierarchy. He uses the market category as a baseline, incorporating all changes in the costs and benefits of exchange relationships. Contracting includes the effects of repeated interactions and reputations, community connotes common knowledge or common values, and hierarchy involves the application of sanctions by some recognized authority.

Lichbach's most striking theme is the incompleteness of the solutions included in any one category – each category of solutions requires that some aspects of the other categories are also in place. Market or contract solutions presume that some pre-existing process has formed individual preferences and cognitive understandings and provided individuals with recognized authority over property. Property rights must ultimately be secured by coercive force, and contracting is facilitated if violations of contracts can be detected and punished. Thus, important aspects of community or hierarchy must be provided if market and contract solutions are to operate anywhere close to efficiency.

Solutions based on community or hierarchy are most effective only when both types of solutions reinforce each other. Communal norms are not self-enforcing, so arrangements for monitoring and sanctioning must be made. It also doesn't hurt if there are some tangible rewards to belonging to a given community. Leaders in a hierarchical organization cannot long rule by force alone, but must elicit some degree of consent from their subjects. Since the production of coercion is itself a form of collective action, an army, police force, gang, or any form of coercive organization must find some way to elicit sacrifice on the part of individuals, through material incentives or the satisfaction that comes from serving one's community.

In short, Lichbach demonstrates that solutions to collective action work best in combination. I find this conclusion compelling, even though I prefer to work with a different set of categories. In the next section I outline a categorization based on actors' motivations for collective action rather than the modalities by which they coordinate their actions.

Multiple agents of overlapping realms of collective action

Reduced to its bare essentials, human behavior is motivated by a desire for wealth, physical security, and emotional attachment to some group. None of these can be accomplished by individual action alone; thus, collective action is fundamental to the pursuit of all individual goals. Elsewhere, I develop a framework for the study of collective action that takes these basic human motivations as given (McGinnis, 1996). I argue that each of these three motivations is most clearly manifested in organizations that specialize in the economic-productive, coercive-protective, and social-communal realms of collective action. Each of the basic three realms is defined in terms of the nature of the good that a given organization is designed to produce or provide. The political realm encompasses all activities related to coordination of activities in the other three realms.

The point of distinguishing realms of collective action is to highlight fundamental differences in the resources available to agents of different types of collective action organizations. Agents of economic organizations have access to financial and tangible assets, agents of coercive organizations can employ force against others, and agents of social-communal organizations have influence over the perceptions and understandings of others. Agents may also have the capacity to transform their basic assets into resources relevant to other realms of collective action, as when a corporate executive uses advertising to shape consumer tastes, a dictator invests in productive enterprises those economic resources extracted from his subjects, or a Pope orders the execution of heretics. Some agents may manage to obtain access to significant levels of resources relevant to all four realms of collective action. In his classic formulation of the resources available to governmental officials, Carr (1964) gives equal weight to economic power, military power, and what he labels "power over opinion." This analysis assigns each of these sources of power to agents of different kinds of organizations in the hopes of later integrating them in a more productive manner.

The familiarity of economic theory makes the concept of a "realm of collective action" easiest to understand for the economic-productive case. Even though firms are typically treated as primitive units, they represent successful responses to the dilemmas of collective action. With rare exceptions, all forms of production entail the coordination of individuals with varied skills or resource endowments. The nature of the firm as an economic organization set up to minimize transaction costs is one of the defining concerns of the new institutional economics (Williamson, 1975, 1985, 1996). The very existence of firms and markets presupposes the prior solution of at least some collective action problems.

Organizations are formed in the economic-productive realm because individuals derive satisfaction from consumption or possession of various goods. Organizations in the social-communal realm manifest the satisfaction that individuals derive from belonging to some groups or community. All individuals go out of their way to participate in families and kinship groups, friendships, clubs, and many forms of organized activity. Calculations of rational choice are certainly relevant to such activities, for individuals must allocate a limited amount of time and effort to a large array of alternative activities and social obligations.

To clarify the nature of collective action in the social-communal realm, consider that economic firms are established in order to take advantage of some "team production externality" (Alchian and Demsetz 1972; Miller 1992). This form of externality exists whenever a group of individuals can more efficiently produce some output by working together as a team rather than as separate individuals. Without this externality, the costs involved in establishing or maintaining any organization could not be offset by the potential benefits of formal organizations. In a similar vein, members of any social group can be said to enjoy positive externalities that offset individual costs of participation (Iannoccone, 1992.)

All social groups must deal with dilemmas of collective action. Social groups can be conceptualized as producers of some collective good, at least for the members of that group. One very important collective good is the production of shared social meanings. At the very least these social meanings facilitate communication among otherwise diverse individuals; they also contribute to a sense of belonging to some larger entity or social identity. Production of shared social meanings provides an important source of power or domination, but social interaction also produces important joint benefits. Shared norms and conceptualization of meanings, concepts included in Lichbach's set of community-based solutions to collective action problems, help set the context within which individuals pursue their interests.

Non-governmental organizations and voluntary associations are important examples of organizations in the social-communal realm. So are familial or ethnic forms of organization. By lowering the expected costs of opportunism in contracts with other members, such organizations facilitate the construction and maintenance of trading networks and other long-lasting economic relationships (Landa, 1994). Any organization that conveys a shared sense of understanding or a common appreciation of norms facilitates social interaction within that group.

The coercive-protective realm is important because all individuals seek security, especially protection from the physical violence of others. To achieve this security requires reliance on the protection provided by specialists in coercion. Armies, police forces, and related organizations are, in effect, "producers" of coercion, and their interactions produce varying levels of protection and threat to different groups.

An important aspect of governance is the ability to punish those who violate laws or regulations. Although it is seldom seen as such, coercion is itself a form of collective action. For coercion to be applied effectively all the standard dilemmas of collective action must be overcome.

Coercion is often seen as a fundamental attribute of the state, or of politics in general. Despite Weber's classic definition of the state as having "a monopoly on the legitimate use of force," few political authorities are directly involved in the application of coercion. I have found it useful to explicitly separate the coercive activities of governments from their other activities. Political agents (or authorities) provide many services, ranging from the mundane tasks of bureaucrats to the more glamorous activities of top policy makers. They pass laws and issue regulations and arrange for the punishment of those individuals or corporations who violate these restrictions. The common element is coordination, providing mechanisms and procedures for collective choice.

Governance, then, involves activities in all four realms. For this reason the political realm, including all activities relating to coordination across realms, is defined as the intersection of the three fundamental realms. The unique location of political authorities at the nexus of economic-productive, coercive-protective, and social-communal realms can be illustrated by consideration of "archetypical" organizations of these realms. Firms are established to make profits, armies to coerce the enemy, and churches to provide spiritual solace and moral leadership. Poor economic performance can cause corporate officials to lose a lucrative job, generals will be replaced if they lose too many battles, and priests must avoid any hint of moral turpitude. Public officials can lose office for any of these reasons.

Although these realms can be distinguished for analytical purposes, any one specific organization typically encompasses some combination of these services. Consider, for example, the family as a form of social organization. Families exist, in one form or another, in all human societies, primarily as a means of socialization and protection. Families are important economic organizations in many societies, especially in agricultural economies. Yet, few families are primarily defined in economic terms. Feminist scholars have alerted us to the coercive and political nature of family organization, particularly its role in perpetuating gender stereotypes and resources inequalities. Despite its economic, political, and coercive overtones, however, the family is fundamentally a social organization.

Any governance structure, then, comprises interactions among a diverse set of organizations, each of which includes services that may overlap with more than one realm of collective action. Yet, these realms remain analytically useful, for they highlight fundamentally different motivations of collective action. One distinction that proves particularly important later in this chapter is that members of any organization have a set of expectations concerning the appropriate behavior of their agents, and these expectations differ systematically across realms.

Governance as a cross-realm activity

In the conceptualization of governance presented here, groups of purposive individuals create a variety of collective action organizations specializing in different types of economic, coercive, and social activities. Whereas Hobbes moved directly from individuals to the state, in this framework political order is attributed to (informal) contracts among agents of productive, protective, and communal groups. These agents contract together (albeit imperfectly) to form a governance structure. Any one agent may seek a degree of "monopoly power" within a given realm, but they face competition from agents of other organizations in that realm, as well as organizations from other realms that have expanded into their own realm. If all four realms of collective action were to be successfully monopolized by a single agent, the result would be a single, unchallengeable center of power even more imposing than Hobbes' Leviathan.

Typically, public economies consist of multiple organizations in all realms. The resulting system of governance is one characterized by multiple contenders for the provision of diverse public services, along the lines of the "polycentric" view of metropolitan governance pioneered by Ostrom, *et al.* (1961).

Organizations specializing in any one realm may compete against each other or collude in various ways, and relationships among organizations specializing in different realms may be very close and long-lasting. Services characteristic of different realms may be incorporated within a single organization, for the same reasons that govern vertical integration within the economic realm. Ultimately, some sort of governance structure emerges from these interactions and/or is consciously constructed by the agents of relevant organizations in all four realms. This is the vision that lies at the heart of my conceptualization of international politics as interactions among multiple agents of organizations specializing in overlapping realms of collective action.

Since governance requires the provision of diverse services, organizations from different realms may specialize in different kinds of services. Infrastructure development and other public goods might be handled by what is primarily an economic-productive organization. Coercive organizations are best at providing monitoring and sanctioning services. Producer groups, professional associations, and the like are social organizations in the sense that they convey shared understandings and norms to their members.

The modern nation-state encompasses activities in all four realms: there can be no nation-state without coercion, some sense of community, the production of at least some public goods, and many forms of coordination. All states claim a monopoly on the legitimate use of violence and assert monopoly control over certain public goods. Socialist states extend this assertion to a larger portion of the economy, and totalitarian states strive to achieve monopoly in all four realms, denying the existence of alternative centers of political power or personal loyalties. But the extent of state monopoly in any of these areas is necessarily incomplete. Secret organizations exist, in one form or another, in all societies. Such organizations can themselves provide the basis for exchange relationships among the group of individuals "protected" by that organization. Governments have a capacity for a broader range of protection, but in some circumstances non-governmental providers can be quite effective.

For example, Milgrom, *et al.* (1990) investigate the role of law merchants as an extra-governmental provider of the collective good of information pro- vision and reputation enhancement. They model one important aspect of fairs in early modern Europe, during which merchants took contract disputes to individuals who adjudicated each dispute and assigned payment from the guilty party. These "law merchants" kept records of which merchants had not paid previous judgments against them, and shared this information with any trader who would ask. Merchants who had failed to pay previous judgments were likely to find it difficult to find other merchants willing to engage in a long-term trade with them.

Governance services can also be provided in the absence of formal organization. Berman (1993: 283) offers as an example:

> the transnational community of exporters and importers, shipowners, marine insurance underwriters, bankers, and others – a community which has a European history dating from the twelfth century and which in the twentieth century has become not merely a Western but a worldwide community, held together by innumerable negotiations and transactions among its participants as well as by its own processes of self-government, including its own . . . procedures for mediation and arbitration of disputes.

Ostrom (1990) is replete with examples of small-scale communities that have managed to resolve their collective task of managing common pool resources with minimal (if any) contribution by established governments. Her list of "design principles" common to successful resource regimes is very suggestive of the range of services needed for the governance of market exchange. Particular importance is attached to monitoring the behavior of other indi- viduals and the sanctioning of rule breakers. Thus, even without direct governmental participation, coercion remains a crucial ingredient in success.

Any form of governance similarly combines aspects of all realms of collec- tive action. The overall combination of service providers is a governance structure or regime.

In the area of international environmental governance, Haas (this volume) demonstrates that NGOs make important contributions towards the pro- vision of several of the basic and supplemental governance services. Environmental scientists and activists have articulated a new scientific under- standing and a new moral vision, thus pressuring governments into signing many international treaties as well as eliciting an emerging market in green products, that is, products produced in an environmentally responsible manner. Several NGOs now routinely monitor the activities of national governments and transnational corporations, as a means to convince individual contributors that these organizations are making a difference in the practical world (McGinnis and Ostrom, 1996). Some sanction environmentally unfriendly governments or corporations via indirect shaming mechanisms or via direct action (such as Greenpeace). Some corporations increase their market shares by developing a reputation for environmentally friendly ("green") products or production processes. By doing so these corporations can be said to contribute to the collective good of individuals and organizations active in that sector of the global economy, in the sense of making it likely that this market will continue despite rise in public concern.

At this point my assertion that patterns of governance at the global level can be best understood as manifestations of realms of collective action defined in terms of individual motivation requires further explanation. The basic connection is that agents must never lose sight of the ever-present need to mobilize and inspire the support and participation of the members of, or contributors to, their organization.

Decisions regarding the investment or allocation of time or money are made by individuals motivated by one or more of these fundamental concerns. By definition, agents of an organization in one realm have control over resources directly relevant to the motivation defined as most central to that realm. That is, agents of firms have direct access to economic resources but not to coercion, and police officers can dispense coercion much easier than bribes. Since efforts to extract additional resources on the basis of any single motivation ultimately reach a point of diminishing marginal returns, an agent of an organization in one realm has an incentive to obtain access to the resources under the control of agents in the other realms.

As a consequence, agents of organizations in different realms can jointly gain by making exchanges of their different types of resources. A warlord, say, might benefit from the economic support provided by landlords, whose property is in turn protected by these specialists in coercion. This form of trade between agents is directly analogous to the basic logic of economic exchange between individuals with different resource endowments and tastes. Governance, then, is a form of exchange through which these potential joint gains are realized. Of course, agents of organizations in different realms confront dilemmas of collective action in their efforts to realize these gains. The organizations that these agents form to realize these joint gains are directly involved in governance, as defined here. Political authorities (that is, the agents of these governance organizations) may make use of any of the solutions in any of Lichbach's categories, but what is particularly important is the ways in which solutions from different categories or resources from different realms reinforce each other.

Rent-seeking, redistribution, and reform

Concerns for equity are ubiquitous in human societies, although criteria remain diverse and disputed. Of particular interest here are the claims of those individuals or sub-groups who fare less well in processes of market competition. Such groups can appeal to those who share with them a common sense of community, hoping they will agree to redistribute some of their winnings to their less fortunate comrades. Although such concerns may be expressed in any communal group, actual redistribution of resources is much easier to accomplish in the context of an hierarchical (coercive) form of organization. Authorities deemed legitimate can then extract resources from one group and redistribute them to other groups. Coercion, coordination, and a sense of community all work hand in hand to facilitate the redistribution of resources.

As they take advantage of their ability to extract and redistribute resources, political authorities need not limit themselves to beneficiaries deemed legitimate by the majority of the population. They may distribute resources to groups simply in order to attract their support. Or they may convey "rents" to particular organizations or market sectors.

The term "rent-seeking" has been defined and used in many different ways (Tollison, 1997), but it is here taken to refer to situations in which an economic actor seeks artificial protection for its economic interests. Since innovations or new products can undermine the market shares of existing firms, winners in market competition try to protect their gains, to convince political authorities to place restrictions on entry into their sectors. By creating and sustaining an "artificial monopoly" rent-seekers can obtain superordinate profits and increase their sense of security in the face of uncertain changes in technologies and markets.

By no means is rent-seeking the only option available to actors fearing the negative consequences of future uncertainty. Groups can arrange to share risks, through purchasing insurance or other means of self-protection. Non-profit organizations and familial ties play important roles in cushioning the dangers faced by individuals in all societies. As such, these formal organizations and informal arrangements contribute to the governance of these societies.

Rent-seeking, as used here, is an ubiquitous phenomenon. Whenever some agent or set of agents has been given or has taken the responsibility for making some policy decisions for a collectivity, then all members can seek to influence the outcome of decisions in their favor. In the purest form of rents, rules are shaped so as to explicitly advantage certain groups, as when firms already operating in a sector of the economy seek protection against new entrants. But even minimal forms of coordination can provide similar opportunities for gain. The definition of product standards, for example, may convey benefits on some producers over others depending on the nature of their production process. Thus, rents can also be sought from agents of non-governmental service providers, if these agents have managed to capture some measure of monopoly control over whatever rules are relevant to their interactions. Again, there is nothing inherently unique to political organizations.

This analysis suggests a conceptual similarity between two terms typically seen as distinct: rent-seeking and redistribution. Both require that certain agents have obtained a monopoly (even if narrowly defined) with regard to the imposition and enforcement of laws and regulations. This monopoly position is crucial to the success of redistribution from winners to losers. Otherwise those groups whose resources are being extracted (for whatever reason) have the option of contracting for law-making and other services from alternative providers, a point made long ago in a classic work by Tiebout (1956).

There remain important differences between rent-seeking and redistribution, as commonly understood. Rent-seeking occurs when some actors successfully change the rules of market competition to ensure their success, whereas redistribution typically takes place after the market has run its course. Those actors who lose out in market competition try to change the rules in their favor, by appealing to normative principles widely shared in their communities. In effect, aggrieved groups can extract rents from the legitimacy of their claims.

How are these concerns relevant to an international political economy in which few hierarchical authorities exist? In short, rent-seeking and redistribution may emerge as unintended side-effects of the provision of governance services, even in the absence of formal government.

First, rent-seeking behavior is ubiquitous even for minimal coordination services, arising whenever any one set of political agents is given exclusive authority over any form of rules related to economic interactions. Second, to the extent that community-based solutions have been used to facilitate the signing and implementation of long-term contracts, then the possibility exists that appeals for redistribution may be given credence. If these appeals are sufficiently compelling to important segments of that community, then the same coercive mechanism that helps facilitate the enforcement of contracts may also be used for redistribution.

Redistribution of resources within a community is a process. It begins when a group disadvantaged by the results of market competition makes claims that redress is merited. Other groups must consider the aggrieved group to be part of the overall community, or else their claims will not be given much credence. The aggrieved group must be organized for collective action, either on their own or by attracting the efforts of agent-entrepreneurs. Their collective actions must also be effective in the sense that their claims ultimately prevail in the rough and tumble of political interactions. All these steps must be present or else claimants will not be satisfied. In short, redistribution is hardly automatic.

In international regimes some or all of these intermediate steps are missing or imperfectly attained. For this reason, aggrieved parties often appeal to other governance structures more attuned to their needs. National governments are a particularly common target of such appeals. Governmental skills at redistribution provide an important reason why the "state" is unlikely to wither away as a consequence of accelerating globalization. Nongovernmental sources of redistribution should not be overlooked, but this particular service remains a speciality of national governments.

The common presumption is that any form of rent-seeking or redistribution hurts economic growth. Yet, the potential for redistribution can have potentially beneficial effects in conditions of rapid change or high uncertainty, as is the case for market globalization. Without some assurance that there exists some mechanism for redress of grievances for those who might suffer substantial losses because of unexpected changes in the market, some risk-averse actors might be particularly reluctant to enter into any exchange relationships.

Aggrieved groups may call not just for a redistribution of resources but also for reform of existing institutions. In general, both the origins of institutional arrangements and their subsequent reform are shaped in important ways by distributional conflict (Knight, 1992). Clearly, some forms of governance structures are more conducive to reform than others. If participants perceive that reform is possible in reasonable circumstances, then they might be more willing to enter into more risky agreements. In this sense, reformability is an important component of a sustainable governance regime.

On the other hand, redistribution and reform cannot be allowed to occur too easily. As has been well demonstrated by North (1981, 1990), economic actors need assurance that their property rights will be respected if their actions are to contribute towards economic growth. In the long run, then, some balance must be struck between secure property rights and the capacity for redistribution and reform.

A basic postulate of transaction cost or new institutional economics is that the existence of a legal system makes it easier for parties to contract by lowering the costs of seeking redress should one party violate a contract. A similarly positive benefit is enjoyed when the potential for redistribution and reform exists. Of course, the process of redistribution or reform is itself costly, as is the establishment and functioning of a legal system. In both cases, benefits resulting from increased trade more than make up for these start-up and maintenance costs. Rent-seeking, redistribution, and reform are important processes in any political order, and so we should expect them to be similarly important in global governance.

Implications for globalization and market governance

Lake (1996; this volume) identifies two forms of cost that will determine whether participants in a sector will organize themselves anarchically or establish a hierarchical organization. Hierarchical organizations are characterized by high costs of governance but lower expected costs of opportunism, since contract violators can expect to be punished by the central authority.

To analyze the decisions of groups seeking to realize the potential gains from successful service provision, I find it useful to disaggregate the Williamson-Lake concept of governance costs into two dimensions: (1) start-up costs involved in establishing a new organization; and (2) costs of opportunism by the agents of an organization. This distinction highlights the difference between establishment of a new organization and reliance on a pre-existing organization.

The cost schedule associated with reliance on a pre-existing organization is determined by the degree of similarity between the organization's existing responsibilities and the services to be provided to this new set of customers. If these services are very similar, then start-up costs would be extremely low, because that pre-existing organization had already had an opportunity to build a reputation and develop an expertise in this form of service provision. However, there may be some concern that the agents of pre-existing organizations would remain more attentive to the needs of their older, more established clientele. To the extent that the interests of these two groups diverge, the new group would face increased concern about agent opportunism. Organizations seeking to expand into dramatically different areas of service provision would have fewer advantages compared to the establishment of an entirely new organization, although there might be some benefits from having an established reputation or expertise in the general area of service provision. Thus, as one moves farther from an organization's original base of expertise the attractiveness of reliance on an existing organization decreases and establishment of a new organization becomes the more likely choice. Finally, costs of agent opportunism should be relatively low for groups establishing a new organization specifically designed to provide specific services to a particular set of clients.

These costs are affected by the behavior of potential suppliers. Agents of existing organizations have personal and institutional interests in obtaining more resources. They can do so by providing new services to the existing set of members or contributors, or by offering services to other groups, that may overlap with the existing group or remain distinct from it. However, their ability to expand into new areas is limited by the degree of similarity between old and new tasks. In all this the role of individual entrepreneurs cannot be overlooked, for dynamic and effective leadership can often make up for differences in relative costs.

National governments are an important class of pre-existing organizations that have specialized in the provision of governance services. Over the years the solid reputations of national governments should help them take on many service provision functions in many different sectors. National governments occupy a unique niche in the institutional field – what other organization (or set of organizations) can credibly claim a range of activities covering all four of the realms of collective action? National governments are uniquely situated to continue to exert influence, despite the fundamental changes occurring in the world today.

The issue of territoriality arises at this point. Territorial control is central to the effective use of coercion but it is not as obviously related to other types of service provision. As globalization proceeds, both economic and social-cultural contacts across territorial boundaries become more and more commonplace. Given the state's relative emphasis on coercion, this makes the services provided by national governments less in tune with the problems raised by accelerating change.

Yet, governments retain advantages in dealing with issues of redistribution and reform. Their combination of hierarchical organizational form and a sense of community makes them particularly adept at redistribution. As the economic and socio-cultural world becomes less territorial, perhaps the focus of governmental activities will shift from coercion to the provision of community-based services of redistribution and reform. As such, governments will continue to play essential roles in the ongoing adaptation to global change.

A capacity for redistribution is not going to be equally efficacious in all sectors of the world economy. In some sectors, those actors most severely hurt by the globalization are also the most marginal to that sector's sense of community; such actors can expect little success within that sector. In such cases governments attuned to the interests (or at least the votes) of these distressed groups must play a major role if any redistribution is to be realized. Even then, major reform of governance arrangements is unlikely to be forthcoming. Conversely, if globalization most upsets groups central to a sector's basic identity, then major governance change will probably follow.

A few cautionary notes about the potentially negative effects of a capacity for redistribution are in order. First is the problem of moral hazard. If individual agents feel assured that any grievances will be addressed, then they will have less incentive to make the possibly painful adjustments needed to avoid losses in the first place. Second, some governments may be rather too successful at redistribution for their own good. Over-indulgence in either redistribution or rent-seeking can have potentially devastating effects on a nation's economy. Nonetheless, a capacity for redistribution would seem, in general, to be conducive towards the long-term survivability of a governance regime. In the absence of some relatively effective method of redress, radical transformations in governance structures seem virtually inevitable, in the long run.

Path dependence and social expectations

In summary, the international political economy contains a complex mixture of sectors in which national governments, firms, IGOs, and NGOs all provide governance services in many different combinations. Some sectors of the global economy are "self-governing," having arranged at some means by which basic rule making, monitoring, sanctioning, conflict resolution, and legitimation services are provided by the members themselves. In other sectors new formal organizations will have been established or arrangements for service provision made with pre-existing organizations. Sectors differ in the relative roles contract, community, and hierarchy play in the provision of governance services, and in the respective importance of productive, communal, and coercive organizations.

One implication of this analysis is that transaction cost calculations cannot tell the entire story of the provision of market governance. Lake expects institutional markets to clear, in the sense that the organizational form adopted in any given sector should correspond to the form of organization that is most efficient in terms of reducing transaction costs, given the characteristics of that sector on the underlying dimensions of scale, opportunism, and governance costs. This correspondence may break down if groups are given the option of contracting with existing organizations. Lower start-up costs may make organizations with otherwise "inefficient" organizational forms be the more preferred option, provided the expansion is into a closely related area of service provision. Of course, if the nature of the services provided are closely related, then so is the organizational form most optimal for that set of characteristics. Still, some governance organizations may come to provide a diverse range of services to a single group, or to overlapping groups, or even to otherwise unrelated groups of customers.

Lake does point to one important source of potential slippage between organizational form and the character of sectors undergoing rapid change. Namely, those actors who benefit from the existing governance structure will strive to maintain that organizational form, even if it begins to prove unwieldy when faced with new situations. The analysis presented here adds another factor, grounded in the ever-present need for agents to maintain the continuing support and participation of the members of, or contributors to, their organization.

The existing set of organizational forms shapes social expectations. Individual members of that society learn to recognize the properties of general classes of social organization, their advantages and disadvantages in different sets of circumstances. But this is more than a matter of adding up the costs and benefits of alternative forms of social organization. Over time, individuals come to associate with each class of organizations a sense of the range of activities considered appropriate for that class. In contemporary Western societies, for example, members may raise concern when a church engages in activities that are too overtly economic (fund-raising) or political (lobbying for certain policy outcomes). But in the Islamic world, exactly the same behavior would seem perfectly natural.

Societal expectations can constrain the expansion of organizations into other realms of activities. An organization expanding into cognate areas should not experience much resistance by its current members, unless this expansion is seen to threaten its capacity to pursue the organization's original goals. However, organizations which encompass diverse services may exceed boundaries deemed appropriate by their own members and contributors, and thus may begin to lose their support. Clearly, the ability of organizations to expand into new areas of service provision is limited.

Expectations concerning the appropriate range of behavior for certain types of organizations become established over time and are an important ingredient of the prevailing culture. Since individuals from different cultures have divergent expectations concerning appropriate forms of social organization, interactions between them are necessarily complicated by these differences. Cultural differences can be ameliorated when a common understanding emerges among experts engaged in a particular sector of the global economy. Still, there is every reason to expect that expansion of governance services in response to globalization will stop well short of comprehensive schemes of governance.

Those sectors in which productive, communal, and coercive arrangements are closely intermixed are best able to weather the disruptions of market globalization. In general, liberal democracies tend to be characterized by governance organizations at multiple levels of social aggregation. As a consequence, groups disadvantaged by market processes have multiple options for seeking redress of their grievances. If they lose in one arena of political competition they can then appeal to governance organizations at other levels of aggregation. Thus far the national scale remains most open to those actors inconvenienced by the disruptions of globalization. However, if similarly disadvantaged actors in different states are able to make contact and develop a common program, they may be able to establish new institutions more amenable to their appeals. To the extent that globalization facilitates contacts across national boundaries for all types of political actors, efforts to bypass national governments may become increasingly effective.

This chapter has demonstrated that the multiple dimensions of governance services can be combined together in many different ways. Sectors of the global political economy are characterized by diverse configurations of organizations even though the same set of basic services is provided, in one manner or another, by the network of governance organizations in that sector. Whatever the configuration of governance, all experience similar tensions, including tendencies towards rent-seeking behavior even if governance services remain minimal.

Transaction cost minimization is one important influence on the ways by which different sectors of the world economy organize themselves for the provision of governance services. But these institutional arrangements in turn have important consequences for the forms of rent-seeking, redistribution, and reform that ultimately shape that sector's ability to weather the uncertainties wrought by market globalization. A capacity for redistribution of resources and for reform of institutional arrangements can be essential to the long-term stability of governance arrangements, even though these abilities to adapt to changing conditions increase the costs of transacting in the short term. Stable governance in times of rapid change requires a meaningful capacity for redistribution and reform.

Note

* I would like to thank Ben Kickers, Brenda Bushouse, David Lake, Elinor Ostrom, John Williams, and the editors for their comments on earlier drafts. All remaining errors are my responsibility alone.

References

Alchian, Armen, and Harold Demsetz (1972) "Production, Information Costs, and Economic Organization," *American Economic Review* 62: 777–95.

Berman, Harold (1983) *Law and Revolution: The Formation of the Western Legal Tradition*, Cambridge, MA: Harvard University Press.

Berman, Harold (1993) "Law and Religion in the Development of a World Order," in *Faith and Order: The Reconciliation of Law and Religion*, Atlanta, GA: Scholars' Press.

Bull, Hedley (1977) *The Anarchical Society*, New York: Columbia University Press.

Carr, Edward H. (1964 [1939]) *The Twenty Years' Crisis 1919–1939*, New York: Harper-Collins.

Friedman, Milton (1963) *Capitalism and Freedom*, Chicago, IL: University of Chicago Press.

Hart, Jeffrey A. and Aseem Prakash (1996) "Globalisation and Regionalisation: Conceptual Issues and Reflections," *International Trade Law and Regulation* 2: 205–11.

Iannaccone, Laurence R. (1992) "Sacrifice and Stigma: Reducing Free-Riding in Cults, Communes, and Other Collectivities," *Journal of Political Economy* 100: 271–91.

Keohane, Robert O. (1984) *After Hegemony*, Princeton, NJ: Princeton University Press.

Knight, Jack (1992) *Institutions and Social Conflict*, Cambridge: Cambridge University Press.

Lake, David A. (1996) "Anarchy, Hierarchy, and the Variety of International Relations," *International Organization* 50: 1–33.

Landa, Janet T. (1994) *Trust, Ethnicity, and Identity: Beyond the New Institutional Economics of Ethnic Trading Networks, Contract Law, and Gift-Exchange*, Ann Arbor, MI: University of Michigan Press.

Lichbach, Mark I. (1996) *The Cooperator's Dilemma*, Ann Arbor, MI: University of Michigan Press.

McGinnis, Michael D. (1996) "Collective Action, Governance, and International Relations: The MAORCA Framework," Working Paper, Workshop in Political Theory and Policy Analysis, Indiana University, Bloomington.

McGinnis, Michael D., editor (forthcoming) *Polycentricity and Local Public Economies: Readings from the Workshop in Political Theory and Policy Analysis*, Ann Arbor, MI: University of Michigan Press.

McGinnis, Michael D. and Elinor Ostrom (1996) "Design Principles for Local and Global Commons," in Oran Young, ed., *The International Political Economy and International Institutions*, Cheltenham, UK: Edward Elgar Publishing, Vol. II, pp.464–93.

Milgrom, Paul R., Douglass C. North and Barry R. Weingast (1990) "The Role of Institutions in the Revival of Trade: The Law Merchant, Private Judges, and the Champagne Fairs," *Economics and Politics* 2: 1–23.

Miller, Gary J. (1992) *Managerial Dilemmas: The Political Economy of Hierarchy*, New York: Cambridge University Press.

North, Douglass C. (1981) *Structure and Change in Economic History*, New York: Norton.

North, Douglass C. (1990) *Institutions, Institutional Change and Economic Performance*, Cambridge: Cambridge University Press.

Ostrom, Elinor (1990) *Governing the Commons: The Evolution of Institutions for Collective Action*, Cambridge: Cambridge University Press.

Ostrom, Vincent, Charles Tiebout and Robert Warren (1961) "The Organization of Government in Metropolitan Areas: A Theoretical Inquiry," *American Political Science Review* 55: 831–42.

Rubin, Elizabeth (1997) "An Army of One's Own," *Harper's Magazine* February 1997, 44–55.

Tiebout, Charles M. (1956) "A Pure Theory of Local Expenditures," *Journal of Political Economy* 64: 416–24.

Tollison, Robert D. (1997) "Rent Seeking," in Dennis C. Mueller, ed., *Perspectives on Public Choice: A Handbook*, Cambridge: Cambridge University Press, pp.506–25.

Wallerstein, Immanuel (1974) *The Modern World-System*, vol. 1, New York: Academic Press.

Waltz, Kenneth N. (1979) *Theory of International Politics*, Reading, MA: Addison-Wesley.

Weimer, David L. and Aidan R. Vining (1989) *Policy Analysis: Concepts and Practice*, Englewood Cliffs, NJ: Prentice Hall.

Williamson, Oliver E. (1975) *Markets and Hierarchies: Analysis and Antitrust Implications*, New York: Free Press.

Williamson, Oliver E. (1985) *The Economic Institutions of Capitalism*, New York: Free Press.

Williamson, Oliver E. (1996) *The Mechanisms of Governance*, New York: Oxford University Press.

3 Globalization and the evolution of rules

Wayne Sandholtz[1]

Rules are the fundamental elements of social systems.[2] Even two strangers from different cultures and speaking different languages, if they met in a remote desert would quickly develop a set of rules to regulate their "society." Social systems exist wherever people interact, as strangers in the wilderness or as currency traders buying and selling on global foreign exchange markets. Such interaction is impossible without rules that delineate roles and the associated bounds of acceptable behavior. Of course, the larger the number of people involved, the more extensive the division of labor among them, and the higher the number of interactions, the greater the need for increasingly differentiated and specific rule structures.[3]

I begin with the premise, developed initially by Hedley Bull and his collaborators, that international relations constitute a social system, and that this international society is defined by rules and institutions.[4] Globalization, defined in this volume as a set of processes leading to the integration of intermediate, factor, and product markets across geographical boundaries,[5] implies increasing density of communication and exchange among persons from differing legal and cultural settings. Those involved in these interactions across (national) social systems experience a need for new, and more specific, rules to govern relationships that are not necessarily covered by domestic laws. One way or another, people who need rules will find or create them – whether that means agreeing to operate under one set of national rules, devising rules outside of state structures (private law), or pressuring governments to establish international or global rules (regimes, international law). A first proposition of this chapter is, then, that globalization promotes the development of transnational society and consequently the elaboration of transnational rules, public and private, formal and informal. New rules do not spring into being out of nothing; they emerge out of, or borrow from, existing rules. A second proposition is that the rules that emerge in response to globalization will be elaborations of, or modeled after, existing rules.

As rule structures become increasingly articulated, they begin to sustain normative discourses that define and redefine the meaning of the rules, and thus the bounds of warranted behavior. The most articulated rule systems have formal, written rules (law), along with specific organizations charged with maintaining the rule system itself (legislatures, courts, police). As rule systems become more elaborate they start to resemble legal systems, with an accompanying tendency toward formalization. A third proposition is, therefore, that if globalization continues, some international rule systems will become increasingly codified and will gradually develop specific organizations for managing the rules and resolving disputes. The development of the European Court of Justice and the strengthened dispute resolution procedures in the World Trade Organization are archetypes of this process.

The main purpose of this chapter is to offer a framework for conceptualizing the dynamics of international rule structures. In the first section I will briefly explain why prevailing approaches to international institutions, based on a transaction-cost metaphor from economics, are inadequate. I then offer a rule-based conception of governance and international institutions. I suggest that governance consists of rule structures, which can exist with or without formal superordinate authority. The conclusion considers what globalization implies for international rule structures.

Limits of the economic metaphor

The dominant approach to analyzing international institutions treats them as passive forums that exist because they enhance the efficiency of state-to-state bargaining. International institutions or "regimes" improve efficiency by reducing the transaction costs associated with negotiating agreements. In the absence of regimes, information about the preferences and compliance records of other states is difficult, or costly, to obtain. By supplying information about the preferences and behaviors of states, regimes reduce information costs that would otherwise prevent states from reaching mutually beneficial agreements.

The transaction-cost account of international institutions traces its origins to Robert Keohane's *After Hegemony*. Keohane imported into international relations discourse the notion of transaction costs, which had been developed by economists, especially Oliver Williamson,[6] to analyze the organizational structures of firms. At the heart of Keohane's theory of regimes, then, is a metaphor: states are like firms and seek to minimize transaction costs, thus enabling them to attain more pareto-efficient outcomes (greater cooperation). Keohane's framework became the standard approach to international governance; any sort of collective action or management of multilateral problems could be depicted as a transaction-cost reducing regime. Indeed, no alternative general theory currently exists.

With the end of the Cold War system, and with increasing economic globalization, international governance has once again become a first-order scholarly and practical concern. The time is therefore right to consider whether or not the transaction-cost (TC) account of international institutions is adequate to our analytical needs. I will briefly argue that conceptual and empirical problems make the transaction-cost approach an incomplete one.[7]

A crucial difficulty is that the TC logic loses something in translation from economics to international relations. In economics, it posits that firms facing constant pressure on prices will seek to minimize costs by using the most efficient mode of organizing production (market, hierarchy, or hybrid). But "competition" among states is not at all like competition among firms. In the United States at least, by far the majority of new businesses fail. In international politics, very few countries cease to exist. In fact, the rules of the international system virtually ensure that, once established, states are not absorbed by their neighbors. It is thus hard to see what the analog in international relations could be to the role that competitive markets play in weeding out firms that choose less efficient organizational forms. If anything, one would have to acknowledge that even the most hideously "inefficient" states survive. An even more fundamental problem is that the market analogy in international relations presumes the ontological status of its basic categories, as if "interests," "actors," and "markets" existed in nature. In fact, of course, markets are social constructs and depend for their existence on deep and dense networks of shared understandings and rules.[8] Thus the social rules that define roles, rights, and responsibilities are logically prior to the cost-benefit calculations of specific agents.

David Lake (this volume) outlines an approach that is also based on Williamson's theory. In Lake's basic metaphor, states are like firms. When entering into relations, or "contracts," with other states, they calculate the costs of opportunism and governance and choose the "governance structure" (from a continuum ranging from anarchy to hierarchy) that minimizes costs. Lake has also sought to provide a functional equivalent for the efficiency imperative, arguing that governments seek to economize on their security relationships because funds saved on defense can be spent instead on politically salient domestic programs.[9] Yet American policy makers during the Cold War made no effort to count the costs of the nuclear weapons program, which was the centerpiece of American security policy.[10] Rather, the obsession with "containing" the Soviet menace justified any expense. If there was no cost comparison for a weapons program in which all expenditures were, in principle, counted in dollars and entered in the federal budget, it seems implausible that policy makers might calculate the diffuse and non-quantified costs of opportunism and governance associated with various interstate contracts. In Lake's perspective, the United States does not absorb Canada and Mexico into an American empire presumably because US leaders regularly calculate that the costs would be greater than they are for the more anarchic relation that exists. A more plausible, and parsimonious, explanation might be that in the normative context of the late twentieth century, among liberal democracies, empire over one's neighbors is illegitimate and unthinkable (it is never subject to any sort of calculation). More generally, as McGinnis argues, governance structures rely not just on low transaction costs but also on legitimacy and consent.[11]

The TC approach also suffers from empirical shortcomings. The first has to do with operationalizing and measuring its central variables. For instance, we do not know how to identify and measure transaction costs themselves. What counts as a transaction cost? How would one determine the size of a transaction cost? The absence of operational definitions is not just a lacuna in international relations; economists have yet to devise workable measures of transaction costs in firms. Equally problematic, without an empirical definition of transaction costs, it is difficult to establish a TC theory's causal claims. We do not really know if transaction costs inhibit interstate agreements, nor if regimes reduce transaction costs, nor if states support regimes because they value the kinds of efficiencies that TC theory posits. Advocates of TC theories provide little guidance on how their fundamental claims could be tested empirically.

Despite his arguments to the contrary, Lake's schema is subject to the same skepticism. Lake asserts that empirical testing of a contracting theory "does not require precise measures of transaction costs or information," nor does it imply the need "to observe the effects of each link in a causal chain" (this volume). But the issue is not that every link must be verified empirically. The question is whether empirical analysis can test even the most fundamental claims of transaction-cost or contracting approaches. Empirical testing requires that the key variables be observable, and in this case the key variables are various kinds of costs. The advocates of contracting theories must be able to show either that those costs are directly and objectively measured, or that the actors' estimates of those costs are observable. If they cannot, there is no way to demonstrate empirically that cost differentials (as opposed, say, to logics of appropriateness or institutional isomorphism) drive the choice of governance structures.[12]

More generally, states and other international actors bargain, pursue self-interests, employ power, and reach agreements (or make contracts). But all of these things happen in social contexts. An actor's interests depend on how it understands its roles, its social situation, and the natural world. These understandings are necessarily social. As Kenneth Arrow puts it, "Rationality is not a property of the individual alone, although it is usually presented that way. Rather, it gathers not only its force but also its very meaning from the social context in which it is embedded."[13] Utility-based or choice theoretic approaches can be useful, but they depend on having first acquired an understanding of the social and institutional context. In the following section I offer the basic elements of an approach that would allow us to analyze the social and institutional context of globalization and governance.

Rules, interests, and choice

As a point of departure, I broadly accept the basic constructivist premise that social structures and agents constitute each other,[14] and Onuf's proposition that rules are what link social structures and individual actors.[15] Any kind of sustained interaction leads to the development of rules that define roles and assign rights and responsibilities to them. I define rules as statements that identify standards of conduct for given sets of actors in given situations.[16] As such, rules are the substance of institutions, and institutions are at the heart of governance.

Rules cause behaviors both directly and indirectly.[17] They produce behavior directly by constraining actor choices. Rules prescribe who can act, how, and when. In formal organizations, the rules are usually supported by penalties or coercive authorities. Rules cause behavior indirectly in two ways. First, they define roles and identities – the "self" in "self-interest." Second, they provide reasons for acting in one way rather than another. That is, when confronted with alternative courses of action, an actor weighs the various rules that are implicated by the situation and chooses according to which rules provide the most persuasive reasons.[18]

The argument so far does not banish self-interested behavior from the social universe. Actors have goals, and prefer to be better off. But what it means to be "better off" depends crucially on one's roles, which are rooted in social contexts, defined by rules. Rules, in other words, are logically prior to self-interest. Rules thus establish the horizons for what people can imagine as their interests and objectives; rules also delineate the range of legitimate means for achieving those ends. People with genuinely autonomous utility functions and those who ignore shared notions of acceptable means are either hermits or psychopaths.

Finally, rules vary in numerous ways, but two key axes of variation for my purposes are along the formal-informal dimension and the specific-general dimension. Formal rules are codified in writing according to institutionalized procedures. Treaties, charters, and constitutions all contain formal rules. Informal rules are shared understandings, nowhere codified, about what constitutes warranted conduct. Informal rules include the non-use of mercenaries and, for a long period of time, the norm that treaties should be observed (which was informal until codified in the Vienna Convention).[19] On the specific-general dimension, the most general rules are those that constitute the actors, that is, that define roles (what is a state) or membership (who can join the United Nations). General rules can embrace broad categories of behavior ("States should promote free trade"). In contrast, the most specific rules concern particular, narrowly defined acts (as proscriptions, prescriptions, or permissions), like: "Do not conduct nuclear tests in the open atmosphere."

Rules and institutions

Rules do not stand alone; they are linked in clusters, or in other words, institutions. In fact, I define institutions as rule structures. Ronald Jepperson similarly defines institutions as socially constructed "program or rule systems."[20]

Organizations are a subset of institutions. Organizations comprise clusters of rules, but they are also composed of people.[21] An organization has members, an institution does not (despite common usage). Though some international organizations (IOs) may serve largely as passive bargaining forums, others are purposive, problem-solving entities.[22] For instance, international organizations like the World Health Organization and the International Whaling Commission exist to solve jointly identified problems. They may, by the way, be the sites of extensive interstate bargaining and they may even enhance the efficiency of that bargaining. But the organizations exist to solve common problems, and bargaining is simply part of the process by which IOs work (not necessarily their *raison d'être*).

Some international organizations provide what Onuf calls "institutional supports" for their rules (I will use the term "organizational supports" but the idea is the same).[23] At the heart of organizational supports are specific kinds of rules. First, organizational supports generally include secondary rules that specify how legitimate behavioral rules are to be produced and applied. Second, organizational supports include formally constituted roles whose inhabitants are authorized (the rules assign rights and duties) to monitor compliance, interpret the rules in specific cases, resolve disputes, impose sanctions on violators, and carry out the penalties. Raz calls these the "primary organs" of an institutionalized normative system.[24] In domestic society, these roles are familiar: police officers, district attorneys, judges, prison wardens (among others). Some IOs similarly (though not identically) constitute actors whose role is to foster compliance with the behavioral rules. Some IOs designate officials whose duties are to monitor conduct, interpret and apply the rules in specific cases, reach determinations as to actors' conformity with the rules, signal violations (or certify compliance), and sometimes even impose penalties.

The European Union is probably the most dramatic example of an international institution with well-developed organizational supports. The Commission of the EC has substantial independent powers, including authority to review and overrule state subsidies to industry, to investigate companies suspected of anti-competitive practices (price-fixing, cartels), to impose fines on firms found to have violated the competition rules, to vet proposed company mergers and impose conditions or disallow them, to take countries to the European Court of Justice for failure to implement Community law, and more. The Commission can in addition act as a policy entrepreneur, offering proposals and mobilizing coalitions.[25] Equally significant, the European Court of Justice (ECJ) has created for itself powers of judicial review. In addition to adjudicating disputes between EU organizations or between them and member states, the ECJ has broad power to interpret and apply EU law in cases referred from national courts. It can hold national governments liable for their failure to implement properly EU legislation, and its decisions are enforced by national courts.[26] These formal organizational supports for its rules distinguish the EU from almost all other international institutions, leading some analysts to conclude that the EU is not an international institution but rather a decentralized or "multi-level" polity. The difficulty in classifying the EU disappears if we think of all political systems as rule clusters (or sets of linked rule clusters).

In this perspective, international society and national states are not different in kind, but only in degree (of formalization and specificity of the rules, and of organizational supports for them). States are highly formalized (codified) rule systems with a high degree of behavioral specificity and full-fledged organizational supports. International institutions tend to have low levels of formalization, specificity, and organizational supports, though there is considerable variation. Since rules vary along two dimensions (formal-informal, specific-general), we can also classify international institutions according to the character of the rules that define them. We can place a cluster of rules (an institution) governing a set of behaviors with respect to both dimensions, yielding the two-by-two matrix shown in Figure 1. The figure illustrates a typology of international institutions. Though it shows discrete boxes for clarity of exposition, the dimensions are actually continuous ranges capable of situating institutions at various points between the poles.

Institutions that are general but formalized – in treaties, charters, and conventions – I call *orders*, since they concern primarily broad frameworks for regulating relations. In other words, orders are primarily rules about rules, governing membership, franchise and decision-making procedures. Examples include the Concert of Europe and the United Nations system. Note that orders can include subordinate clusters of rules that are more specific; the UN, for example, establishes a general order but also includes specific agencies like the UN Environmental Program or the Food and Agriculture Organization (FAO). Specific and informal institutions have rules for specific sets of behaviors, but the rules are uncodified. I call them *tacit regimes*. Tacit

	Informal	Formal
General	**International society:** constitutive rules for international society.	**Orders:** consensus on broad objectives and on the need for an explicit ordering framework; rules of membership, franchise, and decision-making.
Specific	**Tacit regimes:** regularized patterns of interaction in particular domains, with implicit rules but few concrete commitments.	**Problem-solving organizations:** substantial consensus on well-defined ends and means; state claims and actions justified on legal or technical grounds.

Figure 1 A typology of international institutions, with examples

rules generate weaker commitments than formal rules and are more contested, yet they are recognized as rules (albeit with lesser weight or legitimacy) by those participating in the institutions. Decolonization, spheres of
influence, and nuclear deterrence are examples.

Specific and formal institutions are *problem-solving organizations* established
to address quite narrowly defined sets of problems. Specific, formal
institutions will also include more finely-grained behavioral prescriptions,
proscriptions, and permissions. The specificity and formality dimensions
also generate expectations as to the extent of organizational supports in
institutions. General, informal institutions would likely have minimal or no
organizational supports for compliance. Specific, formal institutions could
vary considerably in the degree to which they possess them, but institutions
with highly developed organizational supports will cluster in the southeast
corner of the specificity/formality plane.

Rule structures and international politics

I have suggested that international relations – like all social life – are perva-
sively rule-guided. Since rules are linked to each other in institutions, and
institutions are linked to broader institutions, there are complex structures of
rules that shape international politics. In principle, then, one could map the
rule structures that shape international politics. Scholars have in recent
years undertaken a number of useful studies of the historical development of
specific international rules (usually called "norms");[27] what remains is the
larger task of linking rules into clusters and to larger rule structures. In this
section I outline one way of approaching that task.

I suggest that there are four basic rule complexes that constitute international society: technical rules, system rules, state rules, and liberal rules.
The logic supporting the selection of these four rule structures is that they
cover four essential levels of analysis in the international social realm: the
natural world, the international system, states, and individuals.

Technical rules guide how people (individually and in groups) relate to the
natural world, the broadest or most inclusive level of analysis. The complex
of technical rules is a system for validating knowledge and action, based on
positivism and scientific methods. It grew out of Western rationalism and the
scientific revolutions that began in the fifteenth century and continues to
unfold in the twentieth. Technical rules demystify nature and social relations.
That is, the material and social realms are no longer seen as expressions of the
supernatural or divine. Instead, the universe works according to impersonal,
material laws that are, in principle, discoverable through the methods of
science. Scientifically generated knowledge thus holds privileged status. This
is not to say that technical rules, or scientific knowledge, displace politics,
only that they establish norms for how protagonists must frame their arguments and claims. Peter Haas (this volume) directly addresses the process by
which ideas become institutionalized and thus shape political action.

Scientific epistemology in turn legitimates a "technical" approach to solving problems. In the face of misfortune (floods, epidemics, recessions, gang violence), we seek not to placate the gods but to discover the causes. As it has been constructed, science allows people to uncover causal relations and general laws; solving material or social problems means intervening at the proper point in the causal chain. The basic rules of technical rationality have become so universal that they shape everyday thinking as well as specific collective enterprises (fixing a refrigerator, saving the ozone layer, promoting Third World development). Given the impressive successes of scientific-technical rationality in a number of domains (medicine, agriculture, information technologies, and so on), and the dominance of Western education, it is no surprise that the technical rule complex has covered essentially the entire world; there are no substantial alternatives to scientific rules of knowledge and technical problem solving (even confessional regimes want scientific-technical industries and militaries).[28]

International system rules cover relations among the actors in international relations. The basic principle anchoring this complex of rules is the equality of sovereign states. The system rules thus recognize states as the basic units and provide standards of conduct for their dealings with each other and with other (non-state) actors. The system rules developed gradually, from before the Peace of Westphalia (which represented a formal and collective recognition of a rule of exclusive internal jurisdiction) through the Vienna Convention on the Law of Treaties, and beyond. This complex includes the basic rule that treaties should be obeyed, as well as the rules that govern diplomatic practices.

State rules constitute the internal institutions and structures of states, the dominant political units of the modern era. State rules are not the only normative structures within any given territorial space; there are diverse and overlapping political and cultural rule systems in every state. Nevertheless, states possess the most elaborate and formal of rule structures, as well as the most thoroughly developed organizational supports (in the form of educational, regulatory, investigative, policing, judicial, and penal agencies). The Weberian conception of states as possessing a legitimate monopoly of coercive force within their borders is reasonable as an ideal type, one that also allows us to recognize divergent cases where the supremacy of the state's rules is diminished by internal fragmentation (ex-Yugoslavia, Afghanistan) or supra-national authority (the European Union). International system rules create space for states as rule structures, by recognizing states as the dominant actors in international society. Indeed, to be recognized in the international arena, an entity must in fact be a rule structure that resembles the ideal-typical state – having effective "rule" within a given territory. Meyer and his collaborators take this idea a step further, arguing that "world society" not only legitimates nation-states as the primary international actor but also provides models for the institutional forms and purposes of states.[29] States in turn support the international system rules by sustaining the larger rule complexes (treaties, organizations, diplomatic practices) that validate states. The interaction between international system rules and state rules is a perfect instance of co-constitution.[30]

Liberal rules enshrine the individual as the basic unit of, and ultimate value in, the social world. Liberal rules, growing out of Enlightenment thought, posit the inherent worth, dignity, and freedom of the individual. They define a panoply of individual political and civil rights. Economic freedoms (the rights associated with ownership and control of private property) similarly derive from fundamental liberal values (Locke). Markets are founded on the notion of freely exchanging, autonomous individuals who have exclusive control over their own property. The massive rule systems that have developed to guarantee property rights, market competition, and free trade, all trace back to basic notions of individual freedom and rights (with economic theories attaching a supplementary, pseudo-scientific justification on the grounds of "efficiency"). Later formulations of basic rights include additional economic rights (the right to a basic standard of living, for instance). Group rights (assembly, collective bargaining, and self-determination, for examples) derive from individual rights and in fact exist to protect individuals in the exercise of their fundamental rights. The development of liberal ideals and rules was driven in large part by the desire to fix boundaries to the extraordinary degree of agency accorded to states as rule structures. In theory, if not usually in practice, the prerogatives of monarchs had been absolute; the liberal revolutions delimited state powers by grounding them not in the divine right of kings but in the natural, inalienable rights of people.[31]

Whereas state-system rules cover the entire globe, in that all states participate in international relations on terms established by the rules of sovereignty and diplomatic practice, the liberal rule structure has more uneven coverage. Liberal ideals emerged in Europe and have taken root most deeply in European societies and in countries culturally and historically closely linked to them (North America, Oceania). Colonialism carried European liberal ideas to most of the rest of the world, but the degree to which they became embedded and institutionalized in colonial possessions varies somewhat. Liberal rules have thus become established in Asia, Africa, and Latin America only partially and unevenly. Consequently, the meaning of liberal categories and rules can vary across regions, as evidenced by recurring assertions that "human rights" and "democracy" mean something different in Singapore or Malaysia than they do in "the West."

The gradual encroachment of liberal rules upon international system rules has, in a sense, charted the evolution of international relations. For instance, state sovereignty rules initially granted almost unlimited latitude to rulers in the initiation and conduct of war. Liberal rules have slowly eroded and delimited the war prerogatives, restricting the conditions under which states could legitimately turn to war as well as the methods by which they could conduct the fighting. Norms of intervention in cases of extreme human rights violations or genocide have begun to erode the rule of exclusive internal sovereignty.[32] And some of the thorniest issues for the near future in international politics deal precisely with the tension between international system rules and liberal rules: China's integration into international economic institutions will likely continue to run up against the question of domestic human rights. Ethnic violence within states will provoke calls for international intervention, again pitting liberal rules against sovereignty rules. More generally, the evolution of normative structures, and the resulting tensions between different rule complexes, may be one of the fundamental forces driving international change.

The four basic rule structures thus define the fundamental elements of modern international society. They govern its basic categories of relationships (state-state, state-individual, individual-individual, and relations between people and the natural world). Other elements of these rule structures have emerged or accreted over time, linked by a justifying discourse to the basic rules. The four basic rule structures are general and informal (at least initially, the UN Charter having formalized some of the basic rules of state society as well as some liberal rules relating to human rights).

Dynamism and change

The notion of rule structures might create an impression of fixity. But, in fact, rule change is constant. Change occurs through a ceaseless interaction between rules and practice. What connects rules to practice, and ensures that they evolve together, is the dialogue among actors concerning both the meaning of the rules and the meaning of behaviors. My approach emphatically does not argue that only "texts" exist. Rather, I hold that there are observable behaviors (including speech), but that their significance depends on the principled discussions that occur among actors. Those discussions (or "discourses" or "dialogues") begin with existing rules, but inevitably produce change in the rules. That is, normative and institutional innovations cannot be conjured up out of thin air; they always refer to pre-existing rules and emerge out of the dialogues that actions engender.

I argued earlier that social behavior is rule-guided. This does not mean that the process of linking rules to situations yields unambiguous behavioral directions. Consequently, it is pointless to think of behaviors as falling neatly into the dichotomous categories of "compliance" and "non-compliance." Instead, what matters is the social process by which actors attempt to persuade others that the actions in question did (or did not) constitute warranted behavior. A consensus that a specific act violated rules, instead of establishing the inefficacy of the rules, reaffirms their relevance. Failure to achieve consensus regarding the justifiability of a specific act implies that the meaning of the rules is ambiguous or contested. One actor explains and rationalizes its conduct, perhaps casting it as a justifiable exception to the rules; others respond, criticize, exculpate, or condemn.

Of course, international society is not a debating society, in which those actors with the best arguments and the greatest persuasive skills prevail. Indeed, actors bring to bear both persuasive reasons and material resources. Those with the resources can bribe or compel others to assent to their arguments and interpretations. Thus powerful actors win more arguments than weak ones, as when the British Navy enforced the abolition of the slave trade. But that is not to say that capabilities (or power, or resources) explain everything, for not even the most powerful actors can remove themselves from the webs of rules that define "actorhood" and establish the bounds of the thinkable. Rather, the purposes on behalf of which actors exercise power are shaped by the rules that define roles, interests, and even how to count gains and losses. In other words, power cannot be separated from purpose, and purpose is dependent on socially constructed roles and values. Furthermore, even powerful actors seek to justify their actions. In doing so they can only deploy the categories and normative principles that are available in the existing structures of rules.

What makes the process dynamic is that in the process of dialogue, actors interpret, apply, clarify, and thus modify the rules. The meaning of the rules, and sometimes new rules, emerge from the dialogue. The modified rules then provide reasons for subsequent behaviors; the interpretations from an early discourse shape the terms of later ones. Actors acquire from the dialogues a sense of what range of behaviors can be justified. The new round of action and dialogue again modifies the rules, and the process continues as a cycle.[33] In a sense, then, rules come from rules.[34] Figure 2 is a schematic representation of this dynamic process. Behaviors generate dialogues about the rules, which modify the rules, which in turn provide reasons for subsequent behaviors and discourses, and so on.

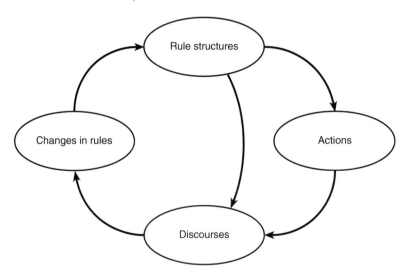

Figure 2 Dynamic relations among rules, actions, and discourses

Globalization and the evolution of rules

I have argued that rule structures, or institutions, are a fundamental and pervasive feature of international relations. Rules provide the context in which actors conceive of their interests and delineate ranges of justifiable action in pursuit of those interests. Rules, then, must be central to any notion of governance. Indeed, I would propose the following as a workable definition: *governance is the process by which rules are generated*. Governance thus defined can include both formal organizations that authoritatively establish and enforce rules, as well as patterned social interactions that produce shared rules without the formal structures of government.[35] The emergence of rule structures, or institutions, is the manifestation of governance.

One powerful question animating this volume is how economic globalization affects international governance. Building on contemporary integration theory, I derive specific propositions concerning the relationship between globalization and governance. The key insight was developed with reference to the European Union, but it is easily generalizable.[36] Globalization, defined as a set of processes leading to the integration of intermediate, factor, and product markets across geographical boundaries,[37] implies rising levels of communication and exchange across national borders. Those involved in these increasingly dense cross-border interactions experience a need for new, and more specific, rules to govern relationships that are outside the familiar and highly structured context of domestic law. For those involved in cross-border interactions (trade, finance, investment, multinational production, distribution, and so on), separate national legal regimes can cast up a variety of obstacles to potentially profitable transnational exchange. In the absence of a transnational or supra-national framework of rules, cross-border transactions are disadvantaged relative to domestic exchange (of course, this is precisely the objective of many national rules). As national markets integrate, cross-border transactions and communications increase, and so therefore does the societal demand for trans- or supra-national rules. Governments can respond to this demand by creating or extending international organizations and rules, or private actors can agree on common standards and procedures without governmental involvement. Of course, governments can resist or obstruct market integration and the associated demand for transnational rules, but only at a cost to cross-border transactors and possibly to the national economy as a whole.[38]

My first proposition is therefore that globalization leads to the expansion of transnational rules. Rule structures will develop where actors need them to guide their relations. This is, to be clear, *not* a prediction that globalization will lead to the expansion of formal international regimes and international law.

A second proposition is that the rules that emerge in response to globalization will be elaborations of, or modeled after, existing rules. New rules cannot be created out of nothing. Indeed, as I have argued above, rule

structures provide the necessary social context in which interactions, normative discourses, and rule making can occur. In one sense, rule structures con-
tinuously generate new rules: behavior triggers discourses that inevitably
reinterpret or modify the rules. Even when groups of actors consciously set
out to create formal organizations or rules (treaties, conventions, charters),
they work with the materials at hand, namely, existing organizations and
rules. A powerful actor can sometimes impose its own forms as models for
international institutions. But institutional design can also be a process
whereby collectivities pattern new institutions on those most widely seen to
be successful or appropriate.[39]

As rule structures become increasingly articulated, they begin to sustain
normative discourses that define and redefine the meaning of the rules, and
thus the bounds of warranted behavior. The most articulated rule systems
have formal, written rules (law), along with specific organizations charged
with maintaining the rule system itself (legislatures, courts, police). As rule
systems become more elaborate they start to resemble legal systems, with an
accompanying tendency toward formalization. A third proposition is therefore that if globalization continues, some transnational rule systems will
become increasingly formalized and will gradually develop specific organizations for managing the rules and resolving disputes.

A caveat is in order regarding these propositions. The term "globalization"
sometimes, and misleadingly, suggests worldwide uniformity in the expansion
of cross-border exchange. In practice, "globalization" means increasing
exchange among certain actors, or among some countries, or within some
regions. As a result, emerging rule structures will *not* be global in their coverage. On the contrary: transnational rules will develop where the growth of
transnational interactions is most pronounced. Transnational rule making
(governance) will shadow rising levels of exchange, producing highly
variegated, overlapping rule structures of different kinds and at different
levels. Some rule structures will develop within geographic regions (the EU),
or among non-contiguous sets of countries (e.g., the OECD). Others will
emerge among sub-state units (along the Rhine river, for example, or
among the US and Mexican border states) or private actors (international
commercial arbitration). Some rule structures will be oriented toward a set
of actors and their relations, but others will be defined with respect to specific
issues or problems.[40] The following empirical examples lend substance to the
propositions. Each of the mini-cases examines the emergence of rules tied to
market integration.

The European Union

The point of examining the European Union (EU) is not that other regions or
the rest of the world are going to follow the path of the EU, toward formal
rules and supra-national organizations. Indeed, the experience of the EU is
unlikely to be duplicated elsewhere. What distinguish the EU are the clarity

and formalization of its rules (the Treaty of Rome and its amendments, legislation, and decisions of the European Court of Justice) and the degree of
autonomy possessed by its supra-national organizations (especially the
Commission and the ECJ). The initial establishment of such institutions is a
hurdle of immense proportions. The founding of the EC was an extraordinary
response to Europe's descent into the abyss of two twentieth-century wars; it
is difficult to envision similar moments of genesis elsewhere. However, the
evolution of the European Union demonstrates both the transaction-driven
development of supra-national rules and the way existing institutions structure the evolution of governance.

The European Community began life as a treaty, an agreement among six
sovereign states. The last forty years have witnessed the remarkable transformation of the EC from an interstate bargain into a quasi-federal polity.
During that period, governance – the capacity to make rules – has shifted
from the national to the EC level in multiple policy domains. One of the
most intractable analytical problems in the study of the EC has been to
explain why governance has shifted faster and farther in some policy areas
than in others. Recent theoretical work, confirmed by empirical research,
offers an answer to that question. Alec Stone Sweet and Wayne Sandholtz
have hypothesized that "rising levels of transnational exchange trigger
processes that generate movement toward increased supra-national governance" in the EC.[41]

The argument is quite straightforward: increasing levels of cross-
border transactions and communications by societal actors will increase the
perceived need for European-level rules and dispute resolution. Separate
national legal regimes (customs and other border controls, differing technical
standards, divergent health and environmental regulations, distinct systems
of commercial law, diverse national currencies, and so on) constitute a major
barrier for those who wish to engage in exchanges across borders. Transactors
can exert pro-integration pressure on their own governments, but when
these are reticent, transactors can access supra-national arenas dominated
by the Commission and the European Court of Justice. National governments
and EC organizations respond to these demands by expanding the reach of
supra-national rules. The institutional structure of the EC shapes the processes by which pressure for integration gets translated into policy outcomes.
That is, the Treaty of Rome, plus subsequent legislation and ECJ decisions,
delineate the legal bases with which actors can frame and justify their
claims, as well as the organizational sites for registering them.

Detailed empirical research, involving both aggregate data and process-
tracing case studies, supports these propositions. Space limitations permit
only a brief summary of some of the results. The European Court of Justice,
through a series of decisions in the 1960s, converted the Treaty of Rome into
a constitution for the EC.[42] Alec Stone Sweet and James Caporaso have
found that after the constitutionalization by the ECJ, cross-national
exchange, transnational judicial activity, and supra-national rule making

rose steadily. Actors seeking to reduce obstacles to cross-border exchange litigate against national barriers (or national failures properly to implement EC law). National courts refer these cases to the ECJ, which systematically extends, and facilitates the production of, EC rules.[43]

Telecommunications is a domain where policy making has migrated to the supra-national level. By the 1980s, Europe's fragmentation into national telecommunications monopolies was increasingly costly to a variety of actors who depended on reliable, advanced telecommunications facilities spanning national borders. European businesses, plus telecoms equipment makers and suppliers of new services and infrastructures, became ready allies of the Commission when it undertook to create a liberalized EC telecoms market. Governments resisted, but found that ECJ rulings and the Commission's use of Article 90 directives (that do not require member-state approval) severely curtailed their ability to prevent telecoms liberalization and rule making at the EC-level.[44] The liberalization of the European airline industry offers a remarkably similar account. At a time of sustained increase in airline passenger and freight traffic, supra-national organizations, in complicity with business and consumer groups, were gradually able to overcome the resistance of governments that had been hostile to deregulation. Once removed from national control, reregulation – at the European level – proceeded.[45] In contrast, areas with minimal cross-border transactions at the societal level (e.g., foreign policy) show little or no movement toward supra-national rule making.

In sum, the relative intensity of transnational exchange across policy domains explains their differential movement toward supra-national governance. The existing institutional structure (rules and organizations) decisively shapes the process of creating supra-national rules.

The WTO

Students of the international trade regime – GATT, now the WTO – refer to its "judicialization," by which they mean its evolution into a formalized system of dispute resolution.[46] What began as an improvised, *ad hoc* process under GATT now looks like a court system. GATT was initially a loose assembly of diplomats who did not view GATT as an international organization and who resisted any form of legalism in resolving disputes. In fact, the diplomats took care to ensure that lawyers were not involved in GATT's decision-making organs. The purpose of the panel system, in place by 1955, was not to adjudicate between disputants. Instead, the panel system was designed to encourage negotiated settlements acceptable to all parties. Because the panels operated on the basis of consensus, either disputant could prevent the creation of a panel, reject proposed panel members, obstruct the panel's work, or veto a panel's ruling.

The panel system fell into disuse during the 1960s, but the period after 1970 saw both its revival and its judicialization. The United States led the way, by lodging the complaints that ended the moribund phase of GATT dispute resolution. Furthermore, the United States initiated the use of legal techniques that contributed to the judicialization of GATT: rather than sending diplomats to negotiate, the US sent lawyers to litigate. The American trade lawyers filed long, detailed complaints and followed up with a full panoply of legal arguments and tactics. This behavior elicited two important kinds of responses. First, GATT panels began to issue longer, more tightly argued decisions, and they began to employ other panel decisions as case law (precedent). In other words, the panels started to act like courts. Second, other GATT parties (e.g., the European Community and Japan) began to send in the lawyers. The Geneva offices of many GATT members included, by the early 1980s, a permanent legal staff. GATT members thus began to treat the panel system like litigation. By the end of the decade, GATT case law had expanded and clarified the quasi-judicial role of the panels.

The Final Act of the Uruguay Round, signed in 1993, created the World Trade Organization and established a formal system of adjudication. In contrast with the old GATT system, the new one is compulsory. The convening of a panel is now automatic upon receipt of a complaint. There are deadlines fixed for each major step in the process. Member states cannot exercise a veto at any point. If a party to a dispute is dissatisfied with a panel decision, it can appeal to the independent Standing Appellate Body, whose ruling is final. The Act also provides for a broader range of sanctions than existed previously. The new dispute resolution procedures seem to be meeting a demand: in the first twenty months of its existence, the WTO received fifty-one complaints from member states, as compared to 196 cases brought to GATT in nearly fifty years.[47]

The steadily rising volume of world trade, coupled with the perceived inadequacies of the GATT dispute resolution mechanism, helped create the impetus for the WTO's more formal, more judicialized system. The WTO case thus demonstrates expansion of rules (as panel decisions acquire the force of case law), borrowing from existing institutions (GATT case law and the use of panels), and increasing formalization.

Transnational business contracts

As companies engage in international activities – investment, trade, franchising, joint ventures, and so on – they enter into contracts with firms (and sometimes governments) from other national jurisdictions. One vexing problem with such transnational contracts centers on the question, "Under what legal jurisdiction will any disputes over the terms of the contract be settled?" International private law developed a body of principles designed to select the appropriate legal system for a specific dispute. The "conflicts of law" norms produce answers to jurisdictional questions, but they have also generated considerable concern owing to the "palpable inconveniences that continue to arise when transnational business disputes must be resolved by national courts applying national law."[48]

In response to the inconveniences posed by national jurisdictions over transnational contracts, global contracting practices and rules have begun to emerge. The globalization of contracting practices and principles has proceeded along two dimensions: formal attempts to codify international rules, and the "spread to the rest of the world of the American style of long, detailed contract concocted by large law firms for a very high fee."[49] Post-war efforts to establish uniform transnational contracting law began with the Uniform Sales Law of the Hague (1964), to which Western European countries adhered. Subsequent projects have included the United Nations Convention on the Contracts for the International Sale of Goods (1980) and the 1986 Hague Convention on the Law Applicable to Contracts for the International Sale of Goods. The United Nations Commission on International Trade Law has generated a Legal Guide on Drawing up International Contracts for the Construction of Industrial Works, and a Model Law on International Commercial Arbitration. Private groups have prepared various model laws for international contracting in more narrowly specialized sectors, like civil engineering. So far, these documents do not create genuinely supranational jurisdictions, but rather offer templates that states may choose to incorporate into their domestic law or private parties may build into their contracts.

A possibly more fundamental change in international contracting has involved the spread of American business contracting practices to much of the world, creating a de facto global standard. Contracts between large companies in the United States are long and detailed, as they attempt to foresee potential future contingencies and questions. The diffusion of American practices could occur in two ways. As US companies moved into other parts of the world, they demanded contracting in the mode that they knew, thus imposing American practices on foreign firms. Or, as businesses of every nationality expanded their transnational activities, they confronted the same kinds of problems that in previous periods had driven the development of American-style contracting. It was relatively easy, then, to adopt the American model that was at hand. Shapiro illustrates these arguments by recounting the spread of American practices in international franchising contracts and mineral development contracts.[50]

International commercial arbitration

Parallel with the movement toward the internationalization of the American style of business contracting has been the development of international commercial arbitration, again with the ascendance of American practices. Arbitration is a consensual procedure, in which the parties to a dispute avoid national legal systems by agreeing to submit their conflict to an arbitrator (or panel of arbitrators). The role of the arbitrator can vary, from being a mediator who encourages the two sides to reach agreement, to acting like a quasi-judge who issues a decision. Yves Dezalay and Bryant Garth, in their comprehensive study of international commercial arbitration, note that the numbers of arbitration centers, professional arbitrators, and disputes submitted have all grown dramatically since the 1970s.[51] The demand for arbitration grew with the expansion of transnational business activity, but received an additional impetus from the growth of the Eurocurrency markets, the rise of OPEC (oil nationalizations, concessions, and petro-dollars), and the expansion of large engineering projects, especially in developing countries. Before the boom in arbitration, the field was dominated by a small club of "grand old men" centered on the International Chamber of Commerce (ICC) in Paris. The ICC both promoted arbitration as a means of resolving transnational business disputes and provided minimal organizational infrastructure. The grand old men were, and are, generally senior European law professors and judges who render decisions on the basis of accumulated experience and wisdom. The growing demand for arbitration in the 1980s overwhelmed the ICC's limited structures and opened the door to outsiders who could compete with the grand old men.

Through that door entered a new kind of player – the legal technocrat, generally based in one of the major Anglo-American law firms. Instead of general wisdom, the technocrats offered "specialization and technical competence."[52] They introduced into arbitration procedures techniques borrowed straight from US or British adversarial litigation. Whereas in the Paris club the role of counsel was to assist the arbitrator in finding an appropriate solution, the role of the technocrats was to attack. Whereas a relative handful of the most established continental arbitrators could invoke principles of *lex mercatoria* in resolving disputes, the new litigators insisted on carefully explicated legal reasoning and attention to evidence.[53] Into arbitration they imported an emphasis on questions of fact and discovery, procedural tactics (motions, objections, delays), references to precedents, and a demand for decisions based on careful legal reasoning. The ICC has leaned toward the Anglo-American litigators, increasing its permanent staff and taking on a more technical role in the management of arbitration procedures. In the competition for business and legitimacy, the technocrats have been in the ascendant, transforming arbitration into a more formalized and routinized process that increasingly resembles American-style litigation.

Conclusions

Rules are the fundamental units of social structure. Linked together into larger complexes, or institutions, rules provide the framework with reference to which people define their interests, objectives, and strategies. This essay outlines a rule-based approach to the study of international governance, which I define as the process by which transnational rules are generated. I have suggested four basic rule structures in world politics, which in turn underpin a wide variety of international regimes and organizations. I have also argued that the rule structures are not fixed but in constant evolution. Rules evolve through a dynamic process that is, in essence, a feedback loop. Rules express shared conceptions of what constitutes warranted behavior in a given set of circumstances. Actors pursue what they take to be their interests, in that rule context. But there are inevitable ambiguities, or disagreements, about what actions the rules justify. Behaviors always, therefore, generate discourses about the meaning of the actions and the meaning of the rules. Repeated rounds of action and discourse reinterpret and thus modify the rules, which in turn shape subsequent behaviors and ground subsequent discourses.

In order to understand the impact of globalization (defined as market integration) on governance (or the generation of rules), I examined the impact of increasing cross-border interactions on rule structures. I offered three propositions: (1) that rising levels of transnational exchange lead to the expansion of transnational rules, public or private, formal or informal; (2) that the rules that emerge in response to globalization will be elaborations of, or modeled after, existing rules; and (3) that some transnational rule systems will become increasingly formalized and will gradually develop specific organizations for managing the rules and resolving disputes.

The empirical accounts illustrate the relationships I proposed, and others could be cited. Ethan Kapstein has documented the emergence of international capital adequacy standards for banks.[54] Security and bond rating agencies (notably American ones, like Moody's and Standard and Poor's) have developed as a private system of regulating access to capital, creating de facto international standards of financial worthiness.[55]

More specifically, with respect to the first proposition, the development of the European Union and of the WTO demonstrate the expansion of rules, triggered by rising levels of cross-border exchange. EU legislation and decisions of the European Court of Justice have generated new rules that respond, broadly, to the needs of persons engaged in cross-border transactions. The judicialization of the GATT/WTO has also been driven by increasing trade and the corresponding need for more efficient means of resolving disputes; panel decisions have become a body of case law, thus expanding the rules of international trade. We also observe the generation of new rules to guide international contracting and arbitration, again in response to the rise in transnational business activity.

The EU and the WTO also illustrate the proposition that new rules evolve out of existing ones. In both cases, new rules (whether legislative or judicial) clearly took shape in the legal context established by the respective founding documents. The contracting and arbitration cases may be even more suggestive with regard to this proposition, since neither domain possessed a basic charter. American practices infused the emerging international contracting rules and arbitration procedures.

Finally, all four cases display a trend toward increasing formalization. In each, the rule systems have become more elaborate and dense. As the rule structures become increasingly articulated, they begin to sustain normative discourses that define and redefine the meaning of the rules – that is, they start to resemble systems of law. The European Court of Justice converted the Treaty of Rome into a constitution for the EC, and then established the supremacy of EC law over national laws. Subsequently, a supra-national legal system developed, involving the ECJ, national courts, national governments, and private parties. The WTO now possesses a highly formalized, quasi-judicial dispute resolution mechanism. International contracts have become increasingly detailed and legalistic in the American style. And commercial arbitration is now based less on the wisdom of distinguished individuals and more on techniques and tactics from Anglo-American litigation.

Globalization is a bit of a misnomer, since there is little in it that is truly global. Transnational market integration proceeds unevenly and partially. But where market integration advances, the level of cross-border interactions will rise, and so therefore will efforts to construct transnational rules.

Notes

1 I am grateful to Global Peace and Conflict Studies at the University of California, Irvine, for supporting this research. I also thank the participants in this project for constructive comments; Peter Haas, Jeffrey Hart, and Aseem Prakash were especially helpful.
2 On this argument see Jepperson 1991, 157.
3 On increasing international social complexity and its consequences for governance, see also Cerny's contribution to this volume.
4 Bull 1977; Bull and Watson 1984. For a recent assessment of the relationship between the "English school" and "American" international relations scholarship, see Buzan 1993.
5 Prakash and Hart, "Introduction," in this volume, p.3.
6 E.g., Williamson 1975.
7 For a more complete critique of the transaction-cost approach, see Sandholtz 1997.
8 On the social construction of markets, see Fligstein 1992 and 1996; Granovetter 1992; Dobbin 1993; DiMaggio 1994; and Hamilton 1994.
9 Lake 1996.
10 See Schwartz 1998.
11 McGinnis, this volume. McGinnis also argues that systems of governance must therefore also include mechanisms for redistribution and reform that raise transaction costs but meet social expectations (norms).
12 Lake's remark (this volume) that one need not "observe gravity to verify its existence" is misleading. Gravity is the law posited; one verifies it by examining the behavior of observable objects. The analog to gravity in Lake's theory is not transaction or information costs, but rather the law to the effect that actors will choose among options so as to maximize expected utility. The costs are not the law, but rather the means of verifying it (by showing that actors minimize costs). Costs in Lake's theory are analogous to variables like "mass" or "distance" in physics – they need to be observable.
13 Arrow 1992, 63.

14 See Onuf 1989 and 1996; Wendt 1987; and Dessler 1989.
15 Onuf 1994, 7. See also Onuf 1989.
16 My definition is close to that of Nicholas Onuf, who has worked to clarify the theoretical deployment of rules. Onuf defines rules as statements that "describe some class of actions and indicate whether these actions constitute warranted conduct on the part of those to whom these rules are addressed." See Onuf 1996, 9.
17 For a more extended argument, see Sandholtz 1998b.
18 See Raz 1975, chap. 2; Kratochwil 1989, 27 and 33.
19 On the former, see Thomson 1990.
20 Jepperson 1991, 149 and 157 Other institutionalists who also see rules as the essence of institutions (but whose theoretical work diverges in other respects) include North 1990, 3 and 6; and Meyer *et al.* 1987, 12.
21 See North 1990, 5.
22 See Haas 1990, 17–18.
23 Onuf 1989, 136–40; see also Raz 1975, chap. 4.
24 Raz 1975, 135–6.
25 See Sandholtz 1996.
26 There is a growing body of research on the role of the ECJ. See Shapiro 1992, 123–7; Weiler 1994; and Stone 1995.
27 See for example: Walzer 1977; Ray 1989; Thomson 1990; Nadelmann 1990; Klotz 1995; Jackson 1993; and Finnemore 1996.
28 In Ernst Haas' formulation, scientific reasoning has diffused sufficiently to create a "universal problem-solving technique." See Haas 1997, 1. Meyer and his co-authors similarly note that the idea of salvation through the church "has been replaced by the belief among almost all elites that salvation lies in rationalized structures grounded in scientific and technical knowledge." See Meyer, *et al.* 1997, 174.
29 Meyer, *et al.* 1997.
30 I owe this point to Nicholas Onuf.
31 Bendix 1978.
32 Reed and Kaysen 1993.
33 See Stone Sweet forthcoming.
34 See Klotz 1995; Onuf n.d.
35 I thus agree with Lake (this volume) that a range of types of governance is possible, from anarchic to hierarchic.
36 The argument that follows builds on Stone Sweet and Sandholtz 1998.
37 Prakash and Hart, "Introduction," in this volume, p.3.
38 See Mattli 1996.
39 For an argument regarding fitness in a given institutional population, see Weber 1994.
40 I am thus in general agreement with other contributors to his volume regarding the institutional forms of the emerging international system. I would expect the kind of institutional pluralism that Kobrin (this volume) has evoked, with over-lapping jurisdictions, multiple loyalties, and the blurring of geographical borders, authority, and the public-private distinction. Though he takes a different path, McGinnis similarly foresees "a complex mixture of sectors in which national governments, firms, IGOs, and NGOs all provide governance services in many different combinations" (this volume). Cerny (this volume) also expects global-ization to lead to cross-cutting, differentiated, multi-layered forms of governance.
41 This section draws on Stone Sweet and Sandholtz 1998.
42 On the constitutionalization of the Treaty, see Stein 1981; Weiler 1991; Burley and Mattli 1993.
43 Stone Sweet and Caporaso 1998.

44 Sandholtz 1998a.
45 O'Reilly and Stone Sweet 1998.
46 Note, for instance the titles of the following articles, on which this section is largely based: Stone Sweet 1997; Hudec 1992.
47 See *Financial Times*, 8 August 1996, 6.
48 Shapiro 1996, 4.
49 Shapiro 1996, 7.
50 Shapiro 1996, 24–32.
51 This section relies on Dezalay and Garth 1995 and 1996.
52 Dezalay and Garth 1995, 37.
53 *Lex mercatoria* in medieval times was a set of customary legal principles, used by merchants (sometimes in their own private tribunals) to supplement the patchy commercial law of states. Though there were some basic rules, much of the *lex mercatoria* consisted of local practices, and it was never codified. With the ascendance of states as the exclusive sources of commercial law, *lex mercatoria* passed into obscurity. Though some modern continental scholars have attempted to revive it as a genuine international commercial law and though some arbitrators refer to it, *lex mercatoria* is insufficiently precise and clear to suit the Anglo-American-style litigators and their clients, whose style of arbitration is in the ascendant. Though *lex mercatoria* is therefore part of private international commercial dispute resolution, it is not the driving force.
54 Kapstein 1992.
55 See Sinclair 1993.

References

Arrow, Kenneth J. (1992) "Rationality of Self and Others in an Economic System," in *Decision-Making: Alternatives to Rational Choice Models*, edited by Mary Zey, Newbury Park, CA: Sage.

Bendix, Reinhard (1978) *Kings or People: Power and the Mandate to Rule*, Berkeley, CA: University of California Press.

Bull, Hedley (1977) *The Anarchical Society*, New York: Columbia University Press.

Bull, Hedley and Adam Watson (1984) *The Expansion of International Society*, Oxford: Clarendon Press.

Burley, Anne-Marie and Walter Mattli (1993) "Europe Before the Court: A Political Theory of Legal Integration," *International Organization* 47: 41–76.

Buzan, Barry (1993) "From International System to International Society: Structural Realism and Regime Theory Meet the English School," *International Organization* 47(3): 327–52.

Dessler, David (1989) "What's at stake in the agent-structure debate?" *International Organization* 43(3): 441–73.

Dezalay, Yves and Bryant Garth (1995) "Merchants of Law as Moral Entrepreneurs: Constructing International Justice from the Competition for Transnational Business Disputes," *Law & Society Review* 29(1): 27–64.

Dezalay, Yves and Bryant Garth (1996) *Dealing in Virtue: International Commercial Arbitration and the Construction of a Transnational Legal Order*, Chicago, IL: University of Chicago Press.

DiMaggio, Paul (1994) "Culture and Economy," in *The Handbook of Economic Sociology*, edited by Neil J. Smelser and Richard Swedberg, Princeton, NJ: Princeton University Press.

Dobbin, Frank (1993) "The social construction of the Great Depression: Industrial Policy during the 1930s in the United States, Britain, and France," *Theory and Society* 22: 1–56.

Finnemore, Martha (1996) *National Interests in International Society*, Ithaca, NY: Cornell University Press.

Fligstein, Neil (1992) "The Social Construction of Efficiency," in *Decision-Making: Alternatives to Rational Choice Models*, edited by Mary Zey, 351–76, Newbury Park, CA: Sage.

Fligstein, Neil (1996) "Markets as Politics: A Political-Cultural Approach to Market Institutions," *American Sociological Review* 61: 656–73.

Granovetter, Mark (1992) "Economic Institutions as Social Constructions: A Framework for Analysis," *Acta Sociologica* 35: 3–11.

Haas, Ernst B. (1990) *When Knowledge Is Power*, Berkeley, CA: University of California Press.

Haas, Ernst B. (1997) *Nationalism, Liberalism, and Progress*, Ithaca, NY: Cornell University Press.

Hamilton, Gary G. (1994) "Civilizations and the Organization of Economies," in *The Handbook of Economic Sociology*, edited by Neil J. Smelser and Richard Swedberg, Princeton, NJ: Princeton University Press.

Hudec, Robert E. (1992) "The Judicialization of GATT Dispute Settlement," in *In Whose Interest? Due Process and Transparency in International Trade*, edited by M.H. Hart and D.B. Steger, 9–43. Ottawa: Center for Trade Policy and Law.

Jackson, Robert H. (1993) "The Weight of Ideas in Decolonization: Normative Change in International Relations," in *Ideas and Foreign Policy*, edited by Judith Goldstein and Robert Keohane, Ithaca, NY: Cornell University Press.

Jepperson, Ronald (1991) "Institutions, Institutional Effects, and Institutionalism," in *The New Institutionalism in Organizational Analysis*, edited by Paul J. DiMaggio and Walter W. Powell, Chicago, IL: University of Chicago Press.

Kapstein, Ethan B. (1992) "Between Power and Purpose: Central Bankers and the Politics of Regulatory Convergence," *International Organization* 46(1): 265–87.

Keohane, Robert O. (1984) *After Hegemony: Cooperation and Discord in the World Political Economy*, Princeton, NJ: Princeton University Press.

Klotz, Audie (1995) *Norms in International Relations: The Struggle Against Apartheid*, Ithaca, NY: Cornell University Press.

Kratochwil, Friedrich V. (1989) *Rules, Norms, and Decisions*, Cambridge: Cambridge University Press.

Lake, David (1996) "Anarchy, Hierarchy, and the Variety of International Relations," *International Organization* 50(1): 1–33.

Mattli, Walter (1996) "Explaining Regional Integration," Working Paper No. 96–4, Irvine, CA: Global Peace and Conflict Studies, University of California, Irvine.

Meyer, John W., John Boli and George M. Thomas (1987) "Ontology and Rationalization in the Western Cultural Account," in *Institutional Structure: Constituting State, Society, and the Individual*, edited by George M. Thomas, John W. Meyer, Francisco O. Ramirez and John Boli, Newbury Park, CA: Sage.

Meyer, John W., John Boli, George M. Thomas, and Francisco O. Ramirez (1997) "World Society and the Nation State," *American Journal of Sociology* 103(1): 144–81.

Nadelmann, Ethan (1990) "Global prohibition regimes: the evolution of norms in international society," *International Organization* 44: 479–526.

North, Douglass C. (1990) *Institutions, Institutional Change and Economic Performance*, Cambridge: Cambridge University Press.

Onuf, Nicholas (1989) *World of Our Making*, Columbia, SC: University of South Carolina Press.

Onuf, Nicholas (1994) "The Constitution of International Society," *European Journal of International Law* 5.

Onuf, Nicholas (1996) "Rules, Agents, Institutions: A Constructivist Account," Working Papers on International Society and Institutions, No. 96–2, Irvine, CA: Global Peace and Conflict Studies, University of California, Irvine.

Onuf, Nicholas (n.d.) "How Things Get Normative," Typescript, Florida International University.

O'Reilly, Dolores and Alec Stone Sweet (1998) "The National Liberalization and European Regulation of Air Transport," in *European Integration and Supranational Governance*, edited by Wayne Sandholtz and Alec Stone Sweet, Oxford: Oxford University Press.

Ray, James Lee (1989) "The Abolition of Slavery and the End of International War," *International Organization* 43: 405–39.

Raz, Joseph (1975) *Practical Reason and Norms*, London: Hutchinson.

Reed, Laura W. and Carl Kaysen, eds (1993) *Emerging Norms of Justified Intervention*, Cambridge, MA: Committee on International Security Studies of the American Academy of Arts and Sciences.

Sandholtz, Wayne (1996) "Membership Matters: The Limits of Functional Theory for Explaining European Integration," *Journal of Common Market Studies* 34: 403–29.

Sandholtz, Wayne (1997) "Rules, Reasons, and International Institutions," Typescript, University of California, Irvine.

Sandholtz, Wayne (1998a) "The Emergence of a Supranational Telecommunications Regime," in *European Integration and Supranational Governance*, edited by Wayne Sandholtz and Alec Stone Sweet, Oxford: Oxford University Press.

Sandholtz, Wayne (1998b) "Rule Structures and International Relations," Typescript, University of California, Irvine.

Schwartz, Stephen I. (1998) *Atomic Audit: The Costs and Consequences of U.S. Nuclear Weapons Since 1940*, Washington, DC: Brookings Institution Press.

Shapiro, Martin (1992) "The European Court of Justice," in *Euro-politics*, edited by Alberta M. Sbragia, Washington, DC: Brookings Institution Press.

Shapiro, Martin (1996) "Globalization of Freedom of Contract," Jean Monnet Chair Lecture, Robert Schuman Centre, Florence: European University Institute.

Sinclair, Timothy J. (1993) "Passing Judgement: Credit Rating Processes as Regulatory Mechanisms of Governance in the Emerging World Order," *Review of International Political Economy* 1: 133–59.

Stein, Eric (1981) "Lawyers, Judges, and the Making of a Transnational Constitution," *American Journal of International Law* 75: 1–27.

Stone, Alec (1995) "Governing With Judges: The New Constitutionalism," in *Governing the New Europe*, edited by Jack Hayward and Edward C. Page, Oxford: Polity Press.

Stone Sweet, Alec (1997) "The New GATT: Dispute Resolution and the Judicialization of the Trade Regime," in *Law above Nations: Supranational Courts and the Legalization of Politics*, edited by Mary Volcansek, Gainesville, FL: University of Florida Press.

Stone Sweet, Alec (forthcoming) "Judicialization and the Construction of Governance," *Comparative Political Studies*.

Stone Sweet, Alec and James Caporaso (1998) "From Free Trade to Supranational Polity: The European Court and Integration," in *European Integration and Supranational Governance*, edited by Wayne Sandholtz and Alec Stone Sweet, Oxford: Oxford University Press.

Stone Sweet, Alec and Wayne Sandholtz (1998) "European Integration and Supranational Governance," in *European Integration and Supranational Governance*, edited by Wayne Sandholtz and Alec Stone Sweet, Oxford: Oxford University Press.

Thomson, Janice E. (1990) "State Practices, International Norms, and the Decline of Mercenarism," *International Studies Quarterly* 34: 23–47.

Walzer, Michael (1977) *Just and Unjust Wars*, New York: Basic Books.

Weber, Steven (1994) "The European Bank for Reconstruction and Development," *International Organization* 48(1): 1–38.

Weiler, J.H.H. (1991) "The Transformation of Europe," *Yale Law Journal* 100: 2403–83.

Weiler, J.H.H. (1994) "A Quiet Revolution: The European Court of Justice and Its Interlocutors," in *The New Constitutional Politics in Europe*, edited by Martin Shapiro and Alec Stone, special issue of *Comparative Political Studies* 26: 510–34.

Wendt, Alexander E. (1987) "The agent-structure problem in international relations theory," *International Organization* 41(3): 335–70.

Williamson, Oliver (1975) *Markets and Hierarchies: Analysis and Anti-Trust Implications*, New York: Free Press.

4 Social constructivism and the evolution of multilateral environmental governance

*Peter M. Haas**

Economic globalization creates transboundary and global environmental externalities. A system of multilateral international environmental governance has evolved over the last twenty-five years as the international community has attempted to address the ecological externalities of economic globalization. Most observers of the 1972 United Nations Conference on the Human Environment (UNCHE), when the international community first acknowledged the urgency of dealing with global environmental threats, were skeptical that effective governance could be established for such issues. Yet governments are now held accountable to new standards of environmental behavior by carriers of values who had no standing in 1945. Not only has a stable set of expectations about reciprocal state practice been established, its form has evolved over time to become more comprehensive, reflecting growing scientific understanding about the behavior of ecosystems and the sensitivity of human societies to such dynamics. The norms, rules and strategies for environmental governance are no longer widely contested.[1] They are now enforced within a multilateral governance structure which systematically limits the role of the state. While states remain the putative sources of authoritative choice, officials are aware of two novel features of international environmental governance: that science is essential for the understanding of global environmental problems, thus shifting the determination of the scope of allocative decisions to the international institutions for science; and that states are increasingly accountable to domestic and transnational constituencies, thus shifting the locus of enforcement upwards and downwards in the international political system: from states toward international institutions and NGOs.

In this chapter I describe the political character of international environmental problems, describe the major features of international environmental governance, analyze their development over the last twenty-five years, and discuss current prospects for this emergent governance structure. Against a backdrop of virtually no systematic governance existing in 1972 the current level is striking. It is far more extensive than in the past, and has been growing increasingly comprehensive (or ecological) in form. This evolution exceeds the theoretical ability of most conventional schools of thought in international relations – neorealism, neoliberal institutionalism, and political economy – to explain in a satisfactory manner on its own terms.

Two complementary definitions of governance underlie my discussion. Michel Foucault uses governance to mean a system of institutional arrangements which "structure the possible fields of actions of others."[2] Similarly, Douglass North writes:[3]

> Institutions are the rules of the game in a society or, more formally, are the humanly devised constraints that shape human interaction. In consequence they structure incentives in human exchange, whether political, social, or economic. Institutional change shapes the way societies evolve through time and hence is the key to understanding historical change.

Governance thus consists of formal institutions designed to obtain collective goals generated from intersubjective beliefs and aspirations. International environmental governance is a process, but one which is principally impelled by changes in formal and informal institutions.

A constructivist approach helps to explain the evolution of this international governance system. The system's structural form – suffrage and decision-making rules – co-evolved with specific norms, rules and strategies for governments' environmental behavior. More than the norms, rules, and strategies which the new institutionalists discuss, this system also entails a set of interlocking social relationships through which such institutional features are developed; enforced; and diffused and reproduced over time. Here I argue that the institutionalization of a new ecological perspective, embodying norms, rules and strategies, was articulated by ecological epistemic communities and disseminated through formal governance institutions. This institutionalization of new beliefs developed concurrently with a general political decentralization at the international level. International decentralization means moving from an international system centered solely on states to more decentralized arrangements in which states share responsibilities with international institutions and a variety of non-state actors. The widespread adoption of new ecologically informed state practices, based on new consensual understandings of the operation of physical ecosystems, is a central element of the explanation offered here, while other elements of the broader picture of international governance – the global decentralization of authority and the emergent influence of NGOs – are exogenous factors, possibly related to economic globalization, democratization, and the end of the Cold War. Once institutionalized within the formal structure of international governance arrangements, new ecological beliefs have acquired a strong role in shaping the policies and practices of member units, and of actors' expectations about those policies and practices. Over time, state practices informed by these ideas have become habitual and internalized, while attendant state regulations seem to be leading to the creation of a green international political economy.

Environmental markets finally emerged in the 1990s; they had not existed before. Donald Connors accurately states that "there is no natural market for environmental technologies, like there is for food or clothing."[4] It seems clear that their creation emerged against a backdrop of a more general evolution of more vigorous domestic environmental management driven by an internationally institutionalized recognition of the scale of new public threats and of convergent beliefs about appropriate unilateral and collective responses. The history suggests that in the absence of strong international pressure on governments to launch new, national environmental policies, domestic practices would not have moved as quickly or as vigorously, and firms would have lacked incentives to invest and commercialize environmental innovations as rapidly as they did.

Ontologically I hesitate to privilege either international systems or state units, or ideas or units. Given the complexity of the international political system as it has developed since 1648, each factor now plays a role. New ecological beliefs did not constitute new units involved in international environmental governance, although they may have privileged the role of non-state actors and thus helped to reinforce other international centrifugal forces that have led to their increasing participation in international politics. These beliefs did constitute institutional regularities: the environmental norms, rules and strategies now widely pursued by governments and firms. In this regard, the new beliefs preceded changes in state practices, making it clear that the system of governance was constituted by ideas associated with a discrete and identifiable group of individuals. This interpretation contrasts with the oft-cited view that practices precede norms, and that norms are merely expedient justifications or codifications of prior practices and the preferences associated with the conduct of those practices.

The constructivist methodology pursued here consists of deductively identifying the possible consequences of ideas on practices, specifying a credible mechanism linking new ideas to changes in practices, combined with process tracing to determine if the hypothesized changes occurred through the proposed mechanisms. Counterfactuals and process tracing help to dispel alternate hypotheses including the null hypothesis about the source of change in environmental governance. Without the involvement of epistemic community members with their ecological perspective, national measures and international regimes would have been much more disjointed. They also would have been weaker, as they would have reflected the overarching desire of many firms and industries to avoid additional production costs and would have reduced the desire of politicians to appear green to domestic voters. Such forces, untempered by an awareness of ecological realities, would have yielded least common denominator agreements at best, agreements which would have been insufficient to drive market change.

Observed changes cannot be explained by technological change alone, as much that technological change has occurred as a consequence of states' efforts to enforce international commitments at home. Even the control of

CFCs, which has been widely hailed as a triumph for technological innovation, occurred as a result of government stimulus.[5] Widespread domestic
environmental concern did not appear until the late 1980s and 1990s, and
thus occurred too late to explain much of the change discussed below. Even
now the depth of public commitment and its political impact remains open
to doubt. State power has not been concentrated in the major areas in which
dramatic changes have occurred, and, to the extent to which US hegemonic
influence was available in environmental issues, it was not systematically
deployed. Thus, neither technological change nor the distribution of power
in the international system explains observed changes in international
environmental regimes.

As I discuss at the end, comprehensive notions of ecological environmental
management have increasingly informed international environmental
regimes over the last twenty-five years, and many governments have adopted
new national practices in accordance with their new international obligations. Less demanding environmental regimes have also been developed
during this period, raising the problem of causal inference for analysts regarding the question as to whether the observed change in governance is due to
ideas or more diffuse multilateral action. In the absence of the application of
more comprehensive ecological policy approaches – that is if all environmental regimes were merely the consequence of compromise between governments, as analyzed by neoliberal instititonalists – the overall tenor of
environmental regulation, including the major markets of Germany, Japan
and the USA, would be much weaker, and thus the incentives and pressure
for adopting new technologies and products would be weaker. Firms in this
counterfactual scenario would be responding to the policies introduced by
governments in order to achieve the more modest goals negotiated internationally, and thus would not have strong incentives for innovation.
Consequently, the role of ideas demands particular analytic attention in
order to explain the governance revolution in the area of the international
environment over the last twenty-five years. Goals, and a more general
theoretical account, should focus on the broad process by which new notions
of governance emerge and diffuse at the international level, and subsequently
become adopted and embedded in national political settings.

Thus my chapter complements those of Lake, Sandholtz and Cerny. But, as
I have just argued, environmental governance does not rest solely or even predominantly on contracting. Irreconcilable differences in principled interests
about transboundary and global environmental threats continues to inhibit
effective North-South cooperation for climate change, among other issues.
Potentially aggregated interests had to be established before international
institutions could be deployed to achieve cooperation. Moreover, empirically
(see below) very few international legal institutions appear to fulfill the contracting functions specified by Lake. More common are institutional arrangements that provide information about the nature of threats and potential
solutions, or even stipulate regulatory responses, rather than providing

information about compliance. Learning takes precedence over assurance, then, in terms of the functional performance of international institutions in the environmental realm, although some degree of assurance occurs as well. Unlike Sandholtz, who focuses primarily on the overarching embedded ideational arrangements within different formal institutional structures, I try to focus on the process by which such institutions become embedded, the potential variation between formal institutional structures, and the potential for embedding dramatically new ideational orientations. Cerny, lastly, focuses on the material underpinnings of global governance. I argue, however, that current environmental technology markets would not have existed without prior concerted international efforts at applying ideas and creating formal institutional structures for environmental governance. As Polanyi argued for markets in the early nineteenth century, and North thereafter, effective markets rest on shared economic beliefs and formal social institutions of information and enforcement.

The nature and scope of international environmental problems

While a sense of urgency has accompanied efforts for the management of environmental risks over the last twenty-five years, due to a fear of non-linear and unanticipated environmental effects of widespread environmental degradation and its possibly irreversible consequences, international environmental problems are singularly difficult to manage owing to both technical and political reasons.

Technically, efforts to cope must be comprehensive if they are to effectively confront the complex array of casual factors associated with environmental threats. Yet this is organizationally difficult to achieve as few governments or international institutions are organized to cope effectively with the multiple dimensions of environmental problems, and many governments lack the technical resources to develop and apply comprehensive efforts.

Effective management is politically difficult because solutions must be negotiated, and there are few strong proponents for vigorous or comprehensive environmental management, either domestically or internationally. Domestically, the costs of action are generally concentrated and short term, while the benefits are diffuse and long term, creating an Olsonian social choice problem in which the collective good suffers. The management of transboundary and global environmental threats requires countries to mutually adjust their policies, but governments are reluctant to participate unless they can be sure that other significant polluters will actively participate in the regime as well. Thus, the difficulty of obtaining international policy coordination also inhibits the pursuit of environmental protection domestically.

Vigorous international action is also difficult because governments often have different policies which must be coordinated, and because national preferences are often at odds. Many less developed countries (LDCs) still have not yet established environmental policies, and those adopted are generally narrower in scope than in the advanced industrialized countries. LDC environmental policies tend to focus on the management of specific resources, rather than integrating environmental considerations in all development planning, such as is emerging in the industrialized countries. Developing country delegates to UNCHE and the 1992 UN Conference on Environment and Development (UNCED) expressed concerns that a focus on industrial pollution and waste management could distract attention from their environmental priorities of deforestation, including unsustainable agricultural practices, population pressures, water quality, and soil erosion. Many LDCs also fear that environmental policy coordination with industrialized states can threaten to retard short-term economic growth by imposing new production and operating costs.[6]

The architectonics of international environmental governance

The current governance system can be described in constitutionalist terms. Governance entails a set of commitments which command obedience (rights and responsibilities, conventions, principles and norms), actual rules and procedures by which these commitments are to be realized, a set of authoritative actors who may participate in decision making (rules of suffrage), a set of formal institutions through which activities are coordinated, and a procedure for adjudicating disagreements and challenges.[7]

No less than in domestic society, governance is exercised through political and administrative processes performed by a legislature, executive and judiciary. Internationally, these functions are performed by international institutions, although the judiciary role is seldom exercised as vigorously as at the national level and is not as equally respected by governments. Authoritative values are developed in international treaty law, through UN General Assembly decisions, and under the auspices of UN agencies. The discussion below of the international environmental governance norms and rules are based on the coding of the texts of 133 of the 142 multilateral environmental treaties signed from 1920 through 1992 as collected by UNEP. A body of "soft law" has also been developed which international lawyers regard as less binding than the formal treaties and customary law developed for the environment. Executive branch and administrative functions are performed by UN specialized agencies. The enforcement and arbitration function is performed only through informal and decentralized channels. Unlike domestic society, these decisions always rest on choice. However, as in domestic society, a lasting and legitimate exercise of governance rests on its legitimacy in the eyes of member governments and their citizenry.

Norms

International environmental norms establish the expectations against which states are willing to be judged. While such instruments of international law may lack the formal requirements of "law" in a more legalistic sense, they do express shared purposes and expectations when voluntarily developed.

Legal scholars concur that a set of principles have been established in international treaties with the effective claim of normative injunctions which constrain the conduct of states by creating new norms and obligations to restore ecosystems' health. States now share the obligations of preventing and minimizing harm and appreciable risk from environmental contamination.[8] Toru Iwama writes that "natural or cultural resources are regarded as international or global commons whose uses are limited by a common interest of mankind. The states are regarded as guardians or custodians of the international community."[9]

More broadly, international treaties concluded since UNCHE reveal an appreciation of the saliency of the issue as well as an acceptance that an increasingly comprehensive approach should be taken toward environmental management.

Environmental governance arrangements have become increasingly "ecological" in form, heeding the ecological laws espoused by scientific ecologists and focusing on the sustainable management of ecosystems rather than containing threats to environmental quality. Species management is cast in terms of a habitat's ability to support multiple species rather than in terms of protecting individual populations living in the area. Environmental impact assessments are now widely required by governments and international organizations in order to weigh the environmental consequences of economic or development decisions. International debates now regularly consider new concepts such as "ecological sensitivity values" to bound the rates of economic growth.

As written, environmental norms complement norms of sovereign rights. In practice, these commitments make governments abnegate claims of sovereignty. While the doctrine of sovereignty maintains an ambiguous standing in UNCHE Principle 21, subsequent international laws establish a clear set of constraints on the actual exercise of sovereignty while leaving the doctrine intact. Governments have become increasingly willing to sacrifice their operational sovereignty in these treaties. Before 1973, only 56 per cent of multilateral environmental treaties regulated domestic activities. Since 1973, 85 per cent of treaties have covered domestic activities. Industrialized countries have been much more willing to sign treaties which circumscribe their sovereignty than have developing countries.

These norms command widespread support from the industrialized countries, and, more recently, from the former centrally planned economies that often lack the domestic resources needed for coping with the ecological devastation caused by central planning. Almost every country is party to at least one multilateral environmental treaty, and most countries are parties to many treaties regulating activities in many different environmental media, be they marine, terrestrial or air. Yet the norms are not universal in their claims to legitimacy. Forty per cent of eighty-five international environmental treaties lack the ratification of at least one country that could play a significant role in resolving the problem at hand. Developing countries have been less willing to cede domestic authority than industrialized countries: China, Brazil, India and Indonesia have each signed fewer environmental treaties which constrain domestic authority than have the USA, Japan, and Germany.[10] Developing countries are also more likely to ratify treaties with general declarative statements than those which deal with operational aspects of environmental management.[11]

Rules

Multilateral environmental treaties and regimes contain a number of concrete rules for national practices. Governments accept the duty to inform each other of risks, to consult in order to assess risks, to notify neighbors in cases of emergency situations and to cooperate in scientific research and systematic environmental monitoring.

Most common are declaratory treaties, which establish collective intent but do not entail concrete domestic commitments for signatories. Thirty-one per cent of all multilateral environmental treaties have been declaratory.

Environmental commitments generally take the form of regulatory injunctions administered through a combination of numerical targets, procedural permits and reporting systems. Twenty-nine per cent of all multilateral environmental treaties entailed some form of operational standards or obligations for management. Air and marine pollution control regimes apply emission and ambient standards for individual and groups of contaminants, typically in the form of "black" (banned) and "grey" (controlled) lists. These lists, too, are becoming increasingly comprehensive in light of the growing ecological sophistication of the regimes' principles, an awareness of possible interactive effects of individual contaminants, and growing scientific confidence in determining specific source-based estimates of ecosystems' abilities to sustain stress from which specific ambient environmental quality standards are derived. Efforts to protect species typically have a set of appendices listing categories of species according to the degree to which their survival is endangered. Rules which stipulate what technologies can be used for various applications have been applied to the management of fisheries (bans on drift-nets) as well as to the control of operational oil pollution from ships.

Ecosystems-based management models have been applied in:

the 1971 RAMSAR Convention on Wetlands of International Importance,
the 1973 Agreement on the Conservation of Polar Bears,

the 1979 Bonn Convention on the Conservation of Migratory Species,
the 1980 Convention on the Conservation of Antarctic Marine Living
   Resources,
as well as for managing the North American Great Lakes (1978).

Management activities based on scientific assessments of the environmental
carrying capacity have been developed for: protecting stratospheric ozone
where the chlorine-loading potential dictates the volume of CFCs which
countries may emit under the Montreal Protocol and its subsequent amendments, and limiting European acid rain, where critical loads appraisals
provide guidelines for national sulfur emissions under the 1994 revised sulfur
protocol.

   Other rule-making techniques are less common, and are declining in
frequency of use. Twenty per cent of multilateral treaties contain actual
bans on prescribed activities. Fewer treaties rely on the use of insurance or liability mechanisms. Insurance funds have been established to pay for oil spill
cleanups and compensation for victims. Clear provisions for liability for
environmental damage have only been developed for: nuclear damage, civil
liability for pollution damage caused by maritime transport of oil, civil
liability for pollution damage caused by offshore operations, and civil liability
for damage caused by inland transport of dangerous substances in Europe.[12]

   Decision-making procedures typically take the form of annual or biannual
intergovernmental meetings to review the activities of international secretariats, authorize new projects, and hash out differences in national
approaches to environmental policy. Increasingly, diplomats apply a set of
legal innovations which have been developed since UNCHE by a small
cadre of ecologically sensitive international lawyers for international environmental treaties. These lawyers participated in a wide variety of negotiations
and tended to reapply their earlier successful legal experiments as precedents
when drafting each new regime. Examples of such legal innovations are: a
framework convention developed in 1976 for the Mediterranean which is
devoid of concrete obligations paired with specific protocols dealing with
environmental protection; technical black and grey lists introduced in the
1972 London Dumping Convention which specify the substances regulated
by the treaty, yet which can be modified by expert agreement without
having to reconvene political parties; an iterated negotiating process first
elaborated by a UNEP committee of legal experts in 1981 and developed for
stratospheric ozone protection in which states first adopt a framework convention signaling common aspirations and goals followed by more technical
and binding protocols; the establishment of dedicated voluntary trust funds
so that regimes may be self-supporting which have the effect of making the
conventions financially self-supporting as well as creating more resources for
programmatic activities; and the creation of committees for monitoring
treaty compliance, first developed for the Montreal ozone protocol, and now
used for the climate change treaty and LRTAP.

Monitoring efforts remain largely the domain of governments, although most treaties require the provision of periodic reports. National reporting to secretariats about their environmental protection activities is often poor, and many secretariats lack the resources or authority to check data submitted by governments. Many NGOs are now capable of monitoring environmental quality, as well as national compliance, and could help compensate for the dearth of effective environmental quality data, as well as providing an independent quality check on data collected through other sources. Much of the environment can be monitored remotely from satellites, and does not require the active collection and submission of data by governments. Remote sensing and satellite monitoring would also enhance verification of trends in natural resource use, marine pollution from organic sources and from oil, as well as in monitoring levels and production of greenhouse gases, although ground truthing is still necessary to confirm remote sensing data. Satellite and airplane based monitoring is less effective at monitoring inorganic marine contamination and urban air quality, for instance, which requires localized sampling and monitoring.

Suffrage

The primary figures in international environmental governance are, of course, representatives of governments who claim the legal authority to take authoritative decisions in international institutions. Governance through the late 1980s primarily occurred through dialogues between environmental ministries and environmental scientists, and with other governmental bodies.

Over the last twenty years, participation in environmental governance has spread beyond the society of states. The scientific community participates widely in international discussions as well as engaging in preliminary discussions at the national level. Environmental issues were initially unfamiliar to policy makers, who often had to solicit technical advice from environmental scientists. Those exercising authoritative control over knowledge command great potential influence because technical information is a critical resource for effective environmental governance. As environmental scientists became systematically involved in decision making at the national level for domestic and international issues, environmental governance came to increasingly reflect their improved understanding of ecosystems. Many regimes have established independent advisory panels, with the effect of institutionalizing the participation of independent scientists in environmental governance. Developing country governments that lack their own indigenous capacity rely on such panels for independent scientific appraisals of environmental risks.

While originally established in the industrialized countries, environmental NGOs are no longer restricted to the North. Many have flourished in Malaysia, the Philippines, India, and Brazil, and umbrella groups exist on every continent.[13] At UNCED, 70 per cent of the registered NGOs came from industrialized countries, with the heaviest representation from the USA, Canada, and the UK. The most heavily represented developing countries were India, the Philippines, Nigeria, Kenya, Sri Lanka, and Pakistan, with over ten NGOs accredited from each. Many of the developing country NGOs are still politically and organizationally weak, lacking large staffs, stable financing, capability to assess science, and experience in dealing with governments.

Multinational corporations (MNCs) kept a low profile in international environmental politics until recently. Many firms decided that environmental regulations did not constitute significant threats to their competitiveness and were content to lobby their governments and temper policies they found onerous. More recently they have responded to growing government intrusiveness and greater interest in the environment on the part of voters and consumers to become more vigorous participants. MNCs could make a positive contribution to environmental governance because they control the products, technologies, and knowledge about markets that are essential for efficient environmental protection.

International administration by international organizations

Many executive branch functions are performed by international organizations. Like executive branches in national governments, the UN specialized agencies and the Bretton Woods institutions can compel or induce action by reluctant members of society as well as legitimating the political participation of members of society. International organizations are engaged primarily in national capacity building, generating and diffusing information, collecting information about actions taken at the national level, evaluating national performance, and building domestic constituencies of sympathetic actors such as scientific networks, environmental NGOs, and, increasingly, private firms.

A number of international intergovernmental organizations have come to design and apply economic development projects and conservation projects which integrate environmental considerations with traditional responsibilities.[14] In the United Nations, the Commission on Sustainable Development (CSD) is now responsible for overseeing and coordinating the environment and development activities of the UN specialized agencies. UNEP has been the environmental catalyst as well as the environmental conscience of the UN system. The World Bank's development style has been transformed to incorporate environmental considerations into project development. The World Health Organization (WHO) publishes environmental standards that are widely accepted in national laws, particularly in developing countries where governmental agencies are unable on their own to set appropriate domestic standards. Other IOs are also expanding their activities to integrate environmental considerations into regular projects.

Enforcement

The judiciary function is weakly performed in international environmental governance. Very few international environmental regimes contain strong provisions for adjudication. Seventeen (including the Montreal Protocol, CITES, the Basel Treaty, and ten species conservation treaties) contain provisions for trade sanctions against violators. Such provisions have rarely been invoked and a few that have are being challenged in the World Trade Court of the World Trade Organization.

Enforcement in practice depends largely upon shame.[15] International institutions provide a key function by collecting and disseminating data and information, receiving reports on treaty implementation by states, facilitating independent monitoring and inspection, and acting as a forum for reviewing the performance of individual states.[16]

Actual enforcement is exercised by political oversight of parties and NGOs at the domestic level in elections. NGOs perform useful functions in international governance by providing information and counterbalancing the claims of both governments and private actors. Some information about governmental performance that influences election outcomes comes from the information provided by international institutions. In addition, a country's reputation in environmental matters is increasingly being considered by multilateral development banks and foreign aid agencies and even private sources of foreign investment. Consequently, enforcement remains voluntary, yet it is subject to fear of opportunity costs of not appearing green. The effectiveness of such decentralized and informal techniques depends heavily on the widespread availability of credible information, the ecological literacy of publics, and the political efficacy of policies.

Many NGOs are now capable of evaluating their government's environmental performance, and could submit their own reports or confirm official submissions to secretariats. Greenpeace now regularly monitors trade in hazardous wastes and in flora and fauna, and publicizes shipments that are in violation of international treaties. The publicity generated by the NGO monitoring is often sufficient to inform recipient governments of activities of which they may have been unaware, as well as pressuring them to enforce their international commitments and to refuse entry of such products. Many NGOs have become virtual watchdogs over private activities in the field as well, replacing or supplementing the monitoring activities of national enforcement agencies. Because governments are often unwilling to cede the semblance of authority to NGOs, private monitoring of governments' actions and of the environment may best be accomplished through independent scientific panels, which have access to a variety of sources of information. Surprise visits by independent inspectors are used in some regimes as a means of verification. Long a part of the Antarctic Treaty System, CCAMLR (Convention on the Conservation of Antarctic Marine Living Resources) provides for such visits, and they have been considered by the

Helsinki Commission in the management of the Baltic Sea area. The concept is accepted by eastern European and OECD countries, but not by LDCs.

Explaining the evolution of international environmental governance

The evolution of environmental governance has occurred within a matrix of scientific understanding, international institutional guidance, market forces, national leadership, and mass concern. While individual regimes and treaties were developed through different configurations of forces, over the last twenty years these efforts have accumulated to form a coherent set of expectations about national behavior and to a lesser degree, a common set of actual practices exercised by governments and by companies. Moreover, these forces have grown stronger over time, leading to an increasingly comprehensive cast to multilateral environmental governance. The combination of knowledge and institutional influence and, more recently, public concern and market pressures has interacted like an isometric set of vector forces to maintain a resilient international regime. The norms, rules and strategies for ecological preservation gain in standing as the domestic and international political costs associated with their violation grow stronger for governments and firms, due to public expectations.

An evolutionary institutional model of environmental governance

The interplay of these factors can be best understood within an evolutionary framework. Ideas provide the genetic material of international governance. This framework accounts for both the frequency with which ideas are adopted and the functional and geographic variation of their adoption.

The loose framework I propose is evolutionary because it consists of independent mechanisms by which new ideas are generated (a variation mechanism, although not purely random since knowledge accretes over time) and adopted by authoritative actors (a selection mechanism); and because past decisions affect present circumstances and choices in ways not apparent to most actors.[17] Ideas become embedded in institutions through standard operating procedures, organizational cultures, and codified routines, and shape subsequent perceptions and decisions taken under their auspices. Ideas condition practical policy choices by actors influenced by institutions, in turn leading to convergent action between those actors, be they governments, firms, or individuals. The impact of ideas persists beyond the initial constellation of factors responsible for their institutionalization as they are internalized to become new organizational routines and institutional incentives to which individuals respond. By creating established roles for all the multiple actors involved in elaborating and enforcing practices which are suggested by these ideas, they create new informal international institutions of shared beliefs and expectations. They inform collective decision making and contribute to the creation of a shared community of understanding. Finally, such ideas are converted to laws and regulatory policy at the national level.

An evolutionary model offers a probabilistic view of trajectories or paths of behavior, with a politically specifiable set of variables likely to explain which idea will be chosen at particular branch points in the trajectories. Branch points follow major crises or systemic shocks because shocks alert publics and leaders to undesirable circumstances and create demands for decision makers to undertake new efforts, and also undermine the authority of policy experts associated with prior policy orientations. Once institutionalized, the new ideas imported at the point of crisis shape perceptions and choices until subsequent crises arise, while also helping to define what would constitute a crisis, because frameworks also help identify plausible anomalies. In the absence of new ideas at such moments, old ideas and perspectives will continue. This model provides essentially a sticky, path-dependent explanation of human behavior, in which many choices or decisions are largely irreversible and the array of possible choices at time (t) is causally related to decisions taken at time (t_{-1}). Ideas may exercise a causal impact later in time regardless of the reasons for their initial selection, as they continue to guide decisions even in the absence of original conditions which contributed to their widespread acceptance. Overall, and over time, the frequency with which decision-makers invoke and rely on the new ideas for policy increases.

The primary actors are states suffering from uncertainty. Leaders and decision makers are driven by a need to survive politically and institutionally. I assume that because of the complex nature of contemporary interdependent international activities, decision makers operate with incomplete and even scanty information about the nature of the physical and social environment they seek to influence. Consequently they are also unsure of their preferences, about their policy alternatives, and about the preferences of other actors with whom they will have to interact strategically. Under such circumstances neither conventional descriptive and prescriptive decision making models based on subjective expected utility or prospect theory apply, because actors are fundamentally unable to identify or choose between the array of choices. Moreover, decision making operates according to a satisficing model in which actors express procedural rationality, at best, subject to the time constraints imposed by bounded rationality, and do not engage in continuous information searches about the state of the policy environment or the efficacy of their own efforts.[18] Lacking experience with environmental problems, few policy makers have sufficient experience or knowledge to draw policy inferences from direct environmental observations. Policy makers are often unclear about how their wealth and power are likely to be affected by new policies, or what measures will promote wealth and power acquisition in the new issue-area.

Thus, changes in information processing are likely to occur following a well-publicized shock or crisis, which imparts a sense of urgency. With tightly interconnected media and communications, the crisis need not be domestic to precipitate national and international calls for prompt state action. At such times, decision makers search for new ways of organizing experience, and they defer to groups with recognized authority. During subsequent, less revolutionary periods these new doctrines or orthodoxies assume the status of taken for granted assumptions, or dogma, which persist until called into question again by external anomalies. In the absence of available consensual knowledge they will remain bound by existing policy paradigms and resort to available techniques based on power and compromise.

The ability to articulate new ideas and control their distribution are critical sources of power because they confer control over meaning and inference. Since the Second Industrial Revolution, experts in science and technology have been regarded as authoritative sources of advice under many circumstances. They monopolize the legitimate use of certain types of knowledge. *Epistemic communities* (networks of professionals who share common normative and causal beliefs, accept common truth-tests and are engaged in a common policy enterprise) serve as the cognitive baggage handlers for knowledge-based epistemes and for less abstract policy-relevant concepts. They transmit new ideas between actors, and articulate ideas' programmatic implications for the formal institutions in which they successfully establish influence.

Once new ideas are established, they diffuse more widely, subject to the leverage commanded by the institution in which the epistemic community has acquired and consolidated its influence. States disseminate the ideas of epistemic communities to other states and to international regimes according to their ability to compel or induce others to apply such practices. Weaker states may adopt new ideas by emulating lessons observed abroad.

Not all states or international institutions are equally likely to consult members of an epistemic community or defer to their advice. Institutions with strong science and technology capabilities, and those representing pluralistic societies will be most likely to be in the first wave of those embracing new ideas. It is there that the scientific culture of epistemic communities will have a close affinity, and new groups will be able to quickly articulate new policy initiatives.

There are several alternatives regarding the likelihood of which ideas will be selected at a moment of crisis. If there is only one new candidate, there is little problem. If there are many, choices may be conditioned by calculations of relative political gain from each idea. In either case, new instrumental ideas will only endure if they are loosely commensurate with deeper seated beliefs and do not threaten strategic political alliances. Table 1 presents a fuller variety of mechanisms by which ideas diffuse internationally.

Institutional learning occurs as groups apply evolving consensual knowledge to institutional practices. Learning may occur directly, through interpersonal persuasion, communication, exchange and reflection, leading

Table 1 Diffusion mechanisms for environmental ideas

From/to	IO	State	NGO	Epistemic community	Firm	Society
IO	• Interagency coordination • Jointly administered programs • Cofinancing	• Training • Demonstration effect[4] • Project funding • Anticipation of project funding • Leadership by IO officials • Sponsor meetings	• Training	• Convene conferences • Support research and monitoring	• Publications • Study groups, workshops, technical panels • Information clearing house • Contracting arrangements • Procurement	• Public education/consciousness raising
State	• Coercion • Recruitment choices • Leadership[3] • Funding	• Coercion/sanctions • Persuasion • Market impacts[2] • Compromise • Demonstration effect[5] • Imitation/mimesis • Leadership[4] • Rewards (foreign aid, bargaining linkages)			• Tax/investment policy • Regulation • Contracting arrangement[5] • Procurement[5]	• Education

NGO	• Publicity • Mobilizing international pressure	• Grants • Publicity • Mobilizing international pressure	• Common campaigns • Communication	• Demonstration effect[1]	• Demonstration effect • Education • Advertising • Publicize and translate • Epicom findings
Epistemic community	• Recruitment • Persuasion • Advisory panels	• Recruitment • Persuasion • Advisory panels	• Persuasion • Communication through overlapping networks	• Communication	• Education
Firms				• Joint venture	• Advertising • Demonstration effect
Society	• Elections • Polls • Civil unrest	• Contributions • Memberships		• Purchasing choices	

Examples:

1 CFC-free refrigerators, energy efficient automobiles, energy conserving household products.

2 A country's ability to affect relative prices elsewhere through unilateral efforts. US unilateral threats of domestic CFC regulation may have had this effect.

3 Leadership is in the entrepreneurial sense of leadership, where the leader identifies a tolerable solution for other parties.

4 Standards and laws which others may borrow. WHO serves this role, as does the US and the EU. Standards elaborated in different institutions are often inconsistent, so that emulation may lead to a diffusion of incommensurate measures.

5 US Green Lights Program.

to the recognition or appreciation of new causal models and shared values. Leaders are socialized to accept new views and to empower their expositors. Alternatively, learning may occur through administrative recruitment, as epistemic community members or their confidantes replace officials informed with alternative perspectives. It may also occur indirectly, as actors alter behavior subject to the influence wielded by institutions that embody the ideas. Different patterns may occur along different time frames, as well. While some effects may be felt immediately through new recruitment decisions, and persuasion, broader shifts in public opinion and societal effects may take decades to occur and make themselves felt as elite decisions.

Once in place, ideas are likely to persist once they acquire a taken-for-granted element and future generations of policy makers are likely to justify their actions through reference to established legitimate principles. It also becomes politically costly to reverse such practices as new interest groups mobilize around them after recognizing that material gains are possible from the application of the new ideas.

Application of the model to explain the evolution of environmental governance

The development of international environmental governance, particularly its increasingly comprehensive form, can best be understood in the light of the evolutionary model presented above. In 1972, most environmental practices by governments were narrow and unconnected to broader social and economic policies. By 1995, international regimes and most national practices were increasingly comprehensive. Both the increasing frequency with which such new ideas about environmental policy are applied and the national and functional distribution of where such policies are applied can both be understood by tracing the development of new ecological management beliefs and their international institutionalization.

The dominant epistemic community in international environmental issues, until the late 1960s, was composed of neoclassical economists and resource managers. They were widely discredited by broadly publicized environmental disasters and the international energy crisis of the 1970s, which they had been unable to predict, and attendant popular fears of widespread resource depletion.

New advice came from an emergent research program with an associated epistemic community: scientific ecology. It had flourished in the United States and Europe in the late 1960s, and is generally regarded as being relatively uncompromised by political and institutional influence.[19] Paul Sears called the new approach "subversive" because it challenged the public and private right to contaminate the environment, regardless of rights of usufruct or other social conventions, and was based on a holistic approach to international policy.

Ecological epistemic communities offered an alternate formulation of environmental problems, replacing a focus on managing discrete resources with a focus on preserving ecosystems through the management of their multiple uses. They shared a perspective that treats environmental contamination as part of a broader set of interconnected problems subject to conditions of high uncertainty, with high potential for surprise and nonlinear effects from environmental stress.

Galvanized by a sense of urgency and environmental crisis accompanying UNCHE, most governments had to create formal institutions to deal with their new environmental responsibility. From 1972 to 1982 the number of industrialized countries with environmental agencies grew from fifteen to thirty-four. Many were staffed by members of the ecological epistemic community, as they were the only legitimate group which commanded a reputation of technical environmental expertise. UNEP was created in 1973 and was staffed principally by young epistemic community members with firm ecological convictions. UNEP elaborated a political process that Maurice Strong had initiated for UNCHE, which pressed states to concurrently engage in environmental research and monitoring while also drafting collective policy measures. By urging states to negotiate before they were confident of their interests he managed to avert some of the more acute Olsonian threats to regime creation.

LDCs were later to appeal to the ecological epistemic community for policy advice. The number of developing countries with environmental agencies grew from eleven in 1972 to 110 in 1982. Developing countries were slower to introduce new environment protection measures than were industrialized countries. Initial attention was directed toward solving domestic environmental problems associated with poverty – water quality, public health, and natural resource conservation. Gradually, measures were adopted to cope with transboundary and global environmental threats as well. By the mid 1980s many developing countries had seriously begun to develop pollution control legislation, although environmental investments and implementation lagged well behind the North. By the end of the 1980s most Latin American and Caribbean governments had adopted legislation protecting water, forests, wildlife, soils, coasts, natural resources and sanitation.[20] Southeast Asian governments started introducing legislation and investing in sewage treatment and pollution control in the 1990s. Few African governments have done so.

While unilateral efforts were taken to deal with domestic environmental threats (some of which occur ubiquitously around the world and thus were subject to international influence from USAID, UNEP and the World Bank), most transboundary and global environmental problems were not seriously addressed unilaterally. This was because the full costs of environmental degradation were not encountered by any single government, and unilateral efforts would not lead to changes in environmental quality unless they were widely reciprocated by other states.

Table 2 Introduction of formal EIA requirements

	−1972	1973–1982	1983–1992	1993–	Total
Advanced industrialized countries	2	4	14	3	23
Former centrally planned economies	0	0	2	0	2
Developing countries	2	5	2	3	12
NIC	2	2	2	0	6
non-NIC	0	3	0	3	6

Source: Calculated by the author from Alan Gilpin, *Environmental Impact Assessment*, Cambridge: Cambridge University Press, 1995, p.3.

Regimes have become increasingly comprehensive over time. In 1973 27 per cent of multilateral environmental regimes (3 of 11) had comprehensive treaties in them. By 1995 40 per cent of the regimes (10 of 25) had such elements. This shift reflects two significant political transitions. First, many new regimes created after UNCHE were designed with ecological management rules in mind, reflecting the increasingly influential ecological epistemic communities, and strong environmentally minded international institutions, such as UNECE, UNEP, and the World Bank. Second, a number of existing regimes became comprehensive, as growing scientific ecological understanding was applied to drafting new treaties within the existing regimes.

From international governance to national governance

National environmental policy styles became more comprehensive over time, as they were caught up in an increasing number of ecological regimes and were subject to influence from a growing number of ecologically informed international institutions, primarily USAID, UNEP and the World Bank (after 1987). National efforts tended to become more vigorous and stringent over time under such institutional pressures. This shift is indicated in part by the increasing use of environmental impact assessments as an obligatory component of environmental planning. Table 2 presents the evolution of use of such instruments by different countries over time.

The use of integrated coastal zone management policies (ICZM), integrative practices which reflect ecosystems management perspectives, has also increased over the last twenty-five years. The planning approach for the management of coastal resources and environments was first developed in the early 1970s and was first converted to national regulation in the 1972 US Coastal Zone Management Act. By 1984, thirteen coastal states had ICZMs and forty-two states had them by 1990. In each instance the numbers are split fairly evenly between industrialized and developing countries.[21]

There are interactive effects between international and national level changes over time. Many of the countries which developed more comprehensive environmental planning approaches – both for transboundary and global environmental resources and also for domestic ones – were directly affected by epistemic communities or were part of a regime which was informed by an epistemic community. While a comparative study of domestic and foreign environmental policy changes in ozone, European acid rain, and marine protection, indicates occasions of changes guided by shifts in public opinion, domestic political alignments, and foreign pressure, these factors do not dominate. They appear in only roughly half of the cases. Individual policy changes are equally influenced by inputs from domestic and transnational epistemic communities, and from international institutional forces which themselves are epistemically informed.

Towards a green political economy

International markets for pollution control technology finally came into existence in the 1990s, following the establishment of international environmental governance arrangements. Green markets were not conceived immaculately. Governmental regulations and emergent popular concern created the demand for new products and processes. Regulations created legal requirements for pollution reduction, creating niches for new products and procedures to reduce pollution. European and US industries report that corporate environmental protection efforts were taken in response to legal requirements.[22]

Estimates vary on the size of these markets. The OECD estimates that current global market for environmental products and services is $300 billion.[23] The largest and most technically advanced environment markets developed in the US (with 45 per cent of the environmental technology market in 1990), Germany, Japan (with 7 per cent of the market); countries with the most comprehensive and effective environmental regulations and also the most competitive environment industries. Environmental technology markets grew most rapidly from 1990 to 1992 in Eastern Europe, Canada, Latin America, Mexico, China, Taiwan, and South Korea.[24] The Worldwatch Institute finds that "some 80–90 per cent of this burgeoning environmental industry, which includes an estimated 30,000 U.S., 20,000 European, and 9,000 Japanese firms, is in industrial nations, though it is now growing rapidly in the Third World as well."[25]

With the combination of market opportunities, public concern and national regulation, there are now incentives for global firms to produce with greenest standards which may be in excess of actual legal requirements in countries of operation. Frances Cairncross, former environmental editor for *The Economist*, observes:[26]

Without a good environmental record it will be harder to find new sites for expansion, because local communities will be less likely to trust a company with a record of being dirty. Good environmental practice reduces the risks of unwittingly committing an environmental offense – breaking one of those regulations and so incurring a large fine or a worse punishment. . . . Reducing toxic emissions means less risk of nasty accidents; using fewer dangerous materials may keep down the bill for insurance premiums; managing to a high standard may be a defense in court for a company charged with some petty environmental transgression.

Some of the largest MNCs have called for global uniform environmental standards based on some of the most stringent measures available.[27] Many MNCs have endorsed a variety of voluntary industrial guidelines and codes of conduct for environmental practices, ecological accounting procedures, and public environmental accounting. The major dynamics of international environmental diplomacy began to change in the late 1980s with the onset of popular environmental concern. Earlier, green parties had failed to exercise widespread influence over national environmental policy in Western Europe, and, while the public expressed widespread concern, it was generally unwilling to commit resources or act based on its concerns. By the early 1990s a growing sense of environmental concern became evident worldwide. A 1992 survey of public opinion in twenty-four countries conducted by the Gallup International Institute demonstrated increasing widespread concern about environmental contamination, in industrialized, developing and formally centrally planned economies, combined with growing demands for international action. Most striking is the universal doubling in the percentage of respondents who felt that their own health was more seriously affected by environmental contamination than ten years ago.[28] Such widespread concern has the effect of reinforcing the institutional and constructivist forces which contributed to the environmental gains of the 1970s and 1980s, making it extremely difficult to reverse decisions which have already been taken.

The future of the international environmental governance

It is now politically inconceivable that there can be a return to pre-UNCED levels of environmental governance, given the isometric interplay between public opinion, economic opportunity and government regulation. A number of potentially limiting factors to future effective international environmental governance remain.

Compliance

National compliance with these prescribed (and nominally accepted) international norms, rules and practices still varies widely. National compliance is often a function of national will, capacity, and institutional design. The correct assignment of enforcement responsibilities may avoid conflicts of interests and thus expedite compliance, although will and capacity are probably the most important factors affecting compliance. Clifford Russell notes that commitments are most efficiently enforced when there is public oversight of private obligations, and private oversight of public commitments.[29]

While states may wish to comply, not all are capable. Many developing countries and formally centrally planned economies have greater difficulties in complying with international obligations than do industrialized countries, due to less developed administrative systems and fewer monitoring and financial resources which can be devoted to enforcement. International institutions may help build national capacity through training, resource transfers, and technology transfer.

Some states lack the will to enforce commitments. International institutions may help build state will. In pluralistic societies they may amplify and refract domestic forces onto governments, through publicizing the state of environmental quality. Elsewhere they help to establish domestic demand by supporting incipient NGOs and grassroots movements, through public education, by disseminating information, and by including scientists in international discussions. Institutions may also directly offer incentives for state enforcement through green conditionality.

Other states are relatively impervious to the shaming elements in the governance structure. Without pluralistic societies and without the need to seek credit or finance from international institutions, governments of many Newly Industrializing Countries (NICs) are relatively insensitive to the array of international and domestic political influences on governments to protect the environment. Future environmental governance for these countries may be a matter of host-country MNC relations. While MNCs, particularly the largest ones engaged in manufacturing, are now part of the new green IPE and will be prone to apply universally the practices they are now pursuing in the North; their domestic counterparts may be resistant to what they see as unnecessary and additional short-term expenses.[30]

The NICs pose a big environmental threat which may not be easily met through international governance mechanisms. Most of the NICs have weak environmental legislation and economic growth is driven by some of the world's most pollution intensive sectors: electronic components, basic metals, vehicle parts, plastics, chemicals, leather products, printing, glass, paper and cellulose, cements and fertilizers.[31] Loss of biodiversity, toxic wastes, heavy metals, sulfur dioxide, nitrogen oxide, and carbon dioxide emissions are likely to rise dramatically with increase in economic growth in China, Taiwan, South Korea, Malaysia, India, Indonesia, and Thailand.[32] While some recent increases in environmental regulation and investment are evident, they are unlikely to be adequate.[33] India, South Korea and China, whose ambitious national industrialization plans offer a potentially devastating impact on the global climate, biodiversity, and on regional seas, remain ambivalent about many global and international commitments.

Emergent environmental threats

Potential environmental threats are numerous. Acid rain in South East Asia, West Africa, and parts of Latin America has been recorded, and will increase in severity as industrialization continues to accelerate. Water quality in the Third World is an overriding national environmental threat to public health because diarrhea remains the major source of infant death in the developing world. Few systematic efforts have been developed to regulate offshore drilling and uses of the seabed, or to collectively manage river basins in sustainable ways. Nuclear decommissioning in the former USSR, and counteracting environmental destruction in Eastern Europe are major items on the future agenda. There is insufficient information for informed public policy for the over 1500 chemicals annually which are widely used globally.[34]

Substantive gaps and inconsistencies

The successes to date in environmental governance raise a new set of problems as well. The multitude of pollution controls needs to be harmonized. Treaties and regimes were developed to cope with discrete problems, or pollutants. The result has been a patchwork of standards for the use of different ecosystems. Industries are presented with different and inconsistent rules for the same substance for different bodies of water, or for emissions into the air or disposal on land. For instance, the Mediterranean and South East Pacific have identical coverage regarding land-based sources of pollution, while they differ substantially from the North Sea and Baltic.[35] Elsewhere, wastes may be incinerated on land although they may not be directly discharged into oceans. This is ecologically problematic as once in the air they reach oceans and thus undermine purely marine-based efforts for environmental protection. Government operations, particularly those connected with national security and defense, remain immune from international governance.

Organizational overload and competition

The proliferation of environmental treaties raises the specter of organizational overload and competition. Few environmental or foreign ministries are adequately staffed to be able to effectively participate in all of the meetings organized under the auspices of the dozens of environmental regimes. Many international secretariats are too small and poorly financed to support the many activities necessary for the maintenance of their regimes. The current crisis of multilateralism further threatens the funding for a number of isolated secretariats, and UNEP has been seeking to consolidate many of them.

Some regimes call for harmonization, as their environmental problems have elements which are consigned to different international organizations. In marine dumping, for example, some activities fall under the jurisdiction of IMO (Intergovernmental Maritime Organization), while others fall under IAEA (International Atomic Energy Agency) or secretariats organized to administer regional regimes. While overlapping institutional jurisdictions may actually improve the strength of international environmental governance because of the possibility of ratcheting up national commitments through linkages and nesting, such a complicated agenda is frustrating for government ministries and inhibits effectiveness.

Financing environmental governance

The costs of global environmental protection are enormous. The cost of implementing Agenda 21's proposals for sustainable development was estimated by the UNCED secretariat at roughly 600 billion dollars a year for 1993–2000. Estimates of the annual capital costs to reduce greenhouse gas emissions by 5 per cent by volume by 2005 are $27 billion for Eastern European states, $18 billion for the OECD states, and $22 billion for the rest of the world. Providing adequate water supply and sanitation services to 90 per cent of the rural and urban populations by end of the century is estimated to require an average annual investment of $28.2 billion. Estimates of containing tropical deforestation are on the order of $40 billion over five years. Containing desertification by the year 2000 can require $2.4 billion per year, and protecting biodiversity may cost $1 billion per year.[36] The World Bank estimates that programs to address the major environmental problems in the developing countries will require an additional annual investment of 66.5–77.5 billion dollars a year by the year 2000. Expenditures for environmental protection would account for between 1.29–1.49 per cent of anticipated aggregate developing country GDP by 2000 (at a projected growth rate of 4.7 per cent from the present), or 3.15–3.65 per cent of actual GDP growth during the period.

Significant distributional problems are associated with foreign investment. From 1991 to 1994, 89 per cent of total private capital flows to developing countries were concentrated in twelve countries: China (29 per cent), Mexico (13 per cent), Argentina (8 per cent), South Korea (6 per cent), Malaysia (6 per cent), Portugal (6 per cent), Brazil (5 per cent), Thailand (4 per cent), India (4 per cent), Turkey (3 per cent), Hungary (3 per cent) and Indonesia (2 per cent).[37] Other developing countries will be hard-pressed to attract sufficient financing for investment in clean technology. This is potentially damaging to the environment, since some of the major potential sources of industrial and consumer greenhouse gases and sulfur dioxide are India and China, which have failed to attract such large volumes of international capital.

Political support by many of the least developed of the developing countries
for many environmental regimes may be threatened by fears of having to
compete with former centrally planned economies for financial resources
from the World Bank and bilateral aid agencies.

Information gaps

Information constraints on many public domain goods inhibit ready recognition of their existence by either sellers or buyers.[38] Many potential users
outside the OECD lack information about environmentally benign technologies and few providers are familiar with these markets. Information
clearing houses are needed to collect information about available environmental technologies and to unite potential buyers and sellers.

Doctrinal backlash

Success breeds backlash. The international environmental principles
and rules which have been assembled over the last twenty-five years are
encountering two forms of ideational backlash. In international regimes,
they are encountering challenges from actors who are involved in trade
regimes that have been developed on entirely different doctrinal foundations.
Aspirations for environmental protection now conflict with regime rules and
doctrines developed for other international activities. While environmental
governance is fundamentally regulatory, international trade governance has
been liberal and free market based. International institutions have varied in
their positions on these matters, depending on the institutionalized beliefs
within them. The WTO, charged essentially to promote liberal trade internationally, has questioned the environmental effects of trade liberalization,
whether trade policies should be used to enforce environmental standards,
and whether environmental standards constitute barriers to trade in two
major decisions. Conversely, the EU, with an eye towards economic integration and political integration, has been less prone to interpret environmental
regulations as threatening free trade.

Summary and conclusion

New forms of environmental governance have emerged with the entry of
new authoritative actors onto the international diplomatic arena. The
international environmental accords concluded since UNCHE establish
normative and procedural benchmarks against which their citizens hold
governments accountable, by other governments, and by influential international organizations. A broad base of environmental governance now
exists.

Substantively, governments are increasingly modifying economic policies
in ways that are believed to be less environmentally destructive. Through

the growing influence of ecological epistemic communities in international environmental institutions and regimes, new ideas about ecologically sustainable development have disseminated internationally, and become increasingly embedded in national regulatory structures; through SOPs (standard operating procedures) of foreign ministries and environmental ministries; through domestic administrative procedures and policies; though patterns of enforcement; and through broader patterns of expectations about governmental behavior. Articulated by epistemic community members, these ideas were first institutionalized internationally in regimes and in programmatic activities by international institutions, followed by national lock in through policies, recruitment of like-minded people to serve in key bureaucratic positions, and enforcement. In turn these efforts have given rise to new economic markets for environmental goods, locking in the governance structure at the national level, and contributing to a better potential for mitigating environmental harm and contributing to clean ups. Further effectiveness depends on easily accessible information about environmental quality and environmental policies, transparent actions by international organizations and governments, the continued participation in environmental diplomacy by non-state actors, sustained levels of public concern in major countries, and improved national capacity for environmental protection.

Such environmental governance is likely to be reasonably robust as the new regulations propagated for environmental protection and the emergent markets for pollution control technology and clean technologies mobilize domestic constituencies to support the international regimes and the national policies which enforce them. As MNCs and firms recognize the potential for financial profits from environmental protection a new transnational political economy coalition emerges behind sustainable development.

Its complete continuation depends of course on the maintenance of the structural underpinnings of the governance structure. Without continued commitment to multilateral institutions and the existence of domestic liberal political structures it would be increasingly difficult for such patterns of governance to persist. While existing commitments might well remain locked in, future environmental threats would not be addressed subject to the rules and values of the current environmental governance framework.

More profoundly, recent patterns of international environmental governance signal a shift in fundamental international governance principles. While units and authority remain territorially grounded, the officials responsible for those units and the effects for which they are responsible are increasingly thinking in non-territorial terms. Decision making occurs primarily in territorially defined and grounded political units, but others whose identities are not defined by political territorial location also make important choices. Ecological epistemic community members' overarching solidarity is with the ecological systems they seek to protect; their identities are expressed functionally at different geographic scales in different issues. Consequently, a shift is underway from ego-based national interests to eco-based ones, as states are informed with such new perspectives and increasingly appreciate that they can no longer regard themselves as discrete entities capable of providing their own wherewithal.

International environmental governance is thus increasingly grounded on notions of connectedness. Problems are no longer easily decomposable. To the extent that such beliefs diffuse more broadly from environmental governance, substantive linkages based on the causal connections between problems may increasingly characterize international negotiations and relations. Future research can profitably address the ways in which regimes initially developed to manage discrete areas of activity are modified to cope with growing appreciation of the increasingly global interconnections between such activities. Under the influence of such a new overarching policy vision, environmental and economic policies may shift from a focus on proximate causes of problems of concern to address more fundamental issues which are believed to be causally implicated within the broader vision of a thick causal tapestry of international politics associated with a deeper recognition and appreciation of complex systems.[39]

Notes

* Financial support was provided by the National Science Foundation (NSF SES-9010101 and SBR- 9123033), the German Marshall Fund, the Commission on Global Governance and the United States Environmental Protection Agency Office of International Affairs. Research assistance was provided by Daniel Carter, Jennifer Koss, Molly Millett, Nicola Poser and Jessica Sowa. For germane comments, either on prior drafts or through ongoing discussions, I thank Hayward Alker, Bob Art, William C. Clark, Tamar Gutner, Ernst B. Haas, Peter Hansen, Jeffrey Hart, Robert Keohane, Robert Knecht, David Lake, Michael McGinnis, Ron Mitchell, Aseem Prakash, Peter Sand, Wayne Sandholtz, Madeline Sunley, Peter Thacher, Craig Thomas, Paul Wapner, and Steven Weber.

1 Norms are principled statements about what states (in this instance) *should* do. Rules are the arrangements by which states intend to fulfill these obligations. Strategies are the policies or practices which states apply domestically to fulfill their international commitments. A convenient glossary of institutionalist concepts is offered in Sue E.S. Crawford and Elinor Ostrom "A Grammar of Institutions," *American Political Science Review* 89, 3 (September, 1995) pp.582–600. Most constructivist authors use a similar vocabulary. John Ruggie prefers "principled and shared understandings." For a selection see Friederich Kratochwil and John Gerard Ruggie "International Organization: A State of the Art on the Art of the State," *International Organization* 40, 4 (Autumn, 1986) pp.753–76; Peter M. Haas "Introduction: Epistemic Communities and International Policy Coordination," *International Organization* 46, 1 (Winter 1992) pp.1–36.
2 Michel Foucault "The Subject and Power," in Hubert Dreyfus and Paul Rabinow, eds, *Beyond Structuralism and Hermeneutics*, Chicago, IL: University of Chicago Press, 1982, p.21, cited by K.J. Holsti "Polyarchy in Nineteenth-Century Europe," in James N. Rosenau and Ernst-Otto Czempiel, *Governance Without Government*, Cambridge: Cambridge University Press, 1992, p.32.

3 Douglass C. North *Institutions, Institutional Change and Economic Performance*, Cambridge: Cambridge University Press, 1990, p.3.
4 Jeff Johnson "Selling Blue Skies, Clean Water," *Environmental Science and Technology* 29, 6, 1995, pp.262A–267A.
5 See Peter M. Haas "Banning Chlorofluorocarbons," *International Organization* 46, 1, (Winter, 1992) p.195; Marc A. Levy, Robert O. Keohane and Peter M. Haas "Improving the Effectiveness of International Environmental Institutions," in Haas, Keohane and Levy, eds, *Institutions for the Earth*, Cambridge, MA: MIT Press, 1993, pp.420–21.
6 Alvaro Soto "The Global Environment: A Southern Perspective," *International Journal* Autumn, 1992; Latin American and Caribbean Commission on Development and Environment, *Our Own Agenda*, Inter-American Development Bank and United Nations Development Programme, 1991; South Centre, *Environment and Development*, Geneva: South Centre, 1991.
7 Robert A. Dahl, *Polyarchy*, New Haven, CT: Yale University Press, 1971; Robert A. Dahl, *Democracy and Its Critics*, New Haven, CT: Yale University Press, 1989. For an effort to understand environmental governance in such terms see David A. Wirth, "Reexamining Decision-Making Processes in International Environmental Law," *Iowa Law Review* 79, 4 (May 1994).
8 Oscar Schachter, "International Environmental Law," *Journal of International Affairs* 44, 2 (Winter 1991) pp.457–93; Toru Iwama, "Emerging Principles and Rules for the Prevention and Mitigation of Environmental Harm," in Edith Brown Weiss, ed., *Environmental Change and International Law*, Tokyo: UNU Press, 1992; Alexandre Kiss and Dinah Shelton, *Manual of European Environmental Law*, Cambridge: Grotius, 1993; Edith Brown Weiss, "International Environmental Law: Contemporary Issues and the Emergence of a New World Order," *The Georgetown Law Journal* 81 (1993); Patricia W. Birnie and Alan E. Boyle, *International Law and the Environment*, Oxford: Clarendon Press, 1992; Edith Brown Weiss, Daniel Barstow Magraw, Paul C. Szasz, *International Environmental Law: Basic Instruments and References*, New York: Transnational Publishers, 1992; Philippe Sands, ed., *Greening International Law*, London: Earthscan, 1993; Winfried Lang, Hanspeter Neuhold and Karl Zemanek, eds, *Environmental Protection and International Law*, Boston, MA: M. Nijhoff, 1991.
9 Toru Iwama, "Emerging Principles and Rules for the Prevention and Mitigation of Environmental Harm," in Edith Brown Weiss, ed., *Environmental Change and International Law*, Tokyo: UNU Press, 1992, p.115.
10 Nazli Choucri, Jan Sundgren, Peter M. Haas, "More Global Treaties," *Nature* 367 (3 February 1994) p.405.
11 Peter Sand, ed., *The Effectiveness of International Environmental Agreements*, Oxford: Grotius Publishers, 1992, p.11.
12 Gunther Doeker and Thomas Gehring, "Liability for Environmental Damage," in Peter H. Sand, ed., *The Effectiveness of International Environmental Agreements*, Cambridge: Grotius Publications, 1992.
13 Robert Livernash, "The Growing Influence of NGOs in the Developing World," *Environment* 34, 5 (June 1992); J. Barnes, "Non-Governmental Organizations," *Marine Policy* (April 1984); Navroz K. Dubash and Michael Oppenheimer, "Modifying the Mandate of Existing Institutions: NGOs," in Irving M. Mintzer, ed., *Confronting Climate Change*, Cambridge: Cambridge University Press, 1992; John Clark, *Democratizing Development*, West Hartford, CT: Kumarian Press, 1990; Julie Fisher, *The Road from Rio*, Westport, CT: Praeger Publishers, 1993; Thomas Princen and Matthias Finger, eds, *Environmental NGOs in World Politics*, London: Routledge, 1994; Leon Gordenker and Thomas G. Weiss, eds,

"Non-Governmental Organizations the United Nations and Global Governance," *Third World Quarterly* 16, 3 (1995).

14 Peter M. Haas and Ernst B. Haas, "Learning to Learn: Thoughts on International Governance," *Global Governance* 1, 3 (October 1995) for additional discussion on international organizations which have added environmental protection to their responsibilities. A baseline of their environmental activities as of 1972 is described in David A. Kay and Eugene B. Skolnikoff, eds, *World Eco-Crisis*, Madison, WI: University of Wisconsin Press, 1972.

15 Abram Chayes and Antonia Handler Chayes, "Compliance Without Enforcement: State Behavior Under Regulatory Treaties," *Negotiation Journal* July, 1991 pp.311–30; Chayes and Chayes, "On Compliance," *International Organization* 47, 2 (Spring 1993) pp.175–206; Ronald B. Mitchell, "Compliance Theory: A Synthesis," *Reciel* 2, 4, pp.327–34.

16 Alan E. Boyle, "Saving the World? Implementation and Enforcement of International Environmental Law Through International Institutions," *Journal of Environmental Law* 3, 2 (1991) pp.229–45; Hilary F. French, "Strengthening International Environmental Governance," *Journal of Environment and Development* 3, 1 (Summer 1994) pp.59–69; Eric Lykke, ed., *Achieving Environmental Goals*, London: Belhaven Press, 1992.

17 Jon Elster, *Explaining Technical Change*, Cambridge: Cambridge University Press, 1983, particularly chap. 6; Richard R. Nelson and Sidney G. Winter, *An Evolutionary Theory of Economic Change*, Cambridge, MA: Harvard University Press, 1982; Stephen D. Krasner, "Sovereignty: An Institutional Perspective," *Comparative Political Studies* 21, 1 (April 1988) pp.66–94; Emanuel Adler, "Cognitive Evolution," in Emanuel Adler and Beverly Crawford, eds, *Progress in Postwar International Relations*, New York: Columbia University Press, 1991; and Emanuel Adler and Peter M. Haas, "Conclusion," *International Organization* 46, 1 (Winter 1992) pp.367–90.

18 Herbert A. Simon, *Reason in Human Affairs*, Stanford, CA: Stanford University Press, 1983; Herbert A. Simon, "Human Nature in Politics: The Dialogue of Psychology with Political Science," *The American Political Science Review* 79 (1985) pp.293–304; James G. March, *A Primer on Decision Making*, New York: Free Press, 1994.

19 For intellectual histories which focus on both internal influences from within the scientific community and external influences from society and government on the development of ecological understanding, see Peter J. Bowler, *The Environmental Sciences*, New York: W.W. Norton, 1992; Joel B. Hagen, *The Entangled Bank: The Origins of Ecosystem Ecology*, Brunswick, NJ: Rutgers University Press, 1992; Donald Worster, *Nature's Economy*, Cambridge: Cambridge University Press, 1987; Robert P. McIntosh, *The Background of Ecology*, Cambridge: Cambridge University Press, 1985; and, grudgingly, Wolfgang Sachs, "Environment," in Sachs, ed., *The Development Dictionary*, London: Zed Books, 1992.

20 Mostafa K. Tolba *et al.*, *The World Environment 1972–1992* London: Chapman & Hall, 1992, chap. 22; Albert Weale, *The New Politics of Pollution*, Manchester: Manchester University Press, 1992; Tony Brenton, *The Greening of Machiavelli*, London: Royal Institute of International Affairs, 1994, pp.67, 70.

21 Jens Sorensen, "The International Proliferation of Integrated Coastal Zone Management Efforts," *Ocean & Coastal Management* 21 (1993) pp.45–80.

22 US Congress Office of Technology Assessment, *Industry, Technology and the Environment*, OTA-ITE-586 Washington, DC: US Government Printing Office, 1994; chap. 4; Dion Vaughn and Craig Mickle, *Environmental Profiles of European Business*, London: Royal Institute of International Affairs, 1993; Ian Christie and Heather Rolfe, *Cleaner Production in Industry*, London: Policy Studies Institute, 1995; *ENDS Report*, 212, September, 1992, p.17; Michael E. Porter, "America's Green

Strategy," *Scientific American* (April 1991); "How to Make Lots of Money and Save the Planet too," *The Economist* 3 June 1995, p.57.

23 Robert U. Ayres and Udo E. Simonis, *Industrial Metabolism: Restructuring for Sustainable Development*, Tokyo: United Nations University Press, 1994; Robert Socolow *et al*. eds, *Industrial Ecology and Global Change*, Cambridge: Cambridge University Press, 1994; National Academy of Sciences, *The Greening of Industrial Ecosystems*, Washington, DC: National Academy Press, 1994.

24 "How to Make Lots of Money and Save the Planet too," *The Economist* 3 June 1995, pp.57–58; Environmental Business Research, *Assessment of U.S. Environmental Technology Strengths and Applications*, Report for US Agency for International Development (December, 1993) p.2.

25 Christopher Flavin and John E. Young, "Shaping the Next Industrial Revolution," in Worldwatch Institute, *State of the World, 1993*, New York: W.W. Norton, 1993, p.182.

26 F. Cairncross, "UNCED, Environmentalism and Beyond," *Columbia Journal of World Business* 27, III and IV (Fall/Winter, 1992) pp.15–16.

27 Stephan Schmidheiny, *Changing Course*, Cambridge, MA: MIT Press, 1992.

28 Riley E. Dunlap, George H. Gallup, Jr. and Alec M. Gallup, "Health of the Planet Survey," Princeton, NJ: Gallup International Institute, 1992. The countries are Germany, USA, Portugal, Great Britain, Canada, Ireland, Switzerland, Norway, Netherlands, Japan, Denmark, Finland, Russia, Poland, the Philippines, Nigeria, India, Turkey, Uruguay, Hungary, Mexico, Brazil, Chile, South Korea.

29 Clifford S. Russell, "Environmental Enforcement," in Tom Tietenberg, ed., *Innovation in Environmental Policy*, Aldershot: Edward Elgar, 1992, p.219.

30 H. Jeffrey Leonard, *Pollution and the Struggle for the World Product*, New York: Cambridge University Press, 1988; Charles S. Pearson, ed., *Multinational Corporations, Environment, and the Third World*, Durham, NC: Duke University Press, 1987.

31 Nigel Harris, "Wastes, the Environment and the International Economy," *Cities* August, 1992, p.179; "World Chemicals: The Challenge of Asia," *The Economist* March 13, 1993, pp.27–30.

32 "Pollution in Asia," *The Economist* October 6, 1990, pp.19–22; "Pollution in Asia," *The Economist* December 11, 1993; Nicholas Lenssen, "All the Coal in China," *Worldwatch* March/April, 1993, pp.22–30; Arthur Zich, "Taiwan," *National Geographic* November 1993, pp.10–32.

33 David O'Connor, *Managing the Environment with Rapid Industrialization*, Paris: OECD, 1994; Michael C. Howard, ed., *Asia's Environmental Crisis*, Boulder, CO: Westview Press, 1993.

34 Mostafa K. Tolba, *et al*., eds, *The World Environment 1972–1992*, London: Chapman and Hall, 1993, chap. 10.

35 Qing-Nan Meng, *Land-Based Marine Pollution*, London: Graham & Trotman, 1987, pp.124–33; W. Jackson Davis, "The Need for a New Global Ocean Governance System," in Durwood Zaelke, ed., *Freedom of the Seas in the Twenty-First Century*, Washington, DC: Island Press, 1993.

36 Lee A. Kimball, *Forging International Agreement*, Washington, DC: World Resources Institute, 1992, p.73.

37 World Bank data in *Finance & Development*, March 1996, p.32.

38 Report of the Secretary-General on Technology Transfer, Cooperation and Capacity-Building E/CN.17/WG.I/1994/2.

39 For a fuller study of this phenomenon see The Social Learning Group, *Social Learning and the Management of Global Environmental Risks*, Cambridge, MA: MIT Press, 1999.

5 Globalization *as* governance

Toward an archaeology of
contemporary political reason

*Ian R. Douglas**

> The development of global governance is part of the evolution of human efforts
> to organize life on the planet, and that process will always be going on. Our
> work is no more than a transit stop on that journey.
>
> (Commission on Global Governance, 1995, p.xvi)

The organization of life is the project, global in scope, an endpoint to which
human societies are inexorably in motion. In *The Poverty of Historicism*, Karl
Popper (1986) warned against the tyranny of any political discourse that
claimed to be riding a tide of inevitability. The 1995 report of the Commission
on Global Governance is a case in point. The epigraph above is representative
of the danger: a whole history of interventions, of misfortunes, scattered
lives, is lost in the grandeur of two sentences. Let us attempt here to regain it.

Unlike one or two of my fellow authors, I argue in what follows that globalization is in no way in tension with governance, indeed each is the logic of
the other. I argue that the root of this equivalence can be found deep within
the genealogy of the modern state. In tracing this equivalence I suggest not
only that we re-examine popular notions concerning the decline of public
authority and the hollowing out of states, but also that we pay greater attention to the political genealogy of concepts such as autonomy, freedom and
participatory democracy. In so doing we can open a space for a fresh evaluation of contemporary discourses and practices of global governance. The
latter endeavour is particularly important, for it is not only what is lost or
not said in the Commission's report that is of interest. Equally significant are
the actions and values sanctioned and affirmed. Above all, it is this *positive*
program of both the Commission and a range of other actors that I wish to
subject to a political and historical reading. What I aim to disturb is not so
much a silence as a monologue of reason that has concealed the intervention
of power, transformed so many real lives – real people – and given dignity, if
not legitimacy, to the violence of a kind of disciplinary governance that
has become our destiny and destination. The "evolution of human efforts to

organize life on the planet" is indeed the type of governance in question, at least in this essay.

I will attempt to outline the archaeology of this reason to the extent that it highlights an alternative reading of the politics of globalization and its intersection with the reality and politics of bringing order to the world.

Governance and the power to govern

In the first volume of *The History of Sexuality*, Michel Foucault described what he saw as a profound transformation at the heart of political governance. "Since the classical age," he wrote,

> "Deduction" has tended to be no longer the major form of power but merely one element among others, working to incite, reinforce, control, monitor, optimize, and organize the forces under it: a power bent on generating forces, making them grow, and ordering them, rather than one dedicated to impeding them, making them submit, or destroying them.
>
> (Foucault, 1979, p. 136)

For Foucault this ascendance marked the threshold of modernity and what he termed the "age of bio-power". Two poles of political intervention emerged; a "great bipolar technology" of power over life. The first centred on the "body as a machine"; an "anatomo-politics" aimed to extort forces and optimize capabilities. The second centred on the "adjustment of the phenomena of population"; a "bio-politics" focused on demography (distribution, longevity, procreation), economy (the synchronization of resources and citizens), and social security (the social constitution of contracts and interests), wherein the health and well-being of the *civitas* became a "general objective of policy" and domain of investment.

In Foucault's philosophical and historical works this theme of the positive constitution of modern society is well established. *Madness and Civilization* (1967) is as much a *tour de force* on the birth of "industrious society" as a history of insanity. *The Birth of the Clinic* (1973) charts the emergence of a medical perception as much concerned with illuminating *social* as corporeal pathology. *Discipline and Punish* (1977) – the history of the prison – is first and foremost concerned with the training (positive sign) of bodies and souls; the dream of a kind of automatic social functioning. And finally – perhaps most profoundly – we have *The History of Sexuality*, which traces the birth of the "knowing subject"; the body that constitutes *itself* as an object of knowledge. *Power* – at least since the eighteenth century – is seen as *productive*; inscripted in knowledge, revealed as truth, operative at the level of the everyday mundane. Foucault gave the name "governmentalization" to the general process of the emergence of self-organizing, self-reliant networks of governance, in which individuals themselves were to play positive roles. *Government* was for

Foucault the "overall effect" of a complex interplay of rationalities and technicalities, as well as – of course – political contingency. The single thread
that linked all modern experiences of politics was the targetting of life above
and beyond death.

This theme dominated Foucault's lecture and seminar series at the Collège
de France between the years 1976 and 1980. Although no comprehensive
study emerged from Foucault's researches, we do have – as well as transcripts
of his lectures – several short essays and papers (Foucault, 1988, 1989, 1991).
These writings are particularly significant in that they portray a continual
sharpening of Foucault's own historical gaze. Rather than be satisfied with
the archaeology of the "dark, but firm web of our experience" (Foucault,
1973, p.199), Foucault increasingly turned his attention to the question of
order; its historical politics, techniques and practices. Foucault sought to
uncover the *inscribed* history of the birth of modern society; the "absolutely
conscious strategy" attested in both political texts and the "mass of
unknown documents" constitutive of the "effective discourse of a political
action" (Foucault, 1996, p.149). This ordering was to be found – argued
Foucault – in,

> 1) The ensemble formed by institutions, procedures, analyses and reflec-
> tions, the calculations and tactics that allow the exercise of this very
> specific albeit complex form of power, which has as its target population,
> as its principal form of knowledge political economy, and its essential
> technical means apparatuses of security.
> 2) The tendency which, over a long period and throughout the West, has
> steadily led towards the pre-eminence over all other forms (sovereignty,
> discipline, etc.) of this type of power which may be termed government,
> resulting, on the one hand in the formation of a whole series of specific
> governmental apparatuses, and, on the other, in the development of a
> whole complex of *savoirs*.
> 3) The process, or rather the result of the process, through which the
> state of justice of the Middle Ages, transformed into the administrative
> state during the fifteenth and sixteenth century, gradually becomes
> "governmentalized" . . .

> (Foucault, 1991, pp.102–3)

The first step toward this "governmentalization of the state" is taken when
populations emerge as a *statistical* problem.[1] Foucault traces this emergence
first in the notion of *raison d'état*, where the greatness of cities and states is
linked to the strength and productivity of the *civitas*.[2] Added to the "great
eighteenth-century demographic upswing in Western Europe" (no doubt in
part a consequence of this new concern with the collective power of people)
and "the necessity for coordinating and integrating it into the apparatus
of production," "'population', with its numerical variables of space and
chronology, longevity and health [emerges] not only as a problem but an

object of surveillance, analysis, intervention, modification, etc. The project of a technology of population begins to be sketched . . ." (Foucault, 1980, p.171).

Epitomized best in what would become known as "cameralistics," *polizei-wissenschaft*, or "police science" – in the writings of Seckendorff (1656), Wolff (1719), Dithmar (1731), Darjes (1749, 1756, 1776), Zinke (1751), Moser (1758), Bergius (1767–74), and Mueller (1790), among others – the aim of this new technology of population was to make individuals "useful for the world" in such a way that "their development also fosters the strength of the state" (Foucault, 1981, p.252).[3] This strength of the state was conceived in two ways: on the one hand, as the material result of the harnessing and channeling of energies (industry) into the productive economy, and on the other, as the securitization of order through workfare, occupation and the incentive to profit (enrichment). Productivity, diligence and happiness emerged as the objectives of the mode of government that dominated the classical age; simultaneously differentiated (in the classification and organization of bodies) and aggregated (in the policing of rhythms and the processes of populations). Freedom, inner strength and security emerged as dominant principles in the discursive constitution of civic order, conditioning the historical development of practical and political government from the eighteenth century onward.

What Foucault's historical studies describe in essence is the simultaneous *spatialization* and *deterritorialization* of political government throughout the course of modernity. In the first instance, government widens its reach (and gaze); intervening in an ever greater number of spaces (psychology, pathology, sexuality, education, etc.), and locations (the asylum, the clinic, the prison, the school, the factory, the boulevard, the playground, and so on). On the other hand, government becomes integral; diffused at the level of the social body as a whole (in law, morality, customs, habits and social knowledge), and assumed within an individual code or structure of command (in disposition, humor, temperament). For heuristic purposes this double movement corresponds to Foucault's identification of "specific governmental practices" on the one hand, and "a whole complex of *savoirs*" on the other, with spatialization constituting the former, and deterritorialization the latter.

What I suggest – again for heuristic purposes, rather than as a strict categorization of the history of power – is that this distinction might also be useful in helping us think of the significance of the ascendance of a discourse of "governance" over that of "government." The latter is indicative of a political reason concerned with the margins and boundaries of civil security (the delinquent, the libertine, the madman). In this sense it is spatialized and territorialized. The former is indicative of a political reason concerned with strengthening the "normality" of the mass. In this sense it is deterritorialized and temporalized (normality defined according to historical expediency). Michel Foucault himself never felt the need to conceptually separate these out, no doubt for good reason. Indeed his notion of "governmentalization" rightly emphasizes both elements of this emerging power over life. I would like to suggest that contemporary discussions of governance would do well to remember this centrality of *government*; both in the sense of the spatiality of power, and in the "government" essentially served in its deterritorialization (the passing of the command structure into the very constitution of the individual).

In this chapter, however, I aim to do more than simply raise that objection. I want also to make a preliminary move toward understanding the technicalities of what I take to be a form of political intervention concerned less with the homology of civil space than with the constitution of civil time; its rhythms, its pace, its motion. In this I want to emphasize the notion of "governance" while not divorcing it from the "specific governmental practices" that lurk behind the outward surface of this deterritorialization. Maintaining this focus on government while trying to describe the parameters of governance is indeed essential as both emerge from the same political reason (the targeting of populations by power).

Let us begin by revisiting the Commission on Global Governance.

Our global neighbourhood

As the report of the Commission continued, I realized that I was reading an historical document, essentially the same in nature to the decrees and lost registers whose vibrations Foucault felt, and whose intensity he dreamt of restoring. I imagined myself surrounded by its forebears – their names rising up through the centuries – Botero, Darjes, Saint-Simon, Bentham. From the discussion of "civic ethics" to "economic stability," from "development assistance" to the "enforcement of law," from the "empowerment of people" to "enlightened leadership," here was encapsulated the grand themes of the modern epoch. The aims of this Commission were clear: to develop a "multi-faceted strategy for global governance," one that would "draw on the skill of a diversity of people and institutions at many levels [building] networks of institutions and processes – that enable global actors to pool information, knowledge, and capacities" (Commission on Global Governance, 1995, pp.4–5). "Governance," in their terms, was to be found in the promotion of security "in its widest sense."

On the Commission's account this was a text about "a new world"; one caught up in the midst of a profound revolution. "Never before" it attests, "has change come so rapidly – in some ways, all at once – on such a global scale, and with such global visibility" (Commission on Global Governance, 1995, p.12). Yet the echoes of all those brief lives, those lowly figures upon whom power, many centuries hence, had turned its attention, kept jumping up as I read. Something was amiss. Though it took me some time to see it, the outline of an equivalence between global governance and the genealogy of modern governmentality and bio-politics was materializing on the very page before me. Where once the theoreticians of police had conceived of the dignity, power and dynamism of the state in terms of facilitating happiness and self-sustenance, now we were being told, "The enormous growth in people's concern for human rights, equity, democracy, meeting basic material needs, environmental protection, and demilitarization has today produced a multitude of new actors who can contribute to governance" (Commission on Global Governance, 1995, p.3). In response, "Nation-states must adjust to the appearance of all these forces and take advantage of their capabilities" (Commission on Global Governance, 1995, p.xvi). Leaders, argued the Commission, must recognize the "collective power of people." "Mobilizing that power to make life in the twenty-first century more democratic, more secure, and sustainable, is the foremost challenge of this generation" (Commission on Global Governance, 1995, p.1).

Despite the fact that "bio-power" emerges as a political rationale and practical strategy in the eighteenth century, popularizing government in its very *modus operandi* (advanced liberal democracy), the picture sketched by the Commission is one of the crisis of government as a whole *because of its decentralization*. In this proposition it is not alone. This mistake is particularly prevalent in contemporary discussion of the state and globalization in the disciplines of international relations and political economy. Susan Strange, for example, in an essay entitled "The Defective State" writes,

> state authority has leaked away, upwards, sideways, and downwards. In some matters, it seems even to have gone nowhere, just evaporated. The realm of anarchy in society and economy has become more extensive as that of all kinds of authority has diminished.
>
> (Strange, 1995, p.56)

The state, for Strange, is "hollowing out." In Strange's view we are witness to a process by which centralized authority over society and economy has become "diffused" in a "neomedieval fashion," with "some necessary authority once exercised by states . . . now exercised by no one" (Strange, 1995, p.71). Governments are the "victims" of a shift in the "state-market balance of power."

Alternatively, take the writings of Phil Cerny. "The essence of the state – and the main practical condition for its viability" he writes,

> lies in the fact that sovereign and autonomous political institutions are capable of deriving legitimacy from a distinct citizenry located in a defined territory. The international system did not present a fundamental challenge [indeed it] constituted a bulwark of the state and the ultimate proof of its sovereignty and autonomy. However, increasing transnational interpenetration has the potential to transform the international system from a true states system into one in which this external bulwark is eroded and eventually undermined.
>
> (Cerny, 1996a, p.123)

Left all alone, the future for the state, in Cerny's view, is bleak. The essential presumption is set up in the first line; states are nothing if not territorially (and ethnically) discreet. Similar themes are developed by Theodore Levitt. "Cosmopolitanism," he writes,

> is no longer the monopoly of the intellectual and leisure classes; it is becoming the established property and defining characteristic of all sectors everywhere in the world. Gradually and irresistibly it breaks down the walls of economic insularity, nationalism, and chauvinism. What we see today as escalating commercial nationalism is simply the last violent death rattle of an obsolete institution.
>
> (Levitt, 1983, p.101)

Here again the metaphor is one of penetration. The hold of the ship of state (its homology) has been fractured. *Per axiom* this entails a crisis of government, indeed its obsolescence. "The Nation State" writes Kenichi Ohmae, "has become an unnatural, even dysfunctional unit for organizing human activity and managing economic endeavour in a borderless world" (Ohmae, 1993, p.78). From its role in the constitution and policing of boundaries, "politics [itself] has entered an age of increasing limits" (Riddell, 1995, p.14). The key index of this limit – it is argued – is found in the inability of governments to control forms of movement. In the words of Mathew Horsman and Andrew Marshall,

> Effortless communications across boundaries undermine the nation-state's control; increased mobility, and the increased willingness of people to migrate, undermine its cohesiveness. Business abhors borders, and seeks to circumvent them. Information travels across borders and nation-states are hard pressed to control the flow. . . . The nation-state [is] increasingly powerless to withstand these pressures.
>
> (Horsman and Marshall, 1994, p.60)

Yet we might ask, from where did man learn the value of motion? Let's return to the question of the deterritorialization of government and the birth of modern notions of governance.

The discovery of motion

In the words of Martin Heidegger, "The breeding of human beings is not a taming in the sense of a suppression and hobbling of sensuality; rather, breeding is the accumulation and purification of energies in the univocity of the strictly controllable "automatism" of every activity" (Heidegger, 1991, pp.230–1). Not least the most important innovation of the classical age was the emergence of a form of political reason that would take as its focus the knowledge and facilitation of this automatism. From Leonardo's anatomical notes and drawings, Versalius' first public anatomy and *De Humani Corporis Fabrica* (1543), Descartes' declaration that the body is no more than an ensemble of "moving machines," Hobbes' assertion that the universe is "corporeal," the flashpoints in that history are no doubt well known. What was emerging was a new spatial imagination of human existence, but also a temporal one. As Jonathan Sawday has so rightly described,

> Mechanism offered the prospect of a radically reconstituted body. Forged into a working machine, the mechanical body appeared fundamentally different from the geographic body whose contours expressed a static landscape without dynamic interconnection. More than this, however, the body as a machine, as a clock, as an automaton, was understood as having no intellect of its own. Instead, it silently operated according to the laws of mechanics . . . The political implications of this process of thought were immense.
>
> (Sawday, 1995, p.29)

One doesn't have to take too many guesses to find the link between the new body of regular motion and the birth of the disciplined and tranquil society dreamed of by the eighteenth-century practitioners of "police science."[4] With the discovery of planetary motion, the psychology of perception and duration, the social diffusion of the clock, the rise of artistic perspectivism, and the mathematical and geometrical revolutions, a new interest in the possibilities and aesthetics of uniform motion was born (Reiss, 1997, Mumford, 1934, 1961). Uniformity *through* space (the automata of movement) fast came to define the parameters of "public safety," good order, and the functioning society.

Though often overlooked, this link between motion and civic order was highlighted in a number of historical works by Michel Foucault. In *Madness and Civilization* (1967, pp.123–34, 160–77), for example, Foucault described how reason itself was constituted in the classical age in reference to extremes of movement; mania related to an "excessive mobility of the fibres," leading to a lightness in disposition, and melancholia to a congestion and thickening of the blood, and subsequent dullness of character. What emerged was not only a medical perception of the corporeal body, but a series of practices, suggestions and knowledges aimed to regulate motion in the *body-politic*. The testing ground was the body of unreason, where mobility,

> must be measured and controlled; it must not become a vain agitation of the fibres which no longer obey the stimuli of the exterior world . . . the cure consists in reviving in the sufferer a movement that will be both regular and real, in the sense that it will obey the rules of the world's movements.
>
> (Foucault, 1967, pp.172–3)

The result, as Foucault described (and also in *Discipline and Punish*) was the gradual emergence of a "science of time" mediating man's relation to motion within the confines of acceptable limits to reason and order defined in the movements of the natural world and celestial heavens. The condemnation of idleness as the "source of all disorders," culminating in the obligation to work (Huizinga, 1927, Foucault, 1967, 1973) is perhaps the most conspicuous indication of the links newly forged between motion, good order and the individual. As Mumford describes, "Time as pure duration, time dedicated to contemplation and reverie, time divorced from mechanical operations, was treated as a heinous waste" (Mumford, 1934, p.197). Evermore, "the 'power' of the soul gave way to a sequence of mechanical movements . . . the silent forces of springs, wheels, and cogs, operating as a contrived whole." As Sawday continues, "The modern body had emerged: a body which worked rather than existed" (Sawday, 1995, p.32).

In *Flesh and Stone*, Richard Sennett takes up the point of how these references to motion (through medical perception and the birth of the productive economy) came to define the early modern city. In doing so, Sennett, like Foucault, makes the crucial link between the organization of bodies and that of the broader body-politic. New principles of urban planning and policing were emerging based upon new medical metaphors of "circulation" and "flow" (Harvey, 1628; Willis, 1684). The health of the body became the comparison against which the greatness of cities and states would be measured. The "veins" and "arteries" of the new urban design were to be freed from all sources of possible blockage.

> Enlightened planners wanted the city in its very design to function like a healthy body, freely flowing as well as possessed of clear skin. Since the beginnings of the Baroque era, urban planners had thought about making cities in terms of efficient circulation of the people on the city's main streets. . . . The medical imagery of life-giving circulation gave a new meaning to the Baroque emphasis of motion.
>
> (Sennett, 1994, pp.263–4)

The regularization of cleanliness and sanitation, and the removal of madmen, beggars and idlers from the highway are but two general projects born of the question of the efficiency of movement that dominates the historical imaginary of the classical age. As Julien Offray de La Mettrie (1748) would remark, only organized matter was endowed with the principle of motion. We may also add that matter endowed with the principle of motion was increasingly regarded as "ordered." What was emerging was a particular relation between politics, space and time, expressed with perfection in the words of Guillaute (a French police officer writing in 1749).

> Public order will reign if we are careful to distribute our human time and space by a severe regulation of transit; if we are attentive to schedules as

well as to alignments and signal systems; if by environmental standardization the entire city is made transparent, that is, familiar to the police-
man's eye.

(Guillaute, quoted in Virilio, 1986, p.18)

Let us not also forget the military, both in its impact on cities and its impact on
bodies. In terms of the former, as Mumford describes,

> To achieve the maximum appearance of order and power on parade, it is
> necessary to provide a body of soldiers either with an open square or a
> long unbroken avenue . . . a moving regiment gives the impression that
> it would break through a solid wall [which] is exactly the belief that the
> soldier and the Prince desire to inculcate in the populace: it helps to keep
> them in order without coming to an actual trial of strength . . .

(Mumford, 1961, p.369)

And before these men could be commanded to run at the enemy they had first
to be taught to stand firm in space and time. The neostoic revival in military
discipline and drill embodied in the practices and procedures of Lipsius,
Maurice of Nassau, Gustavus and Montecuccoli, and passed through to
Eugene, Marlborough, Guibert and the French Revolutionaries, also helped
set the technical parameters of government.[5] Practiced first on the military
courtyard, and then in the field, the hospital, the workhouse, the almshouse,
the prison, the birth of a new age of military logistics is inseparable from the
episteme of organized motion emerging as a political technology of civic
order.[6] The image of society was one of a complex of relays; each to be
synchronized, made efficient and effective. In the remarkable words of
Johann von Justi,

> A properly constituted state must be exactly analogous to a machine, in
> which all the wheels and gears are precisely adjusted to one another; and
> the ruler must be the foreman, and the main-spring, or the soul . . .
> which sets everything in motion.

(Justi, quoted in Parry, 1963, p.182)

Frederick the Great was surely the first statesman to bring together the two
themes that would dominate the historical horizon of the modern period;
bio-power and moving-power. By the turn of the nineteenth century these
themes were running in parallel, a fact of which Foucault seemed well aware.

> At first, [disciplines] were expected to neutralize dangers, to fix useless
> or disturbed populations, to avoid the inconveniences of over-large
> assemblies; now they were being asked to play a positive role, for they
> were becoming able to do so, to increase the possible utility of individuals.
> Military discipline . . . coordinates . . . accelerates movements, increases

> fire power . . . The discipline of the workshop . . . ends to increase apti-
> tudes, speeds, output . . . introducing bodies into a machinery, forces
> into an economy.
>
> (Foucault, 1977, p.210)

A "collective, obligatory rhythm" was emerging; a "meticulous meshing."
"We have passed," Foucault continues,

> from a form of injunction that measured or punctuated gestures to a web
> that constrains them or sustains them throughout their entire succession.
> A sort of anatomo-chronological schema of behaviour is defined . . .
> Time penetrates the body and with it all the meticulous controls of
> power . . . Disciplinary control does not consist simply in teaching or
> imposing a series of particular gestures; it imposes the best relations
> between a gesture and the overall position of the body, which is its con-
> dition of efficiency and speed . . . a positive economy . . . [which] poses
> the principle of a theoretically ever-growing use of time . . . towards an
> ideal point at which one maintained maximum speed and maximum
> efficiency . . .
>
> (Foucault, 1977, pp.152–4)

It was exactly this implementation of a new economy of movement through
time that enabled Frederick to dominate the eighteenth century.

Yet if Frederick was the foreman of this newly constituted machine-in-
motion, Napoleon would surely become its soul. More than anyone prior, he
would embody the next phase of history, defined not so much by the "art of
governing," as what we might describe – with a certain misgiving – as the
"art of motorizing."[7] Again, the crucial link is the birth of bio-politics, and
the transformation of the power to govern. In the words of Carl von
Clausewitz (1968, p.384), "War had suddenly become an affair of the
people, and that of a people numbering thirty million, every one of whom
regarded himself as a citizen of the State." Under the Committee of Public
Safety the *levée en masse* is established providing the first clear model of
modern conscription. Perfected by the hand of Bonaparte, the energy
thrown into the conduct of war was "immensely increased," with whole populations "mobilized for the purpose of wholesale slaughter" (Foucault, 1979,
p.137).

And not only in warfare did the principles of efficiency and movement
dominate, but also in his Civil Code – the *Code Napoléon* – of which he claimed
the "most compact government with the most rapid circulation and the most
energetic movement that ever existed" (Napoleon, quoted in Crawley, 1965,
p.319). All of this was unthinkable without the elaborate ensemble of powers
in which the new *kinetic state* was anchored: the disciplinary codes that would
come to define modern governance. Prefigured perfectly in the words of
French military reformer Comte de Guibert,

What I want to avoid is that my supplies should command me. It is in this case my movement that is the main thing; all other combinations are accessory and I must try to make them subordinate to the movement.

(Guibert, in Crawley, 1965, p.74)

"The best soldier" Napoleon would declare, "is not so much the one who fights as the one who marches" (Napoleon, quoted in Durant and Durant, 1975, p.247). There is no doubt that this marks a threshold in the "evolution of human efforts to organize life on the planet," both militarily and governmentally.

Prolegomenon to global governance

It is this moment in history that serves as urbanist Paul Virilio's point of departure. Like Foucault, Mumford and Sennett, Virilio is also concerned with the birth of a new technical, geometric, chronographic imagination of men and things. What Virilio adds to the story is a more focused description of the nineteenth- and twentieth-century experience of *moving*, and its correspondence with political technology and the genealogy of governance. Virilio also serves as the link to my main argument: that this experience of motion, and its greater facilitation and extension throughout every level of society, is the hidden history of globalism and global governance. Though Virilio has only recently turned his attention to the discourses of globalization (1995b), his writings – I suggest – provide the political and historical reading so lacking in our present discussions. For lack of space let me pick out its main themes.

"Up until the nineteenth century," Virilio writes, "society was founded on the brake" (Virilio and Lotringer, 1983, pp.44–5). Agrarian society then gives way to industrial or transportational society (or what Virilio calls "dromocratic society"[8]). This society is built upon the possibility of "fabricating speed." "And so they can pass from the age of the brakes to the age of the accelerator. In other words, power will be invested in acceleration itself" (Virilio, in Virilio and Lotringer, 1983, pp.44–5). An "unrecognized order of political circulation" was emerging, crystallized in the French Revolution. The events of 1789, he writes,

claimed to be a revolt against *subjection*, that is, against the *constraint to immobility* symbolized by the ancient feudal serfdom . . . the arbitrary confinement and obligation to reside in one place. No one suspected that the "conquest of the freedom to come and go" could, by a sleight of hand, become an *obligation to mobility*. The "mass uprising" of 1793 was the institution of the first *dictatorship of movement*, subtly replacing the *freedom of movement* of the early days of the revolution. The reality of power in this first modern State appears beyond the accumulation of violence as an accumulation of movement.

(Virilio, 1986, p.30)

The stage was set for Bonaparte. "With Napoleon," write the Durants, "the ecstasy of liberty yielded to the dictatorship of order" (Durant and Durant, 1975, p.240).

From this consolidation point (of a broader political investment in motion running parallel to the rise of the money economy, the militant-bureaucratic state, and new advances in the physical and medical sciences), Virilio goes on to chart the active planning of the time and space horizons of whole societies; what he calls the, "primordial control of the masses by the organisms of urban defense" (Virilio, 1986, p.15). For Virilio then, as for Foucault, the aims of modern political rationality are clear; to make mobile the citizenry within the parameters of order, reason and tranquillity. Deterritorializing in a double sense (the investment in motion and the targeting of the populace), individuals become subordinated to a higher realm of ordering beyond terri-torialism: speed. "Revolution" replaces "circulation," automotion supplants motion – the increase in pace acting to secure tranquillity through com-pulsion; what Virilio (1986, p.46) has termed the "peace of exhaustion." In essence (though largely unrecognized, perhaps even by himself) Virilio's work describes in outline the *political technique* through which the "problem" of early modernity – of how to maximize the power of individuals for the pres-tige of the state within the confines of stability and good order – was *transcended* and *neutralized*.

Over the modern period proper, no longer is the dilemma of government how to mediate between the extremes of rapidity and stasis, productionism and docility, circulation and revolution. By the time of Napoleon, not only would political rationality understand the motion of matter and of bodies, it would seek above all to perfect the mechanisms of *producing it*. The "move-ment-of-movement" as a *technical* achievement, emerges at this time (the early nineteenth century) as a societal principle, reordering the whole of the modern world. "What, then" writes N.H. Gibbs, "was Napoleon's distin-guishing mark as a 'great captain'?" "It was his ability to move very large armies, sometimes of 200,000 men and more, across great stretches of the continent at speeds far greater than had hitherto been thought possible . . ." (Gibbs, in Crawley, 1965, p.75). Motion had become speed, and in focusing upon it in the most radical way possible, Paul Virilio begins to answer the question of how efficiency in the governing of men and things was established at the heart of modernity.

Let us imagine the flagpoints of this history in summary form: in early modernity we find a rabble populace, poorly disciplined, wandering, and blighted by the specters of unreason, idleness and environmental destitution. The aim of political reason – in the context of broader societal transfor-mations (the discovery of order through production, the rise of the money economy, commercialism and early mercantilism[9]) – is to navigate a course between the extremes of revolution and stagnancy. Having recognized that (in the words of Botero) the "true strength of a ruler consists in his people," political rationality aims also to "multiply" the citizenry as a productive force. A new politics of order, both of detail (looking into men's souls), and of generality (the new concern with the biology of populations) becomes a technical necessity. Working together, these techniques of intervention ("anatomo-power" and "bio-power") produced at the heart of the classical age an initial stasis; seen best in the military courtyard, the hospital, the prison and the school. The power of movement was subject to a *territorial codification* (in the city, in the workhouse, in the asylum, in the manufactory).

By the beginnings of the nineteenth century the place of the state and political reason in constituting spaces for existence had been secured, and a second "reordering" could now be effected, heralding perhaps less the age of bio-politics as the *age of bio-kinesis*. Rather than charting the middle ground between rapidity and stasis, power would aim to "release" the full productive, dynamic efficiency of the (national) population *in and through time*. "Motion" (or more precisely, motorization) had emerged as the destiny and law of a new politics of order. The full equivalence of Virilio's "metabolic vehicles" to Foucault's "bearers of order" becomes clear. "Dromological power" – or in Foucault, "capillary power" – had emerged as the practical basis and first principle of capitalist modernity established simultaneously with the apparatus of modern governance. Mobility, in other words, had become simultaneously the *means to liberation* and the *means to domination;* the accumulation of men running hand-in-hand with the accumulation of movement, and the illusion of its sovereign release.

Speed was to be taught as a virtue because it had in itself emerged as a *discipline*.

Discourses and practices of contemporary political reason

No doubt this is when "globalism" (though yet to find its linguistic expression) first emerged as the imaginary endpoint to liberal freedom. "To be truly free requires a life without boundaries": the passport to that future is the technical control of motion.[10] As Paul Virilio (1986, p.73) describes, "the dromocrat's look . . . causes *distances to approach*." This negation of "the world as a field" is contained nowhere better than in the very image of the Earth as seen from space. Indeed, if this blue orb is an icon of anything it is of the final frontier in the ascendance of *kinetic political technology*. Hardly a surprise then that Martin Heidegger feared this image more than he did the atom bomb. As he described so perfectly, the "uprooting of man has taken place" (Heidegger, 1993, pp.105–6).

This uprooting, or incitement to motion, is well represented in the discourses and practices of contemporary political reason. Again, our classical themes prevail: *deterritorialization* (disappearances of all kinds of materiality) and *temporalization* (self-constitution and regulation). The former can be regarded as the "modality of becoming" of globalism – the emptying out of all kinds of territory (first of the state, then the world itself). The latter corresponds to the channeling of energies, the optimization of forces, the temporal parameters of modern governance. In practice, like the somewhat shaky distinction between governance and government, these impulses are often intermixed. "You wanted to travel?", asks a promotion for Sky television, "No need to bother." Here speed not only consumes distance, but in bringing everything to hand that is distant (without even the need for physical movement) assures *the ideal political state* of life without boundaries: immobilism. For Paul Virilio this is clearly worrying,

> The end-point is reached when humans have become inanimate. . . . The revolution of the auto, of automobile travel, certainly awakened the illusion of a new nomadism, but in the same stroke the revolution of the audiovisual and electronic media destroyed the illusion once again. With the speed of light the rigor mortis begins, the absolute immobility of humanity. We are heading for paralysis. Not because the surplus of autos brings street traffic to a standstill, but because everyone will have disposal over everything without having to go anywhere.
>
> (Virilio, 1995c, p.103)

As a critique of the dream of globalization Virilio's analysis of the emergence of the "terminal-citizen" is unmatched.[11] Not only does it help us reflect politically upon the dominant discourses of our epoch, but again – like Foucault – it allows us to raise, at least for a moment, the question of the implications of contemporary practices for the constitution of contemporary political governance. What interests are better served by this immobilization of humanity under the illusion of the freedom of speed?

This "space-distortion," for Virilio, finds its origins in the military, but can equally be seen across whole sections of society. "We believe" runs a promotion for Kawasaki, "that to fulfill our potential as a global corporation, we have to continually push back frontiers of space" (*The Economist*, 1994, p.8). "For U.S. Corporations" *The Herald Tribune* affirms, "the Modern-Day Byword Is 'Globalize or Die'" (*International Herald Tribune*, 1994, p.15). In 1989 chairman and CEO of General Electric, Jack Welch, talks of the "global moment," of "lightening speed," "fast action," and "acting with speed." "The world moves much faster today" (Tichy and Charan, 1989, p.115). In 1991 President and CEO of Asea Brown Boveri, Percy Barnevik, prompts, "Why emphasize speed over precision? Because the costs of delay exceed the costs of mistakes" (Taylor, 1991, p.104). In 1994, Vice President, Al Gore talks of a "planetary information network that transmits messages and images at the speed of light," allowing "families and friends" to "transcend the barriers of time and distance" (Gore, 1994). In 1995 a special issue of *TIME* on technology and the "global agenda" begins the cover story article with one word, followed by a full stop. The word is "acceleration."

From Mumford's desire to "get somewhere" to cameralism's investment in motion, a deeper history and practical development lies behind this new vernacular of global-neoliberal *dromoscopic-space;* a fact of which even the advertisers seem occasionally aware. Note, for example, the astounding words that accompanied one of the first promotions to use the image of the globe as seen from "deep space:"

> Who can fail to be moved by the photographs of our Earth – this great globe upon whose surface we dwell – taken from outer space? We gaze downward through the lens and from the vehicles of technology, seeing our planet from the perspectives provided by science. Uncounted centuries of thought and work preceded this moment; the contributions of generations went into its preparation.
>
> (*Harvard Business Review*, 1969, p.17)

A similar point was made more recently in the equally astonishing words of a promotion for Daimler Benz published widely during 1995. Under a double-page spread of the "NASA earthrise," and the subtitle "Progress is the realization of utopia," the dialogue ran,

> Making dreams come true is both a poetic and an accurate definition of progress. Consider man's ancient dream of "automotion," fulfilled at last by the automobile a century ago. But mankind's dreams have always refused to remain earthbound. They have enabled him to soar like a bird, to explore distant planets. And today, science continues to uncover new mysteries and realize ever bolder dreams . . .
>
> (Daimler Benz marketing, 1996)

Automotion fulfills history in the liberation of man from the Earth! Who can fail to be moved by the visuality of the technical result? Clearly the image of the globe is itself essential, now almost obligatory, in the "image bank" of every major corporation. We have the power, it says, to go beyond the critical threshold of orbital speed (the "speed of liberation," "escape velocity"), and in doing so not only separate our existence from the Earth, but destroy in one movement the expanse of the planet. Once even the most seasoned philosophers dared not estimate the size of our Earth. It seemed infinite, immeasurable. But in the middle of this century, we escaped all that, so that now we find – whether we like it or not (and we usually do) – just how small our terrestrial habitat really is. In the words of Buzz Aldrin, "The Earth would eventually be so small I could blot it out of the universe simply by holding up my thumb" (Aldrin, in Kelley, 1988, plate 37).

We should ask questions about this disappearance of geometrical space. We might ask whether communications have not long prepared us for this moment where the necessity of immediacy takes its place as the technical achievement of a political governance in which the absence of distance, of space and expanse serves *specifically* to establish and maintain the equivalence between motion and good order. Are not our discourses of globalism the contemporary monologue of reason that have concealed the political history of the movement of bodies and the extortion of their productive forces? Is not that single snapshot – the NASA Earth – the visual representation of the final stages of the governmentalization of the state and our systems of politics, as globalism, motion and tranquillity become synonymous? Even if we're shy about asking such questions, one can surely see that the implications of the discourses, practices and aesthetics of contemporary political reason have been immense.

Perhaps most conspicuous has been the historical reversal of "motivational crises" (Habermas, 1975), achieved through an intensification of general anxiety about immediacy and the distortion of distance. The specter of "global competition" ("Work smarter, not just harder"[12]), "risk society," the "fear of unemployment," subcontracting, outsourcing and "just-in-time" production; all have collided in the discourses and practices of neo-liberal globalization. The result has not only been an enormous injection of energy into the process of capital accumulation, pulling the failing welfare economies of 1970s into the age of hyper-efficiency. Along with the trajectory we find a wholesale transformation of our perceptions of reality, both in a negative sense of what is disavowed ("There is no alternative," "You have no choice," there is "no place to hide"[13]), and the positive sense of what becomes necessary ("Create a sense of urgency," "involve everyone in everything," establish "friction-free capitalism").[14]

The distant echo of those technicians of government who dreamt of the assembly of men and things in dynamic repose becomes an uproar in every global city, and all their peripheries. "*Activité, activité, vitesse*" – Napoleon's watchword[15] – has indeed become the law of our own world. "Man," write Peters and Waterman (1982), "is waiting for motivation." The long and steady disappearance of the visible markers of the state serves well to conceal the politics behind the decentralization, diffusion and mobilization of the populace as a whole. Yet in the eyes of our favored detectives (Cerny, Strange, Ohmae, etc.), authority is nothing if not holistic, defined negatively against all other constituencies. A naivety that is politically dangerous. All government is equated with negative power (the power to restrict, to confine, to separate and beat-down). It is this presupposition that helps validate globalism as something in which individuals should invest faith. Yet in failing to consider either the history or consequences of the outward deterritorialization it effects, commentators have surely succumbed to the illusion no doubt marked out for them in advance, in order to conceal the real nature of what is at stake; the substitution of governance for government, automatism for autonomy, immediacy for history, dromocracy for democracy.[16]

Rethinking globalization *as* governance

That innovations in political technology were essential to the development of political economy was one of Michel Foucault's lasting contributions to critical politics. As he himself described,

> bio-power was without question an indispensable element in the develop-ment of capitalism; the latter would not have been possible without the controlled insertion of bodies into the machinery of production and the adjustment of the phenomena of population to economic processes . . . it had to have methods of power capable of optimizing forces, aptitudes, and life in general without at the same time making them more difficult to govern.
>
> (Foucault, 1979, p.141)

All of this, for Foucault, was something more than the rise of an ascetic ideal. What occurred in the eighteenth century, "was nothing less than the entry of life into history, that is, the entry of phenomena peculiar to the life of the human species into the order of knowledge and power, into the sphere of political techniques . . ." (Foucault, 1979, pp.141–2).

Why is it that our contemporary commentators believe that this history of political intervention has suddenly "evaporated"?

The reason, as we have seen, is their failure to think deeply about govern-ance and the power to govern. Contemporary transformations, for these commentators, are indicative of (and follow from) a generalized shift in the locus of command from the state to the people. Understood as such it would be misguided to view the consequences of such changes as anything other than, on the one hand, the accidental outcome of technological and market forces, or on the other, as the logic of these forces played out (trans-historically) over the *longue durée*. Yet as we have seen, such a view cannot survive even a cursory reading of the genealogy of governance. Al Gore is indeed right to point out, "Governments didn't do this. People did." But this says nothing about the decline of authority, for as we have seen, this authority, at least from the eighteenth century onward *specifically targeted individuals to become the vectors of their own processes of transformation*. The technology of self-constitution, that Foucault in *Discipline and Punish* described as "panopti-cism," runs hand-in-hand with the ascendance of liberal freedom. As Foucault would describe, "The Enlightenment which discovered the liberties, also invented the disciplines" (Foucault, 1977, p.222). In this light – of the development of mechanics of self-constitution, subjectification, the passing of the command structure into the minds of individuals (what I have referred to in the essay as "governance') – the state cannot be defined merely as the institutions of government. Governance is in that sense a broader phenom-enon; precisely the "efforts to organize life on the planet" that so concerns the Commission on Global Governance.

The question of "authority" then, can only be viewed in its historical setting and against its developmental transformations. That genealogy reveals that for 300 years at least the implicit objective of political reason has been to pass the responsibilities of government onto the shoulders of individuals. Formulated best in the words of von Justi, modern political reason was to be, "concerned chiefly with the conduct and sustenance of the subjects, and its great purpose is to put both in such equilibrium and correlation that the subjects of the republic will be useful, and in a position easily to support themselves." (Justi, quoted in Small, 1909, p.328). The contemporary dissolution of the face of government (institutional fragmentation, dispersion of state authority, diminishing policy autonomy, and so on), says nothing of this longer history of diffusion that lies at the heart of the modern rational order imagined in the classical age. As Paul Virilio has described, the age of visibility (institutions, governments) gives way to the age of disappearance (networks, dispersions), but not as reduction in power. Just as the replacement of the scaffold by the prison was, "not to punish less, but to punish better . . . to insert the power to punish more deeply into the social body" (Foucault, 1977, p.82), so the disappearance of the state has run parallel with the ascendance of new modalities of governance based on the positive constitution of individuals themselves (globalism, competitiveness, self-motivation, rapidity, agility, responsiveness, proactivity, etc.).

Ironically we can agree – in part – with the assessment of Strange, Cerny, Ohmae and others. The state *is* increasingly hollow! What they have failed to consider, however, is the historical reason why it is so. Having considered some of these reasons here (the birth of bio-power made necessary by the birth of the commercial economy and the emergence of populations as a statistical problem) I dispute that our contemporary epoch is a "return to medievalism" (cf. Kobrin's chapter in this volume). What we are witnessing at the level of institutions is simply the replicant process of deterritorialization effected first at the level of individuals during course of the transition from the classical to the modern epoch whereby sovereign power was supplanted by bio-power. As Foucault described, "we should not be deceived by all the Constitutions framed throughout the world since the French Revolution, the Codes written and revised, a whole continual and clamorous legislative activity: these were the forms that made an essentially normalizing power acceptable" (Foucault, 1979, p.144). Perhaps we can now add that our notions of "sovereignty" and "territoriality" have similarly obscured the fate of the state, progressively *emptying itself out* in its own bio-political mutation.

I suggest, then, that the birth of bio-power at the level of subjectivity is the rightful precursor of the globalization of the state. From the point at which this transition took place (with the emergence of the notion of reason of state, police science and the question of "government") this endpoint was established as the logic of political reason. The governmentalization of the state is indeed the globalization of the state. The neomedieval metaphor, in

mistaking this deterritorialization for a "return" to anarchical disorganization, merely obscures further the relations of power that first "discovered
society" (Polanyi, 1957) as the true site of modern governance, followed by
"global society" as the object of *global governance*.

For those that would maintain that this discovery of (global) society signals
the decline in state power, let us remember that Bodin's notion of
"sovereignty" was not first and foremost one of territory, but one of the
supreme power of the state over its subjects ('unique and absolved from the
laws'). As Meinecke describes, "Bodin did not distinguish the question of
what is the supreme authority *within* the State from the question of what is
the supreme authority *of* the State" (Meinecke, 1957, p.57). That said, for
Bodin the reforms of the cameral thinkers and *philosophes* of the Enlightenment
(the birth of active society) would have been unthinkable. The very idea of
participatory "civil society" was, for him, abhorrent. Yet again, we must
return to the notion of bio-power, and note that the birth of active society –
called forth in the writings of the first technicians of the modern state – was
conceived in its origin in terms of the "strength of the state," both commer-
cially and governmentally. In that sense Bodin and the scientists of police
and modern governance would surely have agreed on the basic premise that
underpins each of their actions; the pursuit of public security (*salus populi*)
and the productive society.[17] As Friedrich Meinecke might say, "The difference between the two lay only in the means, not the ends" (Meinecke, 1957,
p.214).[18]

Conceiving "governance" as "diffusion," and diffusion as "civic security,"
one can see that globalization actually *extends*, rather than fragments, state-
ordered power. This form of "government" cannot be reduced instrumen-
tally to the actions of institutions. As Colin Gordon suggests, "the state has
no essence" (Gordon, 1991, p.4). Authority, then – at least over the modern
period – has to be traced *beyond the state*, into the "positive unconscious" and
codes of a culture, "its schemas of perception, its exchanges, its techniques,
its values, the hierarchy of its practices . . . the *space* of knowledge" (Foucault,
1970, pp. xx–xxii). "The question of power," Foucault reflects,

> is greatly impoverished if posed solely in terms of legislation, or the consti-
> tution, or the state, the state apparatus. Power is much more com-
> plicated, much more dense and diffuse than a set of laws or a state
> apparatus. One cannot understand the development of the productive
> forces of capitalism, nor even conceive of their technological develop-
> ment, if the apparatuses of power are not taken into consideration.
>
> (Foucault, 1996, p.235)

In setting up a simple distinction between diffusion (anarchy) and centralization (authority), Strange, Cerny, Ohmae and others simply misread the
history of the modern state, and the genealogy of modern power.

"Until the last few years" writes Cerny, "the long-term development of the 'modern' world order has been characterized by a process of *centralization* and *hierachization* of power" (cf. Cerny's chapter in this volume). The reverse is the case. The modern world order has been characterized over the long term by a political project of *decentralization* and *diffusion*. In highlighting this process as it reaches its final threshold, Cerny actually ends up diverting attention from its own logic, which indeed we are beginning to witness now. This is the reversal now effecting itself at the level of individuals, where this whole technology of power was born. Now, we witness not so much a diffusion and deterritorialization (this has already been achieved). Rather, as Virilio is beginning to describe, we witness a deeper, true centralization and hierachization. The former is effected in the homogenization of whole societies caught up in the necessities of global competitiveness, and "global time" (as well as the imposition of a kind of physical incarceration now that everything arrives without us having to leave). The latter is effected in the very structure of global governance that has emerged to replace the territorial nation-state; the dromological order where the fastest win and the slowest lose, effecting a new and more violent hierarchization of the world.

The pathology of global governance

The final question that a political reading would raise, if only to leave hanging, is the value of global governance in itself. As the history that I have attempted to sketch attests, the development of systems of governance is hardly a neutral process. Any discussion, therefore, of global governance has to confront the question; "to what problem is global governance the solution?" It is that question that makes necessary the opening out of the field of discussion into the interrogation of our deepest presuppositions on the value and politics of governing the relations of men and things. "Imagine *order*" wrote Robert Musil,

> Or, rather, imagine first of all a great idea, and then one still greater, then another still greater than that, and so on, always greater and greater. And then on the same pattern imagine always more order and more order in your own head . . . just imagine a complete and universal order embracing all humanity, in a word, a state of perfect civilian order.

> Take my word for it, it's sheer entropy, *rigor mortis,* a landscape on the moon, a geometrical plague.
>
> (Musil, 1954, pp.197–8)

Our greatest danger might be to underestimate the extent to which order – perhaps entropy – is served by the deterritorialization of the state. This decentralization was imagined first by an ensemble of thinkers who referred to their own work as the "theory of police."

But Musil's words raise the final question, unanswerable here; what are the consequences of universal governance? The works of Paul Virilio – in shifting our attention from the organization of space to the constitution of time – stand, I suggest, as documents charting exactly that universalization of order over the modern period as a whole. Foucault can also act as a reference, in his studies of the internalization of command that goes hand-in-hand with the governmentalization of the state. In each we find a body of work that can be turned profitably to comment on the politics of globalization, and not only that, but a political comment on the nature of governance, that in our current discussions we'd do well to remember. Perhaps it is time, in the words of Gayatri Spivak (1990, p.30), that "the Western theoretical establishment take a moratorium on producing a global solution," if not out of modesty, then the hope of recapturing life's authenticity. We must keep open the debate on globalization and governance.

Notes

* Thanks to Julie Murphy Erfani and Brook Blair for comments and inspiration, and to the editors for including my voice in the dialogue.

1 cf., Hacking (1990).
2 The publication of Giovanni Botero's *The Greatness of Cities* (1588), and *The Reason of State* (1589) are usually taken as a threshold, though he himself emerged in a wider context (e.g., Rosello, Piccolomini, Paschalius and Segni), cf., Viroli (1992) and Tuck (1993).
3 cf., Small (1909), Parry (1963), Johnson (1964), Raeff (1975), Knemeyer (1980), Tribe (1984), Pasquino (1991), and Oestreich (1984).
4 Sawday even goes so far as to suggest that the move from sovereign to republican notions of governance might find their origin in this reformulation of knowledge of the body. In the broader project upon which this chapter draws I investigate corresponding transformations with the emergence of "kinesthetics" and the sciences of human physiology and motion in the mid nineteenth century, and notions of information processing in the mid to late twentieth century. On the correspondence between metaphors of the body and those of the body-politic, cf., Marcovich (1982).
5 cf., Paret (1986), pp.32–213.
6 For detailed historical discussion cf., Crawley (1965), Ward, *et al.* (1909), and Durant and Durant (1963, 1975).
7 Michel Serres (1975) argues a similar point in analyzing the transition from the "clockwork age" to the "motor age," cf., Alborn (1994), Virilio (1986, 1991b, 1995a).
8 From the Greek *dromos*, "the path."
9 In the words of Botero (1956, p.102), "Cities full of tradesmen and craftsmen and merchants love peace and tranquillity."
10 RAC marketing, 1997. The RAC's main theme, "Welcome to the future in motion," sits well with a range of "space/time" marketing campaigns of recent years, from Microsoft's "Where do you want to go today?" to British Airways' "The world is closer than you think."
11 Virilio (1997), p.19.
12 British Telecommunications Ltd marketing, 1995–6.

13 Peters (1987), p.189, Wriston (1988), p.71.
14 Peters (1987), pp.471–7.
15 Durant and Durant (1975), p.248.
16 Virilio (1986), p.46.
17 Saint-Simon is a typical figure; entirely opposed to the overbearing absolutism of the classical age, yet crucially linked to it in his conviction that "industry" (broadly defined) was the best way to ensure individual and civic security, cf., Krygier (1979), pp.34–44.
18 The point is surely reinforced when one notes that the discussion from which this quotation is lifted is one in which Meinecke is comparing the Hobbesian "Leviathan" with the "Nightwatchman State" of liberal rationalism.

References

Alborn, Timothy L. (1994) "Economic man, economic machine: images of circulation in the Victorian money market," in Philip Mirowski (ed.) *Natural Images in Economic Thought: "Markets read in tooth and claw"*, Cambridge: Cambridge University Press, pp.173–96.

Bergius, Johann Heinrich Ludwig (1767–74) *Policey- und Cameral-Magazin*, Frankfurt.

Blair, Brook M. (1996) "Knowledge, Power and the Modern State: Towards a Genealogy of Universal Productionist Order, 1500–1815," Ph.D. Dissertation, University of Newcastle.

Botero, Giovanni (1589) *The Reason of State*, London: Routledge and Kegan Paul, 1956.

Cable, Vincent (1995) "The Diminished Nation-State: A Study in the Loss of Economic Power," *Dædalus: Journal of the American Academy of Arts* 124(2), pp.23–53.

Cerny, Philip G. (1996a) "What Next for the State?" in Eleonore Kofman and Gillian Youngs (eds) *Globalization: Theory and Practice*, London: Pinter.

Cerny, Philip G. (1996b) Book review article, *Millennium: Journal of International Studies,* 25(3), pp. 736–8.

Clausewitz, Carl von (1968) *On War*, London: Penguin.

Commission on Global Governance (1995) *Our Global Neighbourhood*, Oxford: Oxford University Press.

Crawley, C.W. (ed.) (1965) *The New Cambridge Modern History, Volume IX, War and Peace in an Age of Upheaval*, Cambridge: Cambridge University Press.

Dale, Reginald (1995) "Toward the Millennium: the economic revolution has begun," Special Report: Global Agenda, *TIME, International,* March 13, pp.44–8.

Darjes, Joachim Georg (1749) *Institutiones juriprudentiae privatae romano-germanicae*, Lenae.

Darjes, Joachim Georg (1756) *Erste Gründe der Cameral-Wissenschaften*, Jena.

Darjes, Joachim Georg (1776) *Institutiones juriprudentiae universalis*, Lenae.

Dithmar, Justus Christoph (1731) *Oeconomie, Polizei- und Cameral-Wissenchaft*, Frankfurt.

Dorn, Walter L. (1931) "The Prussian Bureaucracy in the Eighteenth Century," *Political Science Quarterly* XLVI(3), pp.403–23.

Durant, Will and Durant, Ariel (1963) *The Age of Louis XIV*, New York: MJF.

Durant, Will and Durant, Ariel (1975) *The Age of Napoleon*, New York: MJF.

The Economist (1994) "Japan Survey," supplement, 9–15 July.

Foucault, Michel (1967) *Madness and Civilization: A History of Insanity in the Age of Reason,* London: Tavistock.

Foucault, Michel (1970) *The Order of Things: An Archaeology of the Human Sciences,* London: Tavistock.

Foucault, Michel (1973) *The Birth of the Clinic: An Archaeology of Medical Perception,* London: Tavistock.

Foucault, Michel (1977) *Discipline and Punish: The Birth of the Prison,* London: Allen Lane.

Foucault, Michel (1979) *The History of Sexuality, Volume 1: An Introduction,* London: Allen Lane.

Foucault, Michel (1980) *Power/Knowledge: Selected Interviews and Other Writings, 1972–1977,* London: Harvester Wheatsheaf.

Foucault, Michel (1981) "Omnes et Singulation: Towards a Criticism of 'Political Reason,'" in Sterling M. McMurrin, ed., *The Tanner Lectures on Human Values,* vol. 2, Salt Lake City, UT: University of Utah Press.

Foucault, Michel (1988) "The Political Technology of Individuals," in Luther H. Martin, Huck Gutman and Patrick H. Hutton (eds), *Technologies of the Self: A Seminar with Michel Foucault,* London, Tavistock.

Foucault, Michel (1989) *Résumé des cours, 1970–1982,* Paris: Juillard.

Foucault, Michel (1991) "Governmentality," in Graham Burchell, Colin Gordon and Peter Miller (eds), *The Foucault Effect: Studies in Governmentality,* London: Harvester Wheatsheaf, pp.87–104.

Foucault, Michel (1996) *Foucault Live,* New York: Semiotext(e).

Gates, Bill (1995) *The Road Ahead,* London: Viking.

Gordon, Colin (1991) "Governmental Rationality: An Introduction," in Graham Burchell, Colin Gordon and Peter Miller, eds, *The Foucault Effect: Studies in Governmentality,* London: Harvester Wheatsheaf, pp. 1–51.

Gore, Al (1994) speech to the International Telecommunications Union, March 21, http://www.freedonia.com/ctheory/

Habermas, Jürgen (1975) *Legitimation Crisis,* Boston: Beacon Press.

Hacking, Ian (1990) *The Taming of Chance,* Cambridge: Cambridge University Press.

Harvard Business Review (1969) July–August, p.17.

Harvey, William (1628) *De Motu Cordis,* Frankfurt.

Heidegger, Martin (1991) *Nietzsche, Volume III,* London: HarperCollins.

Heidegger, Martin (1993) "'Only a God Can Save Us': *Der Spiegel's* Interview with Martin Heidegger," in Richard Wolin (ed.) *The Heidegger Controversy: A Critical Reader,* Cambridge, MA: MIT Press, pp.91–116.

Holstein, William J. (1990) "The Stateless Corporation," *Business Week* May 14, pp.98–100.

Horsman, Mathew and Marshall, Andrew (1994) *After the Nation State: Citizens, Tribalism and the New World Disorder,* London: HarperCollins.

Huizinga, Johan (1927) *The Waning of the Middle Ages,* London: Edward Arnold.

International Herald Tribune (1994), September 3–4, p.15.

Johnson, Hubert C. (1964) "The Concept of Bureaucracy in Cameralism," *Political Science Quarterly* 79, 3: 378–402.

Justi, Johann Heinrich Gottlob von (1755) *Staatswirthschaft,* Leipzig.

Justi, Johann Heinrich Gottlob von (1760) *Moralische und philosophische,* Stettin and Leipzig.

Justi, Johann Heinrich Gottlob von (1769) *Elémens généraux de Police, traduits de l'Allemand*, Paris.

Kelley, Kevin W. (1988) *The Home Planet*, New York: Addison-Wesley.

Kirwin, Peter (1995) "Don't Believe the Hype," *Business Age* 63, December, p 7.

Knemeyer, Franz-Ludwig (1980) "Polizei," *Economy and Society* 9(2) pp.172–96.

Krygier, Martin (1979) "Saint-Simon, Marx and the non-governed society," in Eugene Kamenka and Martin Krygier (eds), *Bureaucracy: the Career of a Concept*, London: Edward Arnold.

La Mettrie, Julien Offray de (1912) *Man a Machine*, Illinois: Open Court.

Levitt, Theodore (1983) "The Globalization of Markets," *Harvard Business Review* 61(3) pp.92–102.

Marcovich, A. (1982) "Concerning the Continuity between the Image of Society and the Image of the Human Body: An Examination of the Work of the English Physician J.C. Lettsom (1746–1815)," in P. Wright and A. Treacher (eds), *The Problem of Medical Knowledge*, Edinburgh: Edinburgh University Press, pp.69–87.

Marshall, Andrew (1995) "Global village rivals the power of the state," *The Independent*, February 27, p.9.

Marsland, David (1995) *Self-Reliance: Reforming Welfare in Advanced Societies*, London: Transaction.

Meinecke, Friedrich (1957) *Machiavellianism: The Doctrine of Raison d'État and Its Place in Modern History*, London: Routledge and Kegan Paul.

Moser, Johann Jacob (1758) *Bibliothec von Oeconomischen-Cameral-Polizey-Handlungs*, Ulm.

Mueller, Johann Nicolaus (1790) *Practisches Lehrbuch ber die Privat- und Cameral-Staatsrechnungen*, Göttingen.

Mumford, Lewis (1934) *Technics and Civilization*, New York: Harcourt Brace.

Mumford, Lewis (1961) *The City in History: Its Origins, Its Transformations and Its Prospects*, New York: Harcourt Brace.

Musil, Robert (1954) *The Man Without Qualities*, Vol. 2, London: Secker and Warburg.

Napoleon I, with the Conseil d'état (c.1960) *Code Napoléon, or The French Civil Code*, Baton Rouge: Claitor's Books.

Oestreich, Gerhard (1984) *Neostoicism and the Early Modern State*, Cambridge: Cambridge University Press.

Ohmae, Kenichi (1993) "The Rise of the Region State," *Foreign Affairs* 72(2), p.78–87.

Ohmae, Kenichi (1995) "Putting Global Logic First" *Harvard Business Review* 73(1), pp.119–22.

Ohmae, Kenichi (1996) *The End of the Nation State: The Rise of Regional Economies*, London: HarperCollins.

Paret, Peter (ed.) (1986) *Makers of Modern Strategy: from Machiavelli to the Nuclear Age*, Princeton, NJ: Princeton University Press.

Parry, Geraint (1963) "Enlightened Government and its Critics in Eighteenth-Century Germany," *Historical Journal* VI(2) pp.178–92.

Pasquino, Pasquale (1991) "Theatrum politicum: The genealogy of capital-police and the state of prosperity," in Burchell, *et al.* (eds), *The Foucault Effect: Studies in Governmentality*, London: Harvester Wheatsheaf, pp.105–18.

Peters, Tom (1987) *Thriving on Chaos: Handbook for a Management Revolution*, London: Pan.

Peters, Thomas J. (1992) *Liberation Management: necessary disorganization for the nanosecond nineties*, London: Macmillan.

Peters, Thomas J. and Waterman, Robert H. (1982) *In Search of Excellence: Lessons from America's Best-Run Companies*, London: Harper and Row.

Polanyi, Karl (1957), *The Great Transformation*, Boston, MA: Beacon Press.

Raeff, Marc (1975) "The Well-Ordered Police State and the Development of Modernity in Seventeenth- and Eighteenth-Century Europe: An Attempt at a Comparative Approach," *The American Historical Review*, 80(2), pp.1221–43.

Reich, Robert (1991) "Who is Them?" *Harvard Business Review* 69(2) pp.77–88.

Reiss, Timothy J. (1997) *Knowledge, Discovery and Imagination in Early Modern Europe: The Rise of Aesthetic Rationalism*, Cambridge: Cambridge University Press.

Riddell, Peter (1995) "Leaders in Cloud Cuckoo Land," *The Times* August 28, p.14.

Sawday, Jonathan (1995) *The Body Emblazoned: Dissection and the Human Body in Renaissance Culture*, London: Routledge.

Seckendorff, Viet Ludwig von (1656) *Teutscher Fürsten Stat*, Hanaw.

Sennett, Richard (1994) *Flesh and Stone: The Body and the City in Western Civilization*, London: Faber and Faber.

Serres, Michel (1975) "It Was before the (World) Exhibition," in Jean Clair and Harold Szeeman (eds), *Junggesellenmaschinen; les machines celibataires*, Venice: Alfieri.

Small, Albion M. (1909) *The Cameralists: The Pioneers of German Social Polity*, Chicago: University of Chicago Press.

Spivak, Gayatri Chakravorty (1990) *The Post-colonial Critic: Interviews, Strategies, Dialogues*, London: Routledge.

Strange, Susan (1994) "Wake up, Krasner! The world *has* changed," *Review of International Political Economy* 1(2), pp.209–12.

Strange, Susan (1995) "The Defective State," *Dædalus: Journal of the American Academy of Arts* 124(2), pp.55–74.

Strange, Susan (1996) *The Retreat of the State: The Diffusion of Power in the World Economy*, Cambridge: Cambridge University Press.

Taylor, William (1991) "The Logic of Global Business: An Interview with ABB's Percy Barnevik," *Harvard Business Review* 69(2), pp.90–105.

Tichy, Noel and Charan, Ram (1989) "Speed, Simplicity, Self-Confidence: An Interview with Jack Welch," *Harvard Business Review*, 67(5), pp.112–20.

Tribe, Keith (1984) "Cameralism and the Science of Government," *Journal of Modern History*, 56(2), pp.263–84.

Tuck, Richard (1993) *Philosophy and Government, 1572–1651*, Cambridge: Cambridge University Press.

Virilio, Paul (1986) *Speed and Politics: An Essay on Dromology*, New York: Semiotext(e).

Virilio, Paul (1991a) *The Aesthetics of Disappearance*, New York: Semiotext(e).

Virilio, Paul (1991b) *The Lost Dimension*, New York: Semiotext(e).

Virilio, Paul (1995a) *The Art of the Motor*, Minneapolis: University of Minnesota Press.

Virilio, Paul (1995b) "Red Alert in Cyberspace!" *Radical Philosophy*, 74, pp.2–4.

Virilio, Paul (1995c) "Paul Virilio," in Florian Rötzer (ed.), *Conversations with French Philosophers*, New Jersey: Humanities Press.

Virilio, Paul (1997) *Open Sky*, London: Verso.

Virilio, Paul and Lotringer, Sylvère (1983) *Pure War*, New York: Semiotext(e).

Viroli, Maurizio (1992) *From Politics to Reason of State: The Acquisition and Transformation of the Language of Politics, 1250–1600*, Cambridge: Cambridge University Press.

Ward, A.W., Prothers, G.W. and Leathers, Stanley (eds) (1909) *The Cambridge Modern History, Vol IX: Napoleon*, Cambridge: Cambridge University Press.

Waterman, Robert (1994) *Frontiers of Excellence: the journey towards success in the 21st century*, London: Allen and Unwin.

Willis, Thomas (1684) *Two Discourses Concerning the Souls of Brutes*, London.

Wolff, Christian (1719) *Vernünfftige Gedanken von der Kräften des menschlichen Verstandes und ihrem richtigen Gebrauche in Erkenntnis der Wahrheit*, Halle.

Wriston, Walter (1988) "Technology and Sovereignty," *Foreign Affairs* 67(2), pp.63–75.

Zinke, Georg Heinrich (1751) *Cameralisten-Bibliothek*, Leipzig.

Part II

Impact of globalization on the Westphalian state

This section provides a conceptual discussion on the impact of globalization (independent variable) on country-level governance. As suggested in the introductory chapter, there is debate on this subject and three categories of scenarios are outlined: the end of the Westphalian state (Stephen Kobrin); the resilient state (Robert Kudrle); and the re-articulated state (Philip Cerny).

The Peace of Westphalia in 1648 is generally considered to have laid the foundations for the modern state-system in Europe. Though this system has continued through numerous upheavals over the last three centuries, the question remains as to whether it will survive the challenges posed by economic globalization. Stephen Kobrin, in his contribution to this volume, does not think so. For him, the modern era is an anomaly. Even though political-economic control based on territoriality has been the norm since 1648, it was not always so. According to Kobrin, medieval Europe may be a better metaphor for the world economy of the next century than the Westphalian system. He identifies four aspects of the medieval world that may apply to the emerging world order: (1) the geography was ambiguous and borders were unstable and ill defined – borders represented a projection of political power on geography; (2) multiple loyalties and allegiances were the norm rather than the exception; (3) elites were cosmopolitan and not tied in their loyalties to a particular territory; and (4) there was a longing for a restoration of the order that was Rome.

Kobrin predicts that the world economy of the twenty-first century will be characterized by technologies whose scale economies require global markets and the replacement of large,vertically integrated multinational firms by intercorporate alliances integrated through information technology. As a result, post-Westphalian governance structures will reflect permeable borders, multiple and perhaps conflicting allegiances, and coexisting levels of authority – transnational, national and sub-national. It will be a relationally rather than a hierarchically structured world in which the meaning of internal and external sovereignty becomes increasingly ambiguous. Kobrin concedes that the medieval analogy has its limits: a new Rome, a supra-national authority is not likely. However, the problems posed by jurisdictional ambiguity and multiple authorities might be dealt with through some combination of harmonizing national legislations on core issues and strengthening international institutions such as the World Trade Organization. Kobrin speculates that a belief in a liberal and democratic world order may serve as the twenty-first century analog of medieval Christendom to provide normative cohesion in the system.

Will the hegemony of the Westphalian state disappear and the Westphalian state become just one of many levels of governance? Philip Cerny predicts in his chapter for this volume that governance will increasingly become functionally and hierarchically differentiated, and as a result, a single level structural hegemony – statism, regionalism, or multilateralism – will not prevail. He draws upon Durkheimian sociological theory that posits that societies advance by becoming more structurally complex; that is, through increasing structural differentiation. This is in contrast to the standard neorealist version of international relations theory where the international system is modeled as a simple structure composed of like units; though differentiated in terms of size or internal institutions, they respond in similar ways to the same stimulus. Such like units are capable of only "mechanical solidarity," not "organic solidarity" which is rooted in cross-cutting division of labor.

Cerny predicts that by encouraging such cross-cutting division of labor, the processes of globalization will lead to structural differentiation both within and outside national boundaries. How would such processes encourage structural differentiation? Cerny first discusses efficiency-based explanations that argue that the Westphalian state is no longer the most efficient unit of aggregation for supplying various collective goods. Inherent in this argument is the notion that the state is an agency for supplying collective goods. Drawing upon Lowi's typology, Cerny identifies four categories of collective goods: regulatory, productive, distributive, and redistributive. He notes that the conditions of supply for each of these would be influenced by the politics as well as the economics of structural changes that are associated with globalization.

Both Kobrin and Cerny suggest that the era of the unquestioned power of the Westphalian state is over. However, they have different predictions about what the new governance systems will look like. It is now commonly asserted that even if the Westphalian state does not wither away in the physical sense, it will be rendered ineffective in enforcing many of its policies within its territory. Robert Kudrle examines the assertion that economic integration has narrowed the scope of effective policy instruments that states can employ to advance the welfare of their citizens. Kudrle debunks four common misperceptions: "reinventing government" can be attributed to globalization, devolution (similar to Cerny's notion of structural differentiation) is a manifestation of globalization, after-tax income inequality in industrialized countries has increased due to foreign trade, and deregulation has been forced by globalization. His conclusion is that most of the challenges associated with globalization admit to effective responses at the national level. And those that cannot be handled at the national level can often be dealt with by cross-national policy harmonization.

Kudrle focuses on three policy domains: trade, capital, and immigration flows. He suggests that globalization is not the cause of many of the domestic problems sometimes attributed to it. He agrees with Krugman that increases in global trade are not the main culprit in increasing inequalities or the shrinking size of middle income groups in industrialized countries. Rather, two more important causal variables are trends in domestic productivity and increases in demand for skilled labor relative to that of unskilled labor.

By carefully analyzing the factors that influence capital mobility, Kudrle questions the assertion that the increased mobility of capital has made redistributive taxation infeasible. He notes that "if fiscal degradation to attract capital is taking place, it certainly has a long way to go" since the levels of taxation on capital in the US, Europe, and Japan range between 50 to 60 per cent. Regarding mobility of labor, he argues that governments have in fact been fairly successful in discouraging certain kinds of immigration (as in the US), if not discouraging immigration all together (as in Europe and Japan), and encouraging emigration of skilled manpower. Further, migration to foreign countries in response to lower personal taxes has also not taken place on any significant scale. Clearly, the Tiebout hypothesis which suggests that citizens "vote with their feet," perhaps valid in the intra-US context, lacks empirical support when scaled up to the inter-country level. This again demonstrates that governments retain the ability to employ tax policy for redistributive purposes. Finally, Kudrle suggests that the political right as well as the political left have vested interests in perpetuating myths about globalization and the obsolescence of the state.

6 Back to the future

Neomedievalism and the postmodern digital world economy*

Stephen J. Kobrin

We are entering a period of turbulent, systemic change in the organization of the world economic and political order – a period comparable to the transition from the feudal to the modern era in the sixteenth and seventeenth centuries. As Hobsbawm (1990: 174) observes, the late twentieth century world economy appears temporally confused, involving a "curious combination of the technology of the late twentieth century, the free trade of the nineteenth, and the rebirth of the sort of interstitial centres characteristic of world trade in the Middle Ages."

In this volume globalization is defined generally as a set of processes leading to the integration of economic activity in factor, intermediate, and final goods and services markets across geographical boundaries, and the increased salience of cross-border value chains in international economic flows. More specifically, I argue that globalization entails two interrelated, technologically driven phenomena.

First, dramatic increases in the cost, risk and complexity of technology in many industries render even the largest national markets too small to serve as meaningful economic units. Second, and more important here, the emerging global world economy is electronic, integrated through information systems and technology rather than organizational hierarchies. Globalization represents a systemic transformation of the world economy that will result in new structures and new modes of functioning (Kobrin 1997).

We are in the midst of what Cerney (1995: 607 and his chapter in this book) and others have called the third industrial revolution, "characterized by the intensive application of information and communications technology, flexible production systems and organizational structures, market segmentation, and globalization." The digital revolution has "dematerialized" manufacturing and commerce; all firms, regardless of sector, have become information processors.[1]

One result of the information revolution is the "deintegration" of the large, vertically integrated "Fordist" firms which organize a significant portion of international economic transactions within their administrative hierarchies (Parker 1992). In their place, a complex system of networks and alliances is emerging in which information technology facilitates the integration and coordination of geographically dispersed operations. An international system of production is being replaced by a complex web of interlaced global electronic networks (Dicken 1994).

The scale and complexity of technology and the emergence of electronically integrated global networks render geographic borders and, more fundamentally, the basic construct of territorial sovereignty problematic. A critical issue raised by globalization is the lack of meaning of geographically rooted jurisdiction when markets are constructed in electronic space. There is a basic disconnect between geographic space and cyberspace.

The neomedieval analogy

The Peace of Westphalia (1648) is taken conventionally as marking the end of medieval universalism and the origin of the modern state system. The medieval to modern transition entailed the *territorialization* of politics, the replacement of overlapping, vertical hierarchies by horizontal, geographically defined sovereign states (Anderson 1996; Jarvis and Paloni 1995).

The modern state system is organized in terms of territorial sovereignty: the division of the globe's surface into fixed, mutually exclusive, geographically defined jurisdictions enclosed by discrete and meaningful borders.[2] Nation states and national markets are defined spatially. Geographic jurisdiction implies that each state's law, rules and regulation apply *within* its territory – within the space encompassed by its borders.[3]

As Carr (1964: 229) noted many years ago, it is difficult for contemporaries even to imagine a world in which political power is organized on a basis other than territory. Geographically rooted, sovereign nation states and the international state system, however, are relatively recent creations which comprise but one of a number of historical modes of organizing political activity.[4]

Furthermore, the current state system may well be unique, a product of a very specific historical context. Agnew (1994a: 65) reminds us that "the spatial scope of political organization has not been set for all time in a particular mode. The territorial state is not a sacred unit beyond historical time." Territorial sovereignty is not historically privileged. There have been other bases for the organization of political and economic authority in the past. There may well be in the future.

Yet we tend to view systemic change as evolutionary by making the very modern assumption that time's arrow is unidirectional and that progress is linear. We assume that each era emerges, in turn, from existing political-economic structures and, in some way, moves beyond what existed previously.

It may be more reasonable to look at modern forms of international political and economic organization as a detour rather than an evolutionary step. The modern era may be a window which is about to slam shut. Guehenno (1995: 4), for example, argues that the nation state is an ephemeral political form, "a European exception, a precarious transition between the age of kings and the 'neo-imperial' age." Anderson (1996: 143) characterizes the political progression from pre-modern to modern to postmodern as a "movement from relative to absolute and then back to (new) relative conceptions of space."

It is critically important to note that I use the terms *modern* and *postmodern* in a very limited sense; they describe distinct (at least from a distance) modes of international political organization. By modern, I mean specifically the post-Westphalian era of territorially sovereign, geographically defined sovereign states. Pre-modern refers to prior non-territorial modes of political organization: empire and medieval. Postmodern assumes a transition to a new, yet undefined, mode of political organization not rooted in geography.

It is, of course, impossible and less than desirable to draw a clean line between postmodern political organization and *post-modernism*. While I am not ready to dismiss meta-narratives, fragmentation certainly plays a major role in any discussion of globalization. Appadurai's (1996) reference to an emergent postnational order comprising a devolution from homogeneous to heterogeneous social units would not be out of place here, nor would Harvey's (1990) discussion of Fordism and flexible accumulation. The emergence of an electronically mediated global civil society is both a manifestation of post-modern fragmentation and of postmodern political-economic organization. Nonetheless, the reader should keep in mind that my use of postmodern refers specifically to the emerging mode of political-economic organization resulting from globalization.

The beginning of the sixteenth century is widely identified as the watershed between the medieval and modern eras (North and Thomas 1973: 102). If we are again at a similar watershed, on the cusp of a transition to a post-modern era, what might it look like? If the post-Westphalian era is coming to an end, can we discern the shape and structure of the emerging, global international political-economy?

A closer look at medieval Europe, the "immediate" past, can help us imagine our postmodern global future. In the *Star Wars* trilogy, Darth Vader is clad in the armor of the traditional villain of medieval epics – the Black Knight – and he and Luke Skywalker duel with laser sabers in a fight that, but for the weapons, would be at home in *Henry IV*. Similarly, the costumes in the futuristic *Waterworld* have been described as neomedieval iron and kelp. In politics and economics, as in science fiction movies, it may help to attempt to visualize the unknown future in terms of the known past.

To be clear from the outset, I do not argue that we are about to return to a world of manors and fiefs, of lords and vassals. If the modern era is an anomaly, however, looking back to medieval Europe may help us understand the rough outlines of an emerging postmodern global economy. The neo-medieval metaphor should be seen as an inter-temporal analog of comparative political analysis. It allows us to overcome the inertia imposed by our immersion in the present and think about other possible modes of political and economic organization.

I am certainly not the first to use neomedieval analogies. Almost twenty years ago, Bull (1977: 254) suggested that one alternative to the modern state system might be "a modern and secular equivalent of the kind of universal political organization that existed in Western Christendom in the Middle Ages." Since that time, a number of other authors have looked back to medieval Europe to try to understand change in the international system.

Hirst and Thompson (1995) observe that international politics is again becoming more polycentric and suggest that its complexity will soon rival that of the Middle Ages. Similarly, Lapham (1988), discussing the emergence of a variety of non-national actors in world politics, suggests that "the hier-archies of international capitalism resemble the feudal arrangements under which an Italian noble might swear fealty to a German prince, or a Norman duke declare himself the vassal of an English king." Anderson (1996) uses neomedieval or postmodern conceptions of territoriality to think about the future of the European Union.

Gottlieb (1993) and Maier (1994) are both concerned about conflicts between nation and state and look to earlier times when sovereignty was "divided" and not inherently territorial for possible solutions. Lipschutz (1992) argues for a global civil society which would mirror the pre-Westphalian, trans-European supra-national civil society.

In an interesting paper, Matthew (1995) suggests an analogy between environmentalism in our era and medieval Christianity as a possible universal ideology. More somberly, many observers, including Kaplan (1994), are con-cerned about parallels between the disorder and violence of the early Middle Ages and the breakdown of civil society and rise of crime in much of the Western world, often noting the similarity between modern suburban walled and gated communities and medieval castles and moats.

Most relevant to the present discussion, Hirst and Thompson (1995) argue that the medieval analogy helps us think back to a period before the mono-polization of governance functions by sovereign states, to a world which was not constructed on the basis of territorial sovereignty. Thinking about the Middle Ages, the last pre-modern period, might help us to imagine possibili-ties for a postmodern future.

This chapter explores the following facets of medieval organization and relates them to changes in the current international political economy: space, geography and borders; the ambiguity of authority; multiple loyalties; transnational elites; distinctions between public and private property; and unifying belief systems and supra-national centralization.

Space, geography and borders

Medieval concepts of perspective and viewpoint were not compatible with territoriality as a mode of political organization. Medieval maps reflected scriptural dogma rather than useful images. The wider world was seen through a screen of symbolism: the idea of external space was only very weakly grasped in terms of a mysterious cosmology comprised of heavenly hosts and other figures of myth and imagination (Harvey 1990; Le Goff 1988).

The revival of Ptolemic geography in the mid-fifteenth century and the development of modern maps over the next hundred years were necessary for the *idea* of a modern international system based on mutually exclusive geography and territorial sovereignty even to become possible.[5] The very idea of conquering and controlling external space requires a modern mindset: the ability to see it as something finite, bounded and "capable of domination through human action" (Harvey 1990: 254).

The concept of international affairs is distinctly and uniquely modern, dating from the late eighteenth century; it was not relevant before the emergence of territorially defined nation states and national markets. International transactions *are* cross-border economic and political interactions which assume the existence of clearly defined, delineated and separable domestic markets and polities.

Medieval European borders were diffuse, shifting and permeable; it is anachronistic to see them as modern jurisdictional limits. Strayer (1970: 83) imagines a situation where in a single day, at the end of the thirteenth century, the King of France might have sent letters to the count of Flanders, who was clearly his vassal, to the count of Luxembourg, a prince of the Empire who held a money fief, and to the king of Sicily, who while a ruler of a "sovereign" state, was also a prince of the French royal house.

In that context, political power and authority could not be based on mutually exclusive geography. Territory was a temporally variable projection of medieval political power rather than its source. As Teschke (1998) notes, territory could be outside of the sovereign's reach yet neither an enclave nor part of a third state; feudal territory should be seen in terms of concentric circles of power projection. Fluctuating frontier zones and overlapping authorities made it difficult to establish precise boundaries.

Given the very complex overlapping systems of authority and the absence of states and fixed boundaries in the pre-modern European world, it was far from clear who was actually independent and what "foreign" really meant as a political construct. In medieval Europe, the difference between domestic and international politics had little or no meaning; it was almost impossible to distinguish between internal and external affairs (Strayer 1970; Krasner 1993).

In contrast, modernity can be seen as built on the notion of the state as a means of organizing and defining political space.

> It is the sovereign state that lays claim to define the boundaries of the political. States partition the global political space into separate polities and the *international* is constituted only in the relations between states. We are

thus left with a vision of the global political space as constituted entirely and exclusively by states.

(emphasis original; Camilleri, *et al.* 1995: 4)

Economic governance in the modern state system assumes that all transactions take place somewhere; that all income streams, production, sales, loans and currency exchanges can be located precisely in geographic space. It assumes that at the end of the day one can determine whose law or regulation applies and in which national market or jurisdiction the transaction takes place.

With the emergence of an integrated global economy, however, it is increasingly difficult to determine what is a national product, a national technology or even a national firm. In today's world, the most important barriers to free flows of international trade and investment are not border restrictions but domestic policies which deal with intellectual property, health and safety standards, worker rights and environmental conditions. The clear line between domestic and international transactions is again becoming ambiguous and blurred.

In 1995, Honda was North America's leading exporter of passenger cars (*Business Week* 1996: 113). Are those exports American and Canadian or are they Japanese? Increasingly, research, development and even production in high technology industries is organized through multinational strategic alliances. Is semiconductor technology developed by the IBM-Siemens-Toshiba alliance American, German or Japanese? Is the question of the nationality of a product, technology or firm even relevant in an integrated global economy? As Reich (1990) asks: "Who is US?"

In our transnationally linked and globally integrated world, both borders, and the attendant sharp distinction between the domestic and the foreign, are again losing meaning. In an interdependent global economy, basic issues such as unemployment and income inequality are no longer domestic problems subject to domestic solutions. Once more, it is far from clear who is independent and who is not.

Going further, one can ask whether the very concepts of geographic space and geographic markets still have meaning when transactions take place in cyberspace. Le Goff (1988) describes medieval typography in terms of a collection of greater or smaller clearings – economic, social and cultural cells – surrounded by a vast impenetrable forest. Our emerging digitally networked world may well come to resemble small cells or clearings surrounded by an electronic forest or no man's land.

Cyberspace is not physical, geometric or geographic. The construction of markets as electronic networks renders space once again relational and symbolic, or metaphysical. External reality seen through the World Wide Web may be closer to medieval Christian representations of the world than to a modern atlas. It is becoming increasingly difficult to determine *where* economic transactions take place or whether geographic space and geo-graphic markets remain relevant.

The Indian software industry, in which exports have grown dramatically in the last decade, provides an example.[6] It is now routine for programmers sitting in Bangalore to work on computer systems in New York and London through real-time satellite linkages. If an Indian programmer upgrades a software system in a bank in New York, there is no question that economic value is being added. It is impossible, however, to specify where the trans-action takes place: in India, in the United States, or in both simultaneously? The Indian programmer working on a bank's computer in New York raises some fundamental questions about the meaning of the term "international trade" as cross-border economic transactions.

More abstractly, the idea of geography as a basis for the organization of politics and economics may be losing meaning. To a very real extent the inter-national financial system, comprised of thousands of monitors located all over the world, is constructed in digitalized electronic space. It is the first global electronic marketplace and certainly will not be the last.

The Internet is at the same time in many places and no place. While the nodes or servers can be located precisely in geometric space, the Internet itself cannot. The Internet has been aptly described as "a nightmare scenario of every government censor" which has "no physical existence and recognizes no national barriers" (Cole 1996: 8).

To be clear, I do not argue that nations or even states are about to fade into the ether. Great Britain, the United States, Japan, Venezuela and Thailand will be here for the foreseeable future. However, I do agree with Strange (1996: 73) that the state is in the midst of a "metamorphosis" resulting from structural change in the world economy and society. The borders between states are losing meaning as discrete limits to jurisdiction, or "lines in the sand," over which flows of people, goods, capital and information can be readily controlled. Distinguishing between internal and external affairs is again becoming difficult. It is thus reasonable to ask whether the clear separa-tion between domestic and foreign, the construct of international or cross-border affairs and indeed the very idea of territorial sovereignty may be unique to the modern era.

The ambiguity of authority

The Middle Ages lacked the singular relationship between authority and territory characteristic of the modern era; geographic location did not deter-mine identity and loyalty (Hirst and Thompson 1995; Spruyt 1994). Over-lapping and competing political authorities were the norm rather than the exception. At times, the spheres of pope, emperor, prince and lord were all interwoven and comprised complex networks of rival jurisdiction.

Citing other sources, Ruggie (1983: 274) describes the medieval system of rule in terms of a "patchwork" of overlapping and incomplete rights of government which were "inextricably superimposed and tangled." He labels the medieval institutional framework *heteronomous*, connoting a "lattice-like network of authority relations." These overlapping, interwoven and incomplete systems of authority often resulted in competing claims to the same geographic area.

To assert singular territorial authority, early modern monarchs had to exert primacy over a patchwork of dukedoms, principalities and other localized authorities as well as transnational institutions such as the papacy, monastic and knightly orders (Kennedy 1993). Until that was accomplished, the concept of an unambiguous relationship between authority and territory was unknown.

Sovereignty – in its modern sense – *is* unambiguous political authority. The idea of exclusive authority over a discrete geographic space which entails the absence of both domestic competitors and extraterritorial superiors underlies the modern political system. It implies that the state is the ultimate domestic authority and bows to no external power, be it pope or emperor (Agnew 1994b; Hirst and Thompson 1995; Spryut 1994).

Singular territorially based authority is once more becoming problematic in our emerging postmodern global political economy. In part, this results from the marked increase in regional economic integration in the last quarter of the twentieth century – integration motivated to some extent by a technologically driven need to increase market size.

Europe provides the most advanced example of regional economic and political integration. While the motivations for European integration are complex, economies of scale in both manufacturing and technology certainly play a major role. Virtually all of the European national markets are too small to allow either competitive manufacture in capital-intensive industries or competitive research and development budgets in technology-intensive industries. This need to integrate is reflected in the record numbers of pan-European mergers and acquisitions in the mid 1990s.[7]

Moreover, despite all of the arguments about federalism, the European Union does have real political authority (see Sandholtz's discussion of the EU in his chapter in this volume). The single market requires that issues such as product standards and competition policy be set at the center. The issue of EU social policy, including collective bargaining rights, length of the working week, hiring and firing conditions, pregnancy leave, sick time and the like, provide an example. While social policy reflects very basic national preferences grounded in differing political-economic philosophies, the single market requires a unified approach. The result is a complex web of overlapping – and at times opposing – European, national and even regional authorities, all responsible for workplace conditions. It is illustrative of the emergence of multiple authorities resulting from regional economic integration.

The European Union also provides examples of the rise of multiple juridical authorities. A British film maker whose film was banned in the United

Kingdom on grounds of blasphemy took his case to the European Court of Human Rights arguing that his freedom of expression was violated and that the statute – which dates from the Middle Ages – was anachronistic and illegal under the broader laws of Europe. If successful, this would have forced the British Government to ask Parliament to reconsider the blasphemy law; however, the censor's original ban was upheld in this case (*Daily Telegraph*, 26 November 1996).

Singular territorially based authority is also compromised by the increased importance and power of international institutions, which in turn reflects the fact that many problems facing states at this point, such as the environment, crime, corruption, the spread of disease and maintenance of an open international system of trade and investment, cannot be solved nationally.

For example, unlike the complex web of bilateral and multilateral treaties which comprised the General Agreement on Tariffs and Trade (GATT), the World Trade Organization (WTO) is an international institution with substantial adjudication authority. This additional authority is, at least in part, a response to the increased frequency, complexity and importance of bi- and multilateral trade disputes in areas such as financial services, intellectual property and trade-related investment issues.

In April 1996, the WTO's tribunal decided that US environmental regulations issued under the Clean Air Act discriminated against imported petroleum. The reaction in the American Congress was immediate and predictable, with complaints about surrendering national sovereignty to so-called foreign judges and calls for withdrawal from the organization.

Attempts to stamp out corruption in international business, or at least limit it, also illustrate the interweaving of international, national and non-governmental authorities. In May 1996, ministers from twenty-six major industrialized countries met under the auspices of the Organization for Economic Cooperation and Development (OECD) and agreed to criminalize the tax deductibility of bribes to foreign officials. This agreement resulted from the intense efforts of a variety of actors: national authorities, especially the US Government, which perceived itself at a competitive disadvantage because it currently has a law on the books criminalizing bribery in international business; Transparency International, a non-governmental international organization (NGO) dedicated to fighting corruption; and the OECD itself (Glynn *et al.* 1997).

There is no question that this represents an interweaving of national and supra-national authority that differs in kind from the conflicts between states and international organizations that were characteristic of much of the twentieth century. Such overlap reflects both the increasing integration of the world economy and the need for multilateral solutions to complex problems.

Non-state actors have also rendered political authority ambiguous. Dramatic advances in communications and, in particular, the convergence of telecommunications and computers, have been a prime cause of the increased number and importance of NGOs such as Amnesty International, Transparency International and Greenpeace, all of which are significant political authorities. These transnational actors are now able to link interest groups directly in a relatively large number of countries through telephone, fax and the Internet. They can share information widely and rapidly, develop a common transnational position on issues, publicize it broadly and effectively lobby both their respective national governments (as concerned citizens) and international organizations.

There is no question, for example, that Greenpeace functioned as a significant political actor in the international political system during the dispute over the disposal of Shell's Brent Spar off-shore drilling platform in 1995. The dispute was orchestrated by Greenpeace, and pitted Shell and the UK Government against Germany and Prince Bernhard of the Netherlands. In the end, Shell backed down from its plan to scuttle the rig in the Atlantic and had to apologize to British Prime Minister John Major for undercutting his support (Tining 1995: 1).

The important point is that Greenpeace was able to do much more than mobilize public opinion through the media. Its affiliates in a number of European countries were able to mobilize the support of their respective governments directly. Shell faced a patchwork of overlapping and incomplete political authorities, both state and non-state.

Similarly, a coalition of over 600 NGOs located in a large number of countries and linked electronically through the Internet and the World Wide Web were able to mobilize sufficient opposition to the Multilateral Agreement on Investment (MAI) being negotiated at OECD that it was effectively tabled in October of 1998. This was a clear manifestation of the potential effectiveness of non-state actors, of global civil society, in an electronically interlinked world (Kobrin 1998a).

A number of observers take the emergence of transnational actors and NGOs as an indication that states are becoming one of a number of – albeit unequal – competing and overlapping layers of authority, and that international politics is becoming more complex and polycentric. Rosenau (1990: 274), for example, foresees the emergence of "a paradigm which neither circumvents nor negates the state-centric model but posits sovereignty-bound and sovereignty-free actors as inhabitants of separate worlds that interact in such a way as to make their coexistence possible." Strange (1996: 73) argues that the state "is becoming, *once more as in the past,* just one source of authority among several . . ." (emphasis added). Similarly, Cerny in his chapter discusses the transformation of world politics into a polycentric system as a result of globalization.

Non-governmental and private international organizations may be one indication we have come full circle to a neomedievalism where sources of authority are "multifarious" (Spiro 1995: 46). They may herald the emergence of what some have called a "global civil society," which provides multiple, interlaced competitors to the singular territorial authority of the state.

In a similar fashion, digitalization and the emergence of electronic markets and electronic commerce may well render the very idea of geographic jurisdiction – and the singular, unambiguous territorial authority characteristic of the modern state system – problematic. A recent US Treasury paper argues that electronic commerce may dissolve the link between transaction and location: "electronic commerce doesn't seem to occur in any physical location but instead takes place in the nebulous world of 'cyberspace'" (Department of the Treasury 1996). Asking *where* the transaction takes place is not relevant in markets constructed in cyberspace.

This is particularly evident in a number of the issues associated with cross-border electronic commerce. For example, it is now technically feasible for a customer in Germany to download a music album to her computer's hard drive from a French music company whose website is maintained on a computer in India, and then pay digitally (perhaps with a smart card) with a deposit of electronic cash in a Cayman Islands bank.[8]

In the modern system, geographic location or jurisdiction determines which authority has the right to tax the income stream arising from the transaction or the sale itself (a sales or value added tax). Where does this transaction take place? Who gets to tax the sale? It is far from clear that buyers and sellers transacting over the Internet actually know *where* the other party is located. If the bytes comprising the album are routed through five countries do they really cross five borders? While the problems posed by overlapping or conflicting tax jurisdictions are certainly not new, the very concept of a singular territorially based political authority may be irrelevant in the Digital Age.

A medieval lord dealt with multiple authorities – emperor and sovereign, sacred and secular – as the norm. It is the modern era, where political authority is defined in terms of unambiguous territoriality, which may be the outlier. The postmodern may well have to learn to accept a heteronomous world of interlaced regional, national, local, supra-national, institutional and non-governmental authorities.

Multiple loyalties

William Marshall, Earl of Pembroke, who was at the same time a vassal of the kings of England and France, actually negotiated with the latter for the former. When in 1204 John Lackland, King of England, ordered Marshall to cross the Channel with him to attack France, he replied: "Ah sire, for the grove of God, it would be an evil thing if I were to go, since I am his sworn liege" (Duby 1985: 141). Marshall, with some difficulty, managed these conflicting relationships well.

Physical location did not define one's place in the feudal political structure. Individuals held multiple titles which could result in complex networks of reciprocal relationships and conflicting duties and obligations (Krasner 1993). As a result, William Marshall and most medieval people saw nothing unusual in situations where allegiances overlapped; multiple and conflicting loyalties were the norm rather than the exception.

Unambiguous political loyalties arise from political identities rooted in territory and geography. Even the most visible modern "dual loyalty" problem – the conflict between loyalty to nation and loyalty to state – is "resolved" by trying to square the circle through self-determination, giving every nation its own piece of geography. Unambiguous political loyalty, however, may be another modern exception, and a relatively recent one at that.

As the conflict in Bosnia so tragically illustrates, self-determination is not the answer to nationalism; it is simply not possible to give every people sovereignty over their own territory. A number of observers suggest that geographic sovereignty rather than nationalism may be the problem. It may not be possible, or even desirable, to root political identity unambiguously in mutually exclusive geographical entities. Maier (1994) argues that solutions such as "confederalism, cantonization and overlapping citizenship" may merit serious consideration. Similarly, Gottlieb (1993) calls for "deconstructing" the notion of sovereignty to allow space for a system of nations to exist alongside the system of states. Both authors argue that multiple political identities are inescapable.

As noted above, the dramatic technological breakthroughs in telecommunications and computing have increased direct transnational contacts, through NGOs and other transnational actors, and have created new common identities that cut across national borders and "challenge governments at the level of individual loyalties" (Spiro 1995: 45). A number of observers see the emergence,or re-emergence, of a global civil society comprised of networks of individuals in distinct locations who link themselves together for specific social and political purposes.

Similarly, Appadurai (1996) notes that with mobile populations linked electronically, the very idea of a nation may now be "diasporic." Nations are increasingly unrestrained by ideas of spatial boundaries and territorial sovereignty. He notes that using electronic media, widely dispersed individuals "imagine" themselves as belonging to a national society.

These developments hark back to arrangements which were common in Europe before the emergence of the Westphalian state system (Lipschutz 1992). The failure of self-determination to solve the nationalities problem and the increasing importance of transnational relations has, in Agnew's (1994a: 62) words, resulted in "a remarkable flowering of alternative political identities."

The pulls of conflicting loyalties are not new.[9] Country, church, corporation and family have always competed with one another, coexisting easily at times and uneasily at others. The issue, however, is not the conflict between overlapping loyalties in general, but between overlapping political loyalties. At least in theory, during the modern era political loyalty was a function of geographic location. Since the French revolution, one is not a subject of a sovereign, but a citizen of a state that is a geographically conceived and determined entity.

What is new, or perhaps not so new, is the emergence of multiple and competing *political* loyalties. The problems with self-determination, the rise of supra-national authorities and modern, often electronically based, transnational relations all loosen the ties to geography and again increase the probability of multiple and conflicting *political* loyalties.

One certainly can be both a European and a Belgian. In the relatively recent past, however, being a European had cultural and social rather than political implications. With the formation of the European Union, that is no longer the case; one is both a European and a Belgian in a very basic political sense and, as noted above, the two authorities can easily overlap and conflict.

Similarly, transnational organizations such as Greenpeace link individuals from a number of countries together to achieve specific political ends. To the extent that environmentalism, for example, has become a transcendent political ideology, it could easily result in conflicts of political loyalty. An English member of Greenpeace could well refuse, at least metaphorically, to cross the Channel to do battle at the side of the prime minister against continental states and continental environmentalists.

Transnational elites

As Hobsbawm (1990: 85) observes, twentieth-century transnational corporations are far more likely to chose their CEOs from their home country than were nineteenth-century nation states likely to choose kings "with local connections." Until recently, and especially in Europe, elites were transnational; the medieval nobility saw itself as European rather than national. Elites might be linked to territories and titles certainly were grounded in place, but they were not territorial in the modern sense.

While I hesitate to draw parallels between executives of the transnational firm and the medieval nobility, geographic place does seem to have lost some of its pull. A cosmopolitan elite is re-emerging as multinational firms begin to draw their top executives from a relatively wide range of backgrounds. There is a considerable managerial corps which is as comfortable in Bangkok as Boston, Mantua as well as Manchester. The World Bank, for example, is often described as composed of citizens of 100 countries who attended six universities.

The emergence of a digital world economy, of electronic commerce and electronic cash, may be another source of emerging cosmopolitanism. The Internet and its associated activities link virtual communities worldwide. It may widen the gap between "haves" and "have-nots," between a global elite with access to information systems and information and those without. The Internet also reinforces the trend, which one may or may not approve, of English becoming the universal language of world business, the Latin of the multinational corporation and the digital world economy.

Public and private property

In the English manor, "the most characteristic version of the manorial village," it was difficult, if not impossible, to separate the subsistence of the villagers from the lord's profit and authority (Previte-Orton 1971: 424). A medieval lord would have found a clear distinction between public and private interests and property alien. He would not have understood an attempt to distinguish his property and interests as duke, for example, from those of his dukedom. Indeed, in the Middle Ages, there was no clear line separating public from private offices. The English sheriff, one of the oldest public offices, began as an estate manager for Anglo-Saxon kings (Strayer 1970).

While there was some concept of common property in medieval Europe, the idea of public (as opposed to common) property or public goods was very underdeveloped. Justice and protection provided by the lord of the manor certainly cannot be described as public goods in the modern sense. Correspondingly, the concept of private property or property rights, especially with regards to land, was very poorly developed. The feudal system recognized multiple rights to land rather than land ownership (North and Thomas 1973; also see Cerny's discussion of public goods in his chapter).

The sharp and clear distinction between the public and private spheres – the idea of private property and private ownership, as well as the corresponding idea of public or collective (as opposed to the lord's) property – is bound up with the modern era and the modern state (North 1981). There are reasons to ask whether the distinction between the public and private is becoming diffuse once again as we enter a period of transition to a postmodern global political economy.

One of the fundamental public aspects of the Weberian state, the domestic monopoly of force and coercive power, does appear to be breaking down. Protection is becoming rapidly privatized, at least among the segment of the populace that can afford it. Even in the United Kingdom, for example, the private security industry employs more people than the entire uniformed police force (*Independent* 1995).

A *New York Times* story entitled "When Neighborhoods are Privatized" reported that when residents of the upper East Side of Manhattan became exasperated with street crime, they tried to create a private security district to hire 500 private officers. While this particular effort ultimately failed, it is indicative of a rapidly growing trend – the privatization of public services. Walled-in, secure, private towns which tax themselves heavily and where all public services are privately performed are becoming relatively common. As of 1995, nearly four million Americans lived in walled-off, gated, secured private communities, which represent one of the fastest growing segments of the residential real estate market (Eagen 1995).

More generally, the postmodern global world economy is blurring the distinction between the public and private spheres. Very large private banks are public actors; the implications of failure or default for the international financial system and national economies are too great to allow. Furthermore, many of the arrangements to mitigate this risk are neither public nor private but a cooperative effort between central bankers, national authorities and private banks.

The Group of 20, for example, is a consortium of leading international banks that work in close association with national central banks. It has recently agreed upon a mechanism to deal with the risk arising from settlement of foreign exchange transactions occurring in different time zones. The agreement, which will be implemented "privately," serves an obvious "public" need of reduction of risk to the international financial system (Graham 1997: 6).

The emergence of significant non-governmental transnational actors in world politics – defined by Keohane and Nye (1971: xi) in their original paper as "contacts, coalitions, and interactions across state boundaries that are not controlled by the foreign policy organs of governments" – makes public-private distinctions difficult. Leaving multinational firms aside, it is impossible to classify Greenpeace, Amnesty International or Transparency International as either fully private or fully public entities. As noted above, there is no question that Greenpeace played a major role in international politics by mobilizing public and governmental opinion against the deep sea disposal of Shell's Brent Spar oil platform. Whether it performed that role as a private or public actor may no longer be a relevant question.

Another major dimension of a postmodern world economy, the digitalization of commerce and the emergence of global electronic networks, also makes the public-private distinction problematic. Is the Internet a public or private "public utility"? It was, in part, created with public funds, but is now entirely managed – if that word is appropriate – privately. Attempts to exert public control over content, whether the problem is perceived as pornography in Washington, DC, or potential terrorist activity in Germany, have been less than resounding successes.

The digitalization of the economy also raises some very basic questions about the meaning and validity of the concept of property rights in the postmodern era. Who owns a digital image? How can the state grant rights to the owner which can be enforced given the often zero marginal cost of reproduction and transmission? Going further, the classic definition of a public good is one where consumption is not diminished by use, and access cannot be restricted (e.g. a lighthouse). But do many privately produced digital goods also fit this definition?

We are certainly not returning to a world of manors and dukedoms. However, it is conceivable that the clear separation between the private and public realms and the very idea of distinct private and public property may be tied to a specific, perhaps exceptional, historical era. The distinction was not relevant in pre-modern times and it may not be relevant in the postmodern future.

Unifying ideologies and supra-national centralization

Malraux has said that during the Middle Ages there was a Europe because there was Christianity – and Christianity was serious. During the Middle Ages, Europe *was* Western Christendom.

The power of the Church *vis-à-vis* the secular authorities varied considerably over time, and even after the settlement of the investiture conflict in the twelfth century never quite achieved Gregory VII's objective of making the papacy the "supreme and autocratic ruler" of both the ecclesiastical hierarchy and the secular potentates. Christianity was, nonetheless, the major unifying force in medieval Europe (Previte-Orton 1971: 500).

All authority, whether holy or secular, was thought to derive ultimately from God; all European thinkers accepted the idea of Christendom as a unified society which was governed by divine law (Krasner 1993). The criterion for inclusion in the political system was based on universal Christianity rather than a particular geographic location. There is no question that a truly universal ideology and political order existed.

Furthermore, the legacy of Rome was strongly felt in the Middle Ages. While the attempt of Charlemagne to recreate Rome was relatively short-lived, and the power and authority of Holy Roman Emperors varied over time, there was a belief in, or perhaps a longing for, the re-establishment of a center: for the order, the law, the culture and the glory that was Rome.

Again, the essence of the modern state system is sovereignty; the idea that there is no ultimate, central or universal authority, such as a pope or emperor, over that of the state. As a result, a defining characteristic of the modern system is anarchy; the absence of a central authority to enforce agreements, sanction offenders or even adjudicate disputes.

It is important to note that anarchy has both positive and normative implications. It is both a property of the system and a belief that there should not be a universal order or supra-national authority. If one accepts a traditional realist view of world politics, even sustained international cooperation is problematic.

In many respects, there is a marked asymmetry between this decentralized structure of the modern state system and the problems we face as we enter the postmodern global era. This perception is not entirely new: over sixty-five years ago, *The Economist* (1930: 652) observed that the tension between a political system partitioned into "60 or 70" sovereign national states and a single, all-embracing world economy has been producing "a series of jolts, jars and smashes in the social life of humanity."

Those "jolts, jars and smashes" now threaten our physical, as well as our social, well-being. There are any number of problems such as environmental degradation, terrorism, drugs, disease and corruption that are inherently transnational. They cannot be solved through unilateral national action and mandate a coordinated, cooperative international response.

While a postmodern analog of medieval Christendom may not be readily apparent, there are a number of suggestions for unifying and universal ideologies, such as liberalism, democracy, a belief in the power of technology or environmentalism. More importantly, as the twentieth century draws to a close, there is increasing interest in stronger institutions at the center; institutions which are short of a real supra-national authority but are not entirely consistent with a world of sovereign states.

Examples abound. The WTO is, at least on paper, a considerably strengthened version of the GATT embodied in an international institution with real adjudication authority. There is increasing pressure for international co-operation and an international agreement on rules for the treatment of foreign direct investment in both the OECD and the WTO (see Sandholtz's discussion of the WTO in this volume). As noted above, efforts, or at least discussions, are underway to find some central international mechanism to deal with corruption in international business, and with worker rights. Most obviously, the EU exists as a supra-national political organization, whether or not a federal Europe, monetary union and political integration are ever achieved.

Again, the point is not that we should expect a new Charlemagne or the moral equivalent of Western Christendom. The point is that the modern ideal of an anarchical system with sovereign states rejecting any superior or central authority may have been an ephemeral product of a specific historical period. The norm may be a recognition of the need for some degree of order, authority and, perhaps, glory at the center.

A neomedieval future?

I believe that we are living through the end of one era and the onset of another; a systemic transformation from a modern to a postmodern political economy. It is a transformation comparable to that from the medieval to the modern era, which Ruggie (1983) has called the most important contextual change in international politics in this millennium.

The structural changes underlying this transformation, the dramatic increase in the scale and complexity of technology, the digitalization of finance and commerce and the emergence of an electronically networked world economy, are clearly revolutionary rather than evolutionary. In many important ways, they represent a clear break from the immediate modern past.

What can we learn from using medieval Europe as a metaphor to help us understand postmodern possibilities? While I do not believe that nation states and the state system are about to wither away, I do think that there may well be very significant changes in their meaning, in their structure and in their function.

The primary argument of this essay is that many aspects of modern political and economic organization may be exceptional and ephemeral – at least when measured on historical time scales. Time's arrow may not be unidirectional. Change may not take the form of an evolutionary progression where each era is built upon the existing foundations or structures of its predecessor.

Mutually exclusive territoriality is not a transhistorical, fundamental principle of political organization. Political power and authority were not geographically defined in medieval Europe and may not be in a digitalized world economy organized through overlapping electronic networks. Discrete and meaningful borders and the clear separation of the domestic from the foreign, indeed the very idea of the international, may be a modern anomaly. Conceptions of space may again become symbolic and relational rather than geometric and physical.

Similarly, the corresponding concepts of unambiguous authority and loyalty may be harder to sustain in a postmodern world of multiple and overlapping authorities: sovereign and non-sovereign, territorial and non-territorial. Multiple and overlapping sources of political authority and multiple and ambiguous political loyalties may once again be seen as the norm.

Perhaps most importantly, the normative belief in anarchy; in the absence of authority at the center, may be crumbling in the face of problems such as crime, corruption, disease, environmental degradation, financial collapse and the like, all of which are well beyond the scope of national or even international action. Absolute territorial sovereignty has always been easier to imagine than to construct. In a postmodern, digitally integrated world economy, however, the idea itself may no longer be meaningful. Control over territory no longer provides a viable basis for control over an economy or economic actors.

The question of what will replace territorial sovereignty, or perhaps more correctly be layered atop and complement it, is critical. At a minimum, effective economic governance in a digital world economy will require markedly increased efforts at harmonization of national legislation and regulations and much more effective and powerful international institutions.

The US Government's 1997 "A Framework for Electronic Commerce" (1997: 3), for example, calls for governance by "consistent principles across state, national and international borders that leads to predictable results regardless of the jurisdiction in which a particular buyer or seller resides."[10] Given the very sharp differences in basic beliefs and values, when one deals with issues such as privacy, encryption and consumer protection, it is clear that harmonization will have to go well beyond a simple reconciliation of national law. This is an area where the needs of technology will compromise national sovereignty; it is but one example of what Strange (1996) describes as a shift of political authority from states to markets.

Yet harmonization will not be sufficient. Although a world government does not appear to be immanent, there is increasing pressure for some sort of authority at the center, an authority which transcends the sovereignty-preserving idea of the international organization. Effective economic governance in the postmodern integrated world economy will require a marked strengthening of international institutions such as the WTO. They may well acquire taxation and enforcement powers if territorial jurisdiction is no longer effective.

At some point, harmonization of policy, the granting of adjudication rights and true enforcement capabilities at the center will result in a real supra-national authority. Perhaps as important, the possibility certainly exists for a universal or unifying ideology, although one is not readily apparent. (Lake and Sandholtz take very different positions in their respective chapters on the possibility of the emergence of supra-national or transnational rules and institutions – of some degree of centralization of authority – as a result of globalization.)

In a widely commented-upon article, Kaplan (1994: 72) used West Africa as a prism to view a future which evokes the dark ages after the barbarian invasions: disease, overpopulation, unprovoked crime, refugee migrations, the empowerment of private armies and security firms and international drug cartels, among other unpleasant possibilities. He clearly foresees the collapse of modernism, the nation state, borders and states' ability to maintain civil order within them. He views political postmodernism bleakly, as an epoch in which "the classificatory grid of nation states is going to be replaced by a jagged-glass pattern of city-states, shanty-states, nebulous and anarchic regionalisms. . . ."

It is a very dark view of the future which clearly evokes the pre-modern, early medieval past. Rising crime and the privatization of security and security forces are a reality. As discussed above, walled suburban communities with very limited entry points and extensive private security forces are becoming far from unusual. There are places in every urban area where security cannot be provided and where one ventures – even in an automobile – at one's own risk. Le Goff's (1988) description of medieval typography in terms of a collection of clearings surrounded by no man's land no longer sounds alien.

While I would hope that Kaplan is a pessimist, one is reminded of Trevor-Roper's (1993, 1933) question in his introduction to Gibbon. He asks whether a philosopher in Imperial Rome would have foreseen that in a few hundred years the barbarians would triumph and the civilization of antiquity would disappear. Could anyone then have imagined the coming dark ages?

One hopes that such an age is not part of the neomedieval metaphor, that a new and more terrifying barbarian is not on the horizon. One hopes that the walled communities and private security forces are themselves ephemeral products of a world in transition and not a permanent characteristic of the postmodern era. The challenge is to ensure that transnational and trans-territorial solutions be found to the problems posed by the emergence of a postmodern, digital world economy.

Notes

* Published by permission of the *Journal of International Affairs* and the Trustees of Columbia University in the City of New York.

  This chapter originally appeared in the *Journal of International Affairs* (Spring 1998: 361–86) in a slightly different form. I would like to thank John Ikenberry, Jeffrey Hart, Daniel Raff, Susan Strange and the editors of the *JAF* for useful comments on the earlier draft.

1 Negroponte (1995) argues that trade in atoms is being replaced by trade in bits. In 1995 *Fortune* combined the service and industrial *500s*, arguing that the central role played by information technology has virtually obliterated the difference between industrial and service firms. *Fortune* cites one source claiming that three-fourths of the value added in manufacturing is now information. See Stewart (1995).
2 Ruggie (1993: 151) notes that "the distinctive feature of the modern state system is that it has differentiated its subject collectivity into territorially defined, fixed and mutually exclusive enclaves of legitimate domain."
3 Formal sovereignty is a legal concept which entails the Weberian concept of ultimate law making and law enforcing authority within a clearly defined territory: the absence of competing domestic claimants and independence from external authority – e.g., emperor or pope. The "undisputed right to determine the framework of rules, regulations and policies within a given territory and to govern accordingly" (Held and McGrew 1993: 265). Spruyt (1994) argues that one of the primary explanations for the spread of sovereign territorial institutions was that respective jurisdictions, and thus limits to authority, could be specified precisely though agreement on fixed borders.
4 Carr, 1964; Kennedy 1993; Ruggie, 1993.
5 The word "geography" did not enter the English language until the sixteenth century. The useful, and surprisingly accurate images created by ancient geographers were suppressed for one thousand years during what Boorstin calls the "great interruption" in European geographic knowledge (Boorstin 1983).
6 The sector has grown dramatically, from a total turnover of $10 million in 1986 to $12 billion in 1996; the estimate for the compound growth rate for the first half of the 1990s was 46 per cent per annum. The industry is export driven; exports – primarily of software services – have grown at over 60 per cent per annum in recent years rising to $734 million in 1996, about 61 per cent of total turnover (Taylor 1996: I and Nicholson 1996: 4).
7 There were $280 billion of European mergers and acquistions in 1996 and $253 in 1995 versus a previous peak of $148 billion in the 1980s (Wagstyl 1997: 17).
8 For more discussion of the impact of electronic commerce on territoriality see Kobrin (1998).
9 It is an overgeneralization to argue that geographic location has been the sole source of political loyalty Socialists in the late nineteenth and early twentieth century certainly called for a transnational working-class identity that would transcend loyalty to nation or state; a concept blown asunder by the enthusiasm the proletariat in virtually every European country showed for mobilization in 1914. More recently, the phenomenon of identity politics has emerged – perhaps as a consequence of postmodern fragmentation – with "political" identity a function of ethnicity, gender, race or sexual preference. My concern here, however, is with competing transnational political identities replacing unambiguous loyalty based on geography.
10 "A Framework for Global Electronic Commerce," Washington, DC, 1997 (http://www.whitehouse.gov/WH/New/Commerce/read.html).

References

Agnew, James (1994a) "The Territory Trap: The Geographical Assumptions of International Relations Theory," *Review of International Political Economy* 1: 65.

Agnew, James (1994b) "Timeless Space and State-Centrism: The Geographical Assumptions of International Relations Theory," in *The Global Economy as Political Space*, edited by S.J. Rostrow, N. Inayatullah and M. Rupert, Boulder, CO: Lynne Reinner Publishers.

Anderson, James (1996) "The Shifting Stage of Politics: New Medieval and Post-modern Territorialities?" *Environment and Planning D: Society and Space* 14: 133–53.

Appadurai, Arjun (1996) *Modernity at Large*, Minneapolis, MN: University of Minnesota Press.

Boorstin, Daniel J. (1983) *The Discoverers*, New York: Random House.

Bull, Hedley (1977) *The Anarchial Society: A Study of Order in World Politics*, New York: Columbia University Press.

Business Week (1996) February 26: 113.

Camilleri, Joseph A., Anthony P. Jarvis and Albert J. Paloni (eds) (1995) *The State in Transition: Reimaging Political Space*, Boulder, CO: Lynne Reinner Publishers.

Carr, Edward Hallett (1964, 1946) *The Twenty Years' Crisis, 1919–1939*, New York: Harper and Row Publishers.

Cerney, Philip G. (1995) "Globalization and the Changing Logic of Collective Action," *International Organization* 49 (Autumn): 607.

Cole, George (1996) "Censorship in Cyberspace," *Financial Times* (March): 8.

Department of the Treasury (1996) "Selected Tax Policy Implications of Electronic Commerce," Washington, DC, November (http://jya.com/taxpolicy.htm.).

Dicken, Peter (1994) "The Roepke Lecture in Economic Geography. Global Local Tensions: Firms and States in the Global Space-Economy," *Economic Geography* 70: 101–20.

Duby, Georges (1985) *William Marshall: The Flower of Chivalry*, New York: Pantheon Books.

Eagen, Timothy (1995) "The Serene Fortress," *New York Times* (November 30): A1.

The Economist (1930) October 11: 652.

"A Framework for Global Electronic Commerce" (1997) Washington, DC (http://www.whitehouse.gov/WH/New/Commerce/read.html): 3.

Glynn, Patrick, Stephen Kobrin and Moises Naim (1997) "The Globalization of Corruption," in *Corruption and the Global Economy*, edited by Kimberly Ann Elliton, 7–27. Washington, DC: Institute for International Economics.

Gottlieb, Gideon (1993) *Nation Against State*, New York: Council on Foreign Relations Press.

Graham, George (1997) "Top Banks Approve Settlement Service," *Financial Times* (June 27): 6.

Guehenno, Jean-Marie (1995) *The End of the Nation State*, Minneapolis, MN: University of Minnesota Press.

Hague, Helen (1996) "Film Maker Aims to Kill the Law of Blasphemy," *Sunday Telegraph* (March 10): 11.

Harvey, David (1990) *The Condition of Postmodernity*, Cambridge, MA: Blackwell Publishers.

Held, D. and A. McGrew (1993) "Globalization and the Liberal Democratic State," *Government and Opposition* 28: 265.

Hirst, Paul and Grahame Thompson (1995) "Globalization and the Future of the Nation-State," *Economy and Society* 24, 3: 408–42.

Hobsbawm, Eric J. (1990) *Nations and Nationalism Since 1780*, Cambridge: Cambridge University Press.

Independent (1995) "Private Lives" (June 11): 14.

Jarvis, Anthony P. and Albert J. Paloni (1995) "Locating the State," in *The State in Transition: Reimaging Political Space*, edited by Joseph A. Camilleri, Anthony P. Jarvis and Albert J. Paloni. Boulder, CO: Lynne Reinner Publishers.

Kaplan, Robert (1994) "The Coming Anarchy," *The Atlantic Monthly* (February): 44.

Kennedy, Paul (1993) *Preparing for the Twenty-First Century*, New York: Random House.

Keohane, Robert O. and Joseph S. Nye (1971) "Transnational Relations and World Politics: An Introduction," in *Transnational Relations and World Politics*, edited by Robert Keohane and Joseph S. Nye, Cambridge, MA: Harvard University Press: xi.

Kobrin, Stephen J. (1997) "The Architecture of Globalization: State Sovereignty in a Networked Global Economy," in *Governments, Globalization and International Business*, edited by John H. Dunning, Oxford: Oxford University Press: 146–71.

Kobrin, Stephen J. (1998) "You Can't Declare Cyberspace National Territory: Economic Policy Making in the Digital Age," in *Blueprint to the Digital Economy*, edited by Alex Lowry, Don Tapscott and David Tiscoll, New York: McGraw Hill: chapter 19.

Kobrin, Stephen J. (1998a) "The MAI and the Clash of Globalization," *Foreign Policy* (Fall): 110–22.

Krasner, Stephen D. (1993) "Westphalia and All That," in *Ideas and Foreign Policy*, edited by Judith Goldstein and Robert O. Keohane, Ithaca, NY: Cornell University Press: 235–64.

Lansdon, Doug and Sue Halpern (1995) "When Neighborhoods are Privatized," *New York Times* (November 30): A39.

Lapham, Lewis H. (1988) "Leviathan in Trouble," *Harper's Magazine* (September): 10.

Le Goff, Jacques (1988) *Medieval Civilization 400–1500*, London: Basil Blackwell.

Lipschutz, Ronnie (1992) "Reconstructing World Politics: The Emergence of Global Civil Society," *Millennium* 21, 3: 389–420.

Maier, Charles S. (1994) "Democracy and its Discontents," *Foreign Affairs* 73, 4: 48–64.

Matthew, Richard (1995) "Back to the Dark Age: World Politics in the Late Twentieth Century," Washington, DC, School of Foreign Service.

Negroponte, Nicholas (1995) *Being Digital*, New York: Knopf.

Nicolson, Mark (1996) "India Emerges as a World Centre for Software," *Financial Times* (July 7): 4.

North, Douglass C. (1981) *Structure and Change in Economic History*, New York: W.W. Norton.

North, Douglass C. and R.P. Thomas (1973) *The Rise of the Western World: A New Economic History*, Cambridge: Cambridge University Press.

Parker, M. (1992) "Post-Modern Organizations or Post Modern Theory?" *Organization Studies* 13: 9.

Previte-Orton, C.W. (1971) *The Shorter Cambridge Medieval History*, Cambridge: Cambridge University Press.

Reich, Robet (1990) "Who is US?" *The Harvard Business Review* (January–February): 53–64.

Rosenau, James (1990) *Turbulence in World Politics*, Princeton, NJ: Princeton University Press.

Ruggie, John Gerald (1983) "Continuity and Transformation in World Politics: Toward a Neorealistic Synthesis," *World Politics* XXXV, 2: 274.

Ruggie, John (1993) "Territoriality and Beyond: Problematizing Modernity in International Relations," *International Organization* 47: 151.

Spiro, Peter J. (1995) "New Global Communities: Nongovernmental Organizations in International Decision Making Institutions," *The Washington Quarterly* 8, 1: 46.

Spruyt, Hendrik (1994) *The Sovereign State and Its Competitors*, Princeton, NJ: Princeton University Press.

Stewart, T.A. (1995) "A New 500 for the New Economy," *Fortune* (May 15): 168–78.

Strange, Susan (1996) *The Retreat of the State: The Diffusion of Power in the World Economy*, Cambridge: Cambridge University Press.

Strayer, Joseph R. (1970) *On the Medieval Origins of the Modern State*, Princeton, NJ: Princeton University Press.

Taylor, Paul (1996) "Exports are Surging Ahead," *Financial Times*, Survey: India's Software Industry (November 6): I.

Teschke, Bruno (1998) "Geopolitical Relations in the Middle Ages: History and Theory," *International Organization* 52/20 (Spring): 325–58.

Tining, William (1995) "Greenpeace Victory as Brent Spar Heads for Shore," *The Glasgow Herald* (June 21): 1.

Trevor-Roper, Hugh (1993) "Introduction," in Edward Gibbon, *The Decline and Fall of the Roman Empire*, 1, New York: Alfred A. Knopf – Everyman's Library, 1933, lxxxiii.

Wagstyl, Stefan (1997) "Mergers a la Mode," *Financial Times* (October 14).

7 Globalization, governance, and complexity

Philip G. Cerny

Analytical issues

Globalization is too easily used to mean different things at the same time. For example, it is often thought to mean the convergence of economics and politics across borders into a single dominant model, a variant of liberal capitalism aligned with neoliberal politics. However, it can also indicate the growth of new forms of divergence – and, of course, the intersection of different forms of both convergence and divergence. These trends are sympto-matic of the growing complexity of providing governance mechanisms in a globalized world (Cerny, 1996, 1999a).

Though governance too takes on several different meanings in the current literature (for example, see Rhodes, 1996), broadly speaking, it consists of fundamental organizational processes characteristic of groups and wider social structures and comprising the institutions or mechanisms which enable them to coexist, whether formal or informal, explicit or implicit. In the new institutional economics literature (and to a greater or lesser extent in other forms of "new institutionalism": Hall and Taylor, 1996), these basic organizational processes are usually thought of as entailing a complex admix-ture of three ideal-type principles of organizational structure – hierarchy, market, and network (Williamson, 1975 and 1985; Thompson, *et al.*, 1991; Cerny, 1997a). In international relations literature, the ideal-type poles are usually rendered as "anarchy" and "hierarchy," with anarchy connoting not chaos but a spontaneously ordered "society without government" (Bull, 1977; cf. Barclay, 1982) – a bit like a market without the central role of the price mechanism.

Globalization impacts upon governance by altering the deeper structures which underlie governance processes and mechanisms, altering various con-ditions or parameters which affect the likely mix of hierarchy, market and network – whether in terms of socio-cultural structures, economic production and consumption, or political processes and institutions. The key question is whether the resulting organizational mix can be understood through tradi-tional analytical lenses or requires a new analytical paradigm. In part, of course, what sort of *political*-institutional mix emerges will result from a redistribution of payoffs determined by shifting economic efficiencies – economies of scale and scope and transaction cost economies in production and distribution – which primarily affect that mix of market and hierarchy within and between firms that Williamson (1975 and 1985) means when he uses the word "governance." However, economically "rational" responses do not emerge automatically in the political sphere; they are bound up in complex processes of social and political intermediation involving values, identities, and social bonds, all located in particular time/space contexts. For example, in terms of what might be called "political globalization," the relationship between various processes of globalization, transnationalization and internationalization, on the one hand, and the political needs, values and desires of a range of local, national, and, indeed, transnational political "publics" (Dewey,1927), on the other, is increasingly becoming the dominant terrain or site of political action and conflict within and between contemporary "competition states" (Cerny, 1997b).

This discourse is transmitted and reproduced less by direct economic constraint, then, and more by a combination of (1) new cross-cutting social, economic and political cleavages and (2) an evolving *discourse* about what globalization might signify for the future of particular individuals and groups as well as for the governance of society in general. Previous conjunctural events and decisions "lock in" future processes in "embedded" institutional structures in "path-dependent" fashion (Granovetter, 1985 and 1992). Granovetter argues that there are always "multiple equilibrium points" available in any specific conjunctural decision or structuration situation. Therefore the particular equilibrium point that is locked in depends not on rational economic calculation *per se* but on a complex mix of rational calculation and other social and political factors. Although in recent centuries the so-called "Westphalian state" (as well as the "modern nation-state", which is often seen to be distinct in several key ways) has, along with the concomitant "states system," been the predominant (locked-in) form of governance at the macrosocial level (notwithstanding its coexistence with other forms of microsocial, mesosocial, transnational and international governance structures), globalization hypothetically involves the emergence and crystallization of new patterns of governance.

These new patterns might be seen to be emerging at a higher, global level or through a complex set of both old and new levels (Cerny, 1995 and 1996), with the old (especially nation-states *per se*) being transformed by their interaction with the new. The broad outline of that transformation can best be characterized through one of the most venerable concepts in social science theory, that of the development of new and more intricate forms of structural *complexity*. Classical sociological theory posits that societies develop by becoming more structurally complex, i.e. through increasing structural differentiation. In contrast, however, international relations theory – especially realism and neorealism – usually starts from the assumption that the international system is differentiated only into "like" units, namely states. Therefore the structure of the system is seen to be determined by the configuration of states (hierarchy, polarity, etc.; see Waltz, 1979). A number of factors have recently brought this assumption under scrutiny. In particular, the rapid collapse not only of the European Communist states but also of the Soviet Union itself does not merely represent a reshuffling of the structure of a "states system." On the contrary, it reflects the increasing difficulties faced both by states individually and by the states system *qua* system in providing stability, security, prosperity and other more specific collective goods. Today, economic structural change is at the heart of globalization. It challenges deeply embedded socio-cultural and political structures in critical ways that cannot be ignored, provoking dynamic responses of promotion, accommodation, and resistance.

In this context, "power" itself inevitably becomes more diffuse, diffracted through an increasingly complex, prismatic structure of socio-economic forces and levels of governance – from the global interaction of transnational social movements and interest/pressure groupings, multinational corporations, financial markets, and the like, on the one hand, to the re-emergence of subnational and cross-national ethnic, religious and policy-oriented coalitions and conflicts of the type familiar in domestic-level political sociology, on the other. World politics – i.e., both domestic politics and international relations, taken together – is being transformed into a "polycentric" or "multinucleated" global political system operating within the same geographical space (and/or overlapping spaces), in a way which is analogous to the emergence of coexisting and overlapping functional authorities in metropolitan areas (Ostrom, *et al.*, 1961). The underlying governance problematic in such multilayered political systems is at least twofold: in the first place, it becomes harder to maintain the boundaries which are necessary for the efficient "packaging" of public or collective goods; and in the second place, it becomes harder to determine what collective goods are demanded or required in the first place – i.e., even to measure what is the "preferred state of affairs" (*ibid*, pp.832–5).

With regard to international relations theory, this collective goods problem can be seen as a challenge to traditional notions of the way "hierarchy" and "anarchy" work, and how they interact with each other. The reason why the modern international system – usually seen to be rooted in political changes symbolized by the Peace of Westphalia (1648) – has been particularly robust has generally been attributed to two dovetailing, mutually reinforcing characteristics of states *per se*. The first is the capacity of individual states – their endogenous structures, processes and institutions – to effectively organize political space and provide public goods *domestically* while fending off outside interference and protecting the domestic society and economy to a significant extent from what economists call "exogenous shocks." Of course, such capacity is only relative, but the cumulative impact over time of wars and of international economic booms and slumps has often been seen as progressively increasing state capacity as states take on a growing range of social and economic functions (compare the two very different approaches found in Polanyi, 1944, and Waltz, 1979).

The second characteristic is the ability of states *in the plural* to evolve a *de facto* system of rules, norms and practices which largely (1) limit or regulate direct conflict between them (although wars are needed to resolve particularly acute systemic conflicts) and (2) permit individual states and groups of states to enter into durable and enforceable – "credible" – commitments about the common resolution of particular problems stemming from their inevitable interaction and interdependence (treaties, trade agreements, monetary systems, etc.). In other words, the lack of a common government over and above states ("anarchy," in the peculiar sense used in international relations theory – i.e., *not* the everyday usage which associates anarchy with chaos) actually enables states to live together relatively freely, because each feels less threatened in its domestic affairs. When you put the two characteristics together, external anarchy reinforces domestic hierarchy, and vice versa. The history of modern nation-states and the "states system" is, then, the history of one specific *equilibrium* between the international and the domestic – an equilibrium seen as both dynamic and self-reinforcing over time. The real "balance of power" in this sense is not just among states, but between the internal and external manifestations of state authority and efficacy.

But this equilibrium between hierarchy and anarchy is a potentially fragile one, something we are prone to lose sight of if we merely view the linear march of the states system from 1648 until the middle of the twentieth century. From the point of view of this chapter, the most significant of these challenges in the last analysis is the capacity of the state to *perform* – i.e., to fulfil a significant proportion of the social and economic aims and dreams of various elites and masses internally, while not allowing itself to be undermined by exogenous economic shocks. This is the bottom line. If a breakdown of the internal hierarchical capacity of states to provide domestic collective goods occurs along with a major challenge to the capacity of the anarchical states system to regulate the relationships between states by undermining the capacity of states to make credible international commitments (i.e., to provide *international* collective goods), then the mutually reinforcing equilibrium of anarchy and hierarchy must inevitably come under greater or lesser strain. What we are concerned with here is how far globalization effectively challenges *both* hierarchy and anarchy, and therefore weakens the historical equilibrium between them, by limiting the capacity of states (separately and collectively) to provide such collective goods in the future. In this sense, then, Williamson's notions of hierarchy and market in the new institutional economics are crucial not just for economic structures, but also for political structures, especially the state itself in both its internal and external dimensions.

Even in terms of the most fundamental traditional concerns of states, those of defense and security, the state is being challenged as the predominant legitimate provider of collective goods (including Weber's "monopoly of legitimate violence"). States almost never fight each other today; virtually all wars are civil and cross-national wars (with the 1992 Gulf War as the exception that proves the rule). At the same time, the power to establish and maintain the world order as a whole – providing stability, security and other crucial collective goods – is increasingly fragmented and/or shared among states, international and transgovernmental coalitions and regimes, and private provision. States can no longer make a full range of credible commitments, whether individually or collectively. Furthermore, state actors themselves – although they continue to have a range of significant economic, financial, political and bureaucratic resources at their disposal and are still crucial actors in regulating particular economic and social activities – paradoxically act in routine fashion to undermine the holistic and hierarchical character of traditional state sovereignty, authority or *potestas* (Cerny, 1997b) – a "hollowing out of the state" (Jessop, 1997). The result is a growing "privatization of the public sphere," not only by selling off or contracting out public services and functions, but in the deeper sense of reducing society itself to competing "associations of consumers" in which administrators are little more than buyers in competing corporations (Ostrom, *et al.*, 1961, p.839).

Now such privatization, marketization or commodification of the state is not something exclusive to globalization; indeed, globalization is often seen as just one of a number of wider "exogenous factors" at work in transforming the nature of governance today, also including decentralization, fiscal constraint, distrust of government, increasing participation (functional representation) by special interests, and the like (Peters, 1997). It is important also to remember the role of other factors which are not directly addressed here, such as the new ideological hegemony of neoliberal thought and the role of individual and group actors or "agents," an issue which I have addressed elsewhere (Cerny, 1999a). Nevertheless, a range of *structural* dimensions of globalization, whether economic, social or political, although limited and uneven in practice are inextricably intertwined with each of these trends both as an independent and a facilitating variable – and even, in the case of the competition state, as a feedback and dependent variable. In essence, this chapter argues that the character of the underlying structural changes involved in globalization alters the "bottom line" parameters or boundaries within which other changes take place. It channels those changes and biases outcomes by altering the payoffs available to individual and group agents when they come to make different choices (the "payoff matrix"), thereby shaping the "structured field of action" within which they operate (Cerny, 1990). Therefore, in order to assess the role of globalization in influencing and/or driving the transformation of governance structures, it is necessary first to characterize those structural changes which are embedded in globalization processes as such.

The dialectic of convergence and divergence

Processes of centralization and hierarchization of the international system, which began with the emergence of the nation-state and culminated in the Cold War system, are being replaced with a much more diffuse, decentralized, and cross-cutting structural pattern. Non-state actors are by no means the only significant agents in this process; indeed, the state, far from being merely a power-maximizing unit subject to the "self-help" imperatives of international anarchy, has become a critical agent of its own – and therefore of the system's – transformation. Key organizational levels of the international system – multilateral, regional, nation-state, and sub-state – have been taking on significant new characteristics; at the same time, a range of transnational "functional" structures have taken shape. Although these developments have roots long before the end of the Cold War, today, with the collapse of the overarching structural constraints built into the Cold War system, a range of permissive conditions exist favouring the consolidation and further evolution of a new structural pattern.

Understanding such a pattern starts from the premise that the system *as a whole* has been transformed, in Durkheim's terms, from a "simple" structure into a "complex" one. A simple structure is "segmented" into "like" units. These units may be very different in size, shape, or internal constitution, and the issue of "likeness," as Waltz has pointed out, is not the same as saying that the units are identical (Waltz, 1986, pp.323–6). What it does mean is that in their interaction with each other, they all *act* in like ways, and that changes in their size, shape or internal constitution do not alter this fact. They retain a fundamental, bottom-line, unit-like character. In this context, they are only capable of what Durkheim calls "mechanical solidarity"; the units may cooperate, but they do not intermingle; they are not characterized by a cross-cutting division of labor. Thus, for Waltz, the international system is inherently a segmented society with a simple structure and held together by mechanical solidarity; this is the basis of the structural logic of anarchy.

From this perspective, then, until there is a single world society with a single legal system to regulate conflict, anarchy remains the rule and mechanical solidarity remains the limit of the possible, although some limited experiments might succeed; Durkheim specifically mentions "a European society which has, at present [1893], some idea of itself and the beginning of organization" (1933, p.405). The only way for a genuine *paradigmatic* shift to take place which would undermine the structural determinism of the neorealist project would be the transformation of the international system into a society with a "complex" structure. Such a structure would involve the emergence of a cross-cutting division of labor, which would permit the development of "organic solidarity," involving both complex exchanges and the development of common rules to regulate such exchanges. But it is not the formation of common rules which is the independent causal variable; it is the spread of the division of labor.

Durkheim argues that "greater societies" are not formed by the evolution or redesigning of rules in and of themselves (*pace* Wayne Sandholtz's chapter in this volume); rather, they are formed out of a reconfiguring of the scale of socio-economic substructures, i.e. of the division of labor. A greater specialization of functions necessarily results from attempts by expanding societies to maintain themselves in equilibrium – and even from the growth in sheer numbers of societies – according to Durkheim. A greater specialization of functions, cutting across societies, induces the development of a *transnational* – not merely an "inter-national" – division of labor. The international system, in what Durkheim admits will be an uneven and long-term process, must however eventually become a complex society linked through organic solidarity. In contrast, Waltz believes that the constraints of the segmental, mechanical, anarchical structure of the international system are still in place and that any paradigmatic shift is both problematic and a long way off.

What sort of "international society" or transnational structure is likely to emerge from this process? I suggest that the system will be controlled and stabilized not by a single hierarchical and legal system of regulation – the development of a single broad regime (which Durkheim himself thought to be the necessary outcome) – but by a complex process deriving directly from structural differentiation, from the new transnational division of labor itself. It is therefore crucial first of all to identify the different variables which contribute to the structure of the contemporary world order. They include both different political variables – other than, and in addition to, the state – and a range of economic and social variables, arranged in complex cross-cutting configurations. The result is likely to involve both an enmeshing of traditional power structures such as the state within a web of overlapping affiliations (what Susan Strange (1988) has called a "web of contracts"), and a cross-fire of fractionalized, cross-cutting conflicts. The basic mechanism by which the system is regulated will shift from a hierarchy of holistic actors – states – which impose order through power and hegemony, to a more complex and diffuse set of interactive self-regulatory mechanisms. These are more than just "webs of power," for they take on an "organic" character (Parsons, 1949, pp.31ff.). It will be the sufficiency or insufficiency of these mechanisms when faced with a multitude of new tasks and challenges that will determine the stability or instability, legitimacy or illegitimacy, performance or non-performance of the overall governance structure of a globalizing world.

Analysts have identified varying ranges of differentiated, cross-cutting structures, each having a particular set of structural characteristics and a differently constituted – but usually overlapping – population of participating agents (e.g., Buchan, 1974; Merle, 1977; Keohane and Nye, 1977; Strange,

1988). The first task, then, is to identify the main kinds of structural differentiation characteristic of the new world order – not holistic categories based
on territorial boundaries, but what might be called functional categories.
Each entails a distinct type of interaction which would otherwise be
aggregated with other types under the institutional umbrellas we have been
discussing.

In attempting to synthesize such "functional" categories, such authors
identify a specific set or range of types of interaction which they see as
characterizing international relations in the contemporary world. First, they
point to a "security" "system," " sub-system," "level," "plane," or "structure." Second, all suggest that there are fundamental differences between
the dynamics of this security structure, on the one hand, and what has usually
been called the "economic" system or structure, on the other; indeed, this
economic structure is often seen as becoming more and more important as
"low politics" displaces "high politics" as the real substructure or infrastructure of the world order. However, the way that the economic structure
actually works is itself contested, as we shall see. Some writers, furthermore,
refer to a "political" system or structure, based on the diffusion of decision-
making authority and sovereignty away from the nation-state, whether
downward to sub-state or cross-national socio-economic groupings or
upward to a variety of multilateral, "minilateral" (see Gilpin, 1987, p.372;
Yarbrough and Yarbrough, 1990), regional, or other categories. Some refer,
finally, to a "cultural" system or structure, based on the transmission and
assimilation of values or the sources of knowledge and understanding in the
contemporary world – whether based on the convergence, or the conflict or
competition, among the values involved.

Analyses of the emerging economic structure have focused on two main
issues: changes in relative economic power; and institutional economies of
scale. The first concerns the nature of international economic stratification
(both vertical and horizontal) in general: locating shifts in the relative distribution of economic resources and power in the world; and suggesting how
these shifts affect the relations between different economic and political
actors (states, regions, multinational firms, etc.). Just how such an increasingly multipolar economic structure might work in the future, however, is
still vague and contested: some writers suggest that it will lead to a more
stable multiple hegemony; others see competitive neo-mercantilism as the
outcome. In terms of institutional economies of scale, the main debate has
been between (1) those who see a trend toward "globalization," whether in
finance, trade, the multinationalization of production, energy, and a range
of socio-economic issues such as environmental depletion and/or protection,
and (2) those who merely see a trend toward increased state imbrication in
a wider range of economic activities, and therefore an increase in "state
capacity".

Perhaps the closest that current analyses approximate to an overall model
of governance is found in the notion that there is an emerging "political"

sub-system or structure. These analyses usually attempt to draw analogies
and identify linkages, overlaps – and discontinuities – between the security
and the economic sub-systems. The trends identified in such analyses tend to
fall into two main categories: (1) a diffusion of power "at the top" of the
system; and (2) the erosion and/or parcellization of national sovereignty –
the diffusion of power "from the bottom up," although the actual impact of
such trends on patterns of governance is problematic. On the one hand, ethnicity, religious revival, sub-state nationalism (e.g., tribalism, Balkanization,
etc.), "multiple channels of interaction," sub- or cross-national "market
segmentation" or "class fractions," etc., are more likely to undermine than
reinforce the state; on the other, internationally linked economic sectors
and/or the development of increased *supra*-national consciousness and
common action may lead from mere interpenetration to real if uneven transnational integration. Clearly many of these perceived trends are in tension
with each other, even mutually contradictory, involving elements of both
convergence and divergence, homogenization and heterogeneity.

Complexity, conflict, and stability

These functional categories are not mutually exclusive, but are closely linked
with each other – interpenetrated and interdependent. We are dealing with
cross-cutting structural categories and not with distinct groups of actors,
eroding the notion that there is such a thing as a "national economy" and
leading many observers to the conclusion that the very concept of "we" in
national terms no longer reflects social and economic realities (see Reich,
1991). Consequently, the idea of the state itself is changing. The twentieth-
century bureaucratic or "national welfare" state developed out of a
movement to control the negative side-effects of the nineteenth-century
"self-regulating market" (itself a product of the liberal state: Polanyi, 1944);
indeed, states have often been thought to be fundamentally and *inherently* hierarchical in structure, in contrast to economic markets (e.g., Gilpin, 1987).
Yet the rediscovery of the role of states historically in promoting markets,
and more recently the popularization of such notions as "competitive governments", "entrepreneurial government," or the "competition state" – along
with the emergence of the "new institutional economics" and the development of the concept of governance in the theory of the firm – have changed
the terms of institutional discourse. The distinction between "state" and
"market" has not simply been blurred.

More than that, *both* state and economic institutions have been shown to
consist of mixtures of hierarchical and market-like characteristics. In an era
when markets, production structures, and firms increasingly operate in the
context of a cross-border division of labor, can the state any longer remain a
structure apart? Today, public policy and management analysis is
increasingly focusing on what has been called the "post-modernist critique"
of "the existing public sector paradigm" (Prowse, 1992). Such concerns

cut across democracy and deal directly with the potential for market-like behaviour in the state apparatus itself – the "commodification" or "marketization" of the state *per se*, both in its endogenous structure and behaviour *and* in its mode of economic "intervention." They also cut across, as does Reich (1991) in the economic literature, the concept of the state as a *territorial* unit (Ruggie, 1993). Similarly, literature on neo-corporatism has shifted its ground from "peak-level" tripartism – the original focus of pioneering writers like Schmitter (1974) – to the more diffuse sectoral and local corporatist forms known as "meso-" and "micro-corporatism" (Cawson, 1985; Cerny, 1990, chap. 6) or even to firm-level "entrepreneurial corporatism" (which, according to Robert Cox (1986), is the product of the transnationalization of social forces). Phrases like "public-private partnership," or the promotion of "competitive advantage" (as distinct from comparative advantage: Zysman and Tyson, eds, 1983; Porter, 1990), have moved from the world of academic analysis into the rhetoric and programmes of politicians on both right and left.

As the transnational division of labour expands, the kinds of things that states can do, and the constraints which derive from external pressures, are constantly changing and becoming more complex. They must act in ways that fit uneasily with, and which increasingly undermine, their traditional hierarchical structures. In addition, at another level, "domestic" societies themselves are coming to be seen not as homogeneous units, but as inherently pluralistic and multicultural – although this can also be a cause of strife in the name of nationalism or "ethnic cleansing." How those conflicts will be managed, in terms of governance, can only evolve within certain parameters.

One of those parameters concerns patterns of identity, belonging, and membership. For example, in "simple" systems such as the states system as conceived in neorealist theory, social identity and membership in the common world were increasingly bound up in externally exclusive, nation-state-based political and social bonds – bonds which are essential for the effective supply and provision of collective goods. Collective goods are those from the enjoyment or use of which *insiders* cannot be excluded, requiring authoritative mechanisms for identifying and excluding *outsiders* (Olson, 1971; Ostrom, *et al.*, 1961; Ostrom and Ostrom, 1977) – a classic task of hierarchical governments (states). Complex systems, in contrast, are characterized by "overlapping memberships" and "cross-cutting affiliations." In the international/transnational/global context – whether we look at states and state actors, multinational corporations, interest groups, and/or individuals – their tasks, roles and activities will cut across the different levels and structures discussed earlier. Without the state and its authoritative capacity to enforce the rules of the game, transnational complexity would seem to imply instability.

However, in Simmel's reformulation of Durkheim, the effect of the development of a division of labor does not merely divide (and thereby unite) discrete, unidimensional individuals into watertight compartments defined in their totality by their specialized functions and roles. Rather, that division of labor is partially reflected and replicated within each individual. Each individual is caught up in a range of different, sometimes competing or even contradictory, tasks, roles and activities. No two individuals represent exactly the same combination of social, economic and political linkages and group affiliations. A "complex social structure" inevitably leads to the formation of complex individuals, whose roles and group memberships overlap with several distinct sets of other individuals and groups – in the family, in employment, in friendships, in leisure activities, in communications, etc. (Simmel, 1955).

Therefore political stability is not derived simply from cooperation, consensus, norms, system equilibrium, etc. Pluralist stability depends instead upon the particular lines of *conflict* which characterize a particular society, as argued by Coser (1956). Conflict has several "functions" in the creation and maintenance of stability. In particular, multilevel *cross-cutting* conflicts can mitigate more entrenched conflict between holistic "close-knit groups," leading to a more flexible social structure. In effect, the unit-like states of the neorealist canon, with their segmental character and their mechanical solidarity, are analogous to Coser's close-knit groups, while the international system today may be analogous to a flexible social structure, characterized by cross-cutting conflicts – thus at least partially counteracting tendencies toward instability.

In this context, the traditional zero-sum character of international relations – the notion that without a tight, overarching structure, the international system is prone to destructive anarchy and zero-sum conflicts – becomes redundant. In effect, each – and perhaps all? – of the structural categories set out earlier can grow stronger simultaneously (although unevenly in space and time) without reducing the (increasing?) strength and/or effectiveness of other levels and structures. They need not be "equal," merely complex. In the context of overlapping memberships across a range of increasingly manifest and "developed" (complex, cohesive, differentiated, etc.) structural categories, the very fluidity identified by such analysts as Keohane and Nye (1977) constitutes the basis not just for an international plurality of "building blocks," but for new dynamic governance processes.

In the post-Cold War world, those governance processes derive from the interaction of different types of social and economic activity, not from the holistic power of the state itself or the unilinear development of a homogeneous "global" society. On the contrary, globalization is a multilayered phenomenon which incorporates the state – and sustains some of its ostensible functions – while at the same time altering its very essence and undermining its constitutional foundations. However, whether the resulting governance arrangements are more likely to resemble Coserian pluralistic stability, or something less coherent and more unstable like the so-called new medievalism, we will address at the end of this chapter.

Globalization and the collective goods problem

The key to understanding the shape of new and complex governance structures in the global era lies in the way that economic competition is changing in the world. On one level, the way the state itself works is changing. The main task or function of the contemporary state is the promotion of economic activities, whether at home or abroad, which make firms and sectors located within the territory of the state competitive in international markets – the competition state. This concept of the "competition state" (Cerny, 1990 and 1997b) therefore goes beyond the idea of the "strategic state" or the "developmental state" of the 1980s (Zysman, 1983; Johnson, 1982). The difference is that, while the state has always been to some extent a promoter of market forces, state structures today are being transformed into market-oriented and even market-based organizations, fundamentally altering the way that public goods and private goods are provided. Indeed, states are transforming – marketizing – *themselves* in the search for effectiveness in an increasingly economically interpenetrated world. On another level, as we have already pointed out, states have promoted the formation of a web of transnational regimes and other linkages which have increasingly been developing the capacity to operate autonomously of those states. However, the authority of such institutions is inherently problematic, making it virtually impossible to establish clear or even operationalizable lines of political (especially democratic) accountability. As a result of this two-fold movement, we are witnessing the transmutation of the state from a civil association into a more limited form of enterprise association, operating within a wider market and institutional environment, but which may be vulnerable to crises of legitimacy.

The significance of economic globalization lies in the way that it has altered the relationship between different kinds of goods and assets, i.e. collective (public and quasi-public) goods on the one hand and private goods on the other (Cerny, 1995). Many of what were thought to constitute collective goods at the time of the Second Industrial Revolution are either no longer controllable by the state because they have become transnational in structure and/or constitute private goods in a wider world marketplace. In the Second Industrial Revolution state, public goods were perceived by virtually all interested parties as national-level phenomena, even by Marxist-Leninists. Of course, the concept of what is "public" about public goods is complex and contested. In terms of etymology, political philosophy and everyday political language, the idea of what is public is essentially normative; it denotes matters that people think *ought* to be treated as common or collective concerns, as distinct from what ought to be left to individuals or private groups to decide and/or do for themselves. Today, the heart of political debate is about choosing among competing conceptions of what should be treated as public and what should not.

In contrast, the economic theory of collective goods argues that only what is most *efficiently* organized and run publicly (i.e. which provides the best possible product at the lowest possible cost when organized according to the definition set out below) ought to be so organized and run. In economic theory (e.g., Olson, 1971), then, the main issue is *indivisibility*, on two levels: goods are truly "public" when both the structure of production *and* the structure of consumption lead to conditions of indivisibility. In a globalizing world, however, such calculations become more complex. In some industries, products that once may have been most efficiently produced on a collective basis (especially on a national scale) may nowadays be more efficiently organized along lines which imply larger, *trans*national optimal economies of scale, making traditional "public" provision uncompetitive. In other cases, technological change and/or flexible production may actually *reduce* optimal economies of scale, turning such goods effectively into private goods, which also are increasingly produced and traded in a global rather than a national marketplace. With regard to consumption, economists refer to the criterion of excludability. Public goods are by definition "non-excludable," which means that collective provision has to be organized in such a way as to prevent non-paying users (free riders) from making the provision of the good too expensive for the rest – i.e., through forced payment (taxes). Again, in a globalizing world it has become increasingly difficult to exclude non-paying users (free riders) from outside national boundaries from benefitting from nationally-provided collective goods in ways that are unacceptably costly in terms of domestic politics and public policy. Thus with regard to both production and consumption, it is becoming more and more difficult to maintain the sort of public or collective boundaries necessary for efficient state provision of public or collective goods.

Different categories of collective goods have different kinds of normative and economic characteristics. I refer to four such categories: regulatory, productive, distributive and redistributive collective goods (adapting the categories developed by Lowi, 1964). Each of these categories has been transformed by the structural changes associated with globalization and the other economic and political trends which, we have argued here, are inextricably intertwined with globalization.

The first category, regulatory collective goods, involves the establishment of a workable economic framework for the ongoing operation of the system as a whole, i.e. it involves the establishment and application of rules for the operation – and interaction – of both market and non-market transactions and institutions. Typical regulatory goods include establishment and protection of private (and public) property rights, a stable currency system, abolition of internal barriers to production and exchange within the national market, standardization of a range of facilitating structures such as a system of weights and measures, a legal system to sanction and enforce contracts and to adjudicate disputes, a regulatory system to stabilize and coordinate economic activities, a system of trade protection, and various facilities which can be mobilized to counteract system-threatening market failures (such as "lender of last resort" facilities, emergency powers, etc.). Real or potential inefficiencies in the provision of regulatory collective goods can have exceptionally wide ramifications, because their provision in and of itself can be said to constitute a sort of "collective collective good" given the role of regulation as a framework within which not only other collective goods, but also *private* goods, are produced and supplied. Regulatory collective goods, therefore, are inextricably intertwined with the very foundations of the capitalist state.

In a world of relatively open trade, financial deregulation, massive international financial flows, the increasing impact of information technology and the like, a range of basic rules and processes necessary for effective governance, from property rights to economic regulation to the promotion of general economic growth, are increasingly complex for states to establish and maintain. In this context, the ability of firms, market actors, and competing parts of the national state apparatus itself to defend and expand their economic and political turf through activities such as transnational policy networking and regulatory arbitrage has both undermined the control span of the state from without and fragmented it from within.

The second and third categories of collective goods involve various specific directly or indirectly state-controlled or state-sponsored activities of production and distribution – *productive* collective goods on the one hand, and *distributive* collective goods on the other. Although these two categories often overlap, and I have previously treated them as a single category (Cerny, 1995), the differences between them can be quite significant, as can be seen in recent theories of public policy, the "new public management," and "reinventing government" (see Ostrom, *et al.*, 1961, for an early example of this argument) – which are themselves closely linked with processes of globalization. In line with the economic definition of public goods set out above, the concept of productive collective goods refers to the production of goods and services, whereas distributive collective goods involve the delivery of those goods and services. Of course, this is often a difficult distinction to make with regard to many areas of state intervention, such as electricity supply or transportation infrastructure (see Helm, 1989). The distinction between these and redistributive collective goods (see below) is also complex.

With regard to productive collective goods, it is their technological and economic characteristics, rather than their normative characteristics, which have been of most significance in distinguishing between public and private. In other words, the validity of the public ownership of politically, economically or militarily "strategic" industries, along with the establishment and maintenance of state monopolies in a range of public services, has usually been seen to derive from economies of scale and transactions-cost savings in their production. Of course, normative considerations have clearly played a major political role for socialists and social democrats both in justifying such policies and in mobilizing support for them, while conservatives and

free-market liberals have similarly argued against such measures in normative terms too.

However, the possibilities for pursuing such policies and for constructing
the post-World War II settlement had, I suggest, more to do with the dominance of Second Industrial Revolution organizational forms, especially as
these forms (and the policies they evoked and enabled) went far beyond the
boundaries of existing ideological debates and created a broad consensus in
most advanced capitalist states – a consensus focused on the mixed economy
and the welfare state at home and increasingly free trade abroad, now
known as "embedded liberalism" – that lasted until the 1970s. More recently,
the interaction of the advent of flexible manufacturing systems, on the one
hand, and competing low-cost sources of supply – especially from firms
operating multinationally, transnationally or globally (whether publicly or
privately owned, based at home or abroad) – on the other hand, has been particularly important in undermining state-owned firms in a range of particular
sectors by transforming both economies of scale and transaction-cost structures. Indeed, both publicly owned firms and privately owned industries
promoted or privileged by the state have been undergoing a complex restructuring process which has not only altered their economic efficiencies but has
also been at the heart of a new neoliberal consensus skeptical about the
possibility and desirability of maintaining a significant public sector and of
pursuing interventionist industrial policy and planning in general.

With regard to distributive collective goods, we are talking about the
supply or provision of products and services to the public (or different publics)
on a collective basis, whether produced in the private sector or in the public
sector. In contrast to productive collective goods, distributive collective
goods are characterized less by their technical indivisibility – economies of
scale and transactions cost economies deriving from "hard" production
systems – and more by potential "soft" scale and transactions cost economies
deriving from their management structures, on the one hand, and from the
collective characteristics of their consumers rather than their producers, on
the other. For these reasons, there is considerable debate over the nature and
amount of any potential transactions cost savings which might result from
their being provided hierarchically rather than through market allocation
processes.

In recent years, policy-oriented economists have come to consider a much
larger range of such goods as being appropriate for market or quasi-market
provision. This changing perspective has resulted both from a re-evaluation
of the nature of demand – the belief that "publics" are essentially collections
of self-regarding consumers rather than embedded in like-minded or homogeneous social collectivities – and from a belief that public sector hierarchies
are inherently costly and cumbersome superstructures. In this sense, many of
those basic public services and functions such as the provision of public
health, street lighting, garbage collection, police protection, certain kinds of
transportation or energy infrastructure, etc., which have been at the bureau-

cratic heart of the modern industrial/welfare state, are being disaggregated and commodified in a range of experimental ways (Dunleavy, 1994; Osborne and Gaebler, 1992).

In this sense, distributive collective goods increasingly overlap with the fourth category, redistributive collective goods – the nature of which has always been seen to be even more fundamentally political, with their public and collective character deriving from political decisions about justice and fairness rather than from the economic efficiency, or inefficiency, of those public allocation mechanisms which they engender. Redistributive collective goods comprise mainly those developed in response to the expanding political and public policy demands of emerging social classes, economic interests and political parties. Clearly many of these goods are only "collective" or "public" goods because political decisions have been made (whether or not in response to public demand) to *treat them* as public. These decisions reflect the belief that such goods *ought* to be supplied on a collective basis for reasons of justice, equity or other normative considerations, rather than as a result of their relative indivisibility in technical economic terms. Redistributive goods have included health and welfare services, education, employment policies, systems for corporatist bargaining, environmental protection, and the like – indeed, the main apparatus of the national welfare state.

Today, the provision of redistributive collective goods is changing dramatically. Corporatist bargaining and employment policies are under challenge everywhere in the face of international pressures for wage restraint and flexible working practices. Although developed states have generally not found it possible to reduce the overall weight of the welfare state as a proportion of GDP, there has been a significant transformation in the balance of how welfare funds are spent – from the maintenance of free-standing social and public services to the provision of unemployment compensation and other "entitlement" programs. The latter have ballooned as a consequence of industrial "downsizing," increasing inequalities of wealth, the aging of the population in industrial societies, etc. – thereby tending to crowd out funding for other services. Finally, the most salient new sector of redistributive public goods, environmental protection, is particularly transnational in character; pollution and the rape of natural resources do not respect borders. Indeed, the main dividing line in a globalizing world between those goods which can generally speaking be efficiently provided as public goods and those which cannot is seen by authors such as Reich (1991) to be whether they involve "mobile" or "immobile" factors of capital – i.e., whether particular goods and assets (including labor) can be easily shifted across geographical spaces in general and national borders in particular, by owners and investors, or not.

Collective goods and complex governance

Particularly central to this transformation, of course, has been the changing technological and institutional context in which *all* goods are increasingly being produced and exchanged, including the rapid development of "post-Fordism," characterized by a wider process of "flexibilization" (see Amin, 1994). At the heart of flexibilization in both production processes and firms themselves has been the explosive development of information technology. Olson (1971), for example, argued that one of the key factors which made collective action difficult in large groups was the inability of large groups to *monitor* the behavior of members who might be tempted (or determined) to free-ride. Electronic computer and communications technology has transformed this problem – bridging one of the oldest institutional conundrums in history and theory, that between centralization and decentralization. This monitoring capability also leaps national borders and brings firms, markets and consumers into a single, global production process in an increasing number of sectors. In addition, as the trade and production structures of the Third Industrial Revolution evolve, they will be increasingly coordinated through the application of complex financial controls, rapidly evolving accounting techniques, financial performance indicators, and the like. These strictures are of course equally applicable to a range of organizations, including government bureaucracies.

But these aspects of the Third Industrial Revolution – flexibilization of production, firm structure, and monitoring – only represent the supply side of the equation. The demand side involves the development of ever more complex consumer societies and the resulting *segmentation of markets*. The technological capacity to produce flexibly – the ability of business to produce at the appropriate scale – has combined with an increasing differentiation of the class system in advanced capitalist societies. These pressures now apply to the provision of public goods by governments as well, with "choice" replacing standardized collective provision.

Thus globalization entails the undermining of the public character of public goods and of the specific character of specific assets, i.e. the privatization and marketization of economic and political structures. Nevertheless, states retain both a certain legitimacy and a range of residual functions – some of which have actually been reinforced by globalization. If we want to look for an alternative way of conceiving of the residual state, probably the best place to look is at American state governments. These governments can claim only a partial loyalty from their inhabitants, and their power over internal economic and social structures and forces has been limited indeed. However, they have been required to operate over the course of the past two centuries in an increasingly open continental market, without there being such a thing as state "citizenship" (only residence, alongside the free movement of persons within the United States as a whole). Nevertheless, they do – like counties, provinces and regions in other countries – foster a sense of identity and belonging that can be quite strong. In economic policy matters they represent the essence of the "competition state." The main focus of the competition state in the world – in a way that is partly analogous to the focus of American state governments – is the promotion of economic activities, whether at home or abroad, which will make firms and sectors located within the territory of the state competitive in international markets. Rather than providing public goods or other services which cannot be efficiently provided by the market – in other words, rather than acting as a "decommodifying" agent where market efficiency fails – the state is drawn into promoting the commodification or marketization of its *own* activities and structures. The state has always to some extent been a promoter of market forces rather than a purely hierarchical or "public" organization; this marketizing quality is especially characteristic of regulatory collective goods. But there is a difference between promoting market activities as a general public good and being itself transformed into a market-based organization *per se*. In effect, it is the transformation of the predominant mix of goods from public-dominated to private-dominated which in turn transforms the state from a primarily hierarchical, decommodifying agent into a primarily market-based, commodifying agent.

By increasingly promoting the transnational expansion and competitiveness of its industries and services abroad and in increasingly competing for inward investment, the state becomes a critical agent, perhaps *the* most critical agent, in the process of globalization itself (Cerny, 1997b). Beyond privatization and deregulation, probably the most extensive experiment in the United States and the United Kingdom has been the subcontracting out of public and social services (Dunleavy, 1994). The state has attempted to replace hierarchical systems with recurrent contracting. What has seemed to make such innovations realistic has been the possibility of vigilant performance monitoring (especially using new information technology) and the application of highly targeted financial controls. Closely linked to subcontracting is the attempt to introduce "internal markets" into previously hierarchical organizations. Britain, for instance, has recently privatized electricity suppliers – thought by many economists to be as near as you can get to a technological "natural monopoly" given the expense of laying parallel cables and the like. The government is promoting competition in each electrical supplier's geographical areas by requiring them each to sell a certain amount of the electricity they produce to industries (and eventually to private consumers) at prices set by their competitors; similar reforms are under discussion in the United States at the time of writing. Some programs to "reinvent government" go much farther, of course, calling for a new entrepreneurialism (and intrapreneurialism?) in the far reaches of government and the public sector (Osborne and Gaebler, 1992). Such internal policy changes, of course, go along with the kind of targeted pro-competitive and pro-business industrial and trade policies analyzed by Hart and Prakash in this volume.

Conclusions: alternative scenarios of complex governance

Rather than globalization leading to the emergence of a more clearly defined and homogeneous global order, it has instead been characterized by the increasing differentiation of both economic and political structures. Against this background, the state is being transformed into a complex mix of civil and enterprise associations. The essence of the problem is whether the very diffusion and decentralization of world politics and the complementary erosion of traditional state capacity will lead to a greater instability of the system as such, or whether it may actually strengthen the stability, resilience and adaptability of the world order at the macro-level.

In this paradoxical situation, a major feature of the new world order may well be the delinking of local and regional conflict from the stabilization of conflict in the system as a whole. Thus the security of the world is no longer likely to be threatened by escalation to total war at a global level, simply because conflicts will remain more localized and therefore less likely to spread. This means, for example, that the well-known rise of religious fundamentalism is not likely to lead to a "clash of civilizations" (Huntington, 1997), but rather to messy, ongoing, multi-level, low intensity conflicts between sub-groups at the local level – often between conflicting factions of the same broad cultural category, for example between Sunni and Shia Muslims, or among those who have been living as neighbors, as in Bosnia and in Rwanda.

The world is most likely to be divided not between conflicting systems but, as Singer and Wildavsky (1993) have argued, between "zones of peace," characterized by relative affluence, expanding trade, financial and communications flows, cross-national cross-cutting cleavages, and low-level consensus around the competition state model with its neoliberal hegemony, on the one hand, and "zones of turmoil," characterized by worsening inequality and poverty, endemic violence, and the decay of both traditional and modern social bonds – what Kaplan (1997) has called "the ends of the earth" – on the other. Economic systems will be permeable at meso- and micro-levels, increasing inequality but at the same time undermining the potential for large-scale international confrontation to which deprivation might otherwise give rise. The world's major powers – especially the United States, by far the strongest military power – will no longer be able to integrate fixed alliance systems under their own command, but will have to construct and reconstruct contingent, shifting alliances in specific crisis situations. And the threat of "balkanization," whether in Eurasia, India, Africa, or the Balkans themselves, will increasingly contrast with the globalization of finance, technology, environmental regulation, etc., in a complex struggle for cultural coherence.

It is clear that a world characterized by complex globalization will not be an easy world to live in, much less to manage, in three ways. First, in the post-Cold War world order, despite the greater number and sometimes the greater intensity of local conflicts, they will not be great enough, nor cumulative enough, to threaten the breakdown of the overarching system. This system will not be based on agreement or consensus on "the rules of the game" among all actors, but on the very cross-cutting nature of conflict in general. Second, the more interpenetrated a particular state, or region, or international organization, or transnational structure – i.e., the more overlapping memberships that are characteristic of its involvement in the world order – then the more likely it will be that specific conflicts are circumscribed, even canceled out, by other, cross-cutting conflicts. Third, however, this new system may well even exacerbate, expand, and deepen some of them.

Within this world of complex globalization and multilayered governance, a range of alternative overall scenarios can be identified. If we postulate the hypothetical existence of two ideal-type poles – a new hierarchization of the international system around global-level governance, at one end of the spectrum, and an unstable anarchy or chaos, at the other – then it is possible to elaborate three intermediate positions. In the middle of the scale is what I have called "plurilateralism" (Cerny, 1993) – the "rosy scenario." In this case, the presence of cross-cutting affiliations may defuse potential conflict situations, leading to the gradual locking in of habits of compromise and market-like mutual adjustment. Governance processes and structures will take the form of self-regulating mechanisms. Such processes may turn out to be extremely powerful in terms of the overall stabilization of the system, but would lack the kind of holistic authority or steering mechanisms to ensure democratic accountability and/or redistributive potential.

Toward the hierarchical end of the spectrum, it is possible to hypothesize that certain layers of the system – particular economic sectors, for instance, which have developed autonomous self-regulatory governance processes, whether in globalized financial markets or through cartel-like behavior among transnational firms – will become the predominant authoritative allocators of collective goods in the global economy. I call this "sectoral hegemony" – kind of a transnational oligopolistic neo-corporatism. Such an overall pattern of governance might indeed be powerful at steering the global economy and undertaking redistributive tasks on behalf of particular business interests; but it would not be responsive in democratic terms to social and political demands – lacking both accountability and authority in a world where nation-states would be increasingly circumscribed and public international regimes too fragmented to be other than agencies open to various degrees of capture. Redistribution would be motivated only by self-interest, although that self-interest would almost certainly include elements of self-restraint in order to preclude destabilization of the system as a whole. International finance is the leading candidate for such a hegemonic role, although its credibility is being sorely tested by the market meltdown at the time of writing (Autumn, 1998).

Toward the anarchic end of the spectrum – "neomedievalism" – the result would not necessarily be collapse. After all, even though we often think of the Middle Ages as a period of chaos, they were actually a time of relative stability and of great social and economic progress. Feudalism was the most productive economic system the world had ever seen prior to the emergence of fully-fledged capitalism; competing authorities and identities – complex feudal hierarchies, the church, the growing cities, corporatist labor and industrial organization in the form of guilds, the flourishing of long-distance trading networks and the development of international banking, both local quasi-tribal and cosmopolitan elite and religious identities, etc. – coexisted uneasily but in a state of dynamic tension. Alain Minc (1993) has called the Middle Ages a time of "durable disorder," which despite the existence of "grey zones" where the writ of any secular or temporal authority did not run, persisted and permitted a wide range of innovative social, political, and economic developments to take place. At the same time, however, such a world runs the risk of deteriorating into a "blade-runner" society.

This picture of change is perhaps more dramatic than some of those found in other chapters in this book. The closest in spirit is Stephen Kobrin's analogy of medievalism and postmodernism, seeing the modern nation-state as the exception rather than the rule in both the history and the future potential of social and political organization. Michael McGinnis's conclusion that a wider variety of social actors will develop new forms of governance through a form of institutional *bricolage* perhaps reflects the "rosy scenario" or plurilateralist model set out above. However, to reprise Granovetter, transaction cost economics do not determine outcomes but merely alter probabilities; the rest is path-dependent. By focusing on the actors he chooses, McGinnis makes a strong case that their choices may create stronger, if more diverse and overlapping, domestic and transnational governance structures in the future. But whether their efforts will result in the sort of coherent governance arrangements he suggests is more problematic. Wayne Sandholtz pictures this process as a rewriting of rules in the face of the challenges of globalization, and indeed the process of rule-writing is gathering steam in a number of issue-areas, as he points out. But rule-writers, like all agents, are not faced with a *tabula rasa*; they do not have unlimited choices as to what rules are both desirable and feasible in practice.

Thus agents – whether McGinnis's social actors or Sandholtz's rule-writers – are increasingly coming up against a range of both old and new constraints and opportunities, brought together in a mix where the landmarks for rule-writing are in many cases vague and untested. These are to a critical extent uncharted waters for governance-building. And one must not forget that among these constraints are the embedded institutions and habits of the nation-state. The residual state retains (at least) two key dimensions of power. In the first place, as Robert Kudrle argues, people are less mobile than capital, and so long as states can effectively regulate the movements of people and extract revenue from them, new structures will be fragmented and partial, and changes may be effectively contained (at least unless or until mass migrations and tax-driven relocation of elites become far more prevalent). I am less sure of this view; changing structures of production and international capital flows may have more of an impact on the ability of states to provide collective goods in general than Kudrle admits. In the second place, as David Lake argues, the very embeddedness of the state closes off many routes to any general refashioning of governance structures. In this context, this chapter therefore argues, there are many routes to change (multiple equilibria), few landmarks to go by, a range of agents with limited and uneven resources and (often short-term) perceptions and objectives, and a number of serious, embedded obstacles to coherent evolution. Thus the most likely outcome of change in this increasingly complex structural environment will also be limited, partial, uneven, multilayered, and potentially riddled with endemic sources of instability. The anarchic, Durkheimian world of mechanical solidarity is fissuring and destabilizing, cross-cut by an ever more complex cross-national division of labor reflected in the development of the "functional" structures described above in the second part of this chapter and in the changing structure of goods and assets discussed in part four. But new forms of organic solidarity at a transnational level have not crystallized to an extent that would be either necessary or sufficient in order to enable a genuinely coherent form of global governance to emerge.

With the collapse of the Eastern bloc and the end of the Cold War, a growing range of structural categories and levels are thus becoming imbricated with each other, intersecting with both traditional and new areas of conflict. The "modern" multitasking, multifunctional, "civil association" character of politics and governance, rooted in the nation-state, is under increasing pressure from both above and below, from new transnational economies of scale to the disaggregation of national culture societies. "Governance" in the future will no longer look so much like "government." Structures and processes of governance must adjust to this multilayered reality, although the precise form it will take will only emerge historically, in path-dependent fashion. The world is now more than ever enmeshed in a process of complex globalization, and the most urgent research agenda in both international relations and political science – not just in the short term but in the long term too – is to identify the myriad dimensions of this complex process and evaluate the structure of the intersections and interactions among them.

References

Amin, A., ed. (1994) *Post-Fordism: A Reader*, Oxford: Basil Blackwell.
Auspitz, J.L. (1976) "Individuality, Civility, and Theory: The Philosophical Imagination of Michael Oakeshott," *Political Theory* 4:2 (August), 261–352.
Barclay, H. (1982) *People Without Government: An Anthropology of Anarchism*, London: Kahn and Averill with Cienfuegos Press.
Blau, P.M., ed. (1975) *Approaches to the Study of Social Structure*, New York: Free Press.

Buchan, A. (1974) *The End of the Postwar Era: A New Balance of World Power*, London: Weidenfeld and Nicolson.

Bull, H. (1977) *The Anarchical Society: A Study of Order in World Politics*, London: Macmillan.

Cawson, A., ed. (1985) *Organized Interests and the State: Studies in Meso-Corporatism*, London and Newbury Park, CA: Sage.

Cerny, P.G. (1985) "State Capitalism in France and Britain and the New International Economic Order," in P.G. Cerny and M.A. Schain, eds, *Socialism, the State, and Public Policy in France*, New York: Methuen, 202–23.

Cerny, P.G. (1990) *The Changing Architecture of Politics: Structure, Agency, and the Future of the State*, London and Newbury Park, CA: Sage.

Cerny, P.G. (1993) "Plurilateralism: Structural Differentiation and Functional Conflict in the Post-Cold War World Order," *Millennium: Journal of International Studies* 22: 1 (Spring), 27–51.

Cerny, P.G. (1995) "Globalization and the Changing Logic of Collective Action," *International Organization* 49: 4 (Autumn), 595–625.

Cerny, P.G. (1996) "Globalization and Other Stories: The Search for a New Paradigm for International Relations," *International Journal* 51: 4 (Autumn), 617–37.

Cerny, P.G. (1997a) "Communication," *Political Studies* 45: 1 (March), 1–2.

Cerny, P.G. (1997b) "Paradoxes of the Competition State: The Dynamics of Political Globalization," *Government and Opposition* 32: 2 (Spring), 251–74.

Cerny, P.G. (1999a) "Globalization and the Erosion of Democracy," *European Journal of Political Research* (forthcoming).

Cerny, P.G. (1999b) "Globalizing the Political and Politicizing the Global: International Political Economy as a Vocation," *New Political Economy* (forthcoming).

Coser, L.A. (1956) *The Functions of Social Conflict*, London: Routledge and Kegan Paul.

Cox, R. (1986) "Social Forces, States and World Orders: Beyond International Relations Theory," in R.O. Keohane, ed., *Neorealism and Its Critics*, New York: Columbia University Press, 204–54.

Dewey, J. (1927) *The Public and Its Problems*, London: Allen and Unwin.

Dunleavy, P. (1994) "The Globalisation of Public Services Production: Can Government Be 'Best in World'?," *Public Policy and Administration* 9: 2 (Summer), 36–64.

Durkheim, E. (1933) *The Division of Labor in Society*, trans. George Simpson, New York: Free Press; original French edition 1893.

Gilpin, R. (1987) *The Political Economy of International Relations*, Princeton, NJ: Princeton University Press.

Granovetter, M. (1985) "Economic Action and Social Structure: The Problem of Embeddedness," *American Journal of Sociology* 91: 4 (November), 481–510.

Granovetter, M. (1992) "Economic Institutions as Social Constructions: A Framework for Analysis," *Acta Sociologica* 35, 3–11.

Haggard, S. (1990) *Pathways from the Periphery: The Politics of Growth in the Newly Industrializing Countries*, Ithaca, NY: Cornell University Press.

Hall, P.A. and Taylor, R.C.M. (1996) "Political Science and the Three New Institutionalisms", *Political Studies* 44:5 (December), 936–57.

Harris, N. (1986) *The End of the Third World*, Harmondsworth: Penguin.

Held, D. (1995) *Democracy and the Global Order: From the Modern State to Democratic Governance*, Cambridge: Polity Press.

Helm, D., ed. (1989) *The Economic Borders of the State*, Oxford: Oxford University Press.

Huntington, S.P. (1997) *The Clash of Civilizations and the Remaking of World Order*, New York: Simon and Schuster.

Jessop, B. (1997) "The Future of the National State: Erosion or Reorganization? Reflections on the West European Case," paper presented to the Conference on Globalization: Critical Perspectives, University of Birmingham, 14–16 March 1997.

Johnson, C. (1982) *M.I.T.I. and the Japanese Miracle: The Growth of Industrial Policy, 1925–1975*, Stanford, CA: Stanford University Press.

Kaplan, R.D. (1997) *The Ends of the Earth: Journey at the Dawn of the 21st Century*, London: Macmillan.

Keohane, R.O. and Nye, J.S. Jr. (1977) *Power and Interdependence*, Boston, MA: Little, Brown.

Lowi, T.J. (1964) "American Business, Public Policy, Case Studies, and Political Theory," *World Politics* 16: 4 (July), 677–715.

Merle, M. (1977) *Sociologie des relations internationales*, Paris: Dalloz.

Minc, A. (1993) *Le nouveau Moyen Age*, Paris: Gallimard.

Oakeshott, M. (1976) "On Misunderstanding Human Conduct: A Reply to My Critics," *Political Theory* 4: 2 (August), 353–67.

Olson, M. (1971) *The Logic of Collective Action*, Cambridge, MA: Harvard University Press.

Osborne, D. and Gaebler, T. (1992) *Reinventing Government: How the Entrepreneurial Spirit is Transforming the Public Sector, from Schoolhouse to Statehouse, City Hall to the Pentagon*, Reading, MA: Addison-Wesley.

Ostrom, V. and Ostrom, E. (1977) "Public Goods and Public Choices," in E.S. Savas, ed., *Alternatives for Delivering Public Services: Toward Improved Performance*, Boulder, CO: Westview, 7–49.

Ostrom, V., Tiebout, C.M. and Warren, R. (1961) "The Organization of Government in Metropolitan Areas: A Theoretical Inquiry," *American Political Science Review* 55: 3 (September), 831–42.

Parsons, T. (1949) *The Structure of Social Action*, Glencoe, IL: Free Press, 2nd edition.

Peters, B.G. (1977) "Globalization and Governance," paper presented at the Conference on Globalization: Critical Perspectives, University of Birmingham, 14–16 March 1997.

Polanyi, K. (1944) *The Great Transformation: The Political and Economic Origins of Our Time*, New York: Rinehart.

Porter, M.E. (1990) *The Competitive Advantage of Nations*, London: Macmillan.

Prowse, M. (1992) "Post-Modern Test for Government," *Financial Times* (21 April).

Reich, R.B. (1991) *The Work of Nations: Preparing Ourselves for 21st-Century Capitalism*, New York: Knopf.

Rhodes, R.A.W. (1996) "The New Governance: Governing Without Government," *Political Studies* 44: 4 (September), 652–67.

Ruggie, J.G. (1986) "Continuity and Transformation in the World Polity: Toward a Neorealist Synthesis," in R.O. Keohane, ed., *Neorealism and Its Critics*, New York: Columbia University Press, 131–57.

Ruggie, J.G. (1993) "Territoriality and Beyond: Problematizing Modernity in International Relations," *International Organization* 47: 1 (Winter), 139–74.

Schmitter, P.C. (1974) "Still the Century of Corporatism?" in F. Pike and T. Stritch, eds, *The New Corporatism*, Notre Dame, IN: Notre Dame University Press, 85–131.

Simmel, G. (1955) *Conflict and the Web of Group-Affiliations*, trans. K.H. Wolff and R. Bendix, New York: Free Press.

Singer, M. and Wildavsky, A. (1993) *The Real World Order: Zones of Peace/Zones of Turmoil*, Chatham, NJ: Chatham House.

Strange, S. (1988) *States and Markets: An Introduction to International Political Economy*, London: Pinter.

Thompson, G., Frances, J., Levacic, R. and Mitchell, J., eds (1991) *Markets, Hierarchies and Networks: The Co-ordination of Social Life*, London: Sage.

Waltz, K. (1979) *Theory of International Politics*, Reading, MA: Addison-Wesley.

Waltz, K. (1986) "Reflections on *Theory of International Politics*: A Response to My Critics," in R.O. Keohane, ed., *Neorealism and Its Critics*, New York: Columbia University Press, 322–45.

Williamson, O.E. (1975) *Markets and Hierarchies*, New York: Free Press.

Williamson, O.E. (1985) *The Economic Institutions of Capitalism*, New York: Free Press.

Yarbrough, B.V. and Yarbrough, R.M. (1990) "International Institutions and the New Economics of Organization," *International Organization* 44: 2 (Spring), 235–59.

Zysman, J. (1983) *Governments, Markets, and Growth: Financial Systems and the Politics of Industrial Change*, Ithaca, NY: Cornell University Press.

Zysman, J. and Tyson, L. d'A, eds (1983) *American Industry in International Competition*, Ithaca, NY: Cornell University Press.

8 Market globalization and the future policies of the industrial states

Robert T. Kudrle[1]

This paper focuses on the mobility of goods and services, capital, and even labor that underlies *market globalization*.[2] A debate has developed about whether the industrialized countries are now experiencing unprecedented levels of trade and investment (Krugman, 1992; Wade, 1996; cf. Bergeijk and Mensink, 1997). In any event, today's linkages are more organic than those experienced in the earlier period and involve an unprecedented degree of "functional integration between internationally dispersed activities" (Dicken, 1992, p.1, cited in Kobrin 1993, p.2).

A study of the complex webs of economic activity involved in market globalization reveals the importance of two developments: technical advances in communication and transportation that have made such integration physically possible and political developments that rendered it socially possible. A huge literature currently debates the patterns of interaction by which these two necessary conditions for market globalization have interacted to produce the observed outcomes (for insightful discussions, see Cerny, 1995 and Cohen, 1996, which also cite much of the relevant scholarship).

This same literature also develops a corollary theme: how market globalization has changed the parameters of state power. Charles Kindleberger wrote nearly thirty years ago that "the state is about over as an economic unit" (Kindleberger 1969, p.207). He saw the state's role declining remarkably in the face of the mobility, and hence the bargaining power, of the multinational corporation. Since Kindleberger wrote, most industrial states have also seen a dramatic increase in portfolio capital flows and in the share of their economies accounted for by foreign trade. The United States joined Europe in gaining a substantial share of direct investment from abroad, although that share in Japan remains very low.

I will argue that the increased mobility of goods, services, capital, and ideas about their interaction lies at the heart of market globalization's challenges to the state. Such mobility now provides some constraint on state action. Over time, this constraint will become more limiting, and the mobility of significant parts of the labor force will also present challenges that are today only dimly descried. Although there are some qualitative changes in modern economies, such as the growth of services, that tend to dampen the rate of growth of international trade (Wade, 1996) (although not necessarily the activities of multinational firms), this chapter does not quarrel with those who predict that globalization by almost any measure will become more important in the future than it is today, unless, as I think most unlikely, nation-states adopt highly restrictive policies. The chapter does argue that the speed of integration has sometimes been exaggerated and, more importantly, that the power of the nation-state to deal with integration issues will remain very strong.

Many have accepted Kindleberger's observation as essentially true today and that the state has already lost its capacity to control its overall level of economic activity, its rate of growth, and – especially – its income distribution. "The state" has, in effect, become much like an American state, an economic entity with little influence over the major forces that affect the material welfare of its citizens. Those who see the emerging state/state similarities as compelling are frequently drawn to the conclusion either that dreadful outcomes impend or that some kind of government above that of the nation-state (and the EU) must be developed to avoid them. I suggest that much of the literature mistakes two other recent developments for the impact of "globalization," and that this has caused many observers to exaggerate the causal power assigned to implacable global forces. Market globalization has developed simultaneously with the a widespread "rediscovery of the market" and also with closer European integration. When considering the European experience, distinguishing the latter two factors from globalization forces beyond Europe therefore presents a formidable interpretive challenge.

This essay rests on six claims

First, most of the economic challenges of the industrial countries, particularly growth and distribution, result from the simultaneous confrontation of similar problems and not primarily from their market interaction with each other.

Second, the economic welfare of each nation-state depends on the wealth it can claim and the group for which it is responsible.

Third, international exchange according to comparative advantage increases national wealth.

Fourth, the globalization of capital sharply raises the importance of relative effective tax rates, international information sharing to prevent tax avoidance, and tax revenue division practices with foreign governments.

Fifth, the possibility of migration together with the economic reality that national wealth is largely determined by the competence of the domestic population implies increased attention to both immigration and emigration.

Sixth, many of the challenges associated with globalization admit to effective responses at the national level, and most of those that do not can be dealt with through policy cooperation that should not be especially difficult to achieve.

National goals and policy

The evaluation of future politics, policy, and institutional developments concerning globalization must rest on judgments about what states seek through
their foreign economic policies and how this quest is likely to develop over
time. I have argued elsewhere (Kudrle and Bobrow, 1982; 1990) that a
small set of general goals is sufficient to motivate most observed policy.
Because these general goals are the collective goods sought by citizens through
foreign policy, they may be regarded as determining individuals' policy
preferences in the absence of the special personal stakes that propel domestic
policy preferences in the simplest public choice models. These goals are
security, autonomy, prosperity and standing.[3] Their relative importance in
the national consciousness varies by state and time period, and policy directions can implicitly support more than one goal or trade off the achievement
of one for another. For most states, standing appears to have been the least
important of the four, and, in a unipolar world, the very meaning of security
is being reconsidered (see Cerny, this volume). Market globalization touches
the prosperity and autonomy goals most directly. Prosperity problems will
receive most attention here.

A policy's apparent fit with general goals is called *ideological consonance*.
In practice, this means that an unusual policy direction will be viewed with
skepticism if it departs from policies that have generally been regarded as
well serving the overall goals – or the goals of some national subgroup – up
to that time. Alternatively, fresh ideas are often embraced in the wake of
failure.

The clarity with which an individual perceives the result of policy is called
impact transparency. Where the relation of a policy either to general goals or to
an individual's self-interest is dimly or confusingly perceived, political leadership is likely to play a particularly important role in determining an actor's
position on the policy.

The *distribution of apparent costs and benefits* drives conventional public choice
analysis. The stakes per political actor play a major role in predicting policy
outcomes because of their influence on the likelihood of political group
formation, cohesion, and effective action.[4]

The mobility of goods and services

Since the early 1970s the rate of growth of living standards in the United
States has fallen to about half of what it had been in the previous two decades,
and the rate of advance in both Europe and Japan is also down sharply. This
poor performance grew *pari passu* with a substantial increase in the size of
the foreign trade sector throughout the industrial world. Great concern
developed about "competitiveness" in both Europe and America. A dominant view among both politicians and the public held that the rich countries
simply could not compete with the rest of the world – and particularly with

the low wage but seemingly very efficient countries of East Asia. Put in formal terms, the gains from trade previously enjoyed were apparently being eroded by the new competitors.

In an article written and placed to cause as much high-level embarrassment as possible, Krugman (1994) put the implicit claim of this huge and highly influential literature to a very simple test. If a lack of competitiveness were really the problem, then a substantial part of the lagging growth of national purchasing power should be assignable to a decline in the terms of trade (the ratio of export to import prices). In fact, Krugman found that only 7 per cent of the US lag could be explained by an unfavorable shift in the terms of trade; the rest was entirely due to falling US productivity growth. While the results of Krugman's approach would vary by country – the US traded goods sector is relatively small – essentially the same argument applies to the fortunes of most industrialized countries. Changes in living standards are overwhelmingly determined by changes in domestic productivity.

The slowdown in productivity growth among the industrial countries after the early 1970s stimulated widespread re-examination of how public policy might be modified to improve national economic performance. Because communication globalization has brought common information and analysis to both elites and publics in all industrial states, reactions to the problem have also displayed much similarity. But this should not obscure the truth that most *common* problems are not centrally problems of globalism, although economic openness frequently adds competitive dimensions to both the problem and alternative avenues for solution. More specifically, in contrast to some other observers (e.g. Cerny, 1995; this volume), I do not regard such phenomena as deregulation, "reinventing government" or governmental devolution as caused by market globalization but rather by a common search for more responsive institutions and higher living standards.

Conventional protectionism implies a loss of both traditional textbook gains from trade and important sources of competition and innovation (Kudrle, 1996). But a larger pie may still leave some with smaller pieces. In particular, both intuition and economic theory suggests that the lagging share of unskilled labor in virtually all of the industrial countries could be partly attributed to the abundance of cheap and alacrious labor abroad. And the relative drop in unskilled earnings has been marked in both the United States and Europe. In addition, the increased trade and investment openness of the 1970s and 1980s had a negative impact on trade union effectiveness. When all sources of a product for a particular market experience the same cost increases together, much more of that increase can be passed on to consumers than otherwise. Openness narrows this avenue of cushioning increases in wage costs and thus increases employer resistance. Nonetheless, most careful studies have concluded that only a minor part of the declining relative wages of unskilled labor can be assigned to foreign trade competition (Krugman, 1995). Moreover, the phenomenon is unlikely to become important in the foreseeable future because less than 2 per cent of national expenditures in the OECD countries goes for manufactured products from poorer countries (Krugman, cited in *Micro*, 1996, p.16–22). Virtually all investigations of declining wages for the unskilled put primary emphasis on changing technology and the increased relative demand for skilled labor that the changes engendered. Commentators differ widely in their optimism about the potential of more education and training for the relatively unskilled to diminish the income dispersion, but this essay contends that, regardless of that potential, states retain sufficient autonomy to redistribute income substantially through the tax system.

The impact transparency of trade policies is very low for most of the public. Protectionist arguments may appear about as persuasive as those for openness, so leadership becomes particularly crucial in policy determination. Moreover, ideological consonance appears to play a complicated role in policies related to trade. Several generations of university students throughout the industrialized world have been taught the doctrine of comparative advantage, which Paul Samuelson has called the most important non-obvious proposition in the social sciences. These persons dominate decision making in most countries and exercise a moderating influence on trade policy across the political spectrum.[5] On the other hand, for much of the working class, particularly in Europe, the apparent decline of labor's bargaining power at the workplace contributes to the ideological dissonance of any policy that seems to ratify or hasten that decline. The leadership of the left and particularly of trade unions understandably portrays a loss of workplace power as inevitably leading to greater income inequality, despite the fiscal potential of the state.

In light of the widespread view among economists that the globalization of trade has not caused either shrinking overall incomes in the industrialized countries nor played a major role in increasing the inequality of its distribution – and at least a partial acceptance of that view by much of the political elite – it may not be surprising that the Left has not succeeded in persuading most of the rest of the voting population in the industrialized countries that a protectionist course will lead to a better society.[6] Instead, much of the Left in Europe, America and Japan has concentrated on controlling trade liberalization to preserve existing jobs.[7] Continued and increased openness depends on a relatively smooth transition to alternative employment. Current European labor policies have made that an elusive goal, although changed labor policies appear more likely than increased protection.

The mobility of capital

In response to persuasive evidence that trade buoyed what would otherwise have been even less impressive productivity growth and that increased income inequality appears to result mainly from technical change, many critics of globalization have developed another line of argument: governments are powerless to engage in corrective action by redistributing income because they must guard against capital flight. This argument badly needs unpacking because some of the evidence adduced in its favor is irrelevant.

Capital flows as speculation

The increase in gross transborder financial activity has dramatically out-paced all other types of exchange. The flow now exceeds $1 trillion a day (Herring and Litan, 1995, p.24). While that growth has been encouraged by volatile exchange rates (Eatwell, 1993) and largely made possible by the com-munications revolution, the virtual unanimity with which the industrialized countries have abolished capital controls (France and Italy as recently as 1986) provided the necessary policy conditions. The actions were taken to complement the commitment to the globalization of trade. Direct investment provides the vehicle for much international production and exchange, and the increasingly frictionless exchange of currencies facilitates such activity.

National authorities committed to defend a certain rate must be prepared for massive purchase of the home currency should the market decide a decline in value of the currency is imminent. This, in turn, raises the issue of why a fixed rate is sought. One frequent reason in recent years is international com-mitment, as embodied in the European Monetary System (EMS) which was developed in the 1980s as a warm-up for full-scale European Monetary Union (EMU) before the turn of the century. This development resulted from a widespread conviction that a single currency (an unbreakably fixed exchange rate among members) would generate benefits that would be worth any attendant costs. These benefits included elimination of the increased cost of protecting against changes in currency values and the political value of a single currency's cementing of the European Union (see Fratianni, this volume).

The situation of the European countries in the 1980s implied enormous difficulties for either pegged rates among them or a single currency. An inde-pendent monetary policy, for example, simply ceases to exist with fixity. Unlike the United States, however, the European Community was, by most measures, not an "optimum currency area" – nor did it come close (Feldstein, 1992b).[8] The costs in aggregate demand and hence short-term employment levels of ceding national policies to the preferences of the German Bundesbank was accurately predicted to produce irresistible pressures for parity changes under the EMS. This, in turn, meant that the "one-way bet" currency specu-lation of the kind that forced devaluations under the Bretton Woods system became a prominent feature of this half-way house to monetary union.

European problems with capital flows resulting from attempts to link cur-rencies scarcely suggests a problem of globalization but rather a determined effort at one kind of economic regionalism. This is not to claim that the yen and the dollar have not been affected by capital flows. Authorities in Japan and the United States still intervened to stabilize output and the price level in the face of disturbances and to slow sharp changes in exchange rates because of their impact on trade (Krugman and Obstfeld 1994, p.588).

In response to the exchange rate volatility that followed the breakdown of the Bretton Woods System, James Tobin (1978) proposed a small (e.g., 2 per cent) tax on foreign investment transactions. He aimed to reduce the volume of short-term speculation because the importance of the tax cost would fall with the duration of the investment. A host of theoretical and practical objections have been raised to the tax, however, and it now seems to be a complete non-starter (for a review of claimed advantages and well as objections from a sympathetic critic, see Eichengreen, 1996). Unless countries reinstitute capital controls, vulnerability to speculation appears to be a permanent element of the present system.[9]

Much of the evidence adduced to complain about the globalization of finance deals either with the torrent of funds that flows because of doubts about the stability of the exchange rate *or,* if that issue is conclusively resolved by currency unification, by the consequent inability of authorities to manipulate the (relatively) risk-free interest rate on government obligations for policy purposes. The EMS frequently displayed aspects of both problems.

For countries without a permanently fixed exchange rate, after-tax interest rates on nominally similar financial instruments denominated in domestic currency can be higher than elsewhere because the price of the domestic currency (in terms of foreign currency) is expected to go down or there is a positive risk premium attaching to the country and its currency. Funds will flow internationally because of changes in these factors.

Capital migration

For analytic purposes it is useful to distinguish financial and risk factors from a more fundamental claim by those attempting to forecast the implications of the globalization of capital. This claim deals, not with the difficulties of maintaining a pegged exchange rate or the inefficacy of monetary policy where such a rate is certain, but rather with the possibility of *sustained* capital outflow from one country to another. Looking behind the "veil of money," the risk-free yield of capital in any country – upon which the returns of financial assets of all kinds are built – depends on its abundance relative to other factors of production. But investors care about risk-corrected yields net of taxes. If the government of country x were suddenly to impose a new tax on all capital earnings, then capital could be expected to flow out of the country, lowering its exchange rate. The flow will not stop until equilibrium is re-established, when the after-tax rate of return has risen to world levels. The equilibrating real capital flow is accomplished by an increase in the country's net export balance facilitated by the depressed exchange rate.

The previous argument contains universal and revolutionary implications about the efficacy of all capital taxation in a world of frictionless capital globalization. Tax incidence theory (Musgrave 1959, pp.288–9) suggests that a factor in completely elastic supply, i.e., any amount is available at a fixed price, cannot bear the burden of a tax. If this condition obtains for capital, then taxes on capital simply denude the country of that factor until it becomes scarce enough for net earnings to rise to their previous level. This, in turn, implies that whatever the law says, the economic burden of a tax on capital must actually fall on labor and land – and with a smaller domestic product into the bargain because an important input is in shorter supply.

If the assumptions hold, this logic has very strong implications for what the law *will* say as states recognize the market forces they confront. States will engage in "fiscal degradation" by competing with each other until they have all "raced to the bottom" of capital taxation, i.e., zero. They will levy only user taxes on capital (taxes that recover the actual cost of services provided) or perhaps go even further in tax-cutting if they perceive various positive externalities.

How realistic are these assumptions, and, in particular, what evidence bears on the actual operation of the mechanism? Risks and the premia demanded for bearing them loom large in the international economy (Frankel, 1992; Gordon and Bovenberg, 1996).[10] The premia relate either to characteristics of the country in question (the country premium) or to the specific currency (the currency premium). The former set includes transactions costs, information costs, tax laws that discriminate by country of residence, default risk, and capital controls or the risk of their revival. Most observers conclude that the country premium for bonds is now quite small among the developed countries (Frankel 1992, p.199) because the last two factors have declined so dramatically. Yet, for other assets, the additional concerns remain to impede market integration. Moreover, the currency premium remains important for all assets in most currencies. The single major factor here lies in the continued exchange rate variability that could only be eliminated by a shift to fixed rates (Frankel 1992, p.200) with all of its attendant rigidities.

A consideration of all of the risks of international investment explains why capital mobility with liberalization remained modest during the 1980s in the face of differing national interest rates (nominal and real)[11] and also why it is likely to increase most (*ceteris paribus*) among those countries in Europe that pursue permanent fixity.

Capital in perfectly elastic supply suggests an extreme case. Subnational governments within the United States, for example, cannot tax most financial investments because of a unified capital market, yet they levy considerable taxes on corporate earnings and mobile real capital.[12] The American case is frequently argued to be a microcosm of the current and future international direct investment competition fueled by globalization. Although the total state tax burden on business dropped moderately over the past several decades (ACIR, 1981; Oakland and Testa, 1996), the states as a group in 1992 were estimated to collect 70 per cent more in taxes on business than the value of services provided to them (Oakland and Testa, 1996, pp.15–16).[13] This suggests that if the American experience is regarded as a precursor of "fiscal degradation" fueled by globalization, dramatic results elsewhere should not be expected soon. And international business tax differences have remained very large. In 1990, the marginal effective corporate tax rate was 24.0 per cent in the US, but 4.6 per cent in Germany and − 72.8 per cent in Italy (Jorgenson, 1993).

The preceding discussion could mislead by appearing to suggest that keeping capital at home is the best policy. Absent externalities and taxes, however, the national income of the capital-owning country is maximized by allowing an outflow if foreign earnings are higher (although labor's market income share falls; MacDougall 1960).

Tax takes and capital flows

International tax issues fall into three broad categories: how taxation changes the geographic flow of productive resources, how revenues are divided among nation-states, and how taxable income disappears through secrecy. For a change in taxes to affect capital flows, the owner of capital must experience an attendant change in net earnings. For most international capital today, this condition holds. Corporate taxes are collected according to two main patterns. Either the host country gets the first and only crack at corporate taxation or, as in the case of the US, the tax paid is credited against the home corporate tax liability. These differences in practice stem from historical developments growing out of two widely used approaches to international taxation: taxation by authorities at the *source* of income and taxation by the authorities of the *residence* of the income claimant.[14] The difference between the two approaches is reduced in practice because residence states, most notably the US, not only allow foreign corporate taxes paid to be credited against what would otherwise be due at home but also for the deferral of residual tax liabilities until profits are repatriated. Thus both the source and the residence approach in fact allow low foreign tax rates to attract home country corporate capital. But in both cases the necessary tax-sparing is typically granted only through specific bilateral treaties.

The burden of all taxes must ultimately fall on individuals. Moreover, most theories of tax equity suggest that, apart from user taxes aimed to compensate for special government services, taxes on individuals are superior to those levied at other points in an economy because burdens can be geared to the taxpayer's ability to pay. This is a strong argument against the corporate income tax as a fiscal instrument and in favor of the assignment of corporate earnings immediately to beneficiaries at their personal rates. This, in turn, implies residence-based taxation. But collecting revenue from residence-based taxation depends on tax liabilities incurred abroad being properly reported, and this is unlikely without some cooperation from foreign tax authorities. The problem is especially important where foreign portfolio (non-controlling) investments are held by individuals, and home country authorities must rely on self-declaration by persons owing the tax.

Most states employ the residence principle for earnings from portfolio investment, apparently to avoid increasing the cost of capital in their own countries, on the assumption that the supply curve is now quite elastic and is becoming flatter over time. This practice can coexist with a substantial corporate tax rate because corporate investments are complex decisions sometimes quite insensitive to tax rate differences (Kudrle, 1998).

When states compete for corporate and portfolio capital with low effective rates for foreign investors or various degrees of transaction secrecy, they are called "tax havens." At the corporate tax level, unusually low tax rates tempt firms to manipulate their intra-firm ("transfer") prices to show profits in low tax jurisdictions.[15] Profit attraction can, of course, occur whether or not differentially low effective rates are offered to foreign investors. Tax havens are also attractive reinvestment points for firms with residual tax liabilities under a residence system.

The residence principle for portfolio investments operating in conjunction with the financial secrecy provided by many tax havens leads to huge amounts of sacrificed revenue in both rich and poor home countries.

Many states, including the US, have continually tightened the rules for individual and corporate use of havens, and limited information sharing has been included in some bilateral treaties. In theory, aggrieved states could unilaterally dissolve all treaties with tax havens that refuse minimum levels of taxation and transparency, essentially reintroducing "double" taxation, and perhaps even forbid their individual and corporate citizens from dealing with the pariahs. Home counties have usually avoided such measures, partly because much of their impact would fall on the operations of home-domiciled business and could cause the departure of some activity from the home country.

A number of cooperative avenues to drain the appeal of the havens have been proposed. The apportionment of worldwide profits according to an agreed formula such as is used within the United States would remove the significance of transfer pricing. A less radical step would see an agreement to confine corporate tax rates to a narrow range. With respect to portfolio investment, the most frequent suggestion is the introduction of a withholding tax that would be forgiven only when earnings are properly reported to the country of residence (Slemrod, 1990, p.20).

The OECD has recently launched a different attack on tax havens. It involves a set of guidelines and a new institution, the Forum, that would investigate and publicize bank secrecy and a failure to share information, tax practices that produce "sham" economies, and differentially favorable taxes for foreign business (OECD, 1998). As is the case with most other reform schemes, the OECD's principal weapon is the forfeiture of tax sparing.

The capital control option

Despite all of the potential for cooperation, if a modern state found itself losing an unacceptable amount of capital for any reason, it would retain all of the technical devices to control capital movements that were developed in the post-war period. Of course, such controls would signal an important reversal of policy with wide implications for the country's gains from trade. In particular, controls would need to be administered in a way that allowed for maximum advantage to multinational firms headquartered in the restricting country. And such action implies a rethinking of previous international commitments. Freedom of capital flows is an important part of most of the 1100 bilateral investment treaties currently in force (UNCTAD, 1996, p.163).

Evaluation

Many international tax experts have predicted that, absent international action, the effectiveness of taxing capital will decline as the elasticity of its supply in any given application increases. The same sources predict that, for this reason, statutory tax rates will also decline (Slemrod, 1990; Tanzi, 1995; McLure, 1997; King, 1997). But this conclusion needs unpacking. First, as some of the evidence cited earlier makes clear, tax rates on capital may erode quite slowly. In a recent study of ten rich countries from 1979 through 1994, Chennells and Griffith conclude that "effective tax rates have not fallen" on corporate capital nor has there been "a significant erosion of the capital base" (1997, p.80), despite business pressure to lower corporate taxes to meet international competition (Cohen, 1996, p.287). Second, corporate abuse of tax havens may at last be getting determined cooperative attention. Third, a decline in the corporate tax rate is not undesirable *per se*. The tax has long been attacked by economists because of its uncertain incidence and its distorting treatment of only part of the economy. In fact, if international agreement on minimum tax rates is struck to avoid arguably excessive competition among states, the agreement should probably include a flexible minimum that would automatically shift down with the weighted average rates of the participants (Kudrle, 1998). Finally, the difficulty of taxing capital in differential uses should not be confused with an inability to tax its earnings at the level of the individual beneficiary. If it is feasible, taxation at this level is both more efficient and more equitable than other taxation, anyway. This problem is largely a function of international economic transparency which the attack on tax havens is aimed to increase. It is also a function of the jurisdictional mobility of individuals, a topic to be treated in the following section.

The absence of greater international tax cooperation so far appears to stem largely from its lack of urgency by comparison with many other issues. For example, a corporate minimum of 30 per cent was recommended for the EU by the Ruding Committee in 1991, but it was rejected by the Commission as excessively obtrusive into domestic policy (Tanzi 1995, p.116–17). The birth of the Euro has brought the issue to the fore once again. What, after all, is the consistency of a strict control on industrial subsidies while activity can continue to be enticed by tax advantages?[16]

Considering the industrial countries as a whole, present and future capital tax challenges resulting from market globalization appear amenable to a fairly modest institutional solution. Foreseeable problems are limited and discrete, and backsliders can gain only if failures to comply are chronic, visible, and unpunished. Adequate performance by the parties should be unambiguous and easy to monitor. The problems appear to admit solution by arrangements that the Brookings "Integrating National Economies" series calls "explicit harmonization," (Aaron, *et al.*, 1995, p.xxii) which seems similar to what Ethan Kapstein terms "cooperation based on home country control" (Kapstein 1994; 1996). Effective action appears fully consistent with "anarchic relations" (Lake, this volume).

More capital tax cooperation appears to be an issue with high ideological consonance across a broad spectrum of opinion in all industrial countries. It promises clear benefits for the overwhelming majority of the population in the form of increased tax effectiveness at a very modest price in national autonomy.[17] There would seem to be broad political potential throughout the OECD for imposing taxes on a great deal of income – most of it flowing to upper income groups in both rich and poor countries – that currently escapes tax altogether because of the absence of comprehensive portfolio withholding taxes. An only minimally informed citizen's mental picture of the impact of the current lack of coordination and information sharing on tax issues should be quite vivid, reasonably accurate, and difficult to refute. Recent activity in the G-7 and the EU as well as the OECD suggests that the problem may finally be getting attention (Allen, 1988).

The mobility of labor

Many ordinary citizens see the apparent inability of nation-states to control immigration as powerful evidence of state obsolescence (Miller, 1994, p.10). The salience of the subject results from the impact transparency of one aspect of a permissive policy: the permanent presence of a large number of foreigners. Immigration is among the foreign policy issues that produce the most continuous visible effect for a typical citizen. In sharp contrast to its political salience, however, immigration has played an astonishingly small role in the political science and general international relations literature (Miller, 1994, p.8). It has also received little attention in international economics.[18]

Economic theory expects non-marginal increments of labor to lower the earnings of that country's labor of the same category – unless there are economies of scale – and to raise the earnings of complementary factors more than the earnings of competing factors fall. The total income of the receiving country should rise more than that of the country of origin falls, so world income also goes up.

Categories of immigrant

Largely on the basis of an overall increase in market earnings of the original national factors, some voices in the industrial countries call for greatly expanded or even unrestricted immigration (Weiner, 1995). But this is a small minority view. Because low market earners in every modern industrial country receive substantial lifetime net subsidies, a *prima facie* prosperity concern about the legal migration of unskilled labor inevitably arises. To the extent that a country's laws and policies apply to illegal residents as well, the sphere of concern is broadened. Borjas (1987) has produced evidence that low earnings by unskilled immigrants in the United States persist over several generations.[19] And unskilled immigration pushes wages down for workers who are already at the bottom of the distribution. One study found that over the period 1980–1995, nearly half the drop in relative wages of native high school dropouts in the US could be assigned to immigration (Borjas, *et al.*, 1997). These results are independent of a perceived threat to autonomy that newcomers inevitably engender, whatever their contribution to economic welfare.

At the other end of the earnings spectrum, Tanzi has recently emphasized the important contributions of what he calls "exceptional labor" (Tanzi, 1995, p.39 based on the work of Murphy, *et al.* (1991)), to the national welfare. He stresses evidence that especially talented people in a broad range of pursuits generate benefits that raise their social contribution far above their wage.[20]

The encouragement of migration by the especially talented need not turn on "externalities." The same logic that makes lower earners particularly problematic holds in reverse for high earners: they pull more than their own weight. Some may regard this claim with skepticism because of the substantial lowering of tax rate progression on personal income that the industrial countries have introduced in recent years, but high income payers of even proportional taxes do not come close to getting their money back.

In addition to migrant labor falling at both ends of the contribution spectrum and a broad range of "normal" labor, there is a fourth category of potential immigrant – and emigrant – to which all states will pay increasing attention: the especially wealthy. This category should receive attention independent of the "talented" group, although the overlap is substantial. A large group of wealthy have done nothing remarkable themselves – they may not even be in the labor force – but are instead the beneficiaries of gifts or inheritances. But where they choose to live can affect the nationality and volume of income, wealth, gift, estate, and inheritance taxes, and that choice may, in turn, be affected by variations in national tax systems.

The varieties of immigration policy

Far more than is the case with the globalization of goods and services or capital, international labor mobility is viewed very differently in Japan, the US and Europe. In most of Europe, after the immediate post-war population shifts, virtually the only planned official labor migration was that of temporary workers. The objective, in retrospect almost universally regarded as naive, was to enjoy the mutual gain of trade in labor services without any permanent effect on the local population. The reasons for the abandonment of such policies suggest why they are unlikely ever to be revived: governments were never successful in getting many migrants and their families to return to their homelands, and their assimilation locally has generally been deemed unsatisfactory. The estimated foreign population in Europe in 1991 ranged from 1.5 per cent in Italy to 7.3 per cent in Germany and even higher rates in some smaller states (Weiner, 1995, p.55; pp.98–9).

Since temporary worker programs were abandoned in the early 1970s, the only legal route for migrants into Europe has been based on claims of asylum or refugee status, and such claims burgeoned with the collapse of political order in the East. In the mind of the typical citizen, a temporary expedient in the service of prosperity and, later, generous treatment of those claiming political persecution became a permanent threat to national autonomy – and, especially in times of high unemployment, to prosperity as well. The cumulative result has been "closed borders and stringent attitudes" (Marie, 1995). The recent politics of migration in Europe has involved greater scrutiny of claims based on political persecution and cracking down on completely illegal immigrants.

Some opinion in labor-short Japan has urged the adoption of a guest worker program. However, the combination of Japan's apparently absolute determination to interpret autonomy partly in terms of ethnic homogeneity – the 700,000 descendants from Koreans who augmented the Japanese labor force in the 1930s are still regarded as "foreign" (Weiner, 1995, p.63) – and the utter failure of repatriation in most of Europe suggest that only token programs will be embraced if at all. The ideological dissonance of such programs in terms of traditional notions of autonomy and the impact transparency of their introduction makes them non-starters. Whatever legal foreign augmentation of the Japanese population develops, it is likely to come mainly from the descendants of previous Japanese immigrants to Latin America.[21] Moreover, Japan's present homogeneity (the foreign population at less than one per cent is among the world's lowest) and island isolation suggest a modest challenge to the prevention of illegal immigration, especially by comparison with the least well placed country, the United States.

Many experts on immigration strongly disagree with the oft-expressed view, particularly in the United States, that illegal immigration cannot be controlled (Freeman, 1994). Instead, case studies stress the historic problem of organizing and maintaining popular opposition against highly concentrated business interests (in the United States, principally agriculture; hotels; and parts of small business, particularly restaurants) abetted by various ethnic and humanitarian organizations. Mobilizing effective political opposition to illegal immigration in the United States has been particularly difficult because of the concentration of settlement in only a few states, the widespread pride in the historic role of American immigrants, and the common view until recently that illegal immigration is a "victimless" crime.

Until recently, the United States devoted only scant resources to border controls or employer sanctions. Europe's greater success has rested on more effective internal controls. It is very likely that Americans' declared aversion to stricter identity checks for employment or government benefits would dissolve if it could be demonstrated that such measures were really necessary as part of an effective attack on illegal immigration. Nevertheless, the public would first demand that the steps already taken be funded and administered more adequately than they have been so far. The mix of policy and enforcement alternatives to reduce illegal immigration to the United States remains to be effectively developed, although 1996 legislation increased border patrolling and tightened procedures for those claiming political persecution (the latter has been about 15 per cent of legal immigration). As is the case of any restrictive public policy, the goal will never be to eliminate illegal immigration altogether.

It appears almost certain that all rich states will reduce even nominally temporary immigration by the unskilled, will attempt to control illegal immigration more effectively than in the past, and will also narrow grounds for admission on claims of persecution. Europe's sensitivity about both unemployment and non-European permanent residents suggests little attention to attracting foreigners; Japan is even less likely to develop any interest in attracting foreign talent. Both of these regions may face another concern in the future, however, and that is the departure of some of their most skilled citizens for other high-income countries that do welcome talented foreigners, especially the United States and Canada. So far, skilled migration from other rich countries to the United States, which generally offers the highest salaries to skilled workers, has remained at low levels, despite higher income taxes and generally lower salaries in Europe and Japan. This could change. Some modifications being considered for US legal immigration policy would move sharply away from the family unification goal, which is responsible for a very large percentage of present total inflow, to a much greater emphasis on human capital within a relatively fixed annual intake.

Personal tax harmonization

Tax policy suggests that the migration of the most capable is not yet regarded as serious among the industrial countries. While personal income taxes over the past fifteen years or so have fallen in nearly all countries, there is little evidence of convergence or of greater moderation by countries with lower per capita income levels. Instead, declining rates apparently reflected the widespread view that lower tax rates generate additional effort – both human capital formation and increased market participation from the existing workforce (Feldstein, 1995). Before economic research developed evidence otherwise, elite as well as popular opinion from the center leftwards regarded claims of a significant tradeoff between equity and efficiency (Okun, 1975) as no more than a rhetorical ploy in the political struggle between the "haves" and the "have-nots." More recently, increasing inequality has resulted from a combination of an increased dispersion of market outcomes and greater doubt that very high marginal tax rates on top earnings help the average citizen.

Some public finance economists in Europe and America now entertain the view that governments may increase both national product and tax revenues by setting the marginal rates on the highest incomes at lower instead of higher rates than those on incomes below (Slemrod, *et al.*, 1994). Although few seriously advocate declining marginal rates, such findings do provide support for proportional rather than progressive tax schedules.

The brunt of meeting the competition in international labor markets has fallen to private business where it will remain. Organized business in high tax countries will lobby for cuts, but in the meantime it will try to adjust net salaries somewhat to avoid migration. The problem will be most acute where salaries are politically determined and difficult to adjust to meet foreign offers in the face of highly transferable skills. British universities have already faced this problem; it was caused by generally lagging British incomes in the 1970s and subsequently by government education budget stringency.

So long as migration in response to tax differences appears to be low, national authorities can be expected to set their personal income tax structures largely for their own purposes. National income redistribution is not now significantly constrained by concern about the escape of those with high incomes, and it should be remembered that growing income inequality is *within* the labor force and not principally between labor and capital; for example, the share of labor compensation in national income in the US has changed very little over the last thirty years (Burtless, *et al.*, 1998, p.65). Moreover, relatively little public investment in human capital formation will likely be written off because of migration. The latter is a very large part of public as well as private investment expenditure. In the United States, for example, Eisner's calculations suggest that adding education and training expenditures to the traditional category of "gross domestic private investment" raises the estimated investment share in US GNP in 1981 from 16.1 per cent to nearly 38 per cent (Eisner, 1989, pp.31–3).

The externalities of the especially talented might lead to a global rethinking about the taxation of labor earnings for services performed outside the home country. The US is currently the only major country that merely allows foreign income tax paid to be credited against home liability, instead of simply abandoning claims to taxation of labor services delivered in another jurisdiction. The American practice clearly provides a better hedge against global tax competition for labor services – except in those, presumably rare, cases where it might cause a person to abandon citizenship rather than pay the higher home rate.

If a serious international migration problem of the talented develops among the industrial countries, it will almost certainly arise first within the EU where variations in personal tax rates remain great, but where – unlike the case with capital taxes – coordination remains to be seriously considered.

Taxes on emigrants

Current tax treatment of those who do emigrate differs greatly by country. Some countries, including Canada and Australia, employ exit taxes, while Germany imposes a special income and inheritance tax on persons who migrate to countries regarded as tax havens but still maintain close economic ties with Germany (US Congress, 1995, Appendix B).

US law now presumes that all those with net worth above $500,000 who renounce citizenship do so to avoid taxes. Although the presumption is refutable, if it stands, the expatriate remains liable for taxation of US income for ten years and can be barred from entering the US.

The rationale for levying a tax on emigrants usually rests on claims that the departed country provided the legal protection or otherwise supportive atmosphere to develop the capacity to earn the continuing income stream or to have experienced the accretion of wealth.

Evaluation

The politics of immigration differs widely by country, but some generalizations are possible. Only in the countries massively populated by immigrants in the past century and a half have permanent newcomers really been welcomed. Elsewhere, permanent foreign settlement has mostly resulted from failed temporary schemes and humanitarian relief. In most countries, even skilled immigrants are viewed as an autonomy threat, and the unskilled are additionally regarded as damaging to overall prosperity and to the distribution of income. Even in the countries generally welcoming newcomers, the unskilled still pose the last two problems, and only a small and decreasing minority favor their admission. In sharp contrast to other states, the concentration of benefits and the diffusion of costs in a generally favorable ideological context has historically led to a lenient US policy on illegal immigration. That is changing, and restriction is almost certain to increase further in the years ahead.

Two developments, the freedom of labor movement within the EU and a likely increased emphasis by the United States on skilled immigration, suggest that the mobility of the skilled may begin to constrain personal income tax rates. The solution for any emerging problem in personal taxation lies in the kind of coordination outlined in the previous section. The probability of success is increased by the fact that currently varying rate structures do not reflect deep conviction about an appropriate level. Most top rates are much lower than in earlier years, and virtually every industrial country has seen top bracket rates that have varied by at least twenty points over several decades. Nonetheless, the vast majority of the population should favor coordination over tax competition that would lighten the burden on those with the highest incomes – beyond that which would be chosen as a trade off between efficiency and equity in a closed economy.

Opting out

One cannot dismiss the possibility that, as the years wear on, some countries may decide that their collective national preferences do not permit the inequalities among their citizens that attend a personal tax and expenditure structure even approximately matching that of the other industrial countries. They might then accept a slide down the table of per capita income, not only as a result of reduced domestic effort, but also because some of their most capable citizens would emigrate, and part of their national savings might flow abroad. Such developments now appear unlikely. An acceptable income distribution is based on value judgments tempered by concerns about efficiency, and the formation of individuals' orientations on these subjects may well be growing more similar across the industrial countries as one aspect of globalization.

Conclusion

The modern nation-state remains enormously different in both power and responsibility from the American state with which it is increasingly compared as an economic actor (cf. Hirst and Thompson, 1995, p.414; Cerny, 1995). International capital mobility is much lower than among the states, and, as it increases, the most important issue will remain earnings transparency. Although corporate tax competition may inconvenience authorities, it is hard to defend an insistence that foreigners levy business taxes higher than the cost of services provided; the taxation of business earnings is more defensible at the level of personal income, anyway. And here the analogy between the national state and the US state misleads most egregiously. The nation-state holds two powerful tools that can be exercised on behalf of the collective welfare that a subnational state lacks. First, it can set personal tax rates with great independence because its citizens can only escape through the major act of abandoning their citizenship. So far, this has been a minor issue for most countries, but future developments may require personal tax coordination and greater fiscal penalties for emigrants. Second, the state can avoid immigration to any extent it chooses. The failure to control immigration is mainly a political and not a technical problem.

Increased trade and investment openness has until now been almost universally selected as an effective strategy to increase domestic prosperity at the price of some autonomy loss in terms of traditional economic instruments. In the future, the threat of loss of the highly skilled may constrain tax rates unless they are coordinated internationally, but states can retard the departure of high earners by special income and wealth taxes. Immigration by the unskilled will be almost completely suppressed. Capital will be welcomed, but enticement will be resisted by others. Capital controls remain a feasible means of restricting outflow; they are almost definitionally inefficient, but they can be made effective. For most states the cost of restriction will continue to appear greater than any likely gain.

Market globalization is frequently assigned as the ultimate cause for largely independent national attempts to deal with similar domestic problems. The Left resists believing that its policies could be found wanting absent exogenous factors, and the Right embraces external necessity as an argument to bolster its own preferences. In fact, market globalization does not lie at the heart of most domestic economic problems, and, although the presently minor role of mobility in exacerbating problems and constraining solutions is likely to grow, the amount of international cooperation necessary to meet serious difficulties successfully should prove quite feasible. The absence of greater cooperation so far may be more an indication of the modesty of the challenge than of the difficulty of finding solutions.

Notes

1 The author thanks Jeffrey Hart, David Lake, E. Philip Morgan, and Aseem Prakash for valuable comments on a previous version of this paper, and Warren Lubline for excellent research assistance. This research was sponsored by the Air Force Office of Scientific Research, Air Force Material Command, USAF, under grant number F49620-94-1-0461. The views expressed herein are those of the author and not necessarily of the Air Force Office of Scientific Research or the US Government.

2 Globalization is widely heralded as the inexorable force of the 1990s, yet it is very infrequently defined. My reading suggests three major usages, each with its own literature and sets of claims: *market globalization* discussed here, *direct globalization* that deals with non-market interactions, and *communication globalization* that powerfully affects the other two and produces its own very strong independent effects as well. (For a discussion of all three types of globalization and their implications for governance, see Kudrle 1998b.) Some environmentalists see market and direct globalization linked in a particularly dangerous way: a phenomenon that is sometimes called "the race to the bottom." In their quest to be "competitive," states may attempt to undercut each other's environmental standards. For a recent analysis of the mechanism and skepticism about its significance, see papers by Wilson, Klevorik and Levinson in Bhagwati and Hudec, 1996.

3 The goals are derived inductively and discussed in the works cited. Standing is meant to capture the psychic income gained from the admiration of others or their subordination. Much foreign policy behavior, especially by large states, can plausibly be explained on these grounds. Autonomy and standing are thus quite

distinct; the former focuses on how a group regards itself, independent of the views of others (Kudrle, 1993; 1995).

4 In tracing the development of policy over time or comparing policy positions among countries, a fourth category dealing with *institutional factors* – must also be considered. Because the treatment here is broad brush and will attempt to stress common elements determining future policy directions across the developed countries, this important set of concerns will receive scant attention.

5 Some recent trade theories suggesting possible prosperity gains from protection are based on specialized assumptions and cannot be used to rationalize most existing protection, (see Krugman, 1987). I am skeptical about Hart and Prakash's argument (this volume) that strategic trade and investment policies (STIPs) may persist and even grow in the future. They acknowledge that such a development cuts against an open global trading system and cannot be a first-best solution for the world economy as a whole. I believe that the Uruguay Round made a good start at scotching some nationalist practices, and that those agreed limitations have been increased by recent agreements on telecoms and financial services. The ultimate success of the OECD's now stalled Multilateral Agreement on Investment talks (Graham, 1996, p.101–19) or the incorporation of restraints into the WTO strike me as far more likely than increased protection, although change may come slowly (Kudrle and Bobrow, 1998).

6 Even economists who emphasize arguments and evidence linking trade and inequality do not frequently suggest protection as a policy response (Rodrik, 1997).

7 For an exposition of the most usual exception from the Left, advocacy of a "social tariff," see Palley, 1994.

8 In particular, the level of international labor mobility within the EU was judged to be far too low. For a representative critique, see Feldstein 1992b.

9 This essay implicitly assumes that there are no fundamental problems in the global real economy, e.g. the problem of chronic deficient demand that so troubled scholars in the 1930s. Nonetheless, market globalization brings with it the likelihood that ephemeral economic problems in one state or region will be transmitted elsewhere. The adequacy of current practices and institutions to dampen and limit such problems is currently very much in question, but the reform of institutions such as the IMF lies beyond the scope of this essay.

10 They can be estimated directly as the covered interest differential.

11 During the decade of the 1980s no OECD country financed more than 15 per cent of its investment from foreign borrowing, and no country sent more than 10 per cent of its savings abroad (Feldstein 1992a, p.62).

12 There would never be hesitancy to levy a tax on land because it is in completely *in*elastic supply at a fixed place.

13 Most of the average rate is borne by capital because of low international mobility. Tracing the real burden of interstate variation in the tax/benefit ratio is complex. The point, however, is about competition and not incidence.

14 Corporate earnings under the source approach do not go completely untaxed by the home country, of course; they are still taxed at the stockholder level.

15 Perhaps half of world trade takes place within corporations, and a huge share of those transactions have no "arm's length" referents.

16 Over most of US history, tax competition among the states was regarded as a minor annoyance rather than a serious problem. While there is evidence of only a minor fiscal degradation to attract business (Fisher, 1996, p.614), politically visible attempts to attract specific businesses have produced calls for Congressional action under the commerce clause of the Constitution (Burstein and Rolnick, 1994).

17 Tax avoidance issues relating to consumption taxes in an era of growing "cyber-commerce" are discussed in Kudrle (1998a). Much unilateral action is possible here, but international cooperation would be far more effective.

18 The best known undergraduate textbooks devote only a few pages of six or seven hundred to the international movement of labor (Caves, *et al.*, 1996, p.199–202; Krugman and Obstfeld, 1994, p.150–5, 181–2, 618–19).

19 A recent National Research Council study of immigration into the US (1997) acknowledges that the costs exceed the benefits of immigration by the unskilled, and some experts believe that the assumptions made may underestimate the extent of the net cost.

20 Tanzi stresses the difficulty of determining who these people are. Serendipitously, the United States appears to have discovered a way of simultaneously identifying many such persons and enticing them to move permanently to the US. A globally-admired American higher education is offered to able foreigners – and especially persons from poor countries – at a price well below its resource cost, and has served as a kind of "loss leader" to induce many foreigners to spend the rest of their lives in the United States. This, of course, has important impacts on the country of origin. As an example, many Indians, highly-trained at public expense, leave the country each year for the high income countries. As a group, however, they make important subsequent contributions in the form of remittances, technology transfers, business contacts, and political influence abroad (Weiner, 1996). For a discussion stressing source country costs and policy suggestions, see Bhagwati and Wilson, 1989.

21 Personal communication with Gary Saxonhouse, March 5, 1996.

References

Aaron, Henry J., Ralph C. Bryant, Susan M. Collins and Robert Z. Lawrence (1995) "Preface to the Studies on Integrating National Economies," in *Taxation in an Integrating World*, Vito Tanzi, Washington DC: The Brookings Institution, VI–XXIV.

Advisory Commission on Intergovernmental Relations (1981) *Regional Growth: Interstate Tax Competition*, Washington, DC.

Allen, Michael (1998) "Tax Evaders Beware: Rich Countries Prepare for Crackdown on Havens," *The Wall Street Journal* May 21: A12.

Bergeijk, Peter A.G. van and Nico W. Mensink (1997) "Measuring Globalization," *Journal of World Trade* 31: 3, 159–68.

Bhagwati, Jagdish and John D. Wilson (1989) "Income Taxation in the Presence of International Personal Mobility: An Overview," in *Income Taxation and International Mobility*, edited by Jagdish Bhagwati and John D. Wilson, Cambridge, MA: MIT Press.

Borjas, George J. (1987) "Self-selection and the Earnings of Immigrants," *American Economic Review* 77: 531–53.

Borjas, George J., Richard B. Freeman and Lawrence F. Katz (1997) "How Much Do Immigration and Trade Affect Labor Market Outcomes?" *Brookings Papers on Economic Activity* 1: 1–67.

Burstein, Melvin L. and Arthur J. Rolnick (1994) "Congress Should End the Economic War Among the States," Federal Reserve Bank of Minneapolis, Annual Report, *The Region* 9(1).

Burtless, Gary, Robert Z. Lawrence, Robert E. Litan and Robert J. Shapiro (1998) *Globaphobia: Confronting Fears about Open Trade*, Washington, DC: The Brookings Institution.

Caves, Richard E., Ronald Jones and Jeffrey Frankel (1996) *World Trade and Payments: An Introduction*, 7th edn. Boston, MA: Little Brown and Company.

Cerny, Philip G. (1995) "Globalization and the Changing Logic of Collective Action," International Organization 49(4): 595–625.

Chennells, Lucy and Rachel Griffith (1997) *Taxing Profits in a Changing World*, London: The Institute for Fiscal Studies.

Chiswick, Barry R. (1991) "Review of *Friends or Strangers* by George Borjas," *Journal of Economic Literature* 29 (June) 627–29.

Cohen, Benjamin J (1996) "Phoenix Risen: the Resurrection of Global Finance," *World Politics* 48, January: 268–96.

Dicken, Peter (1992) *Global Shift: Industrial Change in a Turbulent World*. 2nd edn, New York: Harper and Row.

Eatwell, John (1993) "The Global Money Trap: Can Clinton Master the Markets?" *The American Prospect* Winter.

Ehrenberg, Ronald (1995) *Labor Markets and Integrating National Economics*, Washington, DC: The Brookings Institution.

Eichengreen, Barry (1996) "Conclusion: The Tobin Tax: What Have We Learned?" in *The Tobin Tax: Coping with Financial Volatility*, edited by Mahbub ul Haq, Inge Kaul, and Isabelle Grundberg, New York: Oxford University Press: 273–87.

Eisner, Robert (1989) *The Total Income System of Accounts*, Chicago, IL: University of Chicago Press.

Feldstein, Martin S. (1992a) "The Budget and Trade Deficits Aren't Really Twins," *Challenge* March–April, 60–3.

Feldstein, Martin S. (1992b) "The Case Against EMU," *The Economist* June 13.

Feldstein, Martin S. (1995) "What the '93 Tax Increase Really Did," *The Wall Street Journal* October 26: A22.

Fisher, Ronald C. (1996) *State and Local Public Finance*. 2nd edn, Chicago, IL: Irwin.

Frankel, Jeffrey A. (1992) "Measuring International Capital Mobility: A Review," *American Economic Review* 82(2): 197–202.

Freeman, Gary P (1994) "Can Liberal States Control Unwanted Migration?" in *Strategies for Immigration Control: An International Comparison*, edited by Mark J. Miller, in *The Annals of the American Academy of Political and Social Science* 5(34): July.

Gordon, Roger H. and A. Lans Bovenberg (1996) "Why is Capital So Immobile Internationally? Possible Explanations and Implications for Capital Income Taxation," *American Economic Review* 86(5): 1057–75.

Graham, Edward M. (1996) *Global Corporations and National Governments*, Washington, DC: Institute for International Economics.

Herring, Richard J. and Robert E. Litan (1995) *Financial Regulation in the Global Economy*, Washington, DC: The Brookings Institution.

Hirst, Paul and Grahame Thompson (1995) "Globalization and the Future of the Nation State," *Economy and Society* 24(3): 408–42.

Hufbauer, Gary Clyde assisted by Joanna M. Van Rooij (1992) *US Taxation of International Income: Blueprint for Reform*, Washington, DC: Institute for International Economics.

Jorgenson, Dale W. (1993) "Tax Reforms and the Cost of Capital: An International Comparison," *Tax Notes International* April 19.

Kapstein, Ethan B. (1994) *Governing the Global Economy: International Finance and the State*, Cambridge, MA: Harvard University Press.

Kapstein, Ethan B. (1996) "Shockproof, the End of the Financial Crisis," *Foreign Affairs* 75(1) (January/February): 2–8.

Kindleberger, Charles P. (1969) *American Business Abroad: Six Lectures On Direct Investment*, Cambridge, MA: MIT Press.

King, Mervyn (1997) "Tax Systems in the XXIst Century," in *Visions of the Tax Systems of the XXIst Century*, Proceedings of a Symposium held by the International Fiscal Association, The Hague: Kluwer Law International.

Klevorik, Alvin K. (1996) "Reflections on the Race to the Bottom," in *Fair Trade and Harmonization: Prerequisites for Free Trade?*, edited by Jagdish Bhagwati and Robert E. Hudec, Vol. 1, Cambridge, MA: MIT Press: 459–68.

Kobrin, Stephen (1993) *Beyond Geography: Inter-firm Networks and the Structural Integration of the Global Economy*, William H. Wurster Center for International Management Studies, The Wharton School of the University of Pennsylvania.

Krugman, Paul R. (1987) "Is Free Trade Passé?" *Journal of Economic Perspectives* 1(1): 131–44.

Krugman, Paul R. (1992) "A Global Economy Is Not the Wave of the Future," *Financial Executive* March–April: 10–15.

Krugman, Paul R. (1994) "Competitiveness: A Dangerous Obsession," *Foreign Affairs* 73(2): 28–45.

Krugman, Paul R. (1995) "Technology, Trade, and Factor Prices," Working Paper No. 5355. National Bureau of Economic Research, Cambridge, MA.

Krugman, Paul R. (1996) "Remarks" cited in *Micro* 2(3): 16–22, published by Industry Canada.

Krugman, Paul R. and Maurice Obstfeld (1994) *International Economics: Theory and Policy*, 3rd edn, New York: HarperCollins.

Kudrle, Robert T. (1993) "No Entry: Sectoral Controls on Incoming Direct Investment in the Developed Countries," Chapter 10, in *Multinationals in the Global Political Economy*, edited by Lorraine Eden and Evan H. Potter, New York: St. Martin's Press.

Kudrle, Robert T. (1995) "Markets, Governments, and Policy Congruence Across the Atlantic," Chapter 6, in *Balancing State Intervention*: *The Limits of Transatlantic Markets*, edited by Roger Benjamin, C. Richard Neu and Denise D. Quigley, New York: St. Martin's Press.

Kudrle, Robert T. (1996) "Three Perspectives on Competitiveness: An Introduction to 'Made In America'," *The International Executive* (April/May).

Kudrle, Robert T. (1998a) "Does Globalization Sap the Fiscal Power of the State?" Prepared for the Coping with Globalization workshop, Alexandria VA, July 31–August 1, 1998.

Kudrle, Robert T. (1998b) "Three Meanings of Globalization and Their Implications for Governance," in *Global Governance and Enforcement: Issues and Strategies*, edited by Raimo Väyrynen, London: Rowman and Littlefield.

Kudrle, Robert T. and Davis Bobrow (1982) "US Policy Toward Foreign Direct Investment," *World Politics* (April): 353–62.

Kudrle, Robert T. and Davis Bobrow (1990) "The G-7 After Hegemony: Compatibility, Cooperation, and Conflict," in *World Leadership and Hegemony*, edited by David Rapkin, International Political Economy Yearbook, Vol. 5. Boulder, CO and London: Lynne Rienner Publishers, 147–67.

Kudrle, Robert T. and Davis B. Bobrow (1998) "Competition Policy and Regional Integration: Compatibility and Conflict," *Journal of International Political Economy* March.

Lawrence, Robert Z. (1996) "The Slow Growth Mystery, Can We Cure the Cancer?" *Foreign Affairs* 75(1) (January/February): 146–52.

Levinson, Arik (1996) "Environmental Regulations and Industry Location: International and Domestic Evidence," in *Fair Trade and Harmonization: Prerequisites for Free Trade?* edited by Jagdish Bhagwati and Robert E. Hudec, Vol. 1, Cambridge, MA: MIT Press: 429–58.

MacDougall, G.D.A. (1960) "The Benefits and Cost of Private Investment From Abroad: A Theoretical Approach," *Economic Record* 36 March: 13–35.

McLure, Charles (1997) "Tax Policies for the XXIst Century," in *Visions of the Tax Systems of the XXIst Century*, Proceedings of a Symposium held by the International Fiscal Association. The Hague: Kluwer Law International.

Marie, Claude-Valentin (1995) The E.C. Member States and Immigration in 1993: Closed Borders, Stringent Attitudes (Working Document), *Synthesis Report of the Information Network on Migration from Third Countries* (RIMET), Directorate-General for Employment, Industrial Relations, and Social Affairs. Brussels: European Commission.

Miller, Mark J. (1994) "Preface to Strategies for Immigration Control: An International Comparison," *The Annals of the American Academy of Political and Social Science* July: 8–16.

Murphy, Kevin M., Andrei Shleifer and Robert W. Vishny (1991) "The Allocation of Talent: Implications for Growth," *Quarterly Journal of Economics* 106, May: 503–30.

Musgrave, Richard A. (1959) *The Theory of Public Finance*, New York: McGraw Hill.

Nathan, Richard P. (1995) "Reinventing Government: What Does It Mean?" *Public Administration Review* 55, 2 (March/April): 213–15.

National Research Council (1997) *The New Americans: Economic, Demographic and Fiscal Effects of Immigration*, Washington, DC: National Academy Press.

Oakland, William H. and William A. Testa (1996) "State and Local Business Taxation and the Benefits Principle," *Economic Perspective* Vol. XX: 1 (Jan–Feb) 2–19.

Okun, Arthur (1975) *Equality and Efficiency: The Big Trade Off*, Washington, DC: The Brookings Institution.

Organization for Economic Cooperation and Development (1998) *Harmful Tax Competition: An Emerging Global Issue*, Paris: OECD Publications.

Palley, Thomas I. (1994) "Capital Mobility and the Threat to American Prosperity," *Challenge* Nov/Dec.

Rodrik, Dani (1997) *Has Globalization Gone Too Far?* Washington, DC: Institute for International Economics.

Rosen, Harvey (1995) *Public Finance*, 4th edn. Chicago: Irwin.

Slemrod, Joel (1990) "Tax Principles In An International Economy," Chapter 2, in *World Tax Reform: Cases Studies of Developed and Developing Countries*, edited by Michael J. Boskin and Charles E. McLure Jr. San Francisco, CA: ICS Press: 11–23.

Slemrod, Joel, Schlomo Yitzhaki, Joram Mayshar and Michael Lundholm (1994) "The Optimal Two Bracket Linear Income Tax," *Journal of Public Economics* 53 (February): 269–90.

Tanzi, Vito (1995) *Taxation in an Integrating World*, Washington, DC: The Brookings Institution.

Tobin, James (1978) "A Proposal for International Monetary Reform," *Eastern Economic Journal* 4 (July–October): 153–9.

United Nations Conference on Trade and Development (1996) *World Investment Report 1996: Investment, Trade and International Policy Arrangements*, New York: United Nations.

US Congress, Joint Committee on Taxation (1995) *Issues Presented by Proposals to Modify the Tax Treatment of Expatriation*, Washington, DC: US Government Printing Office.

Wade, Robert (1996) "Globalization and Its Limits: Reports of the Death of the National Economy Are Greatly Exaggerated," Chapter 2, in *National Diversity and Global Capitalism*, edited by Suzanne Berger and Ronald Dore, Ithaca, NY: Cornell University Press.

Weiner, Myron (1995) *The Global Migration Crisis: Challenge to States and to Human Rights*, New York: HarperCollins.

Weiner, Myron (1996) "Nations Without Borders: The Gifts of Folk Gone Abroad," *Foreign Affairs* 75: 2 (March/April), 129–34.

Wilson, John Douglas (1996) "Capital Mobility and Environmental Standards: Is There a Theoretical Basis For a Race to the Bottom?" Chapter 10, in *Fair Trade and Harmonization: Prerequisites for Free Trade?* edited by Jagdish Bhagwati and Robert E. Hudec, Vol. 1, Cambridge, MA: MIT Press: 393–428.

Part III

New institutions and new policies

If globalization processes are indeed creating conditions for changes in policies and institutions, a focus on specific policy domains is required. This is because we expect differing impacts depending on the exposure of a particular domain to international economic pressures, the extant institutions, and the response of actors impacted by it. In this section we focus on three domains: trade and investment policies in the context of industrialized countries (Hart and Prakash), administrative law in the context of the United States (Alfred Aman), and moves towards a common European currency (Michele Fratianni).

Hart and Prakash agree with Cerny that globalization gives states strong incentives to rearticulate themselves. For them, the hallmark of globalization is the technologization of trade, that is, the increasing salience of high technology products in global trade. This creates incentives for states to employ strategic trade and investment policies (STIPs) for developing domestic "architectures of supplies" in critical technologies. Strategic trade theories suggest that state interventions can improve the economic welfare of a country if the targeted industries: (1) generate sizeable positive externalities; (2) show increasing returns to scale; and (3) are embedded in imperfect national and global markets. Imperfect markets create a potential for super-normal profits and such interventions may shift these profits from foreign to domestic firms. In an era of globalization, since the boundaries between the domestic and the global economy are blurred, trade and industrial policies need to react to these new realities. STIPs provide adequate and timely access to new technologies to high technology firms located in a country. Newly created "architectures of supplies" will become a major "pull-factor" attracting investment from both domestic and foreign multinational corporations.

However, STIPs have significant implications for the post World War II politico-economic order based on "embedded liberalism," the coexistence of state interventions in domestic economies and non-intervention in international trade. Specifically, a widespread use of STIPs has two implications: at the international level, it undermines free trade, and at the domestic level, it refocuses a state's resources from demand-side social interventions to supply-side initiatives. Hence, by undermining the current political order

based on embedded liberalism, STIPs create the conditions for the rearticulation of a state that actively intervenes in market processes. Hart and Prakash
predict that redistributive services, which were the hallmark of the Keynesian
welfare state, will come under increasing attack and will be crowded-out by
STIPs.

Any such rearticulation of the state should translate into important changes
in administrative law, "the law that governs the processes by which the
government acts." The question then is, if globalization changes our notions
of state and state policy, then what corresponding changes can we expect in
legal perspectives and doctrines on administrative law? In his chapter for
this volume, Alfred Aman notes that the main function of administrative law
in the nineteenth-century minimalist state was to maximize protection of
citizens from governmental action. In terms of procedural doctrines, the
adversarial model of justice – optimal outcomes result from a contest between
actors, whether in markets or in courts – prevailed. For the Keynesian interventionist state, administrative law was redefined. Since the adversarial
model was viewed as impeding legitimate governmental interventions in the
Keynesian state, adjudicatory proceedings were moved from courts to
administrative agencies. However, administrative agencies did not become
completely autonomous. Courts ensured that agency decision-making processes were transparent. By ensuring that interested parties have standing
rights to participate in administrative proceedings, the courts interpreted
administrative processes as *de facto* political processes.

For Aman, deregulation, emphasis on cost-benefit analysis, movement
toward market-oriented regulatory approaches, declining regulatory
budgets, and privatization are hallmarks of the effects of globalization on
administrative law. States no longer cater to citizens; they cater to consumers
of their services. Aman speculates that the new roles played by administrative
law reflect the erosion of a clear distinction between the domestic and the
global (as well as between the public and the private) that results from economic globalization. He observes that the major transformation in administrative law is that it is moving away from a system primarily designed to
legitimize new extensions of public power, to one that seeks to legitimize new
mixes of public and private power, and to increase reliance on markets to
pursue public goals. The one question that remains is: which branch of the
government is most likely to usher in these changes in administrative law –
the executive, the legislative, or the judicial? He believes that, unlike previous
eras, where courts were the major actors in transforming administrative law,
such changes will be promoted by the executive or the legislature, and the
courts will follow. Aman's conclusion is that it is necessary for courts to provide the doctrinal flexibility to incorporate these new mixes of the private
and the public.

He also discusses the legal changes required for dealing with globalization
within the domestic realm. He asks, in addition, will new supra-national institutions be necessary for providing international collective goods? What are

the challenges in crafting such institutions, especially if their members have diverse economies and political structures? In this context a study of the European experience is instructive in that it constitutes a well-established example of conscious policy integration through the establishment of supranational institutions.

In his chapter, Michele Fratianni looks at the political economy of European monetary integration. According to Fratianni, the original European Economic Community was conceived primarily as a common market that would internalize the economic benefits of liberalized regional trade. In contrast, monetary union is being pushed more for political reasons than for economic ones. Treating the European Union (EU) as a cluster of club goods, Fratianni argues that different policy clubs within the EU correspond to different optimal membership sizes. Clubs are institutional arrangements for providing non-rival but excludable goods. As a result, members are required to fund the production of such goods in order to enjoy the benefits. The excludable attribute of club goods prevents free-riding; if a member does not pay its dues, it can be deprived of the benefits of club membership.

Fratianni highlights the trade-off between the deepening and enlargement of the European Monetary Union. The enlargement issue has emerged in the context of the possibility of admitting new members to the current fifteen member EU club. The enlarged club can potentially have between twenty and twenty-eight members. The aspiring members are generally poorer than the incumbents and have different preferences for EMU policies. Fratianni questions the existing policy paradigm of requiring all members to adhere to universal principles as a precondition for their entry into the EMU. For him, the preferences and the endowments of these actors are far too heterogeneous to be dealt with by a single membership criterion. Instead he suggests that such conflicts can be resolved by introducing more flexible rules of integration. He recommends creating multiple clubs by adopting a multi-speed approach to integration and exempting recalcitrant members from participating in specific policies.

9 Globalization, governance, and strategic trade and investment policies[1]

Jeffrey A. Hart and Aseem Prakash

Introduction

The purpose of this volume is to explore how globalization affects governance. This chapter examines how economic globalization is establishing a political basis for new kinds of state interventions in the economy, what we call the "rearticulation" of the state. We argue that these new types of state interventions are posing new challenges to existing institutions of international economic governance. In the introductory chapter to this volume, economic globalization is defined as the increasing integration of factor, input, and final product markets coupled with the increasing salience of multinational enterprises (MNEs) in economic activity. This is not to say that economic integration is uniform in all markets and countries. However, existing empirical evidence suggests that factor, input, and product markets are indeed becoming more integrated, particularly among the countries in the so-called Triad (North America, Western Europe, and East Asia). The share of MNEs in global economic activity has increased over the last two decades and they are more willing than previously to manage businesses where the value chain for a given product or service is distributed across great geographic distances (for evidence, see Prakash and Hart, 1998).

The activities of MNEs are not fully globalized. MNEs continue to locate most of their research and development (R&D) in their home country or region. They also tend to recruit managers and raise capital from that same territory (Prahalad and Lieberthal, 1998; Pauly and Reich, 1997; for differing views, see Reich, 1990 and Kobrin's piece in this volume). Consequently, states have incentives to become defenders of domestic MNEs' economic interests in global markets and commercial diplomacy has become a key component of states' agendas in international relations. Business executives often accompany politicians on foreign junkets, and politicians claim their visits to be successful if they succeed in securing orders for exports or signing agreements that benefit domestic firms. Even if MNEs were more completely globalized, however, national governments would still pursue policies to favor firms that located more of their value-added activities in their territorial jurisdictions.

Developing new technologies has always been difficult and expensive and often a given industry based on new technologies can sustain only a few players (see Kobrin's piece in this volume). This is occurring in the context of: (1) increased "technologization" of economic activity (increased salience of technology-related expenditures in value-addition processes); (2) a fast pace of technological obsolescence and the constant need for new and improved products; and (3) the ability of "first-movers" in the market to capture substantial rents. Consequently, states have strong incentives to ensure that domestic firms are lead players in key industries. To achieve this objective, they may be tempted to undertake strategic economic policies (SEPs): strategic interventions in trade and investment arenas and/or to establish new rules for international economic activities. For example, India is now the second largest exporter of software in the world. However, since Indian software firms are exporting non-branded and relatively unsophisticated software to MNEs, they create predominantly low-paying jobs (by international standards) in the domestic economy. By being a leader in new technologies and new product development (for which domestic R&D and a domestic supply base are important), the domestic economy of the United States, in contrast, can retain the high end of the value-addition processes and thereby support high-paying jobs. SEPs are attractive to politicians and policy makers, therefore, to the extent that they promote the goal of capturing or maintaining the high end of value-added activities.

This chapter focuses on only one kind of SEP: the kind that seeks to create domestic *architectures of supply* (Borrus and Hart, 1994) through appropriate strategic trade and investment policies (STIPs). An architecture of supply exists if many of the necessary upstream materials and tools are available domestically for strategically important downstream activities. Such architectures of supply constitute a key component of a national system of innovation (Nelson and Winter, 1982). They are critical to ensure timely and cost-effective availability of inputs to firms located within the country's territory. They are a major pull factor for MNEs to locate in a given territory.

How specific or encompassing would such STIPs be and what might be the justifications for them? Even though the theory and practicality of STIPs are contested, they retain their appeal for politicians and policy makers. Here we discuss how globalization creates incentives for states to adopt STIPs and how these policies have created a new agenda for the study of governance in the international political economy. Specifically, STIPs can be designed and implemented to protect uncompetitive domestic industries rather than encouraging the location of internationally competitive value-adding activities in the country. If so, they undermine the free trade order established by the post-World War II international economic system. Thus, to mitigate the incentives for adopting protectionist STIPs, it is important that existing systems of international economic governance be re-examined and possibly reformed.

This chapter is organized into four sections. Section one discusses the three categories of industrial policy theories and focuses on the "technological trajectory" version that provides a rationale for state interventions in high technology industries. Then, the main theories of international trade are briefly summarized and reviewed. Finally, the infant-industry argument, import-substitution policies, and strategic trade theory are discussed. Section two examines STIPs as an intervention game to highlight the incentives for states to intervene in the economy. We then discuss the various criticisms of STIPs. Section three examines how STIPs create a new agenda for the study of international governance, particularly by challenging the post-World War II order based on "embedded liberalism." Section four provides a summary and further conclusions.

Industrial policy and trade theories

State intervention to directly guide industrial activity is called *industrial policy*. State intervention to encourage or discourage foreign trade is called *trade policy*. Industrial and trade policies differ from macroeconomic policies in that they often target only a subset of the economy. Whereas macroeconomic policies (such as tax rates, level of deficit spending, and interest-rate policies) generally do not discriminate among types of firms or industries, industrial policies (such as R&D subsidies, tax subsidies, preferential loans and credit allocations) and trade policies (tariffs, quantitative restrictions, non-tariff barriers, etc.) are targeted at specific firms or industries.

Industrial and trade policies are often compartmentalized in different administrative institutions of national governments. Trade policies are usually handled by commerce ministries and industrial policies by industry ministries. However, trade and industrial policies generally overlap. Trade policies may affect the international competitiveness of domestic firms, while industrial policies may deny domestic markets and technologies to foreign firms. Thus, there is usually some sort of inter-agency coordinating mechanism to deal with the overlap in these two policy areas. As the world trade regime has evolved from the GATT to the World Trade Organization, it has gone from a focus on border measures, such as tariffs and quantitative restrictions, to a broader concern with non-tariff barriers and subsidies, both of which may be instruments of industrial policy. Thus, the interdependence of trade and industrial policies is now recognized and incorporated, not just in domestic policy making but also in the evolving rules of the international trading system.

Industrial policies have a long history. Nationalists of the late eighteenth and early nineteenth centuries, such as Friedrich List (1966 [1841]) and Alexander Hamilton (1964 [1791]), sought state interventions to promote domestic manufacturing in the face of British manufacturing dominance. The infant-industry argument of the German Historical School (Schmoller,

1931 [1895]) suggested that new industries took a while to get established because of startup problems or because a particular country or region was somehow initially disadvantaged and needed to insulate itself temporarily from competition. The infant-industry argument was resurrected after World War II to justify state interventions for the industrialization of the developing countries of Asia, Africa, and South America (Hirshman, 1945, 1971; Singer, 1949, 1950; Prebisch, 1950, 1959; Gerschenkron, 1962).

Debates on trade policy also have a long history. There have been a series of arguments over the proposition that free trade benefits all countries, as Smith (1937 [1776]) and Ricardo (1973 [1819]) asserted, as opposed to the idea that some countries may benefit more than others, especially if they engage in certain forms of state intervention. A recent example of this ongoing debate centers on the work of the strategic trade theorists (Brander and Spencer, 1981, 1985; Tyson and Zysman, 1983; Spencer and Brander, 1983; Dixit, 1984; Helpman, 1984a; Krugman, 1986, 1994a; Stegemann, 1989; Richardson, 1986, 1990, 1993; and Tyson, 1992). Neoclassical trade theorists assume declining or constant returns to scale (growth of output can never grow faster than the growth of inputs), perfect competition in product and factor markets (many producers and very few barriers to entry for new producers), and no information or transaction costs connected with technology flows. Strategic trade theorists relax these assumptions and deduce that domestic firms can benefit asymmetrically from international trade if the state intervenes on their behalf. By doing so, the state can shift not only profits, but also jobs, from one country to another. Therefore, states are tempted to do this.

Industrial policies may or may not be justified in terms of strategic trade theory. For example, some scholars justify industrial policies as being necessary to reduce adjustment costs connected with changes in international markets so as to prevent the creation of protectionist coalitions without reference to strategic trade (Tyson and Zysman, 1983). Others, stressing the differences in national economic institutions which create barriers to technology flows, argue that R&D subsidies are necessary to compensate for these impeded flows (Zysman, 1983; Hall, 1986; Hart, 1992; Encarnation, 1992; and Tyson, 1992).

This chapter examines the implications of the overlap between industrial and strategic trade policies. This overlap has become critical since, with increasing globalization, economic actors are treating the whole globe as the relevant unit for securing inputs, processing them, manufacturing as well as selling the final product. Traditionally, foreign direct investment (FDI) and exports have been treated as mutually exclusive. However, since FDI flows are now recognized as encouraging exports, and since intra-firm international trade exceeds arm's-length trade, impediments to FDI (via industrial policy) are increasingly seen as equivalent to trade barriers (Julius, 1990; Dunning, 1993; UNCTAD, 1995). Hence, trade and industrial policies need to be seen as two synergistic pillars of state interventions to support domestic firms in the global economy. Economic globalization, technologization of traded goods, and the increasing economic salience of multinational corporations (MNCs) constrain contemporary governments; but they also create incentives and new rationales for state interventions in the form of STIPs.

Industrial policy theories

Industrial policies have many rationales; but three broad categories of industrial policy theories can be identified:

1 *technological-trajectory theory* (Borrus, 1988; Tyson, 1992; Weber and Zysman, 1992; and Borrus and Hart, 1994);
2 *structuralist theory* (Servan-Schreiber, 1968; Stoffaes, 1987; Gilpin, 1987; Lake, 1988; Krasner, 1977); and
3 *institutionalist theory* (Zysman, 1983; Hall, 1986; Hart, 1992; Encarnation, 1992; and Tyson, 1992).

Although these categories overlap, they provide different rationales for industrial policies.

The technological-trajectory theorists argue that technological flows across national boundaries are imperfect even when capital is highly mobile. State intervention is needed to secure "first-mover advantages" (Williamson, 1975) for domestic firms in industries where learning curves are steep and supply infrastructures are difficult to reproduce. A good example is the integrated circuit (IC) industry, where average costs decline sharply with cumulative production because of the ability of producers to learn over time how to make the same devices smaller and with higher rates of yield (working chips per wafer) and throughput (faster processing of wafers). Product and production technologies are often difficult to purchase or even license from the original producer and sometimes are also difficult to reverse-engineer.[2] First-movers, such as Intel in microprocessors and Toshiba in dynamic random access memory (DRAM) devices, have experienced rapid growth and high profit levels.

Why is technology not perfectly mobile across national borders? A set of supplier firms develops around the industry leader resulting in internalization of positive externalities within the group. Thus, a supply infrastructure or an architecture of supply comes into existence (Borrus and Hart, 1994) supporting the market dominance of the leading firm. Such infrastructures are difficult and/or expensive to reproduce elsewhere. Hence, the set of core technologies associated with that particular high technology industry will flow only with difficulty across geographic boundaries, and will do so only if that is consistent with the market strategy of the dominant firms. Note that, for such architectures to remain vibrant, it is important that they remain accessible to non-domestic firms as well. In fact, the objective should be that they function as integral parts of the value-chain of key firms, domestic or foreign, in that industry. Both leading firms and policy makers may try to leverage the presence of such architectures of supply to retain high value-added activities in their domestic territory. Thus, policies to create and to maintain architectures of supply do not necessarily undermine free trade, restrict investment flows, or make domestic firms inward-looking. Rather, such architectures seek to influence the location of value-added activities to ensure maximum economic gain for the country.

The structuralists emphasize the differences in the relative positions of countries in the international system, particularly the distribution of economic power across countries. The hegemon, usually the country with the largest GNP, has a self-interest in providing international public goods such as free trade and investment regimes, a stable monetary order, etc., since it receives the bulk of the benefits (Olson, 1965; Kindleberger, 1973). For example, if a high percentage of world trade is denominated in US dollars then the US benefits from monetary seigniorage (Cohen, 1998).

Non-hegemons free ride the liberal trade and monetary institutions by pro-moting exports and capital to the rest of the world while protecting their domestic economy from international competition. If they can do this while also increasing the international competitiveness of their domestic firms (no easy task, of course), then over time they will advance their relative standing in the world economy, thus leading to the relative economic decline of the hegemon. Structuralists argue, in short, that industrial policies are one way that non-hegemons can challenge the power of the hegemon.

Another structuralist argument is that when hegemons face a relative economic decline, they begin to act in a predatory manner by copying the industrial and trade policies of their principal competitors. By doing so, they undermine the liberal economic regimes that they established earlier. Thus, structuralists explain the implementation of industrial policies by both non-hegemons and declining hegemons as part of a larger process of economic competition among countries.

Institutionalists focus on the historically rooted differences in state-societal arrangements and their impact on the competitiveness of domestic firms. They highlight how some institutional configurations systematically create barriers to imports and inward investments, thereby sheltering domestic firms from international competition. In particular, they contrast the relatively open US system with the relatively closed Japanese system, with its incestuous forms of business/government collaboration and its industrial combines (*keiretsu*), and how such differences create advantages for Japanese firms to compete in international markets.[3]

This chapter focuses on the technological-trajectory theory because it pro-vides a rationale for state intervention in high-technology industries. The twin hallmarks of economic globalization are mobile capital (fixed as well as portfolio) and the technologization of trade – the increasing salience of high technology products in global trade. High technology can be embodied in the final product or in the production process. Technologization creates incentives for state intervention to develop domestic architectures of supply in critical technologies, thus enabling firms located in the country to have adequate and timely access to inputs needed to maintain their international competitiveness. Such architectures of supply therefore become a major "pull-factor" for attracting FDI from multinational corporations, thereby furthering the economic agenda of the politicians and policy makers.

Trade theories

Smith (1937 [1776]) made a case for free trade based on absolute advantage. The Ricardian trade theory (Ricardo ([1819] 1973), also known as the classical trade theory, argued for trade based on comparative and not absolute advantage. Ricardo emphasized that for trade to take place, countries need not have absolute advantages in producing different goods. The neo-classical trade theory, pioneered by Eli Hecksher (1991 [1924]) and Bertil Ohlin (1933), also identified comparative advantage as the basis of international trade.[4] Among the main assumptions of the simpler Hecksher-Ohlin models were that:

1   though the factors of production are mobile within the country, they are not mobile across national boundaries;
2   product markets, both domestically and internationally, are perfectly competitive and there are no super-normal profits;
3   there are constant returns to scale in production of all goods (or production functions are homogeneous of the first degree) and firms cannot acquire a monopoly position through "learning curve" advantages;
4   since there are no transaction costs for technology acquisition, access to technology is not a source of comparative advantage; and
5   since goods have different factor intensities, a labor-rich country exports labor-intensive goods and a capital-rich country exports capital-intensive goods.

Note that this specialization results not from access to a superior technology (technology is assumed to be the same everywhere) but from differences in factor endowments.[5]

Though comparative advantage creates gains from trade and specialization, such gains may be distributed unequally across countries. Strategic trade theorists suggest that certain types of state intervention can shift such gains, in special circumstances, from foreign to domestic firms (Brander and Spencer, 1983, 1985; Dixit, 1983; Helpman, 1984a; Krugman, 1986; Tyson, 1992). They suggest that in industries with imperfect competition and super-normal profits, subsidies can shift global profits to domestic firms such that the increase in their profits exceeds the subsidies. Hence, on aggregate, there is a net increase in national welfare.

Strategic trade policies are not the same as governmental interventions in strategic sectors (Flamm, 1996). A strategic sector may generate externalities only for the domestic economy and does not necessarily have international linkages. A good example of this would be a governmental subsidy to promote the construction of fiber optic networks. If such a network does not enhance the global competitiveness of domestic firms, then the subsidy is not a strategic trade policy.

Strategic trade and industrial policies

Strategic trade theories, in conjunction with the technological-trajectory theory of the industrial policies, provide the rationale for STIPs. A case can be made for state support of high technology industries through a combination of trade and industrial policies. The objective is to create and to maintain thriving domestic architectures of supply in critical industries, thereby enabling firms located in the country to be competitive in global markets characterized by super-normal profits and creating incentives for foreign firms in those same industries to invest directly in the country.

Tyson (1992) defends STIPs in the United States as preferable to the incoherence and ineffectiveness of the military-oriented industrial policies of the past. In the Cold War era, the US government intervened in militarily sensitive sectors. Such interventions, however, were designed primarily to assure local sources of supply for key military components and systems, and not to maximize "spin-offs" to civilian sectors. Tyson's message is clear: since states need to intervene anyway, they should do it in a way which maximizes economic welfare, which means they should do it in a manner consistent with strategic trade and industrial policy theories.

Do STIPs have any historical validity and will they be equally efficacious across political systems? Some scholars see STIPs as being the key to the rapid industrialization of Japan and the newly industrialized countries (NICs). It is suggested that Japan followed a phased process of industrial development (Johnson, 1982; Yamamura, 1986; Weber and Zysman, 1992). During the first phase, the Japanese firms were disadvantaged in both development and production costs. To shelter these firms against international competition, the domestic market was closed with a combination of import barriers and inward investment restrictions. Without inward investment restrictions, foreign firms would have been tempted to jump the import barriers by establishing local subsidiaries. This would have impeded the development of local architectures of supply. The import substitution policies adopted in other regions of the world – increased import barriers without investment restrictions – resulted in the establishment of inefficient and international uncompetitive manufacturing facilities. In Japan, fierce domestic competition ensured that domestic firms felt pressure to become first domestically, and later, internationally competitive and they did not become complacent rent-seekers.

In the second phase, Japanese and other Asian firms borrowed and adapted technology from abroad to bridge the technology gap. The state relaxed import restrictions for technological inputs while maintaining inward investment restrictions. The state also encouraged firms to export by linking state support, such as concessional credits, to export performance (Park, 1994). Hence, domestic firms, having established themselves in the home market, were gradually exposed to foreign competition.

The cross-shareholding practices of *keiretsu* member firms in Japan allowed them to compete domestically without fear of hostile takeovers.[6] The role of the Japanese Ministry of International Trade and Industry (MITI) as "gate-keeper" and dispenser of subsidies to specific firms and industries was also important since it created hurdles for foreign firms to sell and to invest in Japan (Johnson, 1982; Encarnation, 1992). Since neoclassical models of industrial economics generally ignored institutions like the Japanese *keiretsu*, they were unable to explain the impact of such "relational structures" (Goldberg, 1980) on business performance. As a result of increased US awareness of the implications of the *keiretsu* system, a major US demand during the Structural Impediments Initiative talks with Japan in 1989–90 was the reform of that system (Kahler, 1996).

In the third phase, Asian producers began to build world market positions without fear of foreign competition. They now tapped foreign markets initially through exports and eventually through foreign direct investment. The international expansion of Japanese and other Asian multinational corporations was now perceived to be impeding the development of architectures of supply in other regions, as Asian component manufacturers followed the main manufacturing companies to foreign locations. Since the main research and development competencies remained in Asia, especially in Japan, the non-Asian firms chafed over their limited access to critical Japanese technologies.

Although the Japanese model has come under attack due to the recent crisis in East Asia and the perceived triumph of the so-called Anglo-Saxon capitalism, Japanese policies have changed the contemporary game of economic rivalry by creating an enormous temptation for other states to copy them. This situation can be conceptualized as a form of prisoner's dilemma game (Richardson, 1986). Suppose state A is debating whether to intervene or not intervene in a particular strategic industry. It faces the following payoff structure as discussed in Figure 1 below.

We assume that: (1) $e > c$ and $e > d$; (2) a,b,c,d, and $e > 0$; and (3) $c > a$ and $d > b$. For B, "intervene" (defect) is the dominant strategy no matter whether A intervenes ($a > 0$) or not ($e > c$). Similarly, for A, the dominant strategy is to intervene irrespective of whether B intervenes ($b > 0$) or not ($e > d$). Thus both countries intervene and the Nash equilibrium (a,b) is pareto inefficient because the highest joint payoffs occur when both refrain from intervening ($c > a$ and $b > d$).

Country A Country B	Intervene	Not intervene
Intervene	Rents shared between A and B (a,b)	All rents to B (e,0)
Not intervene	All rents to A (0,e)	Rents shared between A and B (c,d)

Figure 1 The Intervention Game

Source: Adapted from Richardson (1986: 271)

The intervention game captures the logic of the "cult of the offensive" that arose among the great powers prior to World War I (Snyder, 1984; Van Evera, 1984; Weber and Zysman, 1992). The military and political leaders of that time saw offense as the dominant strategy assuming that wars would be short and the "first striker" would have an overwhelming advantage. The prisoner's dilemma payoff structure of the intervention game creates incentives for a new kind of cult of the offensive leading to the widespread adoption of STIPs. This suggests that new or modified international institutions are needed to change the incentives which make STIPs attractive to politicians and policy makers. We elaborate on this in the next section.

Criticisms of STIPs

The efficacy of STIPs in promoting economic development is disputed. Some scholars attribute the economic successes of Japan and the newly industrialized countries (NICs) of Asia in the 1980s and early 1990s largely to STIPs (Johnson, 1982; Yamamura, 1986; Dore, 1986; Okimoto, 1989; Johnson *et al.*, 1989; Weber and Zysman, 1992; and Tsuru, 1993). Others attribute it to low wage and inflation rates, rapid copying of the product and process technologies of competitors, high domestic savings rates (enabling low interest and high investment rates), and undervalued currency exchange rates (Bergsten, 1991; Krugman, 1983 and 1994c; and Saxonhouse, 1979). The preceding list of alternative explanations is not exhaustive. With the onset of economic crisis in East Asia and economic stagnation in Japan, the long-term efficacy of Asian-style STIPs is increasingly being questioned. Specifically, there is a belief that STIPs provide fertile grounds for "crony-capitalism," that they are inherently corrupt, that they lack transparency and thus impede democratic oversight of economic policies, and that they impede efficient allocation of resources.

STIPs are also criticized for normative, positive, as well as theoretical reasons. The normative critics focus on the dangers of giving too much power to the state. Classical liberals and neoclassical economists argue that the state should be restrained from asserting its authority in new terrains unless there is no other way to resolve market failures. Critics question particularly the need for strategic intervention to increase aggregate economic welfare. Consider a situation where a state identifies a set of strategic industries and provides them with an export subsidy. Suppose that such strategic industries compete for the same scarce factors. In this case, state support drives up the prices of the scarce factor (a pecuniary externality) and no industry benefits (Grossman, 1986). Further, if equity is also an objective of state policy, then such interventions will skew the income distribution in favor of the scarce factor.[7]

Critics also point out that STIPs can advance the interests of a particular country only if others do not retaliate by providing matching supports to their domestic firms and industries. If such retaliation occurs, then the relative gains promised by STIPs may not materialize. It is also suggested that special interests will abuse the willingness of governments to intervene. Firms, as rational actors, have incentives to externalize their problems to avoid painful internal restructuring. Such firms can therefore be expected to lobby for state support (Nelson, 1988). It will be difficult to separate strategic interventions from non-strategic ones.

Many scholars question the implementability of STIPs (Grossman, 1986; Dixit, 1986; Krugman, 1986; Richardson, 1993; Bhagwati, 1993). They consider STIPs similar to infant-industry and import-substitution policies encouraging rent-seeking and leading to misallocation of resources. One of their concerns is that it is difficult, *ex ante*, to specify investments in which industries will have the maximum payoffs. This is, in part, related to the difficulties in measuring externalities. In the absence of reliable and objective measures of externalities, political rather than economic criteria may dominate the choice of strategic industries. Further, STIPs have to be focused on industries with super-normal profits and it is difficult to determine whether a particular level of profit is super-normal. Imperfect competition also does not *per se* signal super-normal profits, since competition among a few rival firms can be fierce enough to drive the prices down to competitive levels.

Critics argue that STIPs cannot explain how domestic firms became R&D leaders in the absence of government assistance or how state-assisted industries failed in the face of massive assistance. Hence, they argue, STIPs can at best be only a facilitating condition for the success of domestic firms.[8]

Scholars also point out that there are different forms of capitalism and that only some forms are consistent with strategic interventions (Gerschenkron, 1962; Shonfield, 1965; Katzenstein, 1978; Johnson, 1982; Zysman, 1983,

Hall, 1986; Lodge and Vogel, 1987; Hart, 1992). An important research question is whether some countries are more willing and capable of using STIPs than others. The US has rarely engaged in strategic interventions in the past, partly because of the ideational and institutional grip of neoclassical economics. On the other hand, since neoclassical ideas are less influential in Japan, the Japanese state faces less opposition to its interventionist role.

STIPs do not show instantaneous results since their effects are usually visible only after considerable time lags, sometimes longer than the electoral cycles. The successful implementation of STIPs requires that firms believe that state support will continue irrespective of political changes. Can every state make such credible commitments (Lenway and Murtha, 1994)? Johnson (1982) identifies two kinds of states: regulatory and developmental. Regulatory states have minimal capabilities for strategic economic interventions and their policies seek to ensure an unfettered working of markets and a correction of market failures wherever they arise. The developmental states, in contrast, are capable of adopting and are willing to stick with STIPs even in the face of temporary difficulties. The United States and Britain are regulatory states; Japan and Korea are developmental states.

Firms' perceptions of state commitments are influenced by the nature of domestic socio-political institutions such as the relative autonomy of the state from domestic interests groups (Katzenstein, 1978; Hart, 1992), the transparency of domestic decision making (Cowhey, 1993), and social and political cohesiveness (Katzenstein, 1985). For example, if political power is dispersed domestically, then it may be difficult for the government to make credible commitments to pursue coherent industrial policies. In a relatively decentralized federal system, the executive may face strong opposition from provincial governments as well as from the national legislature and competing bureaucracies and therefore may not be able to sustain its interventionist policies. Thus, one would expect countries with more centralized and bureaucratic (and therefore relatively autonomous) political regimes to be more likely to adopt and sustain STIPs.

Are developmental states always more credible in providing such assurances or are they credible only in some phases of economic growth? Porter (1990) identifies four phases of economic growth: factor-driven, investment-driven, innovation-driven, and wealth-driven. STIPs are linked with the investment-driven phase in which the developmental state actively facilitates economic growth (Lenway and Murtha, 1994). State support may in fact constitute a credible commitment to deter foreign competitors from engaging in predatory strategies such as reducing prices to drive domestic competitors out of business. However, Lenway and Murtha (1994) argue that, in the innovation-driven phase of growth, the micromanagement of the economy by the developmental state is counter-productive since bureaucrats seldom have the information needed to correctly pick winners. In this phase, the regulatory state (which does not undertake STIPs) may provide a more appropriate institutional setting since it focuses on providing macroeconomic stability, guaranteeing intellectual property rights, and preventing inefficiencies caused by imperfect competition. This argument is also consistent with the literature on "Wintelism" that argues against economic nationalism in certain areas of high technology (Borrus and Zysman, 1997; Kim and Hart, 1998; Hart and Kim, 1998). A recent example which seems consistent with this theory is the successful development of digital television (DTV) in the United States under the guidance of the FCC, as contrasted with the less successful commitment of the Japanese government to a hybrid analog-digital high definition television (HDTV) system called MUSE/ Hi-Vision.

Implications for international economic governance

The debate on STIPs, though inconclusive, highlights the incentives to manipulate market processes created for national governments by the processes of globalization. The recent policy reversals in Hong Kong and Malaysia suggest that some states are feeling compelled to intervene in stock and currency markets, the most hallowed bastions of the "free market." Such interventions have generated support from intellectuals as well as domestic political groups (*New York Times*, 1998). Thus, the debates on STIPs (together with those on coping with the East Asian crisis) remind us once again of the power of ideas in policy making, even when such ideas may not be unanimously accepted within the academy. As Keynes (1937) noted:

> The ideas of economists and political philosophers, both when they are right and when they are wrong, are more powerful than is commonly understood. Practical men, who believe themselves to be quite exempt from any intellectual influences, are usually slaves of some defunct economist.

As highlighted by Kudrle in this volume, globalization has not significantly eroded the fiscal power of the state. The governments of major industrialized nations still command through taxation significant resources for a wide variety of policy interventions. Thus, it is important to realize there is both a demand for such policy interventions and a supply of ideas and resources to undertake them. Krugman (1994a, 1994b), however, one of the original contributors to strategic trade theory, argues that it would be unwise to translate the findings of strategic trade theory directly into policy. He observes that the theories of academic economists as more qualified and cautious than those of the policy makers who implement them.

If STIPs are politically attractive and may be implemented for largely political reasons, what are their implications for international economic governance? Strategic trade theories help to explain some of the increased activity in forming regional economic alliances, particularly the ones in high technology industries. This again can be related to Cerny's argument in this volume that globalization is creating conditions for collective action at multiple levels, including the regional level. For example, the Single European Act of 1987, as well as the Maastricht Treaty, were preceded by a series of programs to promote high technology industries in the region to ensure that Europe did not fall behind Japan and the United States in key technologies and industries. Esprit, Eureka, JESSI (Joint European Semiconductor Silicon Initiative), and the Airbus Consortium are all examples of such programs (Tulder and Junne, 1988; Sandholtz, 1992; Mytelka, 1994).

Similarly in the US, the Sematech consortium for R&D in semiconductor technologies was co-funded by the federal government and industry (Borrus, 1988). Sematech was motivated largely by the success of the Japanese VLSI (very large-scale integrated circuits) program co-sponsored by the Japanese government and Japanese industry. The VLSI program subsidized the imports of US semiconductor manufacturing equipment as well as their reverse engineering. Another US STIPs project, the National Flat Panel Display Initiative, created an umbrella for R&D funding for commercialization of new flat panel display technologies by US firms. This initiative was the US government's answer to the large lead of Japanese electronics firms in the production of thin film transistor liquid crystal displays, mostly for laptop computers (Flamm, 1994, 1995; Barfield, 1994; Hart, 1995).

Recent work on high technology industries suggests that the traditional emphasis on spin-offs from military to civilian technology needs to be supplemented with consideration of spin-ons from civilian to military. An example of this is the use of computer displays and microelectronic circuits developed for commercial products in military avionics systems (Borrus and Hart, 1994). Political arguments over this question have fueled a debate within the national security community over *dual-use technologies*: technologies that have both civilian and military applications. Some advocates of STIPs support strategic interventions to promote dual-use technologies. Critics of industrial policy theories argue that such policies should be avoided because it is impossible to accurately assess the degree of technological interdependence of civilian and military technologies and because such interventions may simply encourage domestic rent-seeking behavior.

In short, the debate over STIPs poses important questions about what kinds of R&D the state should subsidize. Further, if states subsidize R&D, what kinds of safeguards are necessary to prevent the resulting international R&D races from leading to demands for protectionism? Discussions on granting "national treatment" to MNEs in the World Trade Organization and the OECD's Multilateral Agreement on Investment need to be extended to include the right of firms located in a given jurisdiction to participate in state-funded R&D consortia. This will go a long way toward creating a level playing field for firms in international competition, irrespective of their national identity, while at the same time serving the public policy purpose of retaining high-paying jobs within a country.

The recent investigations launched by US Department of Justice against Microsoft and Intel also suggest that in an era where a few firms can dominate industry standards, new laws are needed to ensure that monopolies do not rise in new guises. Similar investigations have been launched against these firms by the European regulators. Lest such investigations begin to assume the form of "they" impeding the functioning of "our" firms, new institutions are required that empower firms to participate in the development of new technologies and products. Thus, new international institutions could ensure that the architectures of supply created by STIPs are not "closed" to MNEs of foreign origin. Such concerns will need to be balanced with the need to protect intellectual property rights and safeguard the interests of the firms investing in R&D. Thus, discussions about intellectual property rights under the aegis of the World Trade Organization and the World Intellectual Property Organization are an important part of the new agenda in international trade negotiations (see Kim and Hart, 1998).

The second major challenge posed by STIPs is that they potentially undermine the post-war international economic order that is based on "embedded liberalism." Ruggie's (1982) notion of embedded liberalism links the rise of the welfare state (which generally combines a variety of social insurance schemes with Keynesian demand management) to an agreement among the major industrialized nations to keep the global trading system as open as possible. In many major trading nations, as long as there was some faith in the efficacy of Keynesian demand-management policies to smooth out economic cycles, the free-traders were able to make side-payments to supporters of social welfare policies in order to secure their acceptance of the liberal trade regime. Within the domestic economy, embedded liberalism combined macroeconomic state intervention with non-intervention in micro markets.

Challenges to embedded liberalism posed by STIPs create pressures for changing the liberal international economic regimes established after World War II (Gilpin, 1987). The World Trade Organization, the successor to the GATT and the main guarantor of an open trading system, will have to adapt to the proliferation of STIPs by a growing number of states. Free-traders, in particular, will have to identify new domestic and transnational coalitions to support non-intervention of the state at both macro and micro levels and the preservation of an open trading system. Putting together such alliances is increasingly challenged by the progressive dismantling of the welfare state that protects the most vulnerable parts of the population. The welfare state permitted governments to promise assistance to elements of society most badly hurt by adjustments to changes in the world economy. It permitted governments to compensate the losers with some of the gains extracted from the winners in international economic competition, to maintain support for free trade policies abroad and the regulatory state at home. As that padding is removed, governments find themselves less and less able to defend free trade and investment policies against the forces of protectionism.[9]

The failure of the 105th Congress to grant President Clinton the fast-track authority for negotiating trade agreements is a testimony to the eroding power of the free-traders. Thus, there is danger that the assaults on the welfare state under the guise of state-shrinking, coupled with the political attractiveness of STIPs, may undermine the post-war free trade order. As of now, the institutions of international economic governance, especially the World Trade Organization and the regional agreements such as NAFTA and the European Union (EU) seem quite robust. However, if the turmoil in East Asia, Latin America, and Russia continues, these economies, especially the Asian economies, may try to export their way out to the US and the EU. If such surges in exports coincide with a cyclical downturn in the US and/or EU economies, there could be revival of demand for adoption of some version of STIPs. This could lead to a bandwagon effect across countries. Hence, it is important that the demands of the STIP proponents be preempted by reforming the existing governance institutions that mitigate incentives for states (especially in East Asia) to support domestic architectures of supplies that discriminate against foreign firms.

Conclusions

This chapter has argued that, in an increasingly integrated world economy, trade and industrial policies need to be viewed as complementary. Globalization is marked by the increasing salience of high technology products and services in world trade. Given that MNEs still continue to be strongly tied to their home countries and that R&D costs have escalated in high technology industries, a given high technology industry can have only few players and the "first movers" will appropriate a significant proportion of the rents. Consequently, states will have strong incentives to ensure that their domestic firms become key actors in critical industries, or that foreign-owned MNEs locate the high end of their value chains in their territories. On this count, STIPs are extremely attractive to politicians and policy makers. They are, at least theoretically, designed to create domestic architectures of supply in critical technologies, enabling both domestic firms and foreign subsidiaries to compete better in international markets.

The recent turmoil in East Asia has not delegitimized STIPs. Rather, it has created a new rationale for this type of state intervention. Due to difficulties in servicing the foreign debt assumed by domestic firms, Asian NICs such as Korea may be forced to permit foreign MNEs and financial institutions to play a larger role in revitalizing their ailing economies. In doing so, however, they will still want to maximize the likelihood that the high end of value-added activities will be located in their territories.

STIPs differ from infant-industry and import-substitution policies in that they are not designed to encourage manufacturing by raising barriers to imports. We hasten to add, however, that STIPS, like infant-industry and import-substitution policies, are inconsistent with classical and neoclassical theories of international trade. According to the neoclassical school, actions by the state to promote specific industries, whether by raising import barriers or by subsidizing R&D, will lead to allocative inefficiencies. This is the heart of the neoclassical criticism on strategic trade and industrial policies.

Even though STIPs are challenged on theoretical as well as practical grounds, they remain attractive to politicians and policy makers. The political appeal of STIPs should not be under-estimated. Ideas influence policies by providing road maps to cause and effect relationships about contemporary societal problems (Goldstein and Keohane, 1993). STIPs provide credible explanations why certain economies are in relative decline and recommendations about what policies are needed to restore or maintain international competitiveness. However, STIPs can lead to competitive interventions, therefore highlighting the need for developing new international institutions that reduce the temptation to adopt them.

Thus the controversy over STIPs, on one hand, is provoking new domestic debates on how to modify the relationships between states and markets to enhance the economic well-being of a country's population: that is, how to rearticulate the state in an era of increasing economic globalization. On the other hand, to the extent that globalization is leading to the proliferation of STIPs, it undermines the international economic regimes that permitted globalization to increase in the first place.

Notes

1 This is a revised version of our paper Hart and Prakash (1997). We thank Marianne Marchand, Henk Overbeek, Larry Schroeder, and the three anonymous reviewers for their comments.
2 Reverse engineering involves improving upon an existing product or production technology by discovering how the product or production technology works, often simply by taking it apart and then reassembling it, and then designing a new product or production technology based on this knowledge. While direct copying of products or production technologies protected by intellectual property laws – such as patent and copyright laws – is often illegal, reverse engineering is usually not illegal.
3 For a review of Japan's industrial policy, see Dore (1986), Friedman (1988), Okimoto (1989), Johnson, *et al.* (1989), Tsuru (1993), and Calder (1993).
4 Since Ricardian and Hecksher-Ohlin models define comparative advantage on a country basis, if countries have comparative advantage in different industries, these theories explain inter-industry flows. However, trade among the major industrialized countries often involves intra-industry exchanges. This led to the development of alternative perspectives such as the product-cycle theory (Vernon, 1966) and other models of intra-industry trade (Balassa, 1966; Grubel and Lloyd, 1971; Helpman, 1984b; and Leamer, 1984). Also, the intra-company trade in multinational corporations makes the patterns of international trade diverge from those predicted by country-based comparative advantage (Caves, 1996 [1982]; Helpman, 1984b; Dunning, 1993; and Markusen, 1984, 1995).
5 Over the years, Hecksher/Ohlin models have been tested for robustness by easing the assumptions about the number of factors of production (Kenen, 1965; Baldwin, 1971; and Leamer, 1984), the number of countries (Jones, 1987), and the mobility

of factors of production (Caves, *et al.*, 1993). In each of these cases the main results still held. In addition, some new theorems relating to the distribution of gains from trade within society (between relatively abundant and scarce factors of production) (Stolper and Samuelson, 1941; Bhagwati, 1959; and Rogowski, 1989) and the equalization of factor prices (Samuelson, 1948) were put forward making neo-classical trade theory a highly compelling approach to analyzing trade matters. Leontief's paradox – a capital rich country exporting labor-intensive goods – pro-vided a major challenge to the Hecksher-Ohlin theory. A significant conceptual contribution of this debate was a more precise understanding of what constituted "labor" and how human capital cannot be equated to "labor." For an overview of the debate, see Leontief (1956, 1957, 1964); Swerling (1954); Valavanis-Vail (1954); Buchanan (1955); and Minhas (1963).

6 The same function is served by the *chaebol* firms in South Korea.
7 Rogowski (1989) argues that trade benefits the relatively abundant factor. Thus exports from a labor rich country benefit providers of labor. Here trade corresponds to natural comparative advantage. Since state interventions through STIPs create comparative advantage, trade may now benefit the scarce factor.
8 For excellent summaries of the positive critiques, see Grossman (1986), Dixit (1986), and Richardson (1993).
9 For a perspective on why states continue to retain an important role in the provision of redistributive services, see McGinnis' piece in this volume.

References

Andrews, Kenneth R. (1971) *The Concept of a Corporate Strategy*, Homewood, IL: Irwin.
Balassa, Bela (1966) "Tariff Reductions and Trade in Manufacturers," *American Economic Review* 56 (June): 466–73.
Baldwin, Robert E. (1971) "Determinants of Commodity Structure of U.S. Trade," *American Economic Review* 61 (March): 126–45.
Barfield, Claude (1994) "Flat Panel Display: A Second Look," *Issues in Science and Technology* 11 (Winter): 21–5.
Bergsten, Fred, ed. (1991) *International Adjustment in Finance: Lessons of 1985 through 1990*, Washington, D.C.: Institute of International Economics.
Bhagwati, Jagdish (1959) "Protection, Real Wage, and Income," *Economic Journal* (December): 732–48.
Bhagwati, Jagdish (1978) *Anatomy and Consequences of Exchange Control Regimes*, Cambridge, MA: Ballinger.
Bhagwati, Jagdish (1993) "Rough Trade," *New Republic* (May 31): 35–40.
Borrus, Michael (1988) *Competing for Control*, Cambridge, MA: Ballinger.
Borrus, Michael and Jeffrey A. Hart (1994) "Display's the Thing: The Real Stakes in Conflict Over High-Resolution Display," *Journal of Policy Analysis and Management* 13(1): 21–54.
Borrus, Michael and John Zysman (1992) "Industrial Competitiveness and American National Security," in *The Highest Stakes*, edited by Wayne Sandholtz, Michael Borrus, John Zysman, Ken Conca, Jay Stowsky, Steven Vogel, and Steve Weber. pp.7–54, New York: Oxford University Press.
Borrus, Michael and John Zysman (1997) "Wintelism and the Changing Terms of Global Competition: Prototype of the Future?" BRIE Working Paper Series, No. 96B, University of California, Berkeley.

Brander, James A. and Barbara J. Spencer (1983) "Tariffs and the Extraction of Foreign Monopoly Rents and Potential Entry," *Canadian Journal of Economics* 14 (August): 371–89.

Brander, James A. and Barbara J. Spencer (1985) "Export Subsidies and International Market Share Rivalry," *Journal of International Economics* 18 (February): 85–100.

Buchanan, N.S. (1955) "Lines of Leontief Paradox," *Economia Internazionale* 8 (November): 791.

Calder, Kent (1993) *Strategic Capitalism*, Princeton, NJ: Princeton University Press.

Caves, Richard E. (1996 [1982]) *Multinational Enterprises and Economic Analysis*, New York: Cambridge University Press.

Caves, Richard E., Jeffrey A. Frankel, and Ronald W. Jones (1993) *World Trade and Payments: An Introduction*, New York: HarperCollins College Publishers.

Chandler, Alfred (1962) *Strategy and Structure*, Cambridge, MA: MIT Press.

Coase, Ronald H. (1937) "The Nature of the Firm," *Economica* 4: 386–405.

Cohen, Benjamin J. (1998) *The Geography of Money*, Ithaca, NY: Cornell University Press.

Cohen, Stephen and John Zysman (1987) *Manufacturing Matters*, New York: Basic Books.

Cowhey, Peter F. (1990) "The Agenda of the Leading Nations for the World Economy: A Theory of International Economic Regimes," in Gunter Heiduk and Kozo Yamamura, eds, *Technological Competition and Interdependence: The Search for Policy in the United States, West Germany, and Japan*, pp.107–47, Seattle: University of Washington Press.

Cowhey, Peter F. (1993) "Domestic Institutions and the Credibility of International Commitments: Japan and the United States," *International Organization* 47(2): 299–326.

Dixit, Avinash (1983) "International Trade Policy for Oligopolistic Industries," *Economic Journal* 94 (Supplement): 233–49.

Dixit, Avinash (1986) "Trade Policy: An Agenda for Research," in *Strategic Trade Policy and the New International Economics*, Paul R. Krugman, ed., pp.283–304, Cambridge, MA: MIT Press.

Dore, Ronald (1986) *Structural Rigidities*, Stanford, CA: Stanford University Press.

Dunning, John H. (1993) *The Globalization of Business: The Challenges of 1990s*, London and New York: Routledge.

Encarnation, Dennis (1992) *Rivals Beyond Trade: America versus Japan in Global Competition*, Ithaca, NY: Cornell University Press.

Flamm, Kenneth (1994) "Flat Panel Displays: Catalyzing a U.S. Industry," *Issues in Science and Technology* 11 (Fall): 27–32.

Flamm, Kenneth (1995) "In Defense of Flat Panel Display Initiatives," *Issues in Science and Technology* 11 (Spring): 22–5.

Flamm, Kenneth (1996) *Mismanaged Trade*, Washington DC: Brookings.

Forester, Tom (1987) *High Tech Society*, Cambridge MA: MIT Press.

Friedman, David (1988) *The Misunderstood Miracle*, Ithaca, NY: Cornell University Press.

Gerschenkron, Alexander (1962) *Economic Backwardness in Historical Perspective*, Cambridge, MA: Harvard University Press.

Gilpin, Robert (1987) *The Political Economy of International Relations*, Princeton, NJ: Princeton University Press.

Goldberg, Victor (1980) "Relational Exchange: Economics and Complex Contracts," *American Behavioral Scientist* 22: 337–52.

Goldstein, Judith and Robert O. Keohane (1993) "Ideas and Foreign Policy: An Analytical Framework," in Judith Goldstein and Robert O. Keohane, eds, *Ideas and Foreign Policy*, pp.3–30, Ithaca, NY: Cornell University Press.

Grossman, Gene M. (1986) "Strategic Export Promotion: A Critique," in Paul R. Krugman, ed., *Strategic Trade Policy and the New International Economics*, pp.47–68, Cambridge, MA: MIT Press.

Grossman, Gene M., ed. (1992) *Imperfect Competition and International Trade*, Cambridge, MA: MIT Press.

Grubel, Herbert and P.J. Lloyd (1971) "The Empirical Measurement of Intra-Industry Trade," *Economic Record* 47 (December): 494–517.

Hall, Peter (1986) *Governing the Economy*, New York: Oxford University Press.

Hamel, Gary and C.K. Prahalad (1994) *Competing for the Future*, Cambridge, MA: Harvard Business School Press.

Hamilton, Alexander (1964 [1791]) *The Reports of Alexander Hamilton*, edited by Jacob E. Cooke, New York: Harper and Row.

Hart, Jeffrey A. (1992) *Rival Capitalists: International Competitiveness in the United States, Japan, and Western Europe*, Ithaca, NY: Cornell University Press.

Hart, Jeffrey A. (1995) "Policies Toward Advanced Displays in the Clinton Administration," Discussion Paper no. 105, Indiana Center for Global Business, Indiana University.

Hart, Jeffrey A. and Sangbae Kim (1998) "The Rise of Wintelism in the United States: Business Strategies and Government Policies," Paper delivered at the annual meeting of the American Political Science Association, Boston, MA, September 3–6.

Hart, Jeffrey A. and Aseem Prakash (1997) "Strategic Trade and Investment Policies: Implications for the Study of International Political Economy," *The World Economy* 20 (July): 457–76.

Hecksher, Eli F. (1991 [1924]) *Hecksher Ohlin Trade Theory*, trans. edited, and introduced by H. Flamm and J. Flanders, Cambridge, MA: MIT Press.

Helpman, Elhanan (1984a) "Increasing Returns, Imperfect Markets, and Trade Theory," in Ronald W. Jones, Peter B. Kenen, eds, *Handbook of International Economics*, Amsterdam: North Holland.

Helpman, Elhanan (1984b) "A Simple Theory of Trade with Multinational Corporations," *Journal of Political Economy* 92: 451–72.

Helpman, Elhanan and Paul R. Krugman (1985) *Market Structure and Foreign Trade: Increasing Returns, Imperfect Competition, and International Economy*, Cambridge, MA: MIT Press.

Hirschman, Albert O. (1945) *National Power and the Structure of Foreign Trade*, Berkeley and Los Angeles, CA: University of California Press.

Hirschman, Albert O. (1971) *A Bias for Hope: Essays in Development and Latin America*, New Haven, CT: Yale University Press.

Johnson, Chalmers (1982) *MITI and the Japanese Miracle*, Stanford, CA: Stanford University Press.

Johnson, Chalmers, Laura D'Andrea Tyson, and John Zysman, eds (1989) *Politics and Productivity*, Cambridge, MA: Ballinger.

Jones, Ronald W. (1987) "Hecksher-Ohlin Trade Theory," in *The New Palgrave*, pp.620–7, New York: Macmillan.

Julius, DeAnne (1990) *Global Companies and Public Policy*, New York: Council on Foreign Relations.

Kahler, Miles (1996) "Trade and Domestic Differences," in Suzanne Berger and Ronald Dore, eds, *National Diversity and Global Capitalism*, pp.298–332, Ithaca, NY: Cornell University Press.

Katzenstein, Peter, ed. (1978) *Between Power and Plenty*, Madison, WI: University of Wisconsin Press.

Katzenstein, Peter (1985) *Small States in World Markets*, Ithaca, NY: Cornell University Press.

Kenen, Peter B. (1965) "Nature, Capital, and Trade," *Journal of Political Economy* 73 (October): 437–60.

Keynes, John M. (1937) *A General Theory of Employment, Interest, and Money*, London: Macmillan.

Kim, Sangbae and Jeffrey A. Hart (1998) "The Global Political Economy of Wintelism: New Modalities of Technology and Power," Paper delivered at a preconference symposium on Information Power and Globalization at the annual meeting of the American Political Science Association, Boston, MA, September 2.

Kindleberger, Charles (1973) *World in Depression 1929–1939*, Berkeley, CA: University of California Press.

Krasner, Stephen D. (1977) "U.S. Commercial and Monetary Policy: Unraveling the Paradox of External Strength and Internal Weakness," *International Organization* 31 (Autumn): 635–71.

Krugman, Paul R. (1983) "Targeted Industrial Policies: Theory and Evidence," in *Industrial Change and Public Policy*, pp.123–56, Kansas City: Federal Reserve Bank of Kansas City.

Krugman, Paul R. (1986) "Introduction: New Thinking About Trade Policy," in Paul R. Krugman, ed., *Strategic Trade Policy and the New International Economics*, pp.1–22, Cambridge, MA: MIT Press.

Krugman, Paul R. (1992) *The Age of Diminished Expectations*, Cambridge, MA: MIT Press.

Krugman, Paul R. (1994a) *Peddling Prosperity: Economic Sense and Nonsense in the Age of Diminished Expectations*, New York: Norton.

Krugman, Paul R. (1994b) "Competitiveness: A Dangerous Obsession," *Foreign Affairs* 73 (March/April): 28–44.

Krugman, Paul R. (1994c) "The Myth of Asia's Miracle," *Foreign Affairs* 73 (November/December): 62–78.

Lake, David A. (1988) *Power, Protection, and Free Trade: International Sources of U.S. Commercial Strategy, 1887–1939*, Ithaca, NY: Cornell University Press.

Leamer, Edward E. (1984) *Sources of International Comparative Advantage*, Cambridge MA: MIT Press.

Lenway, Stefanie A. and Thomas P. Murtha (1994) "The State as Strategist in International Business Research," *Journal of International Business Studies* 25(3): 513–35.

Leontief, W.W. (1956) "Factor Proportions and the Structure of American Trade: Further Theoretical And Empirical Analysis," *Review of Economics and Statistics* 38 (November): 386.

Leontief, W.W. (1957) "Domestic Production and Foreign Trade: American Capital Position Reconsidered," *Proceedings of American Philosophical Society* 97 (September): 332–46.

Leontief, W.W. (1964) "An International Comparison of Factor Costs and Factor Use: A Review Article," *American Economic Review* 54: 335–45.

List, Friedrich (1966 [1841]) *The National System of Political Economy*, New York: Augustus M. Kelly.

Lodge, George C. and Ezra Vogel, eds. (1987) *Ideology and National Competitiveness*, Boston, MA: Harvard Business School Press.

Markusen, James R. (1984) "Multinationals, Multi-Plant Economies, and Gains from Trade," *Journal of International Economics* 16: 205–26.

Markusen, James R. (1995) "The Boundaries of Multinational Enterprises and the Theory of International Trade," *Journal of Economic Perspectives* 9(2): 169–89.

Milner, Helen V. and David B. Yoffie (1989) "Between Free Trade and Protectionism: Strategic Trade Policy and a Theory of Corporate Trade Demands," *International Organization* 42 (Winter): 239–72.

Minhas, B.S. (1963) *An International Comparison of Factor Costs and Factor Use*, Amsterdam: North Holland.

Mintzberg, Henry (1994) *The Rise and Fall of Strategic Planning*, New York: The Free Press.

Mowery, David C. and Nathan Rosenberg (1989) *Technology and the Pursuit of Economic Growth*, New York: Cambridge University Press.

Mytelka, L.K. (1994) *The Growth of Strategic Alliance: A Stock Taking*, Ottawa: Carleton University Press.

Nelson, Douglas (1988) "Endogenous Tariff Theory: A Critical Survey," *American Journal of Political Science* 32 (August): 797–837.

Nelson, R. and Winter, S.G. (1982) *An Evolutionary Theory of Economic Change*, Cambridge, MA: Harvard University Press.

New York Times (1998) September 12: C1.

Ohlin, Bertil (1933) *Interregional and International Trade*, Cambridge, MA: Harvard University Press.

Okimoto, Daniel I. (1989) *Between MITI and the Market: Japanese Industrial Policy for High Technology*, Stanford, CA: Stanford University Press.

Olson, Mancur Jr. (1965) *The Logic of Collective Action*, Cambridge, MA: Harvard University Press.

Park, Yung Chul (1994) "Comments on the 'The Role of State in Financial Markets' by George Stiglitz," in *Proceedings of the World Bank Annual Conference on Developmental Economics*, Washington DC: IBRD/World Bank.

Pauly, L.W. and Reich, S. (1997) "National Structures and Multinational Corporate Behavior," *International Organization* 1: 1–30.

Porter, Michael E. (1980) *Competitive Strategy: Techniques for Analyzing Industries and Countries*, New York: Free Press.

Porter, Michael E. (1990) *The Competitive Advantage of Nations*, New York: Free Press.

Prahalad, C.K. and Gary Hamel (1990) "The Core Competence of the Corporation," *Harvard Business Review* 68(3): 79–91.

Prahalad, C.K. and Kenneth Lieberthal (1998) "The End of Corporate Imperialism," *Harvard Business Review*, July–August: 69–79.

Prakash, Aseem and Jeffrey A. Hart (1998) "Political Economy of Integration," *Business in the Contemporary World* X: 611–632.

Prebisch, R. (1950) *The Economic Development in Latin America and its Principal Problems*, United Nations Commission for Latin America.

Prebisch, R. (1959) "Commercial Policy in Underdeveloped Countries," *America Economic Review: Papers and Proceedings* May: 251–73.

Reich, Robert B. (1990) "Who is Us?" *Harvard Business Review* (January–February): 53–4.

Ricardo, David (1973 [1819]) *Principles of Political Economy and Taxation*, London: Dutton.

Richardson, J. David (1986) "The New Political Economy of Trade Policy," in Paul R. Krugman, ed., *Strategic Trade Policy and the New International Economics*, Cambridge, MA: The MIT Press.

Richardson, J. David (1990) "Strategic Trade Policy," *International Organization* 44 (Winter): 107–35.

Richardson, J. David (1993) "New Trade Theory and Policy a Decade Old: Assessment in a Pacific Context," in Richard Higgott, Richard Leaver, and John Ravenhill, eds., *Pacific Economic Relations in the 1990s: Cooperation or Conflict?* pp.83–105, Boulder, CO: Lynne Rienner Publishers.

Rogowski, Ronald (1989) *Commerce and Coalitions: How Trade Affects Domestic Political Alignments*, Princeton, NJ: Princeton University Press.

Roobeck, Annemieke (1990) *Beyond the Technology Race*, Amsterdam: Elsevier.

Rosenberg, Nathan, Ralph Landau, and David C. Mowery, eds. (1992) *Technology and the Wealth of Nations*, Stanford, CA: Stanford University Press.

Ruggie, John G. (1982) "International Regimes, Transactions, and Change: Embedded Liberalism in the Postwar Economic Order," *International Organization* 36 (Spring): 379–415.

Samuelson, Paul A. (1948) "International Trade and the Equalization of Factor Prices," *Economic Journal* 58 (June): 163–84.

Sandholtz, Wayne (1992) *High Tech Europe*, Berkeley, CA: University of California Press.

Saxonhouse, Gary (1979) "Industrial Restructuring in Japan," *Journal of Japanese Studies* 5: 295–314.

Scherer, F.M. (1992) *International High-Technology Competition*, Cambridge, MA: Harvard University Press.

Schmoller, Gustav (1931 [1895]) *The Mercantile System and its Historical Significance*, New York: Peter Smith.

Schumpeter, Joseph A. (1975 [1950]) *Capitalism, Socialism, Democracy*, 3rd edn, New York: Harper & Row.

Servan-Schreiber, Jean Jacques (1968) *The American Challenge*, trans. by Ronald Steel, New York: Atheneum.

Shonfield, Andrew (1965) *Modern Capitalism*, Oxford: Oxford University Press.

Singer, H.W. (1949) "Economic Progress in Under-developed Countries," *Social Research* 16: 1–16.

Singer, H.W. (1950) "The Distribution of Gains between Investing and Borrowing Countries," *American Economic Review: Papers and Proceedings* May: 473–85.

Skocpol, Theda (1985) "Bringing the State Back in: Strategies of Analysis in Current Research," in Peter B. Evans, Dietrich Rueschemeyer, and Theda Skocpol, eds, *Bringing the State Back In*, pp.3–43, New York: Cambridge University Press.

Smith, Adam (1937 [1776]) *An Enquiry Into Nature and Causes of Wealth of Nations*, New York: Modern Library.

Snyder, Jack (1984) *The Ideology of the Offensive: Military Decision Making and the Disaster of 1914*, Ithaca, NY: Cornell University Press.

Spencer, Barbara J. and James A. Brander (1983) "International R&D Rivalry and Industrial Strategy," *Review of Economic Studies* 50 (October): 707–22.

Stegemann, Klaus (1989) "Policy Rivalry among Industrial States: What Can We Learn from Models of Strategic Trade Policy?" *International Organization* 43 (Winter): 73–100.

Stoffaes, Christian (1987) *Fins des mondes: declin et renouveau de l'economie*, Paris: Odile Jacob.

Stolper, W.F. and Paul A. Samuelson (1941) "Protection and Real Wage," *Review of Economic Studies* 9 (December): 58–73.

Swerling, B.C. (1954) "Capital Shortage and Labor Surplus in the United States," *Review of Economics and Statistics* 36 (August): 250.

Tsuru, Shigeto (1993) *Japanese Capitalism*, New York: Cambridge University Press.

Tulder, Rob Van and Gerd Junne (1988) *European Multinationals in Core Technologies*, New York: Wiley.

Tyson, Laura D'Andrea (1991) "They are Not Us: Why American Ownership Still Matters," *The American Prospect* (Winter): 37–49.

Tyson, Laura D'Andrea (1992) *Who's Bashing Whom? Trade Conflict in High Technology Industries*, Washington DC: Institute of International Economics.

Tyson, Laura D'Andrea and John Zysman (1983) "American Industry in International Competition," in John Zysman and Laura D'Andrea Tyson, eds, *American Industry in International Competition: Government Policies and Corporate Strategies*, pp.15–59, Ithaca, NY: Cornell University Press.

Tyson, Laura D'Andrea, William T. Dickens, and John Zysman, eds (1988) *The Dynamics of Trade and Employment*, Cambridge, MA: Ballinger.

United Nations Conference on Trade and Development/UNCTAD (1995) *World Investment Report*, New York: United Nations.

Valavanis-Vail, Stefan (1954) "Leontief's Scarce Factor Paradox," *Journal of Political Economy* 52 (December): 523.

Van Evera, Stephen (1984) "The Cult of the Offensive and the Origins of the First World War," *International Security* 6 (Summer): 58–107.

Vernon, Raymond (1966) "International Investment and International Trade in Product Cycle," *Quarterly Journal of Economics* 80 (May): 190–207.

Weber, Steve and John Zysman (1992) "The Risk that Mercantilism Will Define the Next Security System," in Wayne Sandholtz, Michael Borrus, John Zysman, Ken Conca, Jay Stowsky, Steven Vogel, and Steve Weber, eds, *The Highest Stakes*, pp.167–96, New York: Oxford University Press.

Williamson, O.E. (1975) *Market and Hierarchies*, New York: Free Press.

Winham, Gilbert R. (1993) "The GATT After the Uruguay Round," in Richard Higgott, Richard Leaver, and John Ravenhill, eds, *Pacific Economic Relations in the 1990s: Cooperation or Conflict?*, pp.184–200, Boulder, CO: Lynne Rienner Publishers.

Yamamura, Kozo (1986) "Caveat Emptor: The Industrial Policy of Japan," in Paul R. Krugman, ed., *Strategic Trade Policy and the New International Economics*, pp.169–210, Cambridge, MA: MIT Press.

Zysman, John (1983) *Government, Markets, and Growth*, Ithaca, NY: Cornell University Press.

10 Administrative law for a new century

*Alfred C. Aman, Jr.**

Introduction

Deregulation, cost-benefit analysis, market-oriented regulatory approaches, declining regulatory budgets, devolution and the delegation of public tasks to the private sector are but some of the hallmarks of what I have called the global era of administrative law.[1] These deregulatory trends are not limited to the United States. In various degrees, they typify new approaches to public law in various countries around the world.[2] Almost all of these reforms are market-oriented; that is, they either substitute markets and the private sector for regulatory regimes or have public agencies use market approaches, structures and incentives to achieve their regulatory goals. Whether such reforms take place in the US, Australia or Germany, the end result is less institutionalized public involvement in decision-making processes that can and often do have widespread public effects. Decisions that were once subject to public law processes and values such as participation and transparency, are now governed primarily by market forces and market values.

The changes occurring in public law have parallels in the private sector. In both sectors, downsizing, decentralizing regulatory (or deregulatory) responsibilities,[3] and increasing efficiency are among the parallel trends that conceptually transform citizens into consumers.[4] As Kobrin describes in this volume, corporate "downsizing," "outsourcing," "off-shore production" and "re-engineering"[5] are indicative of private sector attempts to maximize efficiency and profits in a manner that takes full advantage of new global technologies and newly emerging, worldwide markets. Corporate structures, both for manufacturing and distribution purposes, are changing, with corporate webs – regional and often global in their reach – and smaller, decentralized units of production increasingly typifying the more flexible ways in which businesses organize themselves and operate. In this chapter, I will argue that globalization is having a similar effect on the organization of the regulatory state.

The parallel changes in the public law and private sectors are occurring within a global context whose most significant feature is an unprecedented degree of interconnectedness among national economies. A second characteristic feature of globalization is intense competition among national economies and many of the corporate entities that operate within them. Given today's computer and information technologies, global economic processes also challenge traditional analytical concepts such as core and periphery, or comparative advantage. They involve new patterns of trade and corporate finance.[6] As argued by Cerny in this volume, the essence of globalization today is that these processes occur without direct agency of the state.[7] Thus, they not only are changing the shape of and the ways in which the private sector does business, but these processes also challenge fundamental ideas of what the state is, what its relationship to the private sector should be, and what actions the state can realistically take to deal effectively with perceived social, economic and political problems.

It is within the context of this volume – how globalization impacts governance – that this chapter addresses a basic question: what role can the state effectively play as a regulator, given the collapse of the distinction between domestic and global, as well as that between public and private? Since globalization processes are so varied, globalization is a term with many meanings, some of which have long been a part of our economic and political landscapes. I shall argue, however, that the impact of today's globalization processes on United States administrative law is transforming it in new ways. Indeed, there are changing roles for the state to play based largely on new ways of incorporating market regulatory approaches (and the private sector generally) to public interest ends. Three broad regulatory innovations signal the beginning of a new transformation of administrative law: (1) the delegation of public functions to the private sector; (2) the increasingly common recourse to market regulatory approaches as a substitute for command-control rules; (3) the application of market organizational models such as federal corporations. The effect of such a transformation shifts the role of the legal system primarily from legitimating new extensions of public power and increased state intervention, to legitimating new mixes of public and private power, new uses of private power and increased reliance on market approaches to further public interest goals. This transformation is the major theme of this chapter and the move from the public to the private is a common theme in legal systems throughout the West. To the extent domestic public law processes are viewed and treated as distinct from pure market approaches, global governance conceptions based on cooperation rather than on competition alone are more likely to develop.

To set the stage for this basic shift in administrative law focus, part one of this chapter will examine the role administrative law has played in two different regulatory eras – the *laissez-faire* era of the nineteenth and early twentieth century and the regulatory era of the New Deal and beyond. Part two will then set forth some examples of current regulatory reform approaches involving new mixes of state and private power. Part three will provide various perspectives on these developments, arguing that although we are in the midst of an important transformation in administrative law, policy makers, courts and the public can interpret these changes in various ways. This chapter concludes by arguing that it is necessary to see these changes in a way that can create the legal structures and doctrines necessary to facilitate new governmental approaches to problems and the new public/ private relationships necessary to carry them out. This is necessary if the state is to play a meaningful regulatory role and provide an opportunity for a broad public interest discourse on the many policy questions that will confront our increasingly interconnected global societies. A resort to a *laissez-faire* conception of the state suggests that market competition is all that is necessary for global governance. As we shall argue, more cooperative approaches to global governance require domestic legal structures that facilitate international solutions to complex problems that go well beyond increased economic competition among territorial states.

Administrative law and the state – past approaches

The role of administrative law – past regimes

Examining the philosophical assumptions that underlie domestic law is an excellent way of determining the conception of the state involved when it comes to governance at both the domestic and the global levels. Administrative law is directly linked to the dominant theory of the state in vogue at any given point in time. For most of the nineteenth century, at least until the rise of the Industrial Revolution, it was assumed that the state would play a limited and essentially negative role[8] (see Lake's paper in this volume on this subject). The administrative law that developed in this time was also limited. So-called "red light" theories of administrative law predominated,[9] as the guiding theory of administrative procedure was to maximize protection of citizens from governmental action. This occurred quite naturally, as a function of administrative law's confinement to the courts, thus ensuring that an adversary model of justice would apply, as would basic common law doctrines.[10]

As modern government grew, especially with the creation of various New Deal programmes in the 1930s and beyond, a new theory of administrative law – one that articulated the rationales of a more interventionist state – was necessary. Procedure came to be viewed more functionally, as a means of carrying out the politically legitimate commands of the state. The consistent application of such a theory by the courts, and even the legislature, developed slowly, however, in part because procedural issues were often thought of as separate and distinct from the substantive issues involved. A judicial, adversary model of procedure was usually synonymous with what constituted fairness to the litigants. Prior to the Administrative Procedure Act (APA), there was no generally accepted alternative procedural model to the adversary model provided by the courts, even when policy issues were predominant. Procedures, of course, have substantive effects, as well. The more adversarial the procedures, the fairer the process might appear, particularly to those who objected to the substance of the regulation to be implemented in the first place, but the more difficult and costly it was to carry out the governmental programs involved. The use of procedure to achieve substantive ends, contrary to the substantive goals of a particular governmental program, has a long history in the United States.[11] It was, thus, a major step simply to be able, constitutionally speaking, to move adjudicatory proceedings from the courts to administrative agencies, to which the Supreme Court gave its constitutional blessing in *Crowell* v. *Benson* in 1932.[12]

Quite apart from the procedures used to implement agency programs, however, the fundamental question of agency legitimacy loomed large, especially as the scope of regulation increased. The courts were largely responsible for providing the legal framework that transformed administrative law from the traditional common law model of public law to one more appropriately suited to an interventionist state.[13] Courts did this, in large part, by expanding the opportunities for interested parties to participate in agency and judicial proceedings, thereby making the administrative process a surrogate political process. In his influential article, "The Reformation of American Administrative Law,"[14] Professor Stewart summed up this transition in the following way:[15] "Increasingly, the function of administrative law is not the protection of private autonomy but the provision of a surrogate political process to ensure the fair representation of a wide range of affected interests in the process of administrative decisions."

In the global era, administrative law now appears to be moving from its role as a surrogate political process that legitimates new extensions of public power, to one that legitimates new blends of public and private power and/or private power used for public interest ends. The new administrative law of market approaches and structures is largely the creation of the legislative and executive branches of government.[16] It is unclear just what the role of courts will be, and it may well be that the Supreme Court's interest in reviving the 10th Amendment as well as the Takings Clause of the Constitution could undercut the legislative flexibility necessary to create new regulatory models involving federal, state and local regulation.[17]

The move towards greater political participation and ultimately greater transparency of agency decision-making processes that typified modern administrative law in the 1960s and 1970s was the crucial aspect of the transformation of administrative law that Professor Stewart documents, and it is precisely this aspect of the process that is most in jeopardy from some of the processes of globalization. In a global economy, many significant economic issues are decided before they can even become matters of public concern or involvement.[18] Capital markets function independently of any one nation's concerns but they can place enormous pressure on states to conform to the dictates of the market.[19] The public/private distinction, so long a part of United States public law, shields much of this economic decision-making activity from public law, but financial decisions of this sort are so influential that they can structure the terms in which the public sector will act.

This kind of financial pressure can undercut significantly the ability of a state to engage in traditional forms of economic regulation (for an opposing view, see Kudrle's chapter in this volume). Moreover, in a global economy, investments in plant and labor know no boundaries. If costs in the form of taxes and regulatory burdens are too high, such investment can easily flow to locations where its return is greater.[20] Corporations that do business in various parts of the world may, thus, choose to expand or move their operations to more favorable jurisdictions. Even if such "locational threats" never materialize, they have the capacity to affect seriously the politics and political decisions at federal, state and local levels. Indeed, rather than appear weak, the state may try to be proactive by adopting a "pro-growth" economic policy that affirmatively emphasizes lower taxes and less regulation (see, Hart and Prakash's chapter on strategic trade and investment policies in this context). Such an approach enables the state to "do something," even though the substance of its actions is to minimize its overall role in the economy.

Approaching regulatory reforms, however, as if they are either in the public sphere or the private sphere gives more meaning and significance to the public/private distinction than it should have. In some instances, privatizing a particular policy area may not be accomplished necessarily to eliminate government and public participation, but rather to apply the discipline of the market to the implementation of the public policies involved. In other areas, it may be that the decisions to be made are wholly private and best left to the market – such as the price of gas or oil at the wellhead. The use of private or market discourses to further collective public ends should be seen as separate from the uses of private power intended to be wholly separate from any kind of public, collective decision-making processes.

Administrative law and the state – some current approaches

Recent regulatory reforms at the federal level include some clear examples of privatization – that is, the complete withdrawal of the government and the return of various decisions wholly to the private market. Certain aspects of airlines were deregulated in the 1970s and the Civil Aeronautics Board was abolished, price controls on oil and gas at the wellhead have been repealed, and most recently the Interstate Commerce Commission has been abolished.[21] With the bulk of regulatory reforms, however, the state remains involved, but it increasingly must incorporate aspects of the market to achieve public interest ends. Indeed, market models, approaches, language and concepts dominate the way the federal government now approaches its regulatory role. This is particularly evident in the language, approach, proposals and tone of the Gore Commission report on reinventing government.

In the first *National Performance Review* (NPR), published in September 1993, the Gore Commission outlined both the state of the United States government and a plan to "reinvent" the government so that it might better serve its people and continue to lead the world in this new era of globalization. In this report the Administration stated that its goals were to create a government "that makes sense," "gets results," "puts customers first," and "gets its money's worth." To that end, it directed all agency heads to: "cut obsolete regulations," "reward results, not red tape," "get out of Washington and create grassroots partnerships," and "negotiate, don't dictate."[21a] Since issuing the first report, the Administration has published three updates, one of which proclaims boldly that "The Era of Big Government is Over."[21b]

The application of this new rhetoric in a global context augurs significant changes in United States administrative law that include: (1) new blends of public and private sectors at all levels of government; (2) a redefinition of what is public and what is private, or at least what kinds of public functions can be fulfilled in the private sector; (3) greater reliance on bargaining and negotiation models of decision making when it comes to the exercise of agency discretion; (4) a diminution of public participation stemming from increased reliance on privatization and the delegation of public functions to private entities; and (5) a market discourse that arguably narrows the role of public interest values, and replaces them with the rhetoric of cost-benefit analysis.

To analyze such changes in regulatory direction, emphasis and language, we shall briefly describe three examples of recent regulatory reforms and their impact on administrative law: (1) the wholesale delegation of public functions to the private sector; (2) the devolution of federal responsibilities to the states and the private sector; and (3) the retention of governmental responsibility for implementation purposes, but the privatization of the procedures and structures used to implement these government programs.

Delegating public responsibilities to the private sector

Some might argue with my characterization of administrative law's new "charge" of blending public and private power, by saying that regulation always involves a mix of the public and the private because of the processes used to promulgate them. If a rule is under consideration, comments are requested from the regulated. If adjudication is underway, obviously there is give and take between the private parties and the government during the course of the proceeding. More informal contacts have also been a part of the administrative process, especially if the matters involve future directions the agency might or might not take.

Such contacts, however, usually involve an arm's length set of relationships with the government positioned as a neutral decision maker and the regulated as interested parties to the proceeding. In rule-making proceedings, participation is open to all who have an interest and there is a strong bias in favor of having all communications with the agency in the record.

Recent reforms at the state and federal levels, however, seek to involve the private sector in different ways. One approach is to delegate power and functions, usually thought of as public, to the private sectors. Short of a wholesale delegation, a related approach is to subcontract out a significant portion of those functions normally done by the agency to the private sector. Another is to involve not only the private sector in such new partnerships, but to enlist the cooperation and involvement of state and local government as well. Let me briefly explore two such examples: namely, private prisons and welfare reform.

Private prisons

In its 1996 budget proposal, the Justice Department requested $318 million to build three new federal prisons and fund the activation of seven new prisons, of which five will be privatized.

> In compliance with reinventing government measures, the request proposes the further utilization of private companies, where most appropriate, to manage federal inmates. This expands the private sector's role in federal corrections by contracting for the management and operation of several federal prisons currently under construction. The majority of future pretrial detention, minimum and low security federal prisons will be privatized.[22]

Privatizing prisons differs from deregulating airlines or ending price controls on the price of oil or gas at the wellhead.[23] The airline industry as well as the oil and gas industries are private industries with a substantial number of competitors. Markets can work in setting prices in all of these areas. Prisons, at least in modern times,[24] generally have been thought of as a public function.[25] This does not mean that the "services" associated with running a prison cannot be provided by private companies, but the overall responsibility of providing for prisons has generally been viewed as a governmental responsibility. The implications of privatization of such a function are different from those involved when an industry such as the gas or oil industry is deregulated. When that occurs, public law procedures no longer apply to how the price is set by market competitors. The antitrust laws are thought to suffice. In such industries, what once was public and the subject of elaborate rate-making hearings, is now increasingly private. But when responsibility for prisons is delegated to the private sector, important constitutional questions can persist: can the government delegate these responsibilities and, if so, what are the constitutional rights of prisoners in a private institution?

Courts have begun to resolve some of these issues, usually in favor of extending some aspects of the public sphere to what is now the private sector.[26]

This is accomplished, however, through the application of the state action doctrine, a doctrine that is hardly clear and is highly fact specific.[27] Clearly, this is a doctrine on which much will turn, if there is to be a role for public law in the future. Quite apart from the important legal questions involved, the very nature of this new partnership between the public and private sectors is instructive to us for at least three reasons. First, it suggests that a major source of regulatory reform by means of privatization is driven by the need to lower the costs of government. Competition among private providers of prison services will enable these services to be provided efficiently. Second, by implication, privatization of a public function suggests that government is *not* as good or, at least, not as efficient as it needs to be. Third, the equation of market approaches and efficiency with the public interest suggests that even a function such as imprisoning violators of the law is not so different in its mechanics from a traditional market activity as to exclude the private sector. It is important to emphasize, however, that privatizing prisons in this way enlists the private sector in a way that does more than arguably save money. It also mixes the private and public sectors in a new way and one that is not isolated, but part of a larger, emerging pattern of governmental attempts to accomplish essentially public responsibilities in cost efficient ways. The question that does arise and which will continue to do so, is the extent to which public law applies to the private side of these partnerships? On a more philosophical level, the question that also arises is whether the kinds of values protected by public law are capable of being translated primarily into an efficiency discourse. Is there anything lost in the translation? Welfare reforms clearly raise such concerns, especially since the prior welfare regime was based on the premise that it was the federal government's duty to provide a safety net for those who could not be accommodated by the market economy.

Welfare reform

Quite apart from traditional federalism concerns and the role that states are to play in our federal system, devolution of federal responsibilities to the states is also driven by cost considerations and increased competition for foreign investment among individual states. Indeed, many states now have their own trade representatives in various countries around the world and they aggressively seek foreign investment, the jobs that come with this investment as well as new global markets for the products produced in their states. Having a greater chance to control more closely the regulatory and social costs incurred in the state can make efficient states more competitive in the global economy. This is one of many reasons for the drive towards greater state control of welfare assistance programmes.[28] Indeed, the Clinton Administration has issued countless memoranda and orders endorsing the devolution of federal power to the states. Its reason is similar to those given by large corporations that seek to decentralize their operations, and that is, to increase efficiency. According to the federal government, the states "should have more flexibility to design solutions to the problems faced by citizens in this country without excessive micro management and unnecessary regulation from the Federal Government."[29] Welfare reform is one of the most dramatic examples of this kind of governmental decentralization.

The Welfare Reform Act of 1996, also known as the "Personal Responsibility and Work Opportunity Reconciliation Act of 1996," removes the responsibility of administering welfare to needy families from the federal government and transfers the task to the states through the conferral of "block grants." In so doing, the federal government has given up its traditional safety net function for protecting the poor. The relinquishment of the safety net role is based, in large part, on the belief that individual states can devise their own programs to deal with the poor and make their own choices as to how best to meet the needs of their poorest citizens. A federal presence, however, remains. A state is eligible to provide welfare under this Act only if it has first submitted a plan to the Secretary of Health and Human Services that meets several requirements, including how the state intends to conduct a program that: (1) provides assistance to needy families with (or expecting) children and provides parents with job preparation, work and support services to enable them to leave the program and become self-sufficient; and (2) requires a parent or caretaker to engage in work (as defined by the state) once the state determines that the parent or caretaker is ready to engage in work, or once the parent or caretaker has received assistance for twenty-four months (whether or not consecutive), whichever is earlier. Such loose stipulations imposed on the states by the federal government pay homage to the federal government's oversight authority, but also substantially liberate the states to craft a welfare reform plan suitable to their own needs. Because of the states' newfound freedoms, many of them are interested in employing the private sector in the implementation of their programs. As the *New York Times* has noted: "[t]he new law allows states to buy not only welfare services but also gatekeepers to determine eligibility and benefits."[30]

Any number of private companies are lining up to take over these functions, including Lockheed and Electronic Data Systems. Whether a conflict of interest develops between the private sector's need for profit and the public interest values that militate in favor of eligibility remains to be seen. Once again, there will be problems of translation when one balances the needs of our poorest individuals with the efficiency concerns of a private firm whose primary task is to determine the eligibility of welfare applicants as efficiently as possible and within the constraints of a relatively small budget. For such a system to work, policy makers, and perhaps courts as well, will have to find ways of blending this kind of public-private partnership and creating the kind of legal discourse necessary to achieve the benefits learned from the discipline of the market, without ignoring important values not fully susceptible to narrow cost-benefit calculations. Also, as McGinnis argues in this volume, governments perhaps still remain the most credible and efficient players for providing redistributive services such as welfare due to lower "start-up" costs.

Federal corporations – corporatizing government

Another approach to regulatory reform that blends the public and private, if not in new ways, at least in increasingly common ways, is to leave certain public functions in the public sector, but to use a private sector structural model for the supervision and delivery of those services.[31] Federal corporations have long provided a structural framework for such an approach. The federal government's authority to charter corporations is well established and authorized by the Necessary and Proper Clause of the Constitution.[32] The United States Postal Service, the Federal Aviation Administration (FAA), the Federal Railway Administration, and the Overseas Private Investment Corporation (OPIC) are just a few examples of the federal government's use of private models for delivering public services.

These federal corporations take various forms and the state action doctrine looms large in determining the extent to which administrative law or constitutional law will apply to these entities. If the federal government can simply avoid constitutional protections by corporatizing governmental agencies, form will clearly have triumphed over substance. This, the court concluded in *Lebron* v. *National Railroad Passenger Corporation*[33] should not be the case. In *Lebron* the court held that Congress' decision that Amtrak was a private entity was not determinative for the courts when asked to decide whether the state action doctrine applied.[34] The Supreme Court held that a

> corporation is an agency of the government, for purposes of constitutional obligations of the government rather than "privileges of the government", when the state has specifically created that corporation for the furtherance of a governmental objective and does not merely hold some shares but rather controls the operation of the corporation through its appointees.[35]

Recalling its stance as to the status of the Reconstruction Finance Corporation, the Court went on to note that the fact "that . . . Congress chose to call it a corporation does not alter its characteristics so as to make it something other than what it actually is. . . ."[36]

The conclusion that Amtrak is "an agency or instrumentality of the United States for the purpose of individual rights guaranteed against the Government by the Constitution," is founded on the history of government-created and controlled corporations. As the Court noted:[37]

> a remarkable feature of the heyday of those corporations, in the 1930s and 1940s, was that, even while they were praised for their status "as agencies separate and distinct, administratively and financially and legally, from

the government itself, which has facilitated their adoption of commercial methods of accounting and financing, avoidance of political controls, and utilization of regular procedures of business management", it was fully acknowledged that they were a "device" of "government", and constituted "federal corporate agencies" apart from "regular government departments".

Lebron may be the new day, but it is important to note that the courts have not always been so accommodating when it comes to seeing through the "private veil" of the corporate form. Courts have held that the Legal Services Corporation, the Corporation for Public Broadcasting and Communications Satellite Corporation (COMSAT) are all essentially private concerns.[38]

As with privatized prisons, however, both the approach to governing federal corporations and how the courts choose to view them is essential to the development of our understanding of administrative law in the future. Indeed, the use of these various corporate agency forms are increasingly common.[39] The government frequently is now expected to look like as well as perform in a manner consistent with private sector models. This is particularly true for the various commercial activities that the government carries out, but the dominance of the market and market models is not so limited. Market discourses have also been used frequently to structure various non-commercial regulatory approaches and incentives, such as the use of market approaches in the amendments to the Clean Air Act.[40]

All of the above examples of market structures and market regulatory discourses imply a different relationship between the regulated and government and, more importantly, between government and its citizens. It is possible, however, to view this as simply a change in the means of regulation, but I believe that more is at stake. As the ends of regulation increasingly mimic market results, this inevitably affects not only the regulatory discourse, but the processes by which these results are reached. Moreover, if one adopts a *laissez-faire* view of these various returns to the market, the domestic law that results makes cooperative regulatory approaches at the intellectual level difficult to achieve. Not only are there fewer regulatory structures in place, but the approach one takes to domestic regulation helps define what is possible at the international level. If a cooperative model of governance is to develop at the global level, a cooperative view of regulation and the market will be necessary at the domestic level.

Three perspectives on regulatory reform

The market-oriented regulatory reforms that globalization processes encourage states to pursue can be conceptualized in different ways. Indeed, globalization itself is a term of art that refers to a variety of complex, dynamic legal and social processes in which states increasingly are "actors" only indirectly. In many instances, these processes significantly undercut a state's autonomy, though the state may not wish to see it that way. For example, a state may wish to implement certain domestic political solutions to ease unemployment caused by increased off-shore production, but regulatory solutions that raise manufacturing costs at home can exacerbate the off-shore problem. If the state imposes higher regulatory costs on domestic industries, these measures can encourage further relocation or expansion off-shore. Thus, a state might make a deregulatory response to this kind of situation. A *laissez-faire* interpretation of this response would stress that markets can and should be allowed to work and that states, by implication, are essentially powerless in the face of such trends. Another interpretation would see the state as initiating a new policy approach, but one that embraces the market. The state can, in effect, appear to mimic the market, adopt its language and to some extent its goals, and in so doing, retain an active role in mediating the impact of global economic, political trends. Whether this is the strategy of a weak or a strong state is hard to discern because many of the market-oriented goals a state may set for itself are sympathetic with, if not the same as, what an unregulated market approach would achieve. By taking "credit" for these results, however, the state may appear to remain a viable actor in processes that it may ultimately be able to influence, but not control.

A state's action or inaction in the face of changing economic forces is thus subject to many interpretations, but it can also trigger different bodies of judicial administrative law precedents and the underlying political theories of the state that these cases represent. Moreover, different interpretations of these changes can fuel various kinds of domestic regulatory politics that suggest very different regulatory visions for the future.

This part of the chapter considers three such perspectives on current reforms. In discussing them, it is important that we differentiate the various uses of the market inherent in each of these conceptualizations. This is important because some state action or inaction can appear to be consistent with very different regulatory philosophies and goals. By recognizing the various interpretive possibilities that exist, we can help, when necessary, to create, or when possible, to preserve ways of seeing these changes that provide for the kind of legal flexibility or interpretive space necessary for a new administrative law to develop, one appropriate for the new mixtures of public and private power suitable for the regulatory problems in today's global economy.

Back to the future

Kobrin suggests in this volume that the medieval analogy may be appropriate to describe governance systems of the future. Along the same lines, one could easily contend that private prisons and state welfare programs, significant portions of which are privatized, as well as the use of federal corporations – especially those that avoid the state action doctrine – are all steps back to a nineteenth century *laissez-faire* conception of the state. Such a theoretical approach to state power resonates deeply with a body of case-law that was developed in the early stages of United States administrative law, emphasizing the economic rights of individuals. It also resonates with a constitutional framework that minimizes federal power and maximizes that of the states.

Moreover, the political regulatory debates that accompany these and similar reforms easily fall on a unidimensional spectrum, with the free market at one end of that spectrum and – in the United States at least, where nationalization of industries has been rare – some form of extensive command-control regulation at the other. With this spectrum in mind, the regulatory debate appears to be a zero-sum game. One zero-sum view of the overall direction of market-oriented regulatory reforms is that they take us "back to the future" – representing a return to a nineteenth-century *laissez-faire* conception of the proper relationship of the state to the market; that is to say, the state's role is expected to be minimal, especially at the federal level, and most problems are viewed as essentially private and amenable to market solutions or aid provided by institutions thought to be part of "civil society." The administrative law for such a conception of the state would consist largely of the common law doctrines and approaches that dominated the so-called traditional model of administrative law discussed above.[41]

The view that we are, in fact, moving away from an interventionist state to one that relies primarily on free markets coincides with the resurrection of the importance of constitutional provisions and interpretations long thought relatively unimportant to defining the role of the state. These include such provisions as the Takings Clause of the 14th Amendment,[42] the 10th Amendment[43] and a narrowly read Commerce Clause.[44] In addition, recent cutbacks in the doctrine of standing by the Supreme Court also challenge some important assumptions of modern administrative law, by making it more difficult for affected parties to challenge administrative actions in court.[45] If American administrative law was once transformed by the courts, as Professor Stewart has written,[46] no such transformation appears in these opinions, unless it is the beginnings of a return to the traditional model of administrative law. Though an analysis of these recent Supreme Court cases is beyond the scope of this paper,[47] these opinions all rely heavily on, and tend to reinforce, bright line distinctions between such categories as public and private, state and federal, as well as party and citizen. Though these opinions too are capable of alternative interpretations, the overall thrust of these cases and the constitutional matrix which they imply may undercut the kind of governmental flexibility that is necessary to react effectively to new global regulatory contexts. Collective approaches to societal problems that blur public/private distinctions may be a source of important, new regulatory reforms that are appropriate for a state that no longer is as autonomous as it once was. Constitutional flexibility when it comes to the respective roles of the federal, state, and local governments, as well as the private sector, will be required for the kind of experimentation that may be necessary.

Quite apart from the potential impact of recent decisions by the Supreme Court, many legislative proposals set forth in the Republican Party's "Contract with America" in the 104th Congress, in fact, provide very specific examples of a back to the future scenario for regulatory reform, one that includes not only attempts to abolish some government agencies and programs outright, but also one that utilizes a *laissez-faire* procedural approach to effectively curtail the power of agencies too popular to abolish.[48] Some supporters of these proposals undoubtedly see procedural reforms as but a way station on the road to a substantive *laissez-faire* approach. Short of abolition of certain agencies, however, procedures advocating elaborate cost-benefit review are the next best approach because they are likely to ensure that any new regulatory action will be unlikely.[49] For legislative proponents of a back to the future view of regulatory reform, the state is like a rubber band that has been stretched too far. At a minimum, a procedural *laissez-faire* approach resists any additional or new role for the state and, over time, the state must be allowed to snap or slip back to a minimalist starting position.

This kind of hard-edged, philosophical view of regulatory reform, also drives a certain kind of domestic politics, a politics that sees government as a major contributor to a national problem characterized by declining competitiveness, fewer industrial jobs, high taxes and governmental institutions incapable of offering or implementing any constructive solutions. The public-private dichotomy is often emphasized to the point where almost any governmental attempt to rectify a problem is assumed to be doomed to failure, but the market consistently is seen as a major source of liberation[50] (in the context of the politics of the globalization discourse, see Douglas' piece in this volume). Such an approach, however, fails to create the kinds of domestic governmental structures and approaches necessary for the global level.

Corporatizing government

Closely related to a *laissez-faire* approach to government is another version of the back to the future thesis, but one which is more optimistic in nature, and one which does not necessarily reject a role for government to play. This approach, which we might call the "economic growth model," posits as free a market economy as possible as the ultimate goal, with the explicit assumption that less regulation and less costly government will increase economic growth in a manner that will benefit everyone. But rather than emphasizing a pure philosophical belief in the value of individual freedom from government intrusion, this view places more emphasis on the consequences that can flow from markets and efficient government – namely, economic prosperity for all.[51] Though government will have a role to play, that role should be made to adhere to corporate organizational forms and structures whenever possible and be subject to the discipline and rigors of the market.[52] If it is necessary to enlist the private sector to carry out certain governmental tasks, such as the management of prisons, mental hospitals or public housing, that may be necessary, if it is the most efficient way of proceeding.

Besides reliance on the market, either as a form of bureaucratic organization or as a substitute for government, another aspect of this perspective on regulatory reform involves some relatively new ways in which interest groups may interact with the government. Corporatism is a political theory with a great variety of meanings.[53] But there are aspects of the political theory developed to support corporatism that have resonance with certain trends in United States administrative law, especially those aspects of the theory that assume a bargaining relationship between the government and selected, representative interest groups and an outcome that is really a brokered policy in which the government often plays more of the role of mediator, than judge. These aspects of corporatism thus focus on:[54]

> the outcome of a bargaining process between state agencies and those organized interests whose power in the political marketplace means that their co-operation is indispensable if agreed policies are to be implemented. The state is not sufficiently powerful for officials to dictate policies and impose them unilaterally, but at the same time it is sufficiently powerful to resist capture by those interests. This notion is clearly implicit in the concept of bargaining: each party must have resources to bargain with; otherwise the relationship is one of subservience or submission.

The need for increased bargaining on the part of the state to achieve goals that are realistically enforceable, is indicative of a state that can no longer accomplish its objectives by direct command-control regulations. This is true for a number of reasons. First, as noted above, the processes of globalization can weaken the state in various ways, not the least of which is that they make it relatively easy for some industries to move production around the globe, avoiding excess costs, but often affecting local employment opportunities as well. There is thus a greater premium on the part of the state to negotiate with potential regulatees, perhaps to convince them of the necessity of the regulation and that what it proposes is as cost-effective as possible. This relates closely to enforcement. As the funding of agencies decreases, effective enforcement of the regulations promulgated increasingly requires the co-operation of the regulated. They need to be given the discretion to reach the desired results in ways that make sense for them. Industries also increasingly need to be part of the planning and regulatory process.

The increasing reliance on markets and market approaches as substitutes for more direct forms of regulation highlights efficiency concerns and it also suggests a regulatory discourse that is much closer to market concerns and modes of operation. This is likely generally to be more in tune with business interests, but a market discourse applies especially easily to companies doing business in multiple countries. They are freer to reject the political costs of doing business in any one jurisdiction if they can move production around the globe relatively easily. Thus, these market approaches and discourses also suggest new roles for the private sector to play when designing new rules or regulatory approaches, and new bureaucratic structures for government to use, structures that seek quite consciously to copy the form and disciplines of corporate structures.[55]

Finally, since so many regulatory reforms are driven by cost considerations in both the industries to which they apply and in the agencies that promulgate them, localities in competition for foreign investment also wish to have these functions performed in the most efficient way possible and in a manner that is closest to the level of government actually affected. Thus, devolution of regulatory responsibilities to the states and even to localities within those states is increasingly common, as we have seen with welfare reform, discussed above. But the farther one gets from the national level, the easier it is for forms of interest group-government negotiation to occur that begin to approximate even more directly a kind of corporatism with very selected representatives of key industries and labor unions agreeing on the governmental actions necessary to, for example, attract foreign investment to their particular jurisdiction.[56] The "deals" that ultimately are struck often involve tax breaks that provide added incentives for multinational companies to locate in that area.[57]

Market cooptation

A third view of regulatory reform begins with the assumption that government regulation can be positive. This view is held by those who philosophically believe in an active government and, more importantly, the ability collectively and legitimately to define something called the public interest. It is not inconsistent, however, for such proponents of regulatory reform also to believe that regulation need not only be the traditional, so-called "command-control" type. New forms of regulation that seek to coopt the market as a regulatory tool can be both effective and efficient. Such reformers thus seek to enlist the private interest for the public good but the public good is not defined by the market alone. The market is a means to an end, not an end in itself.

Using the market in this way represents the public uses of the private interest. Markets are used not just to maximize wealth, however it might be distributed, but to structure incentives in such a way as to achieve public interest goals. The government itself also can function more efficiently and in less expensive ways. In an era of intense global competition and scarce resources, incorporating some of the accountability and the discipline of the market into government activities is, thus, also viewed as an important reform. The more efficient government becomes, the better it can accomplish its public interest goals. Such a view, however, does not see the use of federal corporations or privatized prisons as essentially relieving the state of the responsibility for policy outcomes reached by these privatized structures, but simply as a new, hopefully more effective way of advancing the public interest. If it can be shown, for example, that the cost savings anticipated from privatizing prisons do not materialize or that important non-economic values were inappropriately excluded from the decision-making processes of federal corporations or privatized welfare programs, these reformers would be open to different mixes of the public and the private, including a return to older forms of regulation.

It is important to emphasize that, in this perspective, uses of the market and market incentives as a means to further public ends do, indeed, differ significantly from reforms designed to return to the market as an end in itself or from those that seek to have government approximate market structures and outcomes, as ends in themselves. Different conceptions of the roles of the state, the private sector and the public interest are involved in each of the perspectives sketched above and each generates the need for somewhat different legal doctrines or, at least, different conceptual and interpretive approaches to these doctrines. For those who see the market as an end in itself, be they advocates of back to the future or economic growth advocates who see the federal corporate form as an end in itself, a clear distinction between the state and the private sector is necessary. It is, therefore, important that the line between public and private be a bright one. From a constitutional point of view, this means that what falls within the private realm is the domain of the market and private, individual decision making. The role of law is to assure that such private activity can occur safely beyond the reach of the state. Given the assumption that such a public or governmental role will be relatively small compared to the private sector, there is also a presumption against state intervention in economic matters and in favor of maximum private involvement.

For those who wish to coopt the market for public purposes, the public/private dividing line is problematic. Given that it may be sensible to have a more market-oriented state, the state must still be an independent public interest force. But if the state is to forge new alliances with the private sector to carry out public interest goals, a constitutional structure that too rigorously defines what is private in opposition to what is public can hamper the creativity of these new state/private partnerships or inappropriately shield activities and decisions that have broad public impact from the kinds of procedures that "public" law can provide. Moreover, for those who see the market as a means to achieve public interest ends and believe government agencies can carry out these programs, the role of the state remains important in setting goals, standards and structuring incentives in new ways that can funnel private interests in public interest directions.

One could argue that with the market cooptation perspective, the interest group model of administrative law remains intact because only the form of regulation has changed. It would be a mistake, however, to assume that even with the more public interest emphasis of the third perspective, the role of the state continues to be the same or, arguably, as powerful or as extensive as in previous eras. Further, the more the market and market approaches are used to reach public interest results, important values that are not easily quantified may, in effect, be omitted entirely from consideration. Costs are usually easier to quantify than benefits. Similarly, while equating citizens with consumers may clarify the role or duties of the state in certain contexts, there is something lost from this translation as well. The concept of citizenship is a deep one that can both include and transcend the role of individuals as mere consumers of state services.

The market metaphor has its limits; its rhetoric can and often does limit the roles the state may play and many of the factors described above as market-oriented can more easily come into play in such contexts. Indeed, as market-oriented regulatory schemes have become common, there also is more need for cooperation between the regulated and the state. As noted above, this is especially true in an era of declining regulatory budgets and the consequent inability of the state effectively to enforce the law. As a result, the bargaining process between the state and the regulated increasingly takes place on more equal footing, with both the state and the regulated concerned about minimizing costs.

At the same time, market-oriented regulatory schemes that are not steeped in a back to the future mindset raise interesting and important questions concerning, for example, the efficiency of the processes used to formulate and then carry out governmental rules. The interest group model of administrative law errs in the direction of inclusiveness when it comes to who may participate in policy-making processes, whether or not there is some repetition of views. But a model that emphasizes efficiency may not. It seeks to minimize overlap and militates in favor of selected interest group representatives. Similarly, an explicit cost-benefit approach to regulation yields a different and arguably more narrow public interest discourse when it comes to, for example, solving value-laden regulatory problems that require some translation of the regulatory issues involved into a cost-benefit calculus. Even greater tensions can arise when the regulation involved has been delegated wholly to the private sector, operating, as it were, as a service provider to the government and thus concerned primarily with profitability.

The tensions these newer approaches to regulation produce raise important questions involving what is public and what is private and, more importantly, the extent to which the public interest retains any viability as a concept beyond efficiency. Regulatory reforms that rely on the private sector and market incentives do not represent a return to the past or simply more of the same, but the beginnings of a new model of administrative law in which the line between the public and the private is no longer distinct, and the lines between and among levels of government – international, federal, state and local – should not be so sharp as to prevent synergistic interplay among them and the creation of new combinations or partnerships between government and the private sector. Indeed, the future role for administrative law will be to incorporate and justify new mixes of private and public power as well as to try to ensure the opportunity for a broad based public interest discourse, one that resists the idea that narrow, technocratic cost-benefit analyses are always determinative. Such a role would be compatible with more cooperative approaches to governance at the global level.

Conclusion: the new administrative law

The cumulative effect of various market approaches to regulation, regulatory structures and procedures is to introduce a new mix of private and public power, as well as state and federal power. The overall context of globalization frames these developments. The emphasis on global competition and economic growth coupled with the general weakness of any single individual state in the face of globalization processes, encourages more negotiation on the part of the state as well as regulatory approaches more sympathetic to the cost-conscious demands of multinational businesses and government as well.

For these approaches to evolve into a new administrative law, however, it is necessary for the courts to provide the doctrinal flexibility to incorporate new mixes of the private and the public without, necessarily, opting for one extreme or the other. Judicial approaches that maximize the differences between public and private power can easily shelter private power used for public interest purposes. At the same time, the automatic judicial imposition of "activist procedures" in situations that call for more nuanced and efficient governmental approaches can be counter-productive. In one instance, essentially public decisions are shielded from procedural protections. In the other, new governmental approaches are made inefficient or unduly burdensome by the imposition of procedural models that fail to take into account the need for efficiency that new global realities dictate. Finally, the new administrative law also will be one that must effectively interact more often and with more flexibility with state and municipal law.

If the state is to play a realistic role in the changes brought about by globalization and a public interest discourse is to remain an important part of policy making, it is necessary that a new model of administrative law be developed, the outlines of which are already apparent. This new model will need to legitimate new forms of public, private, state and federal partnerships. A domestic public law of this kind can provide the kind of legal and philosophical foundations necessary for cooperative global governance approaches to develop in the future.

286   *Alfred C. Aman, Jr.*

Notes

* I wish to thank Professors Carol Greenhouse, Jost Delbrück and Lauren Robel for their very helpful comments on this chapter, as well as Ursula Doyle, for her excellent research assistance. An earlier version was published in: Michael Taggart, editor, 1997, *The Providence of Administrative Law*, pp.119–34, Oxford: Hart Publishing.

1 A.C. Aman, *Administrative Law in a Global Era* (Ithaca, NY: Cornell University Press, 1992).
2 See "Symposium, Project: Privatization: The Global Scale-Back of Government Involvement in National Economics" (1996) *48 Admin LR 435*. See generally *The Province of Administrative Law*, Michael Taggart, ed., Hart Publishing, 1997).
3 See generally Albert Gore, *National Performance Review* (Sept. 7, 1995), Annual Report: Common Sense Government.
4 Idem.
5 Peter Dicken, *Global Shift: The Internationalization of Economic Activity* (New York: Guilford Press, 2nd edn, 1992), 169.
6 Idem. For an excellent analysis of the fundamental changes brought about by globalization on various industries, especially the information technology industries, see S. Sassen, *The Global City: New York, London, Tokyo* (Princeton University Press, Princeton, NJ, 1991). See also S. Sassen, *Cities in World Economy* (Pine Forge Press, Thousand Oaks, 1994).
7 See J. Delbrück, "Globalization of Law, Politics, and Markets – Implications for Domestic Law – A European Perspective" (1993) 1 *Ind. J. Global Legal Stud.* 9. See also A.C. Aman, "The Earth as Eggshell Victim: A Global Perspective on Domestic Regulation" (1993) 102 *Yale LJ* 2107 and S. Sassen, "Towards A Feminist Analytics of the Global Economy" (1997) 4 *Ind. J. Global Legal Stud.* (forthcoming).
8 See C. Harlow and R. Rawlings, *Law and Administration* (Weidenfeld and Nicolson, London, 1984), 9–10. As Harlow and Rawlings have noted:

> its role was to act as a "policeman", providing the framework in which citizens could go about their business. According to Locke, the state's functions are limited to the presentation of the rights of its members against infringement by others. . . . It is this and nothing more; a state exceeds its legitimate function if it endeavors to go beyond these limits. (idem)

9 Ibid., chaps 1 and 2.
10 See P. Verkuil, "The Emerging Concept of Administrative Procedure" (1978) 78 *Colum. L. Rev.* 258.
11 For a case study of the uses and misuses of procedures, see A.C. Aman, "Institutionalizing The Energy Crisis: Some Structural and Procedural Lessons" (1980) 65 *Cornell L. Rev.* 491.
12 *Crowell* v. *Benson*, 285 US 22 (1932).
13 R.B. Stewart, "The Reformation of American Administrative Law" (1975) 88 *Harv. L. Rev.* 1667.
14 Idem.
15 Ibid., 1670.
16 It appears that, once again, courts may be in the "red light" position, but this situation is not the same red light – this is a different junction with different traffic. See A. Aman, "The Globalizing State: A Future-Oriented Perspective on the Public/Private Distinction, Federalism and Democracy," 32 Vand. J. *Transnal'l L. 769.*
17 Idem.

18 See generally S. Strange, *Casino Capitalism* (Blackwell, Oxford, 1986).

19 Ibid., 3.

20 D.M. Andrews, "Capital Mobility and State Autonomy: Toward a Structural Theory of International Monetary Relations" (1994) 38 *International Studies Quarterly* 193. For an analysis of capital mobility and its relationship to labour mobility, see S. Sassen, *The Mobility of Labour and Capital* (Cambridge University Press, Cambridge, 1988).

21 Interstate Commerce Commission Termination Act of 1995, Pub. L. No. 104-88, 109 Stat 803 (1995). With airlines and trucking and other industries as well, privatization should be coupled with the application of the antitrust laws.

21a Albert Gore, Report of the National Performance Review, From Red Tape to Results: Creating a Government that Works Better and Costs Less (Sept. 7, 1993).

21b Albert Gore, National Performance Review, 1996 Annual Report: The Best Kept Secrets in Government (Sept. 1996).

22 Department of Justice, News Release, "Justice Department Seeks 20 Percent Increase in FY 96 Budget to Reduce Violent Crime and Illegal Immigration" (6 Feb. 1995).

23 Historically, private prisons, like private fire departments, were prevalent in the eighteenth and nineteenth centuries, but they have been, almost exclusively, a state function ever since. See B.B. Evans, "Private Prisons" (1987) 36 *Emory L. J.* 253. For a discussion of the constitutionality of the delegation of these functions, see J. Field, "Making Prisons Private: An Improper Delegation of a Governmental Power" (1987) 15 *Hofstra L. Rev.* 649.

24 See J.J. Misrahi, "Factories with Fences: An Analysis of the Prison Industry Enhancement Certification Program in Historical Perspective" (1996) 33 *Am. Crim. L. Rev.* 411.

25 See above at n. 23.

26 See, e.g., *Edmonson* v. *Leesville Concrete Company*, 500 U.S. 614 (1991). See also *Lugar* v. *Edmondson Oil Company Inc.*, 457 U.S. 922, 939–42 (1982).

27 See R. Krotoszynski, "Back To The Briarpatch: An Argument In Favor of Constitutional Meta-Analysis In State Action Determinations" (1995) 94 *Mich L. Rev.* 302, 303.

28 See A.C. Aman "A Global Perspective on Current Regulatory Reform: Rejection, Relocation or Reinvention?" (1995) 2 *Ind. J. Global Legal Stud.* 429.

29 Executive Order No. 12875, 3 CFR, reprinted in 5 U.S.C. § 601 (1993).

30 Nina Bernstein, "Giant Companies Entering Race to Run State Welfare Programs," *New York Times*, September 15, 1996.

31 Some of these constructs take the form of "mixed-ownership government corporations." Examples of such corporations are: Amtrak; the Central Bank for Cooperatives; the Federal Deposit Insurance Corporation; the Federal Home Loan Banks; the Federal Intermediate Credit Banks; the Federal Land Banks; the National Credit Union Administration Central Liquidity Facility; the Regional Banks for Cooperatives; the Rural Telephone Bank when the ownership, control, and operation of the bank are converted under § 410(a) of the Rural Electrification Act of 1936 (7 U.S.C. 950(a)); the United States Railway Association; the Financing Corporation; the Resolution Trust Corporation; and the Resolution Funding Corporation.

32 See *McCulloch* v. *Maryland*, 17 U.S. 316 (1819); see also *Osborn* v. *Bank of the United States*, 22 U.S. 738 (1824). The *Osborn* Court echoed the *McCulloch* Court's reasoning. See A.M. Froomkin, "Reinventing the Government Corporation" (1995) *U. Ill. L. Rev.* 543, 551.

33 115 S. Ct. 961 (1995) (hereafter referred to as *Lebron*).

34 Ibid., 971.

35 Ibid., 974.

36 Idem.

37 Idem (quoting from Pritchett, "The Government Corporation Control Act of 1945" (1946) 40 *Am. Pol. Sci. Rev.* 495).

38 See, e.g., *Network Project* v. *Corporation for Public Broadcasting*, 4 Media L. Rep. (BNA) 2399, 2403–8 (D.D.C. 1979); *Texas Rural Legal Aid Inc.* v. *Legal Services Corp.*, 940 F. 2d 685, 699 (D.C. Cir. 1991); *Warren* v. *Government National Mortgage Association*, 611 F. 2d 1229, 1232–5 (8th Cir. 1980), cert. denied, 449 U.S. 847 (1980). See also *Jackson* v. *Culinary School of Washington*, 788 F. Supp. 1233, 1265 (D.D.C. 1992) (holding that the Federal Student Loan Guaranty Association is "not a governmental entity" because Congress designated the corporation "private"). *Lebron*, above at n. 33, itself is not without its own ambiguities. See Krotoszynski, above at n. 27, 301–14.

39 See Aman (1995), above.

40 See Clean Air Act Amendments of 1990, Pub. L. No. 101-549 (1990).

41 See *Stewart*, above at n. 13; see also Verkuil, above at n. 10, 264.

42 US Const. amend. XIV. See, e.g., *Dolan* v. *City of Tigard*, 114 S. Ct. 2309 (1994).

43 US Const. amend. X. See, e.g., *United States* v. *Lopez*, 115 S. Ct. 1624 (1995).

44 Idem.

45 See *Lujan* v. *Defenders of Wildlife*, 504 U.S. 555 (1992), in which the Court held that the defendant environmentalists did not show sufficient "imminent injury" to have standing.

46 See Stewart, above.

47 See Aman at n. 16, above.

48 Most of these proposals involved environmental regulation, such as, e.g., those dealing with wetlands or toxic dumps.

49 For example, the proposed Comprehensive Regulatory Reform Act of 1995 (S 343) restricts agency action to only those issues specifically required by statute; requires peer, congressional, and judicial review of each rule; and mandates a cost-benefit analysis for every rule.

50 Many of the tax reform proposals fall into this mode of reform, too. Abolishing the IRS and minimizing the sources of revenue the federal government has to fund its programs, of course, would make their passage in the first place less likely.

51 See generally Peter Passell, "Asia's Path to More Equality and More Money for All," *New York Times*, 25 Aug. 1996, E5.

52 See text accompanying nn. 31–9 above.

53 See, e.g., P.P. Craig, *Public Law and Democracy in the United Kingdom and the United States of America* (Clarendon Press, Oxford, 1990), 148–53 and A. Cawson, *Corporatism and Political Theory* (Blackwell, Oxford, 1986), 22–46.

54 Ibid.

55 Gore Commission, above at n. 3, 1.

56 See R. Perrucci, *Japanese Auto Transplants In The Heartland* (Aldine De Gruyter, New York, 1994).

57 Idem.

11 Governance of the EU in the twenty-first century

Michele Fratianni

The issues

The European Union (EU) is bound to change the integration rules as expansion takes place. There is a trade-off between deepening and enlargement and the conflict can be resolved by introducing more flexible rules of integration. This is the basic theme of this chapter, which intends to make two contributions. The first contribution – which fits squarely the central theme of this volume – is to show that governance structures are "endogenous" relative to the integration process. The second contribution concerns the application of club theory to international organizations. The EU is an institution *sui generis:* it is neither purely supra-national nor purely inter-governmental. It is a mix of the two, with weights changing over time. The tension between member countries that desire more centralization and countries that resist it can be resolved by sorting out preferences through the creation of smaller clubs. These clubs can pursue either different integration objectives or similar objectives with different intensity.

The original European Community (EC) was conceived primarily as a trade bloc. While it is true that the Treaty of Rome has articles defining external equilibrium, full employment, price stability, and exchange rate stability as common objectives, these are too vague and cannot in any way be interpreted as a blueprint for monetary union, let alone political union. Economic and monetary union (EMU) was elevated to an objective of the EC by European leaders in the Hague Summit of 1969, three years before the accession of Denmark, Ireland and the United Kingdom. Over the years the EC has invested a great deal of its political capital in EMU. Yet, the economic case for monetary union is rather marginal compared to the large, and relatively certain, net benefits of trade integration. But monetary union is more important for its political implications than its economic ones. History shows that monetary union and political union go together. A common currency carries the symbolic value of unity. For many European politicians, especially those in France and Germany, monetary union was understood to be a catalyst for political union.

The Treaty on European Union (TEU) represents a great leap forward with respect to the Treaty of Rome.[1] It imbeds the great aspirations of most EU members to be not only an economic union, but also a monetary union and ultimately, although in an as yet unspecified way, a political union. The TEU charts the deepening of the integration process in the EU. Of all the non-trade policies, EMU is the most clearly delineated. The TEU, in fact, establishes that EMU will be reached in three stages and that in the final stage the newly formed European Central Bank will operate at the center of a European System of Central Banks. The Treaty creates two other "pillars," the Common Foreign and Security Policy and the Justice and Home Affairs, which are much less developed and clearly need the test of time. The former includes principles for a common defense and political cooperation; the latter deals with asylum, immigration, citizenship, and judicial cooperation.

The TEU has changed decision making as well; the changes favor centralization and represent another step, albeit small, towards a federal structure. Qualified majority voting has been extended. Although unanimity still applies to most critical decisions, the possibility of resorting to a qualified majority has altered decision making in the EU. The introduction of the co-decision procedure and the extension of the cooperation and assent procedures have given the European Parliament more power.

Enlargement of the EU is bound to slow down the deepening process just described. The membership of the Community doubled from 1958 to 1986 with the accession of Denmark, Ireland, the United Kingdom (1973), Greece (1981), Portugal, and Spain (1986). It then expanded by an additional 25 per cent by 1995 with the new member states of Austria, Finland and Sweden. Another round of accession is in the making. Thirteen applications for membership are pending: Turkey applied in 1987, Cyprus and Malta in 1990, Hungary and Poland in 1994, Romania, Slovakia, Latvia, Estonia, Lithuania, and Bulgaria in 1995, and the Czech Republic and Slovenia in 1996. The European Council, at the Copenhagen Summit of July, 1993, signaled its intention to open the EU doors to the ten Central and Eastern European countries, specifying that the requirements of memberships are "stability of institutions, guaranteeing democracy, the rule of law, human rights and respect for and protection of minorities, the existence of functioning market economy as well as the capacity to cope with competitive pressure and market forces with the Union" (Baldwin 1994, p.155). The European Council, at the Madrid Summit of December, 1995, goes further on the enlargement issue: it sets accession negotiations with Malta and Cyprus to start six months after the end of the 1996 Intergovernmental Conference; it expresses hope that accession negotiations may also start at the same date with the ten Central and Eastern European countries; and acknowledges the approval of the European Parliament to form a customs union between the EU and Turkey. The guarded language of the European Council with respect to the ten Central and Eastern European countries reflects the concern of many incumbents about the ability of the EU to absorb so many aspirants quickly. More on this later.

While it is difficult to predict the actual timing of the Eastern enlargement, it is clear that sooner or later thirteen more countries will be part of the EU. In the early part of the twenty-first century EU membership could virtually double once more, this time bringing much more heterogeneous and diverse countries than was true when the Community went from six to fifteen members. In Table 1 I have listed two possible expansions of the EU: one to twenty members and the other to twenty-eight members. EU-20 would add to the existing group of fifteen members the four Visegrad countries and Slovenia. This is the expansion that is likely to occur before the other eight countries are added. The few basic statistics shown in the table give a sense of the diversity of the aspirants relative to the incumbents.

Three features emerge from the table. The first is the wide income dispersion between EU-15 and the larger groups. The ratio of the highest to the lowest GNP per capita income, expressed in purchasing power terms, would go from 1.7 in EU-15 to 6 in EU-20 and 6.4 in EU-28. The aspirants are much poorer than the four poorest incumbents (Greece, Ireland, Portugal and Spain) and have a relatively large fraction of the labor force working in agriculture; the two statistics tend to go together. This implies that the aspirants would be net recipients of significant transfer payments.[2] The prospects of raising these revenues at the Union level are small, in light of the fact that the bulk of the financial burden would fall on incumbents. The sober prediction is that the EU would be forced to drastically reform the Common Agricultural Policy and reduce other net transfers to poor regions.

The second feature that emerges from the table is the shift in the balance of power from well-to-do to poor members (Baldwin 1994, Table 7.14). Assuming that aspirants would receive votes in the Council on the basis of population and holding unchanged existing voting rules, the four poorest incumbents plus Hungary and Poland could form a blocking coalition. The desire by many incumbents to integrate more deeply could be held hostage to more generous transfers from rich to poor members. The third and final feature of the table is that inflation rates are much higher among aspirants than among incumbents, in turn implying that the prospects for an enlarged EMU would have to be considered rather small.

The push for enlargement has more to do with politics and security matters than economics. Germany fears political instability in Central and Eastern Europe and believes that EU membership may be decisive in transforming the former socialist countries into viable market economies with stable democracies. Opposition against expansion to the East comes from two groups. The first group consists of poor regions – Greece, Ireland, Portugal, and Spain – and protected sectors – e.g., agriculture – which are net beneficiaries of the EU redistributive policies and fear that the new entrants will take away from the pool of common resources.

Table 1 Enlargement: basic data

Countries	Mid-95 pop. (millions)	PPP estimates of GNP per capita, 1995, US = 100	% labor force in agric., 1990	Av. infl. 1996–97	Votes in Council
Germany	81.9	74.4	4	0.80	10
France	58.1	78.0	5	1.05	10
Italy	57.2	73.7	9	3.80	10
U.K.	58.5	71.4	2	2.85	10
Belgium	10.1	80.3	3	1.50	5
Luxembourg				1.00	2
Netherlands	15.5	73.9	5	1.70	5
Denmark	5.2	78.7	6	2.05	3
Austria	8.1	78.8	8	1.85	4
Finland	5.1	65.8	8	1.25	3
Sweden	8.8	68.7	–	1.50	4
Spain	39.2	53.8	12	2.65	8
Portugal	9.9	47.0	18	2.80	5
Greece	10.5	43.4	23	7.75	5
Ireland	3.6	58.1	14	1.35	3
EU-15 max/min	**22.7**	**1.7**	**11.5**	**9.70**	
Czech Rep	10.3	36.2	11	8.60	5
Slovak Rep	5.4	13.4	12	6.00	4
Hungary	10.2	23.8	15	20.90	5
Poland	38.6	20.0	27	17.45	8
Slovenia	2.0	–	5	9.40	3
EU-20 max/min	**50**	**6**	**13.5**	**9.7**	
Cyprus				3.05	2
Malta				2.50	2
Bulgaria	8.4	16.6	14	606.20	5
Romania	22.7	16.2	24	96.80	8
Lithuania	3.7	15.3	18	16.75	4
Latvia	2.5	12.5	16	13.00	3
Estonia	1.5	15.6	14	17.20	3
Turkey	61.1	20.7	53	83.85	10
EU-28 max/min	**54.6**	**6.4**	**26.5**	**757.7**	

Source: IMF (1998), World Bank (1997).[10]

The second opposition comes from the old EU members that would prefer deeper integration to a larger EU. But to proceed in a more flexible way the rules of the integration games need to change, and this is the heart of my argument.

This chapter proposes a flexible form of governance of the integration process (von Hagen and Fratianni 1999; Dewatripont *et al.* 1995). This proposal is compared to another proposal, that of the German Christian Democratic party, which would divide the Community members into either core or periphery countries. The core countries would be those that intend to achieve the deepest form of integration, whereas periphery countries would cooperate on specific policy dimensions. Countries could graduate from one periphery to another and all the way to the core only if they followed a prescribed path. The flexible integration approach redefines core and peripheries in terms of policy dimensions instead of countries. The core is defined by the minimum level of integration and universal rules of the game accepted by all incumbents and aspirants. Peripheries are optional policy areas. In this proposal all incumbents and aspirants must subscribe to the Single Market Program; in contrast monetary union, social union, joint defense union, and political union are optional areas of integration. The two proposals stand as sharp alternatives and reflect two different views of the Community: one strictly hierarchical where each member shares the same objectives, the other flexible where each member pursues different objectives subject to a minimum level of integration.

The chapter is organized as follows. First, the existing rules and institutions of the integration process are described. In particular, I underscore that the universal application of these rules has broken down. The next section argues that the Single Market is the core activity of the EU, that is the activity without which the EU would lose its *raison d'être*. This is not to say that the Single Market is the only objective, but rather that it is the bare minimum incumbents and aspirants must agree to. I then present two alternative approaches to integration. Conclusions are drawn in the final section.

Rules of the game and institutions

It is useful to think of rules as defining a regime or an order. For international monetary economists rules evoke immediately "the rules of the game" of the classical gold standard (1879–1913). A set of rules constitutes a "framework of laws, conventions, regulations, and mores that establish the setting of the system and the understanding of the environments by the participants in it" (Mundell 1972, p.92). Not all rules are written; some can be informal or based on custom. The important point is that, regardless of the degree of formality, participants behave as if these rules exist (McKinnon 1993, p.2). Rules confer rights and obligations, but also direct participants on how to act under specific circumstances (Sandholtz, this volume). Institutions are part of the rules of the game; indeed different rules generate different institutions. It is hard to conceive of international institutions as totally disconnected from the underlying order.

Some examples may clarify the potential usefulness of the above definitions. The Treaty of Rome, the TEU, the *acquis communautaire*, and the decisions of the European Court of Justice are clearly part of the integration rules in the

EU; but so are informal understandings, such as the old Luxembourg Compromise – invoked whenever a critical national interest was involved – which had the effect of postponing voting until consensus was reached (Nugent 1994, pp.144–5).[3] The Exchange Rate Mechanism codifies the rules of limited exchange-rate fluctuations for those member countries participating in the European Monetary System (EMS). Many of these rules are clearly spelled out; others are not. For example, EMS participants thought that "intramarginal" interventions (i.e., interventions before the exchange rate touches the intervention limits defined by the Exchange Rate Mechanism), while not compulsory, were desirable for the functioning of the EMS. In 1987 an Accord was reached, the Nyborg Accord, that made intra-marginal interventions of up to 200 per cent of a member's quota eligible for financing by the EMS institutions and thus forcing a country with an appreciating currency to essentially create more money. The Accord tried to formalize – though in the form of a gentlemen's agreement – a previously ambiguous and informal rule; yet the formalization did not remove all ambiguities on rules of interventions. The French interpreted the Accord as giving a participating country the automatic right to use EMS resources; the Germans interpreted it as giving the central bank of the appreciating currency the discretion to decide on individual cases (Fratianni and von Hagen 1992, pp.25–6).

Institutions evolve as the rules of the game change. The European Parliament and the Council of Ministers are evolving as the process of democratization deepens. New rules create new institutions. EMU will usher a new institution, the European Central Bank, whose existence will weaken old institutions, the national central banks. The TEU is more specific on what the new institution will do than what the old institutions will not do. But as EMU will grow the rules of the game governing monetary unification will become more precise and the role of new and old institutions more delineated.

The complexity of the rules of the integration game in the EU has spun an intricate web of EU institutions that defy simple categorizations. EU institutions are too strong to be thought of as international organizations and yet not strong enough to supplant national institutions. In areas such as agriculture, competition policy, external trade, and money EU institutions and rules dominate national institutions and rules. In other areas, most notably fiscal policy and defense, national powers remain sovereign. Supra-nationalism cohabits with intergovernmentalism, with the former gaining over the latter as time goes on. Rules evolve because the process of deepening is inevitably leading some member countries to question the value of deeper forms of integration. Up to the TEU rules and institutions had general universality: all member countries accepted all the integration rules. The speed of the integration train was identical for all, with the speed determined by the slowest moving locomotive. Maastricht changed all of that.

The breakdown of the universality of rules

In the bargaining process over Maastricht three different positions emerged: those who wanted EMU soon and without preconditions, those who wanted EMU later and with preconditions, and those who did not want EMU at all. The UK belonged to the last camp. Among the others a dispute developed which was reminiscent of the controversy of the 1970s between "economists" and "monetarists" (Swann 1992, pp.192–4). Germany – with Belgium, Luxembourg, and the Netherlands – was the leading exponent of the "economic" view of EMU, namely that economic convergence must precede EMU. France was the leading exponent of the "monetarist" view of EMU, namely that EMU facilitates economic convergence. Germany favored a long transition period and formal convergence criteria before the final stage of EMU; France, with Italy, on the other hand, wanted EMU quickly and without strong preconditions. Both groups agreed on the desirability of the end state, but disagreed on the speed with which each member would reach the end state. The German position was consistent with a multi-speed approach to European EMU (Garrett 1993); the French position with a one-speed approach. The UK position rejected EMU outright as undesirable.

In the end the German position prevailed, and the UK and Denmark were given opt-out clauses for not participating in EMU. The UK also broke ranks with respect to social policy.With the signing of the TEU the long tradition of the universality of the integration rules was broken. The TEU, in fact, accepts the principle that certain types of integration rules – those outside the Single Market – have less than universal applicability. Furthermore, the Treaty also accepts the principle that countries may reach end goals at different speeds. Multi-speed integration is an implication of the entry conditions to Stage III of economic and monetary union.[4]

The breakdown of the universality of rules is no more evident than in today's EMS. In the heated discussion of the ministerial meeting of 2 August, 1993, the French proposed that Germany leave the EMS. The Dutch, Belgian, Danish and Luxembourg delegations protested very loudly and said that, if that were the case, they too would the leave the EMS, leaving France in the system with Spain and Portugal (*Financial Times*, 3 August, 1993). The compromise was that the Exchange Rate Mechanism bands would be widened to plus or minus 15 per cent, except for the Dutch who voluntarily preferred the narrow to the wide bands. Within a few days Belgium, Luxembourg and Denmark signaled that they too wanted to return to the narrow bands very soon (*Financial Times*, 10 August, 1993). This declaration was equivalent to the formation of a fixed exchange-rate club which France, Ireland, Spain, and Portugal elected not to join. Indeed these four countries formed a different kind of fixed exchange rate club, one which enjoyed more flexibility than the German-led club. A third group of member countries – Greece, Italy and the UK – elected not to participate in either club.[5]

Why the breakdown

As the EU has tried to deepen integration, some member countries have challenged the notion of a "common EU vision" beyond the implementation of the Single Market. This breaking of the ranks arises either because the economies are structurally different or because national policy preferences diverge.

Jacquemin and Sapir (1995) have made an attempt at identifying possible dividing lines in the EU-12. These authors tried to form clusters of countries, taken from EU-12, using principal component analysis. Two components explain 66 per cent of the total variance and three components 79 per cent.[6] Using two components, two separate groups of countries emerge: a northern group and a southern group, consisting of Greece, Ireland, Portugal, and Spain. Italy is fairly unstable and can be classified as either the most southern of the northern countries or as the most northern of the southern countries. Two results stand out from this exercise. The first is that there is significant heterogeneity among incumbents, a result that is not altogether surprising. The second observation is that Denmark and the UK belong to the same northern clusters and yet these two countries have dissented, in different degrees and manner, on the desirability of EMU. In essence, differences arise either because the economies differ or because policy preferences differ.

I have noted that structural or policy differences do not undermine the universal acceptance of the Single Market but of deeper forms of integration, such as EMU or political union (PU). In what follows I will argue that there are plausible arguments for treating the Single Market as the core activity of the EU and other forms of integration as non-core or optional activities.

Core and non-core activities

The core activity of the EU is the Single Market which combines a common market (freedom of movement of goods, services, and inputs) with a set of uniform competition standards. Other policy areas, such as EMU or PU, are more controversial. Some members outright challenge the wisdom of pursuing EMU and PU. Other members, while not challenging the goal, recognize the heterogeneity of the membership and would like to set entry conditions so as to minimize the risk of pooling members with different economic structures and policy preferences.

Core activity

The traditional argument in favor of the welfare-enhancing properties of the Single Market comes from customs theory. Let us start from the benefit side. So long as trade exceeds trade diversion, an incumbent will have an incentive to join the EU. There is general agreement that static trade creating flows have outweighed trade diverting flows in the EC customs union (Swann 1992, pp.119–20). But the Single Market goes much beyond a customs union. The estimates of the net gains from the completion of the Single Market range from a minimum of 2.5 per cent to a maximum of 6.5 per cent of Community GDP (Commission 1988, p.19). The highest estimate includes the important but more difficult to quantify competition and restructuring effects, but excludes dynamic aspects such as the interaction between technological innovation and competition. The insights of the new growth theory suggest that, under specific circumstances, integration (i.e., more competition) may lead to a permanent increase in the economic growth rate of the area through a positive interaction between innovation and integration. In sum, the net gains from the completion of the Single Market are large.

Total costs to run the enlarged EU will also be higher. Two critical factors are at work. The first is that, for a given decision rule, the larger the membership the more difficult it is to obtain agreement and to accommodate the objectives of different interest groups. Under existing voting rules, EU enlargement implies a loss of decision-making power of the large countries in favor of small countries. Blocking coalitions are easier to form in EU-20 than in EU-15, implying that agreement will be more costly after enlargement. The second factor is that marginal costs of decision making respond to different decision rules. Unanimity is the most costly voting rule for the club because this rule protects the minority of one. The larger the number of countries the more costly is unanimity in the sense that one small member can prevent all other members from implementing a policy of their choice. Simple majority, on the other hand, is the least costly voting rule. Typically, voting rules within a nation state are either of two types: simple or qualified majority. Simple majority applies to ordinary laws, whereas qualified majority applies to higher-level laws, e.g., constitutional amendments. Unanimity, instead, applies to intergovernmental agreements where each member state wants to retain sovereign rights.

The EU is a mixture of intergovernmentalism and supra-nationalism, with the former clearly prevailing over the latter. Unanimity remains the dominant voting procedure. Yet, over the years the pendulum has swung, albeit in a minor way, towards supra-national decision making. The three institutions that best represent supra-nationalism are the Commission, the European Parliament, and the European Court of Justice. The Commission has agenda power on what the Council of Ministers decides and is a busy secondary legislator, regulator, and enforcer of EU laws. The European Parliament, the weakest EU institution, has gained influence relative to the Council by virtue of the so-called cooperation, codecision, and assent procedures that have forced the Council to act more like a partner than as an autonomous body (Martin 1993, pp.137–40).[7] Finally, the European Court of Justice has consistently decided in favor of integration whenever governments were reluctant to implement directives and regulations to protect national markets and specialized groups. Now, the Court is also able to fine member states for violations of EU legislation.

Both aspirants and incumbents seem to believe that in the aggregate additional benefits exceed additional costs. However, distributional issues play a critical role in the enlargement negotiations. Aspirants can no longer protect industries and seek compensation for the adjustment costs that fall on those industries. Incumbents understand that to expand trade they need to compensate new entrants for the adjustment costs. Thus, each enlargement has given additional power to the Union to effect transfers on behalf of new entrants. The European Regional Development Fund was established in 1975 on the wake of the British and Irish accession; the size of the Structural Funds doubled after the accession of Portugal and Spain and further expanded to target the unpopulated area of Sweden and Finland (Begg 1996, p.9). Aside from the Common Agricultural Policy, the EU's primary transfer criterion is regional inequality: a region is undeveloped and eligible for transfers if its per capita GDP is less than 75 per cent of the Community average. This spatial approach to redistribution was further consolidated by the TEU whose Article 2 states that one of the Union's objectives is "to promote throughout the Community a harmonious and balanced development of economic activities." A Cohesion Fund was established with the purpose of funding transportation and environmental projects in member states whose per capita GDP is less than 90 per cent of the Community average.

In sum, geographical expansion of the Single Market is accompanied by "side payments" from the richer incumbents to the poorer new entrants. Furthermore, these payments are handled at the Union level. The centralization of redistribution eliminates the incentives for individual states to compete on taxes or secede from the Union. In the absence of redistribution some member states would be tempted to attract resources from other states by offering advantageous tax treatment or by protecting local industries. Centralized redistribution protects the Single Market. The negative aspect of centralized redistribution is that member states would have diminished incentives to implement policies that raised incomes.

The next wave of enlargements poses serious challenges to the redistribution process. To begin with, the aspirants are much poorer than the poorest incumbents (Table 1). Given existing rules on Common Agricultural Policy, Structural Funds, and Cohesion Fund the aspirants would be entitled to significant flows of resources. Just to cite an example, Greece and Portugal are expected to receive ECUs 400 per person by 1999 from the Structural Funds. Applying the same sum to the new entrants, Begg (1996, p.6) calculates that Slovenia would receive transfers equal to 7 per cent of its GDP and Lithuania 51 per cent. The increase in the EU budget would require substantial further funding by the richer incumbents. While such transfers may be part of the long-run equilibrium result, in the short run rich incumbents may find it in their interest to either delay access to aspirants or accept them under restrictive conditions. The other consequence of enlargements is that the Community average GDP will fall and push many regions from poor incumbents such as Greece, Ireland, Italy, Portugal, and Spain above the

75 per cent threshold. Thus, poor incumbents would tend to resist new accessions unless the redistribution rules were revised in their favor. Such a revision would exacerbate the burden on richer incumbents. In sum, redistribution is going to be a critical part of the accession of the new entrants. Without a resolution of these issue the Single Market will be in jeopardy. The conclusion is that Single Market and side payments are intertwined. Side payments must be placed with Union institutions to avoid incentives to compete at the tax level or erode the substance of the Single Market.

Non-core activities

Unlike the Single Market, inclusive of side payments, EMU and PU are not considered vital to each member state. Some member states have indeed preferred to opt out of EMU, indicating that participation in it reduces national welfare. Similar considerations hold for PU.

The arguments in favor and against EMU are fairly well known and need not be repeated here at length (see, for example, Fratianni 1994, pp.220–4). Here I summarize the main points. The move from flexible exchange rates to monetary union yields two benefits, one cost and one uncertain outcome. The two benefits are the lower transaction costs associated with one money and the saving from not having to cover forward contracts denominated in different currencies. The inability to vary the exchange rate represents a cost, which is higher the more unevenly distributed the shocks are in the EMU area, the more rigid real wages and the less mobile is the labor force. For the Eastern countries that are undergoing a deep economic transformation the cost of fixing the exchange rate is potentially high. Finally, there is no a priori reason to believe that the quality of monetary policy in a EMU would be better than in all of the separate regions. While the construction of an independent and price conscious central bank represents a positive development for the European EMU, the strong possibility that national representatives in the European Central Bank Council will vote according to national preferences tends to make a EMU more inflationary than the lowest inflation region, which in the European context is Germany.

In sum, EMU is not as attractive as the Single Market to some of the incumbents as well as to many of the new entrants. Given the fact that an EU of twenty or twenty-eight will have members with vastly different economic structures, a German-style EMU is not likely to suit the interests of all members.

PU is more difficult to analyze than EMU because it involves agreements over sensitive issues such as taxation, police, justice, foreign policy, and defense. The long history of nation states has conditioned individuals to think in terms of national sovereignty and national character. Yet, the globalization of markets and crimes, and the emergence of nuclear power have reduced the power of the nation state to control or affect decisively economic and political events. In many areas nation states have had or will have to share their power or their sovereignty. A good case in point is defense. Technological changes, such as nuclear power, have transformed defense from a national to an international public good, in turn giving incentives to countries to form alliances or defense clubs. NATO is the most successful defense club; yet, it does not run without difficulties. The biggest one comes from the tendency of the smaller members to free ride at the expense of the larger members (Olson and Zeckhauser 1966; Frey 1984, Table 7.1). This is so because the larger members enjoy the highest benefits from a peaceful world and, thus, are willing to bear a disproportionate share of the club's costs. This situation clearly fits the motivation of Germany to include the four Visegrad countries in the EU to protect her from political instability. This incentive leads other members of the EU to ask Germany to pay a disproportionate share of the cost of the new wave of annexation.

A couple of general comments can be made on political integration. The first is that the push for political integration has tended to follow economic integration. Second, there is much more resistance to political integration than to economic integration. This resistance exists because integration has been effected by policy makers and the people at large have not participated in the process. In addition, national and supra-national political leaders have failed to formulate a clear and coherent view of what political union may mean in the EU. Fuzzy concepts and a lack of democratic participation have inevitably retarded progress towards political integration.

Policy complementarity

Historically PU implies EMU and a Single Market. The EU was created as a customs union but had a vocation of ultimately arriving at PU. The separation of core from non-core activities was based on the revealed preference of some member states that there was no complementarity among the various policy dimensions, that is economic integration does not necessarily lead to EMU and EMU does not necessarily lead to PU. Yet, European federalists have counted on policy complementarity to achieve a Federal union (Persson *et al.* 1996). Policy complementarity is at the heart of what Tsoukalis (1977) and van Ypersele and Koeune (1985) call the "cumulative logic of integration": the process of integration spreads from one area to another. For example, the formation of a customs union eliminates commercial policy as a national policy instrument; this in turn creates an incentive for member countries to use exchange rates to gain competitive advantage over other member states. The principle of the cumulative logic of integration leads member countries to fix the exchange rates or, better, to create a monetary union. Monetary union implies the emasculation of national monetary policies; member countries will want to use fiscal policies more intensely. But a centralized monetary policy may feel the pressure to bail out member states with profligate tendencies. So to lessen the incentive for fiscal profligacy, a push will be made to coordinate or centralize fiscal policies (Persson *et al.* 1996). Once fiscal policies are coordinated the next step of political unification becomes compelling.

Those member states that object to deeper forms of integration are afraid exactly of this cumulative logic. There is nothing inescapable about the cumulative integration logic. For example, the proposition that a centralized monetary policy is more prone to bail out national governments stems from the unstated assumption that there is solidarity among member states. If one were to drop this assumption a centralized monetary policy can act quite independently of national fiscal policies. Member states will borrow at interest rates that reflect country risk. US monetary policy is not held hostage by the profligacy of the State of New York. Explicit no bail-out rules are in the Maastricht Treaty. The credibility of these rules will be tested and an independent monetary authority, like the European Central Bank, can refuse the financial excesses of a member state.

The complementarity between customs union and monetary union exist only if one ignores the type of monetary policy the union will pursue. A monetary union eliminates the possibility that a member country may pursue competitive devaluations, but also reduces the voice of the member state in determining its own preferred inflation rate. For a country with a poor tax administration inflation may represent a significant source of tax revenues; such a country may not be necessarily better off joining a low inflation EMU. In other words, one complementarity can be offset by other considerations, so that there is nothing inherent about going from customs union to a single EMU.

Flexible integration

We have seen that both old members and aspirants of the EU desire more choice and flexibility than available at present. Some members prefer to speed up the process of integration, others opt for wider membership before effecting deeper integration; and others finally want both. The differences in objectives and the large discrepancy in economic structures between incumbents and aspirants have generated and justified proposals of flexible integration. These proposals range from "pick and choose" integration to a supra-national body that would decide integration for all members (for an evaluation of these proposals cf. Dewatripont *et al.* (1995) and Fratianni (1995)). Here I want to concentrate on a governance structure that would be able to accommodate the flexibility required for a very heterogeneous membership of twenty-eight countries.

We have noted that the EU has implicitly accepted the principle of multi-speed integration. But this approach has three disadvantages. The first disadvantage stems from the possibility that those who qualify early for a specific type of integration may create new rules that would block the participation of other members. The EMU provides an obvious example. The first group of member countries that is likely to meet the entry condition for Stage III –

Germany, France, Belgium, Luxembourg, the Netherlands, and Austria – may want to exclude Italy, Spain, Portugal and Greece from EMU for fear that these countries would be too inflation pone (Alesina and Grilli 1993). The second disadvantage is that politicians may object to two or multiple speeds because the electorate may associate slower countries as being inferior to faster countries, even though all of them will end up at the same point. The third and most fundamental disadvantage is that multi-speed integration allow countries to pursue shared objectives at different speeds, but not different objectives. Multi-speed integration does very little to meet the concern of the UK about EMU and social policy, or the prospective fear of some aspirants that a German-dominated EMU would be too disinflationary. In sum, multi-speed integration does not add enough flexibility.

Let us now see two sharply different governance structures that address the issue of diverse national policy preferences.

The German proposal of variable geometry

The German Christian Democratic party (CDU 1994) has advocated variable geometry to deal with the diversity of the EU membership. In the German document a distinction is made between a center and a periphery. The center would consist of those EU countries that want to achieve the deepest level of integration over a broad range of policies. The selection of such countries would presumably be based on the criteria that, not only the economies of these countries are structurally equivalent, but that their policy preferences are virtually identical. Structurally equivalent economies with divergent policy preferences could not qualify for the core group. Once defined, the group would aim to integrate at the deepest level, all the way to political unification. Those countries that are not part of the core fall into peripheries. Members can move from one periphery to another and eventually graduate to the core following a precise sequence. One possible configuration would be as follows. The Single Market would be the first, and farthest from the core, periphery and would include all members. Social policy would be the second periphery (closer to the core) and would include all those members that integrate in this policy dimension; monetary union the third periphery and would include all those members that had integrated social policy and now integrate monetarily; joint defense the fourth periphery and would include all those members who had qualified for the third periphery and now wanted to integrate their defense systems; and so on until the core which would include all those members that wanted to integrate on all policy dimensions.

There are two drawbacks to the German proposal. The first drawback is the stigma associated with the distinction between the core and the periphery. Since this distinction emphasizes countries and not policy dimensions, membership in the core will be identified with the elite group of "insiders" and membership in the peripheries as being "outsiders" (von Hagen and

Fratianni 1999). The second drawback stems from the precise sequence of moving from the farthest periphery to the core. The rigidity of the sequence creates a potential for externalities: members of a periphery can arbitrarily raise entry conditions and thus determine the integration process of the outsiders. To eliminate such externalities all incumbents and aspirants would have to decide on the entry conditions and the operation of the peripheries. Without such an *ex-ante* agreement, conflicts would emerge between those who belong to the periphery and those who are on the outside. The rigidity of the integration sequence and the monopoly that a club has on a given integration area severely restricts non-club members in completing the integration process. This concern was expressed during the negotiation over EMU, and the TEU imbeds the principle that all members have a voice in determining entry rules to Stage III of EMU.

Common core and flexibility

The alternative proposal is based on the fundamental distinction between core and non-core activities, rather than on the identity of countries (von Hagen and Fratianni 1999; Fratianni 1995; Dewatripont *et al.* 1995). Participation in the core activity is compulsory; participation in the non-core activities is optional. Rules and institutions defining optional activity are part of the core activities.

The motivation of the proposal is: how much flexibility to put into the system without emasculating the *acquis communautaire*. Flexibility should be constrained by a minimum set of policies and decision rules without which the EU loses its distinctiveness. Thus, it is important to distinguish between a common *core* of integration, to which all EU members must adhere, and a set of *peripheries* or optional integration areas. Note that, unlike the CDU document, core and peripheries are here defined in terms of policies and not countries. In the German document the core is formed by a restricted number of members; in this proposal the core represents the basic common values all EU members share. The core is the necessary minimum for joining the EU. The Single Market is undoubtedly part of the core. Without the Single Market the EU loses its most fundamental identity. The Single Market is expected to generate large net benefits. Those sectors or economic regions that stand to lose from the implementation of the Single Market may obtain compensation from other sectors or regions that stand to gain enough to compensate the losers. The process of compensating those who lose from integration is also part of the activities of the core club.

Full membership implies participation in the core, that is in the activities of the Single Market. Other policy areas, such as EMU and social policy, do not belong to the core for two reasons. The first reason is based on the fact that the EU has already granted "derogations" in these policy domains to some member countries.[8] The second reason is that the economic case for both EMU and social policy is much less clear-cut and more controversial than the economic case for the Single Market.

The core should also contain the constitution of the EU and the "rules of the game" that would regulate the entry, operation, and exit of the peripheries. In the CDU document there is the danger that peripheries may set exclusive entry conditions and create negative externalities for outsiders. The rules of the game cannot permit peripheries to interfere with the integrity of the core, i.e., activities that would compromise the Single Market. All EU members must agree on entry, operation, and exit conditions of peripheries.

This proposal would offer more choices than the CDU document, which prescribes a strict sequence in moving from one policy area to another and does not allow the formation of competing clubs. In this proposal, for example, members would have the option to join a MU of their choice or not join one at all. In light of the wide heterogeneity of the future membership of the EU, there is no reason to expect that the conditions for a single EMU will be satisfied. Homogeneous members will have an opportunity to pursue deeper levels of integration without being held back by others. On the other hand, those who want a more superficial form of integration do not feel threatened by countries that have a deep commitment to integration.

Implications for Eastern enlargement

I have noted that the aspirants are, in relation to EU-15, poor, agricultural, and populous. There are two possible accession strategies. The first strategy is the full integration approach: aspirants would join the EU at the level of integration reached by incumbents, including EMU, social policy and incipient forms of political integration. Given the great disparities between incumbents and aspirants, full integration translates into a very distant accession. The waiting period could prove too long for some aspirants who may face the risk of a return to the past. The alternative strategy is flexible integration, whereby aspirants commit themselves to reach a level of integrating consistent with the core. Participation in the core would in turn facilitate the process of democratization and economic transformation in the East. The flexible integration strategy would remove the obstacles for a distant accession date.

The Eastern enlargement is proving to be very difficult because the hurdle the aspirants must jump is high. Flexible accession breaks down one high hurdle into a smaller required hurdle and smaller optional hurdles. A second complication with Eastern enlargement has to do with the sizable transfer payments that current EU rules would bestow on new entrants. There are four possible ways to handle the transfer issue: (1) large increases in the EU budget; (2) deep modifications in the EU transfer system; (3) unequal treatments of incumbents and new entrants; and (4) delay the enlargement until (1) and (2) are no longer relevant. Option (4) is the most damaging for the democratization and economic transformation of the aspirants. Option (1) is politically difficult in the rich EU countries, particularly in Germany (Baldwin 1994, p.176). Option (3) would create an undesirable and unacceptable caste system.[9] Option (2) offers the most promises. Accession could be made conditional on the reform of the Common Agricultural Policy and regional redistributional policies. Aspirants would expect the redistribution rules to change. One possible reform would be to nationalize the income support of farmers, as Austria, Finland and Sweden did before they joined the EU (Baldwin 1996). In sum, it is preferable to enlarge sooner by adopting flexible integration and a reform of the redistribution rules than to enlarge much later under the full integration strategy.

Conclusions

The European Union is pursuing two objectives, deepening and enlargement, which are increasingly in conflict with each other. Dissent in the membership has been handled by accepting multi-speed integration and exempting recalcitrant members from participating in specific policy dimensions. The governance structure resulting from this approach is *ad hoc*, with certain rules and institutions having universal application and others not. More flexibility appears to be needed. Two approaches have been presented here: the proposal by the German CDU and a more flexible version of this document.

The German CDU proposal envisions a hierarchical model where members pursue exactly the same goals. Given the large and heterogeneous membership, common goals imply that only some members can pursue deep integration; others will be relegated to shallow integration. The alternative proposal envisions a union where members participate in the integration process with different intensities. It is not clear a priori whether the second approach will yield a lower average level of deep integration than the German approach. Much would depend on the flexibility of moving from shallow to deep integration. What the second approach assures is that each member can select the depth of integration at its own will and pace.

As a concluding note, let me place the study within the broader theme of this volume, governance. As stated at the outset, I wanted to use the "case study" of the EU enlargement to drive two fundamental principles: governance is endogenous relative to the forces of integration (i.e., market forces), and all-inclusive, non-overlapping institutions (clubs) cannot handle a heterogeneous membership. On the first point, governance's endogeneity, my essay must be paired with Sandholtz's (this volume), where globalization is viewed as promoting "the development of transnational society and consequently the elaboration of transnational rules, public and private, formal and informal" (p.77). Prakash and Hart, in the introduction to the volume, speak of globalization as the "proximate" long-term independent variable and governance as the dependent variable (in a more general equilibrium framework, as the volume's editors point out, governance responds to forces such as technological change and government-initiated policies). My two alternative rule structures of the integration game offer an example of the necessity to adapt old rules to new circumstances, that is to a much larger and more diverse EU. While I argue for one particular structure over the other, both structures represent an evolution with respect to existing governance. The latter cannot survive deepening and/or enlargement. On the second principle – the creation of institutions that are not all-inclusive, but overlap – my essay resonates with Kobrin's "Back to the Future" and Cerny's "Globalization, Governance, and Complexity," both also appearing in this volume. For Kobrin, "multiple and overlapping sources of political authority and multiple and ambiguous political loyalties may once again come to be seen as the norm" (p.182). For Cerny, "world politics . . . is being transformed into a 'polycentric' . . . global political system within the same geographical space (and/or overlapping spaces), in a way which is analogous to the emergence of coexisting and overlapping functional authorities in metropolitan areas" (p.186).

The end product of more flexible forms of integration does not add up to a clean-cut design; in fact, it is rather messy. But so are the underlying economic, social, and political processes. For example, the proliferation of regional trade arrangements is not the solution economists would have designed from scratch. We do not know yet whether it will promote world trade or impede it, the reason being that regional governance structures are promoting both trade expansion and protection. Trade regionalization permits countries with similar preferences to integrate over a defined range of activities. As regionalization expands, preferences become more diffused. Old governance structures creak. It is well known that international organizations with universal membership tend to be ineffective, to the point of being no more than talk shops. Effective solutions are taken by organizations with relatively homogeneous memberships. These organizations compete with one another and their domains are constantly changing as they redefine their functions, geographical area, and membership.

Notes

1 The Treaty on Monetary Union was agreed upon by the Heads of State at the Maastricht European Council in December of 1991; signed by the Foreign and Finance Ministers in February of 1992; and came into force in November of 1993.

2 Baldwin (1994, p.176) concludes that "an enlargement by 2000 that included only the Visegrad-4 would require an increase of the EU budget of about 70%."

3 The Luxembourg Compromise was never codified as a formal decision-making procedure and was made irrelevant by the Single European Act of 1986. Yet, it "may not be quite completely dead" (Nugent 1994, p.145).

4 There are six entry conditions relating to inflation rates, long-term interest rates, government budget deficits, government debt, exchange rate realignments, and independence of national central banks. Elsewhere (Fratianni *et al.* 1992, Fratianni 1994) I have argued that on strictly economic arguments a two-speed EMU is preferable to a one-speed EMU. Reliance on fixed exchange rates to signal the political commitment to price stability and monetary union is a basic

flaw of the Maastricht strategy for European EMU. It has forced EMS participants to give up valuable flexibility needed to adjust to country-specific shocks
during the transition and has created a fragile environment because national policies are not yet coordinated; at the same time the safety valve of capital controls
has been removed.

5 Italy and the United Kingdom left the Exchange Rate Mechanism, following the
turbulent exchange market events of September, 1992. Greece never joined the
Exchange Rate Mechanism.

6 The data set consists of a total of twelve economic dimensions: the unemployment
rate, youth unemployment, working hours, working week, industry employment,
service employment, public employment, per capita gross domestic product,
labor productivity, public expenditures on R&D, R&D personnel, and state aids.

7 The cooperation procedure makes life harder for the Council. Two readings are
prescribed. The first reading is similar to the opinion stage in the consultation procedure. The Council adopts a common position by qualified majority. In the
second reading the European Parliament has three months to take actions. If the
European Parliament rejects the common position, the Council can go ahead
with the common position by voting unanimously. If the European Parliament
amends the common position, the latter is sent back to the Commission for revision.
Within three months the Council can either accept the amendments by qualified
majority or fail them to accept by unanimity.

In both the co-decision and assent procedures the European Parliament has veto
power. With respect to the cooperation procedure, the co-decision procedure
starts after the Council approves the common position. The European Parliament
can approve, modify or reject the Council's common position. Either one of the
two last instances triggers a Conciliation Committee consisting of an equal
number of Council's members and European Parliament's members. If the
Conciliation Committee finds an agreement, the European Parliament and the
Council must adopt the compromise, otherwise the compromise becomes null. If
the Conciliation Committee does not find an agreement, the Council can approve
the common position with the amendments proposed by the European Parliament;
alternatively the Parliament can reject the proposal.

As the name suggests, the assent procedure requires the European Parliament to
approve the proposal.

8 The Maastricht Treaty grants derogations on MU to Denmark and the UK; and
derogation to social policy to the UK.

9 Unequal treatment is equivalent to letting the member states provide redistributive services to those actors who have been negatively affected by the integration
process (McGinnis this volume).

10 World Bank (1997) is the source of the first three columns; the GNP per person
index is based on purchasing power parity; IMF (1998) is the source of the fourth
column; inflation rates are based on GDP deflators for EU-15 and on consumer
prices for the rest; the votes in the Council of potential new entrants were based
on population and existing rules.

References

Alesina, Alberto and Grilli, Vittorio (1993) "On the Feasibility of a One-Speed or
Multi-Speed European Monetary Union," *Economics and Politics* 5 (July): 145–65.
Baldwin, Richard E. (1994) *Towards an Integrated Europe*, London: CEPR.
Baldwin, Richard E. (1996) "Concepts and Speed of an Eastern Enlargement," Paper
presented at "Quo Vadis Europe?" Conference, Kiel, June 26–27, 1996.

Begg, Ian (1996) "Inter-regional Transfers in a Widened Europe," Paper presented at "Quo Vadis Europe?" Conference, Kiel, June 26–27, 1996.

Bofinger, Peter (1999) "The Political Economy of the Eastern Enlargement of the EU," in Barry Eichengreen and Jeffry Frieden (eds), *The Political Economy of European Integration: The Challenges Ahead*, Ann Arbor, MI: University of Michigan Press.

Cerny, Philip G. (this volume) "Globalization, Governance, and Complexity."

CDU (1994) CDU/CSU Fraktion des Deutschen Bundestages, "Überlegungen zur europäischen Politik," Bonn: mimeo.

Commission of the European Communities (1988) "The Economics of 1992," *European Economy* 35 (March).

Commission of the European Communities (1990) "One Market, One Money," *European Economy* 44: 5–347.

Dewatripont, Mathias, Francesco Giavazzi, Jürgen von Hagen, Ian Harden, Torsten Persson, Howard Rosenthal, Gerard Roland, Andre Sapir, and Guido Tabellini (1995) "Flexible Integration," *Monitoring European Integration* 6, London: CEPR.

Financial Times (1993) "ERM bands Produce Sort of Harmony," 3 August.

Financial Times (1993) "Commission Determined to Hold Line on EMU Strategy," 10 August.

Fratianni, Michele (1994) "What Went Wrong with the EMS and European Monetary Union," in Berhanu Abegaz, Patricia Dillon, David H. Feldman, and Paul F. Whiteley (eds), *The Challenge of European Integration: Internal and External Problems of Trade and Money*, Boulder, CO: Westview Press.

Fratianni, Michele (1995) "Variable Integration in the European Union," Paper presented at Forum CEIS Q8, Porto Cervo, September 22–23, 1995.

Fratianni, Michele and von Hagen, Jürgen (1992) *The European Monetary System and European Monetary Union*, Boulder, CO: Westview Press.

Fratianni, Michele, von Hagen, Jürgen and Christopher Waller (1992) *The Maastricht Way to EMU*, Essays in International Finance N. 187 (June), Princeton, NJ: Princeton University Press.

Frey, Bruno S. (1984) *International Political Economics*, Oxford: Basil Blackwell.

Garrett, Geoffrey (1993) "The Politics of Maastricht," *Economics and Politics* 5 (July): 105–23.

International Monetary Fund (1998) *World Economic Outlook* (May), Washington, DC: International Monetary Fund.

Jacquemin, Alexis and Sapir, André (1995) "Is a European Hard Core Credible? A Statistical Analysis," CEPR Discussion Paper.

Kobrin, Stephen J. (this volume) "Back to the Future: Neomedievalism and the Postmodern World Economy."

Martin, Lisa (1993) "International and Domestic Institutions in the EMU Process," *Economics and Politics* 5, 2: 125–44.

McGinnis, Michael D. (this volume) "Rent-Seeking, Redistribution, and Reform in the Governance of Global Markets."

McKinnon, Ronald I. (1993) "International Money in Historical Perspective," *Journal of Economic Literature* 31, 1: 1–44.

Mundell, Robert A. (1972) "The Future of the International Monetary System," in A.L.K. Acheson, J.F. Chant, and M.F.J. Prachowny (eds), *Bretton Woods Revisited*, Toronto: University of Toronto Press.

Nugent, Neil (1994) *The Government and Politics of the European Union*, Durham, NC: Duke University Press, 3rd edn.

Olson, Mancur and Zeckhauser, Richard (1966) "An Economic Theory of Alliances," *Review of Economics and Statistics*, 48: 266–79.

Persson Torsten, Roland, Gerard, and Tabellini, Guido (1996) "European Integration and the Theory of Fiscal Federalism," Paper presented at "Quo Vadis Europe?" Conference, Kiel, June 26–27, 1996.

Prakash, Aseem and Jeffrey Hart (this volume) "Introduction."

Sandholtz, Wayne (1996) "Rules, Reasons and International Institutions." Paper presented at the International Studies Association, San Diego, Calif. 15–21 April.

Sandholtz, Wayne (this volume) "Globalization and the Evolution of Rules."

Swann, Dennis (1992) *The Economics of the Common Market*, London: Penguin Books, 7th edn.

Tsoukalis, Loukas (1977) *The Politics and Economics of European Monetary Integration*, London: George Allen and Unwin.

van Ypersele, Jacques, and Koeune, Jean-Claude (1985) *The European Monetary System: Origin, Operation, Outlook*, Brussels: Commission of the European Communities.

von Hagen, Jürgen and Fratianni, Michele (1999) "Banking Regulation With Variable Geometry," in Barry Eichengreen and Jeffry Frieden (eds), *The Political Economy of European Integration: The Challenges Ahead*, Ann Arbor, MI: University of Michigan Press.

World Bank (1997) *World Development Report 1997*, Oxford: Oxford University Press.

Globalization and governance: conclusions

Jeffrey A. Hart and Aseem Prakash

International relations scholars are interested in debates about globalization and governance partly because of a deeper concern about change versus continuity in the international system. One important focus of theorizing in international relations in recent years has been to set the beginning and end points of the anarchic international order identified by realists and neo-realists as the basic building blocks. There is a tendency for realists to claim that anarchy is universal across time and space (Waltz, 1979; Grieco, 1988). Critics of realism, in contrast, argue that the anarchic international system may have been a useful way of thinking about the world for the relatively short period in history dating from the Treaty of Westphalia in 1648 until some time in the recent past, but that it may be losing its value. Kobrin's essay (Chapter 6) builds on this theme to argue both that there is now a new world order, and that it may be more like the world order that prevailed in the Middle Ages than the one that existed between 1648 and the recent past. He argues that economic globalization, made possible by the wider availability of computers and fast telecommunications systems, is the main reason for this change. Similarly, Cerny in Chapter 7 argues that the dominant actors of the realist's anarchic system, the governments of nation-states, are not as dominant as they once were and that the system is evolving in the direction of greater complexity. Globalization is one of the reasons for this in Cerny's view, but there are other factors as well. For example, Cerny sees factors like the rise of the "competition state" and the "hollowing out" of the Keynesian welfare state via privatization of state functions as also contributing to changes in governance, independently of globalization. Both Kobrin and Cerny question the applicability of realist models in the contemporary world, but for somewhat different reasons.

Globalization and governance are of interest to policy makers because of the growing attention paid by the media and the general public to the globalization theme. A good example is a statement made by President Clinton at the Economic Summit in Denver in the summer of 1997: "Protectionism is simply not an option because globalization is irreversible. . . . If we try to close up our economy, we will only hurt ourselves." He added:

"It seems to me difficult to imagine that this is even a serious debate right now." (*New York Times*, 1997)

Clinton's statement raises two important but debatable points: that globalization is irreversible, and that the openness of the economy is positively associated with the welfare of the nation. It is typical of attempts by various interested parties to "naturalize" globalization; that is, to portray it as a natural force which is beyond the ability of mankind to channel or direct.

This volume has focused on three main questions: (1) what is meant by governance in the study of international relations and international political economy; (2) how globalization affects governance; and (3) what kinds of policy innovations may be required for dealing with the challenges of globalization. Two competing perspectives on governance – the new institutionalist and the constructivist – were introduced and defended in Chapters 1–4. The essence of the debate among the authors of these chapters is whether one should adopt a narrow or broad definition of rationality to explain decisions about the provision of collective goods, which the editors of this volume have equated with governance. The new institutionalists (Lake and McGinnis) have argued that a narrow definition of rationality is superior because it provides more parsimonious and testable theories of governance. The constructivists (Sandholtz and Haas) contend that the definition of rationality has to start from the idea that rules and rule systems (also called institutions) are constituted by political actors who use those rules not only as guides to their own behavior but also as guides to the interpretation of the behavior of others.

The constructivists question the ability of new institutionalists to operationalize key variables in their models; transaction costs being one of these variables. Lake has responded to this criticism by arguing that his theory does not require "precise measures of transaction costs." Both institutionalists and constructivists appear to agree that the heart of the problem of governance is providing actors with rules and incentives to mitigate opportunistic behavior and that such rules and incentives do not always have to be provided at the national or global levels to be effective. They also agree that the appropriate level of establishing and enforcing rule systems varies with the specifics of the problem at hand (see the chapters by McGinnis, Sandholtz, Haas, Cerny, and Fratianni).

The editors equated governance with the organization of collective action in the introductory essay. We are not alone in this view. Oran Young (1986), for example, has adopted the same definition. Defining governance in this manner allows us to tap into the work of scholars who have studied the resolution of collective action problems for more than three decades. One of our new institutionalist authors, David Lake, has decided in Chapter 1 to define governance as the establishment of contracts, by which he means "the enforcement of bargains." In our view, contracts are one way to resolve collective action problems, but not the only way. There are times when the coercive power of the state or local government is the primary pathway to resolving collective action problems, although sustainability may be a problem when coercion is not part of a larger social contract and coercion is therefore viewed as illegitimate. Lake has decided to restrict his definition of governance in this manner in order to create a more parsimonious theory. Because the study of governance (and especially that of global governance) is still not well developed, it is not yet clear which of these two approaches for defining governance will yield the best results.

Making global governance the object of study inevitably brings with it a potential bias toward order in the international system, which was also inherent in the earlier study of international organizations, regimes, and institutions. While no one would argue that there is too much order in international relations, the kinds of order that people are seeking can be quite different, and it is always necessary to maintain a critical perspective when claims are made about the superiority of any given type of order over its alternatives (including chaos). This message can be found explicitly in the chapters by Sandholtz, Fratianni, and Douglas, and implicitly in a number of others. Sandholtz in Chapter 3 invites us to examine the fundamental rules that constitute a given order; Fratianni in Chapter 11 suggests we carefully distinguish between orders that provide public goods versus "club goods"; while Douglas in Chapter 5 asks us to beware of a global order which perpetuates an oppressive "dromological order where the fastest win and the slowest lose, effecting a new and more violent hierarchization of the world."

Another interesting controversy in this volume is about the likelihood that the overall system is evolving toward greater stress on the resolution of collective action problems at the global level. Lake, in particular, questions that there is a trend toward effective global governance. Environmental politics appears to be one of the most likely places for this to occur, but even there many forms of opportunistic behavior can be prevented at the subglobal levels and only a select set of environmental problems have to be dealt with globally (Haas in Chapter 4). A leading example of the latter was the successful negotiation of the Montreal Protocol to deal with the problem of reversing the destruction of the ozone layer in the upper atmosphere produced by the release of ozone-destroying chemicals. Even though the bargaining for the Montreal Protocol was conducted at the global level, responsibility for monitoring and enforcement of the agreement rests primarily on the national governments who signed the Protocol.

All the authors in this volume focused on economic globalization rather than other forms of globalization. The editors have defined economic globalization to mean the increasing integration of factor, goods, and services markets across geographical boundaries. Globalization, thus defined, can be thought of as either an independent or a dependent variable (or both). The editors argued in the introduction that globalization processes (as dependent variables) were initiated and encouraged by factors such as technological change, domestic politics, inter-state rivalries, and the spread of market-based systems. Economic globalization has been posited to lead to new or modified governance institutions because of the challenge it poses to existing institutions. In Chapter 6, Kobrin argues, for example, that the economic globalization that resulted from the deployment of high-speed global tele-communications networks, creates difficulties for the governments of nation-states by making it more and more difficult to identify the location of economic transactions, and to monitor the costs and benefits of those trans-actions. This is particularly problematic when it comes to taxation, where the establishment of the location of wealth-creating activities is crucial to the administration of tax laws. Kudrle in Chapter 8 argues, in contrast, that existing laws already provide the necessary instruments for dealing with this issue.

Most of the contributors to this volume have treated globalization as an independent variable and examined its implications for governance, but that is not the only way to study globalization and clearly there is a lot of potential benefit to viewing it as part of a larger set of global processes, as David Lake does in Chapter 1 and Ian Douglas does in Chapter 5. Lake sees globalization as a product of the effort by hegemonic liberal countries to remain hegemonic. Lake argues that economic globalization is at least partly a function of the policy preferences of powerful actors like Britain in the nineteenth century, and the United States in the twentieth, and that global governance is such a threat to that order it is unlikely that it will be supported by hegemons. Douglas argues that the debate over global governance is a continuation of earlier debates connected with the rise of what he calls "bio-politics" in the Enlightenment and the democratization of societies in the nineteenth century (epitomized by the Napoleonic *levée en masse* – mobilization of the entire citizenry for war).

In the remainder of this chapter, we discuss two issues. First, we summarize the principal lessons learned from the essays in this volume. Second, we out-line new questions in need of further research.

Lessons learned

Economic globalization is a process which is multidimensional and in-complete. Charting the actual course of economic globalization is a research task that is still in its infancy. Measurement of globalization processes is spotty and inadequate. Financial integration appears to be the dimension of economic globalization that is farthest along, but even in that area, data on globalization are hard to come by. There are still many policy instruments available to states who are willing to opt out of the global system, so one interesting line of inquiry for researchers is determining the perceived and actual costs of doing this.

Globalization is a focus of political organization and activity. Some people oppose it, while others rally to its defense. The identification of supporters and opponents of globalization is an empirical question worth pursuing. But it is equally important to understand the sources of support and opposition. The prevailing focus in political science literature on globalization is the extent to which it has weakened or strengthened the state. Many of the authors in this volume consider that focus to be overly restrictive. They think it better to see the state as one of a large family of collective goods-providing institutions that may play a greater or lesser role in the future, and for a variety of reasons. Thus, it makes sense to begin examining the political strategies of local communities, local and regional governments, interest groups, religious groups, non-governmental organizations, and other types of human aggregations with regard to globalization and its consequences.

Peter Haas, in Chapter 4, argues that environmental regimes are growing stronger because of the spread of environmental knowledge and consensus among experts. Haas' work suggests that there is a cognitive dimension to the politics of globalization that affects the resolution of collective action problems, and hence has implications for governance. Haas sees technical experts as playing a very important role in this area because of their ability to convince people to change the way they "frame" problems cognitively. These technical experts are not usually organized along national lines, but rather transnationally, as is the wont of intellectuals. The same is true of many environmental interest groups that concern themselves with global environmental issues. The reader may question the desirability of a system which grants so much persuasive power to transnationally organized technical elites, especially as this goes against the grain of many theories of democracy. Nevertheless, in areas where many people would like decisions to reflect knowledge gained via scientific inquiry such elite influence, as Haas argues, is probably inevitable.

Robert Kudrle in Chapter 8 argues that economic globalization constrains the behavior of nation-states, but that governments still retain the power to deal with integration issues. He argues that globalization has developed side by side with a "rediscovery of the market" and increasing European integration, and that these three phenomena together create challenges for national governments which those governments can deal with effectively often via harmonization of policies with other governments. Kudrle focuses particularly on the problems created by globalization for the administration of reasonable and equitable national systems of taxation. Tax havens, rapid shifting of funds across national boundaries, and a declining inability of governments to control the movement of people across geographic boundaries may create incentives for a "rush to the bottom" – that is, the adoption of lower and lower standards for social policy, based on competitive tax cutting which leaves the national governments incapable of cushioning the impact of increasing international competition on the least productive workers and the least efficient enterprises. McGinnis in Chapter 2 and Cerny in Chapter 7 also seem to share this worry. Kudrle, however, is optimistic that national governments will not rush to the bottom but instead will maintain the essential and effective social policies associated with the welfare state and focus on increasing productivity in order to continue to attract domestic and foreign private investment. This view is echoed, for the most part, in the essay by Hart and Prakash in Chapter 9, although they are more concerned than Kudrle (and therefore more in agreement with Cerny and McGinnis) about the possible negative consequences of the breakup, or what they call the re-articulation of the state.

Kudrle points to the relatively little known fact that US tax laws make it easier than they should for foreign nationals with assets in the United States to evade taxes on those assets as part of an overall system of inducing foreigners to invest in the United States. He argues that the dangers of tax competition among national governments (part of the rush to the bottom thesis) are overstated, and that governments will find a way to harmonize their policies to prevent major distortions in capital flows (which are not that strongly affected by tax rates anyhow). Kudrle seems much more worried about the evil consequences of the untaxed outflow of highly productive individuals out of, and the relatively unrestricted inflow of poor and uneducated immigrants into, the wealthier industrialized countries, than he is about the rush to the bottom via lowered taxes and lower social spending. Indeed, he advocates stricter enforcement of restrictions on immigration and the re-establishment of restrictions on capital flows as reasonable defensive policies for those countries.

Kudrle attacks a number of general propositions about the impact of globalization that he believes are not well grounded in fact: that (1) reinventing government is a manifestation of globalization; (2) deregulation was forced by globalization; (3) the shift in decision-making power to subnational levels of government (devolution) is a consequence of globalization; and (4) increased inequality (higher unemployment and lower wages for workers in import-competing manufacturing industries) is a consequence of globalization. These propositions have indeed been part of the debate over globalization, and Kudrle does us all a service in summarizing the counter arguments against them.

Alfred Aman in Chapter 10 provides an excellent discussion of the implications of globalization for the US legal tradition. He focuses, in particular, on the distinctions embedded in US law between private and public institutions which are increasingly problematic in the new international environment. The desire of the US government to effectively address the consequences of the growing competitiveness of other countries in world markets is helping to create a new form of administrative law which permits the government to work cooperatively with the private sector to enhance US economic competitiveness. This administrative law, however, runs against the grain of a large number of judicial decisions, based on constitutional grounds, legal precedents, and the legacies of nineteenth-century and early twentieth-century capitalism, designed to establish firm boundaries between the public and private spheres. Aman eloquently states the problem but does not advocate a simple answer, leaving it (in our view properly) to be debated in a larger forum.

Thus, the essays by Cerny, Hart and Prakash, Kudrle, and Aman all deal in different ways with the impact of globalization and other factors on the organization of advanced industrial nations, and particularly on the welfare state and the competition state. As such, these essays bridge the gap between international relations and comparative politics. We believe they should be seen as precursors of a larger agenda for research about the roots of the post-war welfare state and its ability to withstand the challenges that have been posed by neo-conservatives, neo-liberals, and neo-fascists in recent years. Neither Keynesianism nor the welfare state is dead, but the pressures on both are increasingly intense and they are coming from a variety of political locations, so this is not purely an "academic" question.

An agenda for future research: coping with globalization

This volume, despite the many arguments that it contains among the various authors on relatively fundamental issues, constitutes an advance in the conceptual foundations for globalization research. The concepts of globalization and governance have been clarified in such a way that it is now considerably easier to undertake systematic, empirical research on both and the relation between them. Also, the current volume focuses attention particularly on the limitations of international relations research that focuses solely on the implications of globalization towards the ability of national governments to maintain their primacy as authoritative actors in the world system and emphasizes the importance of considering the impact of globalization on other actors as well, where the concern is to observe changes in governance and not just government.

Based on our reading of the globalization literature in preparing this volume, we think that another bias in the existing literature on globalization needs to be corrected. Globalization is often projected as an inexorable and inevitable development that is radically altering the ways in which human societies organize themselves. Two kinds of responses are suggested to deal with it. First, globalization is viewed as an opportunity for economic growth and development. To tap into that opportunity, scholars recommend that collective organizations such as governments and firms should adapt to the demands of an increasingly globalized world economy. Of course, there is disagreement about how to do this. Scholars have different views on the appropriate pace and extent of governmental leadership in liberalizing domestic economies. Some scholars of business strategy suggest that firms should globalize and establish a physical presence in all their major markets. Others suggest that firms should focus on deepening their core competencies and not worry so much about establishing a market presence in all major markets.

The second perspective views globalization as essentially a disruptive force that benefits few but impoverishes many while also undermining the ability of the state to redistribute wealth and income. Thus, the recommendation is to resist globalization. The objective is to slow down its pace and dilute its impact, if not reverse it altogether.

These strategies emanate from opposing perspectives: globalization is either essentially beneficial or disruptive. Consequently, they represent the polar ends of the "response to globalization" continuum. We believe that future research on globalization should start with the idea that most governments and firms perceive globalization to be taking place without prejudging the essential character of globalization. Thanks to the work in this volume, we now view globalization as a set of related processes that are incomplete and reversible. Depending on factors such as resource endowments, preferences, and internal institutions, governments and other social actors have some ability to cope with globalization. We think that future research should focus on the coping strategies of governments and firms, evaluate the success of these strategies, and suggest some possible lessons to be drawn from them.

References

Grieco, Joseph, M. (1988) "Anarchy and the Limits of Cooperation; A Realist Critique of the Newest Neoliberal Institutionalism," *International Organization*, 42: 485–507.

New York Times (1997) "In Denver for Economic Talks, Clinton Calls for Freer Trade," June 20: A6.

Waltz, Kenneth N. (1979) *Theory of International Politics*, Reading, MA: Addison-Wesley.

Young, Oran (1986) "International Regimes: Towards a New Theory of Institutions, *World Politics* 39 (August).

Name index

Subject index